CREATING FREEDOM

Creating Freedom

THE LOTTERY OF BIRTH, THE ILLUSION OF CONSENT, AND THE FIGHT FOR OUR FUTURE

Raoul Martinez

PANTHEON BOOKS

NEW YORK

Library of Congress Cataloging-in-Publication Data
Name: Martinez, Raoul, author.
Title: Creating freedom : the lottery of birth, the illusion of consent, and the fight for our future / Raoul Martinez.
Description: New York : Pantheon Books, 2016. Includes bibliographical references and index.
Identifiers: LCCN 2016023448 (print). LCCN 2016026687 (ebook).
ISBN 9780307911643 (hardcover : alk. paper).
ISBN 9780307911650 (ebook).
Subjects: LCSH: Liberty.
Classification: LCC B824.4 .M335 2016 (print). LCC B824.4 (ebook).
DDC 123/.5—dc23.
LC record available at lccn.loc.gov/2016023448

www.pantheonbooks.com

Jacket design by Janet Hansen

Printed in the United States of America
First United States Edition
2 4 6 8 9 7 5 3 1

To Mum, Dad, Chess and Kev

Contents

Preface

Free markets, free trade, free elections, free media, free thought, free speech, free will. The language of freedom pervades our lives, framing the most urgent issues of our time and the deepest questions about who we are and who we wish to be. Freedom is a stirring ideal, central to the concept of human dignity and visions of a fulfilling and meaningful life. Its universal appeal, its ability to unite and inspire, have long made it a powerful political weapon. For some it is a clarion call for revolution, for others a justification of the status quo. Academics, think tanks, religions, political parties and activists have recast the concept in different ways. In the scramble to define it, the ideal of freedom has been pushed, pulled, twisted and torn; expertly moulded to suit the interests of those with the power to shape it.

Even as they steer our economies, democracies and judiciaries, today's dominant conceptions of freedom are unknown to most people. They are part of the conceptual foundation upon which society has been built, framing our thinking on everything from punishment and reward to capitalism and democracy. But this foundation, mixed as it is with myth and illusion, is crumbling. Plagued by civilisational crises – economic, political and environmental – the towering edifice it supports is not only unstable and unsustainable, but unjust. For too long the language of freedom has been used as a tool of control, helping to justify poverty, erode democracy and lend legitimacy to barbaric punishment.

As inequality soars, economic crises erupt, people work longer for less, as refugees surge across borders, corporate power intensifies, forests disappear and sea levels rise, it is time to engage in a fundamental reassessment of this hallowed ideal. When a society fails on multiple fronts, its foundational ideas must be questioned.

A simple principle animates these pages: the more we understand the limits on our freedom, the better placed we are to transcend them. We may well be less free than we like to think, but only through understanding the freedom we lack can we enhance the freedom we possess. Ignorance of our limitations leaves us vulnerable to those able to exploit them. Facing up to the limits on our freedom explodes a number of persistent myths – myths surrounding individual responsibility, justice, political democracy and the market. Some of these myths persist because they advance the interests of those in power; others because they flatter us, offering false comfort. All come at a price. The way we think about freedom shapes our view of the present and our vision of the future. It is a lens through which we interpret and evaluate the world, a compass by which we set our course. But not all conceptions of freedom are created equal. Each is based on assumptions about the world, some of which fly in the face of evidence and logic.

A sharp distinction is often drawn between questions of free will and those of political and economic freedom. Traditionally, these concepts have been separated into distinct categories, but this obscures more than it reveals. We dissect reality into manageable parts for study, but, if we do not put those parts back together in order to gain an understanding of the whole, we risk losing sight of the big picture. We risk losing touch with reality. This danger is inherent in modern education where the price of progression through the system is specialisation. Too often, where we should discover connections, we are taught to see impassable subject boundaries, but the limitations on our freedom are interconnected. A thorough understanding in one area enriches and changes our perception in others. To delve deeply into the meaning of freedom we have to breach disciplinary boundaries along the way. Insights and evidence from philosophers, psychologists, economists, historians, scientists, criminologists and environmentalists all play a role in the discussion to come. By building connections and teasing out their far-reaching implications, a radical, cohesive framework emerges – one that provides a much-needed overview of where we are and where we could be.

On the one hand, parts of society remain passive and deeply cynical about the possibility of change; on the other, social movements are rapidly growing around the world in response to the interlocking crises facing us. More and more people are questioning the systems that dominate their lives and diminish their liberty. Against this backdrop, it is time to reclaim the ideal of freedom for the urgent task of putting people and planet before profit and power.

We need a movement born of a shift in consciousness, one that will challenge the assumptions upon which our society is founded. To value truth – that elusive but all-important ideal – is to try and follow it beyond the shell that encloses our present understanding: to break through the defining labels of our inherited identity, the disciplinary boundaries that characterise our education and the limits set by society on our imagination. This book challenges ingrained assumptions about ourselves and the world and calls for an urgent transformation in our thinking and behaviour. It is a manifesto for deep and radical change. Through the prism of freedom, it examines the limitations of our dominant ideas and the failings of our current system, but it also explores the great potential that exists to create something better. The ideas and means to do this already exist, but we need to share them with each other, connect with each other and act on them. We need a revolution in our thinking that will spark a revolution in the way we organise our lives and structure our societies. A better world is possible, but if we take our freedom for granted we extinguish the possibility of attaining it.

PART ONE

THE LOTTERY OF BIRTH

I

Luck

We do not choose to exist. We do not choose the environment we will grow up in. We do not choose to be born Hindu, Christian or Muslim, into a war-zone or peaceful middle-class suburb, into starvation or luxury. We do not choose our parents, nor whether they'll be happy or miserable, knowledgeable or ignorant, healthy or sickly, attentive or neglectful. The knowledge we possess, the beliefs we hold, the tastes we develop, the traditions we adopt, the opportunities we enjoy, the work we do – the very lives we lead – depend entirely on our biological inheritance and the environment to which we are exposed. This is the lottery of birth.

We meet the world primed to adopt the way of life we encounter. The society that greets us takes our potential and shapes it. Ancient Greece, Confucian China, Renaissance Italy, Victorian England, Communist Russia – across millennia of human history there has been a spectacular multiplicity of cultures, each with the power to mould us in radically different ways. Early interactions, the treatment we receive and the behaviour we observe, begin the process of constructing an identity. Gradually, imperceptibly, we are inducted into a community.

Cultural transmission is a powerful process, one that has produced both beautiful and ugly outcomes. A glance at history reveals that there is neither a belief too bizarre nor an action too appalling for humans to embrace, given the necessary cultural influences. As much as we condemn the injustices and prejudices of past societies, there is no reason to assume that, under those circumstances, we wouldn't have embraced the same values and defended the same traditions. We might have developed loyalty to any group, nation, ideology or religion, learned any language, practised any social custom, partaken in any act of barbarism or altruism.

Thinking about the lottery of birth draws our attention to a simple fact: we do not create ourselves. The very idea entails a logical contradiction. To create something, you have to exist, so to create yourself you'd have to have existed before you had been created. Whether we're talking about flesh and blood people or immaterial souls, there is no way around this simple fact.[1] The implications are far-reaching: if we don't create ourselves, how can we be responsible for the way we are? And if we aren't responsible for the way we are, how can we be responsible for what we do? The answer is: we cannot.

The kind of freedom that would make us truly responsible for our actions – truly worthy of credit or blame – is a dangerous illusion, one that distorts our thinking on the most pressing economic, political and moral issues of our time. Yet it's an illusion central to our lives. As we will see, examining it exposes as false a number of assumptions at the heart of our culture – ideas about punishment, reward, blame and entitlement – and demands a revolution in the way we organise society and think about ourselves and each other.

It can seem hard to reconcile the fact that we are not truly responsible for the lives we lead with the countless choices we make every day – what to eat, what to wear, whether to lie or tell the truth, whether to stand up for ourselves or suffer in silence. After all, I'm choosing to type these words and you're choosing to read them. However, the act of making a choice does little to confer responsibility. The reason for this is simple: *we make choices with a brain we didn't choose.*

No one creates their own brain. No one even really understands the workings of their brain, let alone anyone else's. Just as computers do not programme themselves, we do not 'wire' the grey matter inside our skulls. This feat is accomplished through endless interactions between our genes and environment, neither of which we control. The upshot is that I did not choose to be me and you did not choose to be you, yet who we are determines the choices we make in any given situation.

Intuitively, we understand this. We are good at predicting the behaviour of those we know well. If a child, partner or sibling shows a drastic change in behaviour, we look for some external cause – drugs, bullying, overwork. Take the real-life case of a middle-aged married man – let's call him 'John' – who developed an overwhelming addiction to child pornography.[2] After several incidents of highly inappropriate sexual behaviour, as well as some time on a rehabilitation programme, John faced a stretch in prison. Suffering from increasingly painful headaches, John was hospitalised the night before he was due to be sentenced. A brain scan revealed a massive tumour in his orbitofrontal cortex. The surgeons operated, removed the tumour, and John's sexual appetite and behaviour returned to normal. After six months, however, the paedophilic tendencies returned. His wife took him back to the surgeon, who discovered that a portion of the tumour had regrown. After a second operation, John's behaviour returned to normal.

With the discovery of the brain tumour, John seems more a victim than a moral deviant – someone worthy of compassion rather than punishment. We tell ourselves that the tumour is to blame for his troubling behaviour and, of course, no one chooses to have a tumour. But what if there had been no tumour? Would that have made John more responsible? Would you feel more justified in blaming John if, say, his addiction had been the product of childhood abuse rather than the abnormal growth of brain tissue? If so, why? We no more control our upbringing than we do cell growth in the brain, and formative experiences have a profound impact on the way we develop.

In the 1950s, British psychiatrist John Bowlby showed that a child's relationship with its primary care-giver has a decisive impact on emotional and mental development. Today, it is widely accepted among child psychologists that if a child fails to form a secure attachment to a care-giver, the likelihood increases of developing a range of behavioural problems related to depleted self-worth, lack of trust in other people and an absence of empathy.

The Adverse Childhood Experiences (ACE) study, one of the largest of its kind, looked at the long-term effects of childhood trauma on health and behaviour.[3] Its findings confirm what many might expect: 'stressful or traumatic childhood experiences such as abuse, neglect, witnessing domestic violence, or growing up with alcohol or other substance abuse, mental illness, parental discord, or crime in the home . . . are a common pathway to social, emotional, and cognitive impairments that lead to increased risk . . . of violence or re-victimization, disease, disability and premature mortality.'[4] The prevalence of and risks associated with these problems are greater in people who have experienced more abuse. For instance, each traumatic event in a child's life makes them two to four times more likely to develop an addiction.

Most brain development takes place after birth. This is a distinctive feature of human beings. Dr Gabor Maté, a physician specialising in the treatment of addiction, argues that physical and emotional interactions determine much of our neurological growth and that addiction is largely a product of life-experience, particularly in early childhood:

> [E]ndorphins are released in the infant's brain when there are warm, non-stressed, calm interactions with the parenting figures. Endorphins, in turn, promote the growth of receptors and nerve cells, and the discharge of other important brain chemicals. The fewer endorphin-enhancing experiences in infancy and early childhood, the greater the need for external sources. Hence, a greater vulnerability to addictions.[5]

At any moment the state of our brain is a reflection of countless forces – genetic and environmental – over which we have little or no awareness. Advances in science and improvements in technology are gradually increasing our understanding of the brain. Today we can detect and identify brain tumours; two hundred years ago we could not. Back then, John would have been held completely responsible for his actions. No account would have been taken of the effect of the abnormal growth of tissue in his brain because no one would have known about it. The default assumption would have been that an adult is morally responsible for his or her actions.

As modern scientific instruments have increased our perceptual reach, our knowledge of the brain has improved. Observation and experience have taught us that a tumour can have a dramatic effect on an individual's behaviour, radically changing their personality. We have learned to attribute responsibility for abnormal behaviour to the tumour instead of to the person who happens to suffer from it. The problem with this line of thinking is that our assessment of blameworthiness is constrained by our current level of scientific understanding. A hundred years from now, with better scientific instruments and a better understanding of the brain, we may be able to detect subtle changes in the brain's neuro-chemistry that give rise to all kinds of behaviour which today we attribute to the 'free agency' of the individual. Neuroscientist David Eagleman writes:

> The underlying cause [of a form of behaviour] could be a genetic mutation, a bit of brain damage caused by an undetectably small stroke or tumor, an imbalance in neurotransmitter levels, a hormonal imbalance – or any combination. Any or all of these problems may be undetectable with our current technologies. But they can cause differences in brain function that lead to abnormal behaviour. . . In other words, if there is a measurable brain problem, that buys leniency for the defendant . . . But we *do* blame someone if we lack the technology to detect a biological problem.[6]

The more we understand the brain, the more we will be able to account for our behaviour by reference to its specific features, which will be attributable to genetic inheritance and life-experience. We may be able to show that the violence and aggression of an abusive father is rooted in a particular hormone imbalance, which itself could be rooted in childhood trauma. Scientific advances will help us to view a person's choices in a far wider context, one that includes the forces that created the brain making the choices we observe. The notion of 'individual responsibility' is just a fig leaf that covers the current gaps in our knowledge.

Our understanding of the brain is still extremely limited. In one cubic millimetre of brain tissue there are a hundred million synaptic connections between neurons. Current imaging methods rely on blood-flow signals that cover tens of cubic millimetres of brain tissue.[7] The upshot, as Eagleman vividly puts it, is that 'modern neuroimaging is like asking an astronaut in the space shuttle to look out the window and judge how America is doing'.[8] Though it may never be attained, a total understanding of the brain would eradicate the idea of individual responsibility entirely. But we do not have to wait for advances in science to understand that if someone behaves differently from us in a given situation, it is because they *are* different from us. We may lack the technology to identify the relevant way in which their neuro-circuitry differs from our own, but the evidence of the difference lies in the behaviour. If we had exactly the same brain state and encoun-tered the same situation then, all else being equal, we would behave in exactly the same way. This principle holds whether we are using it to explain the exceptional intellectual gifts of Einstein (which, inci-dentally, led him to reject the myth of responsibility) or the extraordinary moral failings of Stalin.[9]

Simon Baron-Cohen, Professor of Developmental Psychopathology and a leading researcher in empathetic development, suggests that when it comes to varying degrees of empathy, 'perhaps we should see such behaviour not as a product of individual choice or responsibility, but as a product of the person's neurology'.[10]

> We do not hold someone with schizophrenia responsible for having a hallucination, just as we don't hold someone with diabetes respon-sible for their increased thirst. In the case of the person with diabetes, we 'blame' the person's low levels of insulin, or the person's cells for not responding normally to insulin. That is, we recognize the biomedical causes of the behaviour. Equally, if someone's behav-iour is the result of their low empathy, which itself stems from the underactivity of the brain's empathy circuit, and which ultimately is the result of their genetic make-up and/or their early experience, in what sense is the 'person' responsible?[11]

Perhaps the biggest obstacle to seeing things this way is the intuition that, although as children we are not responsible for our identity and actions, we can choose to change ourselves as we mature and, by doing so, become truly responsible – bad habits can be broken and patterns from childhood overcome. On the face of it, this seems a reasonable claim. People can change and often these changes can be brought about very consciously – that is not in doubt – but it cannot make us truly responsible for who we are. To see why, think of a new-born baby endowed with a genetic inheritance it did not ask for and exposed to a world it played no part in creating. At what point does it become a truly responsible being, worthy of credit and blame?

The problem is that, by the time we have developed the intelligence necessary to contemplate our own identity, we are already very much in possession of one. How we think about ourselves and the world around us will already be framed by the conditioning we have received up to that point. This conditioning informs any choices we make, even the choice to rebel against aspects of that conditioning. It is still possible for new influences, encountered by chance, to have a deep impact on what we think and do, but we're not responsible for what we encounter by chance – and the influences that we consciously seek out are sought because of who we already are. As the philosopher Galen Strawson put it: 'Both the particular way in which one is moved to try to change oneself, and the degree of one's success in the attempt at change, will be determined by how one already is as a result of heredity and experience.'[12]

Most of what goes on in the brain is completely inaccessible to the conscious mind. Rather than its functioning being a product of consciousness, it makes more sense to say that consciousness is a product of the brain's functioning. Eagleman writes:

> The first thing we learn from studying our own [brain] circuitry is a simple lesson: most of what we do and think and feel is not under our conscious control. The vast jungles of neurons operate their own programs. The conscious you – the *I* that flickers to life when you wake up in the morning – is the smallest bit of what's transpiring in your brain . . . Your consciousness is like a tiny stowaway

on a transatlantic steamship, taking credit for the journey without acknowledging the massive engineering underfoot.[13]

When you take into account the influence of genetics; environmental toxins; the treatment we receive from parents, teachers, friends and foes; the role models we have access to; the life options available – among many other salient factors – it's clear that the machinery with which we make our decisions has been constructed by a process far beyond our control. Collectively, these influences determine the chemical make-up of our brains: the balance of hormones, the functioning of neurotransmitters, the architecture of our neural circuitry – all central to the decision-making processes that result in the choices we make. Confusion about responsibility arises because the act of making a choice blinds us to the causal relationship that links a choice to a brain, and a brain to the array of forces that shaped it.

The philosopher Ludwig Wittgenstein once said, 'Philosophy is a battle against the bewitchment of our intelligence by means of our language.'[14] In light of this, what do we mean by 'responsibility'? It's fair to say that, with few exceptions, adults are more responsible than children. Here the word 'responsible' is a synonym for 'dependable', 'capable' or 'trustworthy', as in: 'Let her take care of it, she is a responsible adult.'[15] This meaning needs to be distinguished from the kind of responsibility that would make us deserving of blame, punishment, credit or reward – what we might call 'true' or 'ultimate' responsibility.

To think clearly about responsibility it is important to bear in mind this distinction. On the whole, adults are more reliable, rational and capable than children, but this doesn't make them more responsible for the way they are or for the actions that follow from the way they are. Being more capable may make us more effective at pursuing our goals, but it doesn't make us more responsible for the goals that we choose to pursue. Education, cognitive development and political freedom all increase the power we have to act on our environment, but this does not make us more responsible for what we do with that power. What we do in a given situation is determined by the way we are – and for that we are not responsible.

Another source of confusion is the difference between so-called 'voluntary' and 'non-voluntary' actions. The distinction is really between actions that reflect intentions and those that do not. If you discovered that I had intentionally poisoned someone, you would draw very different conclusions about me than if you learned I had poisoned someone accidentally. In the first case, you might conclude that I am malicious and not to be trusted whereas in the second case you might just advise me to be more careful. Intentions reveal character; accidents reveal incompetence. However, since we do not create ourselves, we are not responsible for either character or competence. The distinction between voluntary and non-voluntary actions has no bearing on questions of ultimate responsibility (although it remains extremely important for other reasons, such as assessing the risk a person may pose). To be morally accountable, it is not enough to establish someone's intent, it must be shown that they are ultimately responsible for that intent, and that, as we have seen, is impossible. A psychopath may make many morally horrendous choices, but they will not include choosing the brain of a psychopath. Malicious choices may be voluntary; possessing a brain that makes them is not.

The nature/nurture debate also has no bearing on the question of ultimate responsibility. What counts is the fact that we are created and shaped by forces for which we are not responsible, not the combination or origin of these forces. We know that our species has been shaped, moulded and modified, and our genes divided, combined and recombined, to meet the survival challenges faced by our ancestors. Who we can become has been determined by this evolutionary process. Who we actually become is determined by the interaction with the environment we encounter thereafter.

Our genetic inheritance, which limits both our physical and mental potential, is the reason we grow arms instead of wings and noses instead of beaks. It's also the reason we struggle to hold more than a few items in our short-term memory yet have no trouble recognising the face of an old friend. The basic blueprint for the stages of human development is encoded in our DNA and, since natural selection tends to standardise the design of a single species, our genetic similarities far outweigh our differences. The outcome is that any human child can learn any language and adopt any culture.

Evidence of this emerged in 1938 when a Stone Age society was discovered in the forests of New Guinea. Roughly a million people had lived in isolation from the rest of the world for 40,000 years. In spite of this, the genetic differences between a New Guinean baby and any other human baby turned out to be trivial: a New Guinean infant raised in any other human culture can learn its language, adapt to its diet and adopt its traditions as easily as any other child.

Interesting as such findings are, the question of ultimate responsibility is unaffected by the scope and limits of our biological potential. Whether we believe that people are born 'blank slates' and shaped almost completely by their environment, or in genetic determinism, which emphasises the influence of genes, or in some combination of the two (the only plausible position), the result is the same: we are the product of forces beyond our control. We do not create ourselves.

Another topic that has no bearing on the question of responsibility – even though it can often be found at the heart of debates on free will – is determinism, the idea that there is only one possible future. Whether our universe is deterministic or not, the concepts of self-creation and ultimate responsibility remain incoherent.[16] A choice is either part of an unbroken chain of cause and effect or it is the product of chance. Neither option leaves any room for ultimate responsibility. If every effect has a cause, then a complete explanation of any action will take us back to the birth of the universe. Even if the chain that links a choice to its cause and that cause to a preceding cause is broken, it still does not make us any more responsible. An uncaused, arbitrary event is random and a random event in our decision-making process is not compatible with any meaningful notion of responsibility. If a random event in the brain causes your arm to move, clearly the movement was not intentional.

We are not, and can never be, free from the forces that shape us. The kind of responsibility that would make us deserving of punishment or reward, credit or blame, is an illusion, a sacred myth passed on from one generation to the next with no rational basis. The impossibility of ultimate responsibility is taken for granted when we talk about anything else in the natural world – sharks, trees, apes or amoebas – but for some reason we assume humans possess it. Aspects of our culture betray an awareness of the limits on our freedom – think of the proverb, 'There, but for the grace of God, go I' – yet, on the whole, we go about our lives, form our opinions, educate our young and organise society according to the myth of responsibility.

No scientific finding offers any support for this myth. It is hard to imagine how any finding could. On the other hand, what we do understand about human behaviour and the brain directly contradicts it. And we have a growing number of eminent psychologists, neuro-scientists and physicists to tell us so.[17] Still, with or without scientific evidence, all it takes is elementary logic to expose the myth of ultimate responsibility because the idea itself is incoherent, confused and contra-dictory. The nineteenth-century philosopher Friedrich Nietzsche called it a 'perversion of logic'. The belief that we can truly bear responsibility for our actions is, he wrote, 'to absolve God, the world, ancestors, chance, and society' – it is to believe that we can pull ourselves 'up into exist-ence by the hair, out of the swamps of nothingness'.[18]

The blame game

The idea of ultimate responsibility is buried deep in the foundations of our religious traditions, political ideologies and legal systems – implic-itly assumed but rarely stated. Its existence is implied by concepts like heaven, hell, sin and eternal damnation at the heart of the Abrahamic faiths. A cosmic system of condemnation and salvation only makes sense if people deserve the fates handed down to them. The concept of karma – central to Hinduism, Buddhism and Jainism – has similar implications. For millennia, formal religions have played a powerful role in perpet-uating the responsibility myth, justifying all manner of cruel and vicious punishments in this life and the next, often in stark conflict with other values central to their teachings.

Crude formulations of the myth also occupy a prominent position in popular culture. It has been given a huge boost by the growing 'self-help' movement, whose blend of materialistic values and pseudo-spirituality has fostered a multibillion-dollar industry. One of its chief exponents, Deepak Chopra, perfectly embodies the synthesis. Boasting clients from Madonna to Hillary Clinton, the appeal of Chopra's message to the affluent and aspirational is not hard to discern: 'People who have achieved an enormous amount of success are inherently very spiritual . . . Affluence is simply our natural state.'[19]

Perhaps the most successful branding of the idea came with Rhonda Byrne's hugely popular book and film, *The Secret* (2006). In it we are introduced to what Byrne claims is a universal natural law – the law of attraction – which states that 'like attracts like', and that we can change our situation by changing our thoughts. Desirable outcomes such as good health, wealth and happiness come to those with 'positive' thoughts and feelings. And, by implication, undesirable outcomes come to those with 'negative' thoughts and feelings. Even natural disasters costing thousands of lives, the book claims, can be traced back to the negative thought patterns of the devastated communities. Byrne quotes a Dr Joe Vitale: 'If people believe they can be in the wrong place at the wrong time . . . those thoughts of fear, separation, and powerlessness, if persistent, can attract them to being in the wrong place at the wrong time.'[20]

This view of human freedom is at the extreme end of the ideological spectrum, but these attitudes are influential and pervade our culture. Take, for instance, the growing problem of obesity. In a 2005 study, Abigail Saguy and Rene Almeling looked at 221 newspaper, medical and book sources and found that, while two-thirds cited individual causes of obesity, less than a third gave any mention to structural factors such as geography, longer working hours, the fast food industry or reduced income. Revealingly, the tendency of the sources to focus on personal responsibility increased when discussing particular social groups: 73 per cent of articles mentioning the poor or people of colour blamed obesity on bad food choices, whereas in articles that did not mention these groups, the figure dropped to only 29 per cent.[21]

Raj Patel, in his book on the food industry, *Stuffed and Starved* (2007), shows that this approach ignores important realities. Poor neighbourhoods, while boasting a higher concentration of fast food restaurants, have on average four times fewer supermarkets than affluent areas. In other words, people of colour and the poor live in environments that are far more likely to result in obesity. By contrast, richer, whiter areas are more likely to provide access to healthier, fresh, nutritious food, lower in salt and fat. Patel writes:

> [M]any choices have already been made for us by our environment, our customs, our routine. Choice is the word we're left with to describe our plucking one box rather than another off the shelves, and it's the word we're taught to use. If we're asked why we use the word 'choice' to describe this, we might respond 'no one pointed a gun to our head, no one coerced us' as if this were the opposite to choice. But the opposite of choice isn't coercion. It's instinct. And our instincts have been so thoroughly captured by forces beyond our control that they're suspect to the core.[22]

Our food choices have been restricted and shaped before we ever really think about them. Consumption habits, like all habits, are shaped by forces 'beyond our control'. In the case of food, they are formed at an early age and are lifelong – the $10 billion spent annually on marketing food to children in the US is clearly a long-term investment.[23] The ideas, values and images we encounter in our environment shape our dietary habits. A striking example is Fiji, where, in 1990, eating disorders were unheard of. In 1995, television was introduced, mostly from the US and packed with advertising. Within three years, 12 per cent of teenage girls in Fiji had developed bulimia.[24]

Today, those wishing to control their weight are offered a different strategy in *The Secret*: 'If you see people who are overweight, do not observe them, but immediately switch your mind to the picture of you in your perfect body and feel it . . . Attracting the perfect weight is the same as placing an order with the catalogue of the universe. You look through the catalogue, choose the perfect weight, place your order, and then it is delivered to you.'[25] Byrne's writing verges on the comical but her message is symptomatic of a powerful trend. *The Secret* reached the top of the *New York Times* bestseller list, where it remained for 190 weeks. It has been translated into fifty languages and has over 20 million copies in print.[26]

A modern secular manifestation of the responsibility myth is found in the promise of 'The American Dream' – that anyone can become rich and those who do, deserve it, whereas those who don't only have themselves to blame. Its roots can be found in classical liberalism, the intellectual forerunner of today's dominant political ideology, neo-liberalism. The tendency to hold individuals ultimately responsible for their lot in life was emboldened in the late nineteenth century by the emerging doctrine of Social Darwinism, drawing its inspiration from Darwin's theory of evolution.

According to this view (which was not held by Darwin), individuals, groups and races are subject to a law of natural selection so that in-equalities of wealth and power between groups can be explained as products of biological differences – imperialism and colonialism can be viewed as a form of evolutionary progress. In other words, it is natural that the weak perish, while the strong grow in power. Its most vocal American advocate, William Sumner, asserted that 'the drunkard in the gutter is just where he ought to be' and that 'the millionaires are a product of natural selection . . . They get high wages and live in luxury, but the bargain is a good one for society.'[27] At a time when governments are simultaneously cutting taxes for the rich and welfare for the poor, it is clear that, although the language may have changed, the ideas of Social Darwinism are alive and well.

Political scientist Charles Murray writes: 'I want to reintroduce the notion of blame, and sharply reduce our readiness to call people "victims".'[28] His concern lies more with the 'youngster who is studying hard, obeying the law, working hard, and taking care not to have a baby' than with the 'youngster who fails in school, gets in trouble with the law, does not hold a job, or has a child without being able to care for it'.[29] He also writes, 'The standard to which I hold myself, and which I advocate for other commentators on social policy, is: do not apply a different moral standard to strangers – including poor strangers – from the standard which applies to the people one knows and loves.'[30]

This is dangerously simplistic. When moral evaluations of behaviour are made, this view places a high value on equality of criteria – 'we should apply the same moral standards to everyone' – but ignores the inequalities that gave rise to the behaviour under evaluation: a blatant double standard. In a partial concession, Murray claims that 'even if it is true that a poor young person is not responsible for the condition in which he finds himself, the worst thing one can do is try to persuade him of that'.[31] This is an extraordinary statement. Knowledge, not ignorance, is what empowers us. What freedoms would have been won if slaves, serfs and exploited labourers had blamed themselves for the degraded condition of their existence? What rights, wages and government assistance would the poor have secured if their explanations of inequality had been restricted to personal failings? Understanding the source of our problems – individually and collectively – is a crucial step on the path to solving them.

A vast amount of intellectual effort has been expended by theologians and philosophers to 'make the world safe for blame'.[32] Many thinkers have taken up the task; none have succeeded. Much has been said about the social utility of blame, our instinct to hold people responsible, and the different forms blame can take, but no argument or evidence has been produced that gives us any reason to suppose that people are truly responsible for their actions. In light of bad behaviour, we may justifiably withdraw trust, express disapproval, feel upset, cut ties and, if it safeguards the welfare of society, support measures such as fines and imprisonment, but none of this requires that we apportion blame. The belief that people are blameworthy finds no support in science or logic and ignores the most basic truths about human beings. It is an anachronism held in place by instinct, tradition and fear.

The myth of responsibility also has great political utility. As legal scholar Barbara H. Fried writes, 'enthusiasm for blame is not confined to punishment. Changes in public policy more broadly – the slow dismantling of the social safety net, the push to privatize social security, the deregulation of banking, the health care wars, the refusal to bail out homeowners in the wake of the 2008 housing meltdown – have all been fueled by our collective sense that if things go badly for you, you've got no one to blame but yourself'.[33] The more responsibility that is laid at the feet of individuals, the easier it is to justify the many inequalities in our world. If addicts, sinners, refugees, prisoners, the homeless, the obese, the unemployed and the poor can be blamed for their condition, there is little obligation to help them.

If we believe that each person bears ultimate responsibility for their lot in life, it is far easier to justify discrepancies in power, wealth and opportunity. If the rich deserve their privilege and the poor their destitution, perhaps things are as they should be. As Herman Cain, former Republican Party presidential candidate, declared: 'Don't blame Wall Street. Don't blame the big banks. If you don't have a job and you're not rich, blame yourself.'[34] But no behaviour occurs in isolation. Every choice is the result of heredity, experience and opportunity. Billionaire Warren Buffett recognises more clearly than most the decisive role of luck: 'Most of the world's seven billion people found their destinies largely determined at the moment of birth . . . [F]or literally billions of people, where they are born and who gives them birth, along with their gender and native intellect, largely determine the life they will experience.'[35]

As soon as we place human behaviour in the wider context of cause and effect, a framework that takes into account the steering power of genes and environment, the decisive role of luck in our lives becomes obvious. Simply to exist is extraordinarily lucky, the odds are so incredibly small. Over 90 per cent of all the organisms that have existed on this planet died without producing offspring.[36] The fact that you're reading this means that every one of your ancestors, since life on Earth began, escaped that fate. Luck continues to dominate after birth. A baby born in Japan is fifty times more likely to reach its first birthday than a baby born in Angola.[37] An African-American infant is twice as likely to pass away in its first year as a white American child.[38] From 1990 to 2015, the number of children who died before their fifth birthday – mostly from preventable diseases – is roughly 236 million.[39] And if we make it into adulthood free from abuse, violence, neglect, war, famine, malnutrition, physical or mental illness, extreme poverty, debilitating injury, or the loss of a parent or sibling, we are luckier than most.

The abilities and capacities we possess can also be chalked up to good fortune. Whether we have the brain of an Isaac Newton or the speed of a Usain Bolt is really a matter of chance. What's more, the psychological tools to make the most of our opportunities and talents are themselves down to luck. Confidence is key to taking advantage of opportunities – to embarking on an ambitious task or showing resilience in the face of setbacks and failure. Yet our levels of self-belief are highly sensitive to the treatment we receive in childhood, and for that we are not responsible. Be it patience, innovation, concentration, creativity, perseverance or self-control, no capacity is equally distributed across the population. Walk into any classroom and you will find some children who can sit happily for hours studying and others who find it unbearable, some who are brimming with self-belief and others undermined by self-doubt. Different brains have different capacities and, as we know, no one chooses their own brain. Whether we are the star pupil or a dropout, disciplined or distracted, motivated or lazy, is ultimately a matter of luck.

Decades of research have revealed the impact of early experiences on the development of our innate capacities. For instance, children from lower-income families with less-educated parents enter school far behind their wealthier counterparts in language skills. The amount of time our care-givers spend conversing, reading and playing with us – and the quality of those interactions – all makes a difference to our development. Stanford psychologists have shown that two-year-old children from poor families may already be six months behind in language development.[40] By age four, children in middle- and upper-class families hear in the region of 30 million more words than children from families on welfare.[41] A study conducted by the Scottish Centre for Social Research (SCSR), which tracked the abilities of 14,000 youngsters, found that by age five, children with degree-level educated parents are, on average, a year and a half ahead of their less privileged counterparts in terms of vocabulary and around thirteen months ahead on problem-solving.[42]

A life-journey depends on a wide range of unpredictable factors. Variations in genes and experience do not need to be large to have an impact on the paths we take. Small variations can have significant repercussions, setting in motion events that result in completely different outcomes. In chaos theory, this is known as the 'butterfly effect'. With a slight tweak in starting conditions, the man who dies at twenty-five from a drug overdose might have lived to hug his grandchildren. The woman who wins the Nobel Prize in Literature might, with a small change in early circumstances, have spent her life as a housewife never to discover her talent. When we hit a crucial fork in the road – whether or not to steal, cheat, retaliate, take a risk, quit a job, revise for an exam or remain in an abusive relationship – apparently trivial variations can make all the difference, nudging us one way or another. At decisive moments, an attentive friend, an inspiring book, a caring teacher, a strong role model, a smiling stranger, even good weather or a long night's sleep, may be enough to prevent us making a costly error.

Some people defy every expectation, achieving remarkable things in the face of adversity. It is tempting to view such lives as evidence that we can, after all, be the masters of our own destiny, but to do so would be a mistake. Forces beyond our control determine the resources – psychological, physical and material – at our disposal to carve out a new path, and these resources, along with countless other twists of fate, ultimately determine how successful we will be in our attempt. For every unlikely success story there are countless people of equal potential who died in poverty and obscurity due to the crushing force of circumstance. Just because the odd person wins the lottery does not mean the game isn't rigged for everyone else to lose.

By casting off the defunct ideology of credit and blame, we can get to work on understanding the deeper roots of behaviour: familial, genetic, economic and political. This is a necessary antidote to the lazy belief that the buck of responsibility stops with the mystical 'free agency' of the individual. Such thinking is reminiscent of primitive attempts to construct theories of the natural world. In order to explain why some things rise and others fall, Aristotle spoke of how 'bodies' move to their 'natural place': apples fall because it is in their nature to fall; steam rises because it is in its nature to rise. Such wordplay serves only to conceal our ignorance. Just as for falling apples and rising steam, there are reasons why people behave the way they do, reasons that take us far beyond the will of the individual.

Our talents, attitudes, inclinations and opportunities are the products of forces we do not control. Debate still rages over the relative importance of biological and environmental factors but the responsibility myth has been debunked and, with it, the grounds for credit and blame.[43] It may be intuitively compelling, flattering for the fortunate and expedient for the powerful, but ultimate responsibility is a myth, an irrational dogma that causes great harm to many people.

Luck has been the decisive force in the life of every person who has ever lived. And, be it good or bad, nothing we do makes us more or less deserving of the luck we receive. If ultimate responsibility is an incoherent concept, the notion of desert – that we can be truly deserving of reward or punishment – also loses meaning. If we are not truly responsible for what we do, then what we do cannot make us more or less deserving of pain or pleasure, suffering or joy. Punishment and reward may serve important pragmatic functions, providing incentives for the kinds of behaviour we want to cultivate in society, but that is a separate issue – one to be explored in the following two chapters.[44]

I should add that there is another use of the word 'deserve' that is not affected by these views on responsibility. A frail old lady on a bus deserves a seat more than a healthy young woman. A single mother of three deserves a state subsidy more than a multimillion-dollar corporation. Why? In each case, it is clear who has the greater need. The word 'deserves' in these examples is just another way of saying 'has greater need for'. In the same way, if you are exhausted and I am well rested, we might say that, of the two of us, you deserve a holiday, not because you have worked harder – though that might be one reason why you are exhausted – but simply because of your greater need. As we will see, a needs-based system of rewards is the only one that passes the test of fairness.

A dangerous idea?

Is it dangerous to expose the myth of responsibility? According to philosopher Daniel Dennett, 'Deeming that nobody is ever really responsible for anything they do is step one on the way to a police state that medicalizes all "anti-social" behavior, and that way lies the Gulag.'[45] He also warns that it could 'rob us of our dignity' and reduce our inclination to engage in moral behaviour. Are these fears legitimate?

That an idea may be used to serve destructive or oppressive ends tells us very little about its truth or value. There is always a battle to decide who will interpret important ideas, to determine whose interests they will serve. In the heat of such conflicts, ideas are stretched, twisted and mangled as the stakes increase. A case in point is the theory of evolution, which revolutionised the way we think about our species and the natural world. Exploring this revolution in *Darwin's Dangerous Idea*, Dennett writes:

> From the moment of the publication of *Origin of Species* in 1859, Charles Darwin's fundamental idea has inspired intense reactions ranging from ferocious condemnation to ecstatic allegiance, sometimes tantamount to religious zeal. Darwin's theory has been abused and misrepresented by friend and foe alike. It has been misappropriated to lend scientific respectability to appalling political and social doctrines.[46]

If Darwin's idea can be used to justify 'appalling political and social doctrines', should it be ignored, suppressed, obfuscated or publicly discredited? Dennett thinks not: 'There is no future in a sacred myth. Why not? Because of our curiosity.' The only way to protect what is of value 'is to cut through the smokescreens and look at the idea as unflinchingly, as dispassionately as possible'. Facing up to Darwin's dangerous idea shows that 'what really matters to us – and ought to matter to us – shines through, transformed but enhanced by its passage through the Darwinian Revolution'.[47] Dennett's reasoning can equally be applied to the 'sacred myth' of individual responsibility. If it were to be widely rejected, society would need a conceptual revolution to adjust to its implications. As we will see, understanding the limits on our freedom has the potential, just as with the theory of evolution, to provide a 'transformed but enhanced' perspective on what matters most in our lives. Darwin himself rejected the responsibility myth and believed that 'This view should teach one profound humility, one deserves no credit or blame for anything' and 'nor ought one to blame others'.[48]

Before exploring what this transformation might look like, it is important to recognise that the belief – tacit or explicit – in ultimate responsibility comes with its own dangers. It has been used to justify the cruellest of acts, lending bogus credibility to notions of sin, retribution and 'just deserts'. It vindicates feelings of entitlement and strengthens the impulse to blame and punish. Recent research has demonstrated empirically the ugly attitudes associated with this way of thinking.

To measure how strongly people identify with the idea that the world is just – that good things happen to good people and bad things happen to bad people – psychologists use the 'Just World Belief' scale. A person who scores highly on this scale strongly agrees with statements such as 'By and large, people get what they deserve' and 'People who meet with misfortune have brought it on themselves'. Another measure used is the 'Right Wing Authoritarian' scale, which asks how strongly people agree with statements like 'The established authorities generally turn out to be right about things, while the radicals and protestors are usually just "loud mouths" showing off their ignorance' and 'Our country desperately needs a mighty leader who will do what has to be done to destroy the radical new ways of sinfulness that are ruining us'. Those who score highly on this scale are more willing to submit to authority and more likely to feel hostile towards those who do not.

Psychologists Jasmine Carey and Del Paulhus found that a strong belief in the responsibility myth correlates with high scores on both scales. Their work is part of a growing body of empirical research which strongly suggests that, as our belief in the myth strengthens, so does our tendency to blame victims, advocate harsher punishments, submit to those in power, and perceive extreme economic inequality as fair and just.[49] Perhaps it is the promotion of the myth – rather than its rejection – that risks the return of 'the gulag'.[50]

A series of studies published in *Psychological Science* found that when people's belief in ultimate responsibility was diminished – through exposure to arguments against free will or scientific findings about the brain – they became less punitive.[51] Such evidence suggests that dispensing with the responsibility myth would actually be conducive to ethical behaviour rather than an impediment to it, and be an important step towards compassion rather than a rejection of morality. After all, if we are not responsible for our achievements and failings, we are all on an equal footing: ultimately, no one deserves more joy, happiness or freedom than anyone else. This does not oblige us to treat everyone in the same way, but it does demonstrate that the deprivation experienced by some and the privilege enjoyed by others cannot be justified on the grounds that each group deserves what it gets. From this perspective, we discover a sturdy foundation for equality, empathy and compassion.

It would be immoral to ignore just how much luck is involved in moral behaviour itself.[52] Actions that we regard as unethical are – like any behaviour – ultimately a product of formative conditions, which is why those who lack compassion for others are no less deserving of it themselves. Nevertheless, there are times when it is difficult to be compassionate. Invariably, when we suffer at the hands of someone else, there are powerful and complex emotions to work through before compassion is a viable response – and for some of us, in certain situations, it may never be within our grasp. Recognising this is itself a requirement of compassion.

It can be hard to forgive ourselves for the pain we cause others. Yet there is evidence to suggest that doing so is important for our physical and, especially, our mental health.[53] Feelings of self-loathing, it seems, exacerbate cycles of destructive behaviour. As the saying goes, 'hurt people hurt people'. We should never forget that the world marks us before we have a chance to mark it. This perspective invites us to look beyond our own guilt and failings to the systemic and cultural basis of our identity. Perhaps a broader perspective can help to break cycles of self-destructive behaviour. What is done cannot be undone: the important question is always 'What will be done next?'[54]

We are rooted in our environment and depend on its offerings no less than a tree whose health is inextricable from the sunlight, air and soil that surround it. We, too, begin as a seed whose growth and development depend on its environment. Our capacity for happiness, confidence, ecstasy, empathy, love and hate, is not of our own making. None of this means that we cannot change, learn and grow, or that making the effort to do so is unimportant – on the contrary, it is essential – but it does mean that the extent to which we succeed in our attempt, relative to others, is not something for which we can take credit. Just as the tiny seed that grows into a giant redwood cannot take credit for its height, we cannot take credit for what we become. In an important sense, our achievements are not really *our* achievements. We are notes in life's melody, not its composer.

To deny that we are truly responsible is not to deny the possibility of principled and ethical behaviour. We do not need to hold a person responsible for some admirable trait to value what they are. We treasure the vivid colour, elegant shape and aesthetic beauty of the rose without imputing any responsibility to it. The same is true for all of nature in its complexity and magnificence – including human beings. Why should we need to hold Nina Simone responsible for her genius to treasure what she created? Why do we need to hold Martin Luther King responsible for his courage to revere what he achieved? To expose the myth of responsibility is not to deny the existence of inspiring and admirable human attributes; it is simply to view them as gifts of nature in the same way that we view the splendour of a sunset. Such beauty is meaningful and uplifting in itself.

Perhaps what Dennett and others really fear is that by doing away with the responsibility myth we will encourage 'irresponsible' – thoughtless or even reckless – behaviour, that we will have less reason to be caring, conscientious, respectful and dependable. This fear is misplaced. Values motivate us to act, not belief in ultimate responsibility, credit or blame – and values are the product of a wide range of complex forces. Einstein may have rejected the myth of responsibility, but this did not stop him dedicating his life, with vigour and passion, to unlocking the mysteries of the universe, campaigning against the proliferation of nuclear weapons and arguing for a fairer society. There is no reason to think that exposing the illusion of responsibility will undermine the determination to meet our needs or achieve our goals. It does not diminish the cherishing of loved ones, the thirst to learn, or the outrage we feel at injustice. As I will explore in the final part of this book, it is in the pursuit, creation and experience of what we truly value that we discover our deepest freedom.

There is another benefit to exposing the myth of responsibility: doing so highlights the fundamental importance of questioning. If we are not responsible for the way we are, if we are not the authors of our own identity, then who or what is? Awareness of just how susceptible we are to forces beyond our control gives us a compelling reason to investigate those forces and, if necessary, transcend their influence. This is important. If democracy is to have any meaning, and the dangers of centralised control are to be averted, it is essential to have a questioning citizenry.

It is no coincidence that the majority of Sudanese are Muslim, the majority of Thais are Buddhist, and the majority of Italians are Catholic. (In each case the figure is close to 90 per cent.) Our entry into this world may be arbitrary, but the world that greets us is not. Numerous forces vie for our attention and loyalty. Our minds are a battleground for competing ideas. The outcome of this battle determines who we become and the society we create. But the forces that win out are not necessarily the ones that serve us best. Over the course of human history, countless people have been conditioned to defend oppressive ideologies, support destructive regimes and believe downright lies. It once served the interests of monarchs to spread among their subjects the idea of the divine right of kings, just as it served the interests of colonialists to spread the idea of racial superiority. Today, it serves certain interests to spend billions of dollars a year marketing fast food to children, at a time when child obesity is a major public health problem.

Although the ideological, cultural and religious labels that divide us are not inherent in our nature, history suggests that the capacity to identify with them for arbitrary reasons is. This capacity enables the easy transmission of bias, prejudice and ignorance from one generation to the next. If we are to expand our freedom, we need to question our beliefs and values and the forces that brought them about. Why do we hold the beliefs that we do? Why have we formed the habits that we possess? And, crucially, whose interests do they serve? Questioning the religious, economic, social and political paradigms of our time is as urgent as it has ever been. To shape identities is to fashion the future – but what future are we creating? Today the world is scarred by war, extreme inequality and environmental devastation. If we're to create an alternative future, we can't just reproduce the thinking that shaped the past.

Look at these two lines.

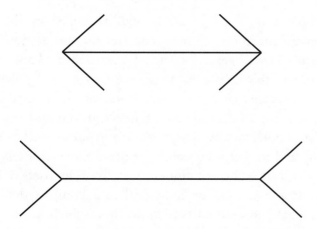

If you are familiar with the Müller-Lyer illusion, you'll know that though the bottom line appears to be longer than the top one, both lines are equal in length. Psychologist Daniel Kahneman writes:

> To resist the illusion, there is only one thing you can do: you must learn to mistrust your impressions of the length of lines when fins are attached to them. To implement that rule, you must be able to recognize the illusory pattern and recall what you know about it. If you can do this, you will never again be fooled by the Müller-Lyer illusion. But you will still see one line as longer than the other.[55]

For many of us, the psychological experience of making choices feels incompatible with the idea that we are not truly responsible. However much we ponder the philosophical arguments and scientific findings, it may not be possible to overcome this feeling. The illusion of responsibility persists, like an optical illusion, even when it has lost intellectual credibility. Perhaps this is not a problem. We are what we are and must work with what we have.

The experience of an illusion may persist but our beliefs about it can change and our response to it can be modified accordingly. As Bertrand Russell put it, 'A hallucination is a fact, not an error; what is erroneous is a judgement based upon it.'[56] This holds for the cognitive illusion of ultimate responsibility. The perennial debate over the existence or non-existence of 'freedom of the will' is fuelled by the cognitive illusion that we make free choices. The fact that the notion of a truly free choice has never been coherently formulated has had little impact on the vigour of this debate. Although we may never be able to break the illusion completely, we can prime ourselves to respond differently by developing our understanding of freedom and responsibility. On issues of real significance we can inform our judgements with a more intellectually and morally defensible perspective, one that takes account of the fact that our will is conditioned, not free. The roots of behaviour go far beyond the will of the individual to encompass the economic, political, familial and cultural conditions from which it emerges.

The philosopher Thomas Nagel wrote that to 'acquire a more objective understanding of some aspect of life or the world, we step back from our initial view of it and form a new conception which has that view and its relation to the world as its object. In other words, we place ourselves in the world that is to be understood.'[57] As we contemplate what we are and the forces that have shaped us, we do just that: we view our beliefs and values, loyalties and prejudices, assumptions and affiliations, not as free choices, but as outcomes of a complex process whose roots predate our existence. Taking this perspective, adopting this 'objective attitude' – which is really just an exercise of the imagination, like putting yourself in someone else's shoes – exposes the arbitrary nature of many aspects of our identity. It provides a rationale for questioning the inevitably flawed maps of reality we hold in our heads, and weakens our ties to the labels, traditions, habits and beliefs that commonly define who we are, at least enough to question, evaluate and reflect on them.

The attempt to view our identity and world from new and challenging perspectives is part of a process that has the power – over time – to profoundly change the self being viewed. It provides a potent antidote to the worst excesses of arbitrary identification; to the sorts of narrow, entrenched, dogmatic worldviews that drive us to kill and die for flags, symbols, gods and governments whose connection to us is no more than accidental.

★

Fatalism is the view that our fate is predetermined, by the gods, the stars in the heavens, or some other external force. It is the belief that destiny is inevitable and that making our own deliberations, choices and actions is largely pointless. To be absolutely clear, this is not the argument being made here. Yes, luck plays a decisive role in all of our lives but neither this fact nor anything else in this chapter implies that we are powerless. This book is not an exercise in submissive resignation. The point of identifying our limitations is to give ourselves the best chance of transcending them. It is through understanding the way we are that we increase the possibility of being as we wish to be.

Later chapters will return to these arguments in various ways, exploring the long shadow cast by the myth of responsibility over politics, economics and the wider culture – and asking how society might look if it escaped this shadow. As we will see, a great deal depends on our capacity to cultivate a more accurate understanding of ourselves and each other. The notion that we are somehow truly responsible for the way we are and what we do has led to absurd beliefs and cruel policies. It legitimises the claim that people deserve the privileges they enjoy and the punishments they receive. It promotes the view that the fates of the prosperous and the poor, the celebrated and the reviled, are merited. It offers a tacit yet powerful endorsement of inequality and oppression. To expose the responsibility myth is to expose these pernicious ways of thinking and place a powerful tool in the hands of those fighting for a fairer allocation of wealth, power and opportunity. It is also a significant step towards creating a more compassionate world, in which the impulse to blame is overcome by a desire to understand, and feelings of entitlement give way to humility. By shattering the myth of responsibility we give ourselves the best chance of expanding the freedom that is available to us, personally and politically. The more we understand the effect the world has had on us, the more we can control the effect we have on the world.

2

Punishment

The idea that people who do bad things deserve to suffer is deeply embedded in our culture. It has been expressed over the centuries through the doctrine of 'an eye for an eye'. In practice, religious traditions have gone far beyond the spurious equality this implies. The Bible has often been interpreted as prescribing capital punishment for transgressions such as adultery, sodomy, blasphemy, breaking the Sabbath, worshipping other gods and cursing a parent. The Koran supports capital punishment for, among other things, 'spreading mischief', interpretations of which have included treason, apostasy, adultery and homosexual behaviour. The belief in a divine system of retribution and punishment, that unrepentant sinners deserve to suffer for eternity in hell, remains a core tenet for much of humanity.

Echoing religious doctrine, philosophers, judges and political leaders have for millennia claimed that the primary purpose of punishment is retribution, in which the suffering of the perpetrator is an end in itself.[1] This remains a popular view. Opinion polls on the death penalty give a good indication of contemporary attitudes. A YouGov survey in 2014 found more UK citizens in favour of reinstating the death penalty than against, while a 2010 survey showed that 74 per cent would support the death penalty 'under certain circumstances', though not for all murders.[2] In the US, support for the death penalty hovers at around 61 per cent.[3]

This cultural commitment to retribution may be rooted in human nature. When someone engages in the act of punishing a perceived cheater or exploiter, brain scans have revealed increased activity in the 'pleasure centres'.[4] There is even evidence that babies as young as eight months exhibit a desire to punish perceived wrongdoing.[5] Evolutionary psychologists argue that punishment evolved as a means of preserving mutually advantageous forms of group cooperation. Drawing on the theory of reciprocal altruism, they claim that punishing 'cheats' who receive benefits without bearing any of the costs acts as a powerful incentive for cooperative social behaviour.

Whatever the evolutionary reasons for developing an instinct for punishment, it is worth remembering that natural selection is an amoral process. Nature, as Tennyson put it, is 'red in tooth and claw'. To the extent that they have an evolutionary basis, righteous indignation and the thirst for revenge are part of who we are only because they enhanced the survival of our ancestors long enough for the associated genes to find their way into subsequent generations. Robert Wright, author of *The Moral Animal*, a book on the evolutionary roots of our moral instincts, remarks that perhaps 'The intuitively obvious idea of just deserts, the very core of the human sense of justice . . . the fury of our moral indignation, the visceral certainty that . . . the culprit deserves *punishment* [is no more than] a by-product of evolution, a simple genetic stratagem.'[6]

Viewing our instincts with a degree of scepticism – questioning, analysing and appraising them in light of other ideas, beliefs and values – is essential for social progress and self-knowledge. Moral anger can be a dangerous force. The sense that we have the *right* to inflict suffering on a perceived wrongdoer has justified some of the most inhumane practices in history, from stoning and impaling to burning at the stake, disembowelling and decapitation. It has also shaped our criminal justice system, moulding it to conform to stubborn intuitions about just deserts, retribution, blame and responsibility.

The most advanced legal systems on the planet are committed to the idea that most people, most of the time, enjoy the kind of freedom that makes them truly responsible for their actions. According to the US Supreme Court, 'belief in freedom of the human will' is a 'universal and persistent' element of the law, and 'a deterministic view of human conduct . . . is inconsistent with the underlying precepts of our criminal justice system'.[7] Explicit commitment to 'freedom of the will' can be found in a number of court rulings and in the work of many legal scholars.[8] It is embedded in the foundations of the criminal justice system, the same foundations that are now cracking under the weight of scientific knowledge.

In response to this pressure, some legal theorists have staked out a fall-back position. In the eyes of the law, we are practical reasoners: through conscious deliberation we decide how to act in order to achieve our goals. According to legal scholar Stephen J. Morse, and many others who share his view, to hold people responsible for their actions we do not have to establish whether they possess sufficient 'freedom of the will', only that they have sufficient rationality. As he puts it: 'rationality is the touchstone of responsibility'.[9] If a crime reflects clear conscious intentions, this is what counts (never mind the deeper origins of those intentions). Morse acknowledges that free will may be illusory and determinism true, but rejects the idea that this has anything to do with responsibility, arguing that as long as a person's rational capacities 'seem unimpaired' they should 'be held responsible, whatever the neuroscience might show'. In practice, courts need only presume that with few exceptions 'adults are capable of minimal rationality and responsibility and that the same rules may be applied to all'.[10]

This view of responsibility sheds light on many of the procedures employed in the contemporary courtroom but it is fundamentally confused. It concedes that our behaviour may ultimately be the product of forces beyond our control, yet claims we can still be held responsible for it.[11] It smacks of trying to have your cake and eat it. As we have seen, rationality and other forms of competence certainly increase our ability to achieve goals and understand the consequences of our actions, but they do not make us responsible for the goals we choose to pursue – that depends on the way we are, and for that we are not responsible. To repeat an earlier formulation: a rational psychopath may make morally horrendous choices, but they will not include choosing the brain of a psychopath. The implications of neuroscience are clear: biology cannot be separated from behaviour, and we do not choose our biology. In some cases the courts already accept this – as demonstrated by the growing list of 'syndromes' and 'disorders' being employed as a legal defence – but they remain exceptions. Given the huge variation in genetic potential, life experience and social opportunity that we see in the world, to presume that, with few exceptions, 'the same rules may be applied to all' is plainly a recipe for injustice, not a solution to it.

As a society we can agree to define responsibility any way we wish – in terms of rationality, annual income, educational attainment or even height. But changing definitions does not alter the underlying facts. Relaxing the criteria for responsibility may help to conceal the cracks snaking through its foundations, but, for the modern criminal justice system, these problems will only become more apparent with time. Although the best of science and logic have shown it to be a meaningless question, the courts continue to ask whether lawbreakers are deserving of punishment, whether they are blameworthy. As long as this question beats at the heart of criminal justice, its methods will remain irrational and its outcomes unjust.

It does not have to be this way. Instead of submitting to misleading intuitions, our justice system could yield to the findings of science and the demands of reason. This would involve acknowledging that no one is truly blameworthy, rejecting retribution as a legitimate justification for punishment and focusing on improving the future rather than exacting revenge for the past.

Dispensing with blame and responsibility does not necessarily mean dispensing with all punishment. The evidence we have from psychological studies suggests that 'the motivation to punish in order to benefit society' remains in place even when 'the need for blame and desire for retribution are forgone', so society could keep the 'social benefits of punishment intact while avoiding the unnecessary human suffering and economic costs of punishment often associated with retributivism'.[12] Once we know someone is guilty of committing a crime, the important question is what the *effect* of punishment would be on both the guilty lawbreaker and the rest of society. In a rational criminal justice system, the justification for punishment would derive solely from the positive effects it has on society, not from notions of blame or desert.

The benefits of punishment

Once retribution is ruled out, the most influential justification for punishment is to be found in the logic of deterrence. The idea is that criminal punishment not only deters lawbreakers from reoffending but acts as a deterrent to the wider population, a common assumption being that more severe punishments are more effective deterrents. Although in some contexts the logic of deterrence is compelling, it has its own serious flaws and fails as a justification for many of the punishments currently endorsed by governments – democratic or otherwise – around the world.

Deterrence strategies often fail to produce the outcomes we expect. For instance, prisoners in countries with longer and harsher punishments are more likely to reoffend than prisoners in countries with more lenient sentencing. The incidence of recidivism in the US and UK hovers between 60 and 65 per cent. This is roughly 50 per cent higher than rates in less punitive nations such as Sweden, Norway and Japan.[13] Bringing together the results of fifty different studies involving over 300,000 offenders, Canadian criminologist Paul Gendreau found that not one reported that imprisonment reduced recidivism. In fact, longer sentences were associated with a 3 per cent increase in reoffending rates, supporting the theory that prison can function as a 'school for crime'.[14]

In the US, almost seven out of ten males will find themselves back in jail within three years of release.[15] A 2010 UK government paper showed that 68 per cent of adults who either left prison or started a community sentence in the first three months of 2000 had reoffended within five years.[16] After decades of research, prison psychiatrist James Gilligan concluded that the 'most effective way to turn a non-violent person into a violent one is to send him to prison' and that 'the criminal justice and penal systems have been operating under a huge mistake, namely, the belief that punishment will deter, prevent or inhibit violence, when in fact it is the most powerful stimulant of violence we have yet discovered'.[17]

Objects, natural disasters, animals, small children and (sometimes) people with a mental illness are exempted from punishment precisely because they lack the cognitive capacity – the 'minimal rationality' – to be deterred by threats of punishment.[18] This seems reasonable enough, but the problem is that anyone who commits a crime belongs, by definition, to the category of people undeterred by the punishments of society. At least when they commit the crime, every lawbreaker clearly possesses a brain that is not put off by the possibility of being arrested, tried, imprisoned or, in some cases, even executed. The high percentage of reoffending former prisoners confirms that those who end up being punished are not the ones the deterrent is primarily acting on.

If punishment often fails to deter lawbreakers from offending and reoffending, what purpose does it serve? The standard answer is that if criminals were not punished for their crimes, those members of the public who were previously deterred would in future have less reason to abide by the law and the crime rate would go up. It is the effect on this second category of people (the deterred public) that is used to justify the punishment on the first (the lawbreakers), that is, the criminal population are being punished to prevent the rest of the population from turning criminal. But if people are not truly responsible, then using the deterrence argument to justify harsh punishment is, as Daniel Dennett points out '. . . doomed to hypocrisy. Those whom we end up punishing are really paying a double price, for they are scapegoats, deliberately harmed by society in order to set a vivid example for the more ably self-controlled, but not really responsible for the deeds we piously declare them to have committed of their own free-will.'[19]

Disturbing though this reasoning may be, it lies at the heart of the deterrent argument. It was candidly recognised by the influential American jurist Oliver Wendell Holmes, Jr: 'If I were having a philosophical talk with a man I was going to have hanged (or electrocuted) I should say, "I don't doubt that your act was inevitable for you, but to make it more avoidable by others we propose to sacrifice you to the common good. You may regard yourself as a soldier dying for your country if you like."'[20] Expressed in this way, the injustice of the deterrent argument is apparent. It advocates punishment, even execution, for people who are not truly responsible for what they do – people who in many cases have suffered excessive hardships and deprivation – in order to prevent the more self-controlled, and often more privileged, from breaking the law.

As well as being morally dubious, the strategy of harming some to deter others can easily backfire. Severe punishments can function as an 'anti-deterrent', increasing violent crime rather than diminishing it. For instance, both the US and Nigeria experienced an increase in murder rates after introducing the death penalty, while its abolition in Canada saw a drop in homicides.[21] And of the countries with the highest homicide rates, the top five that employ the death penalty average 41.6 murders per 100,000 people, whereas the top five with no death penalty average roughly half that number at 21.6 murders per 100,000 people.[22] One explanation for these facts is that severe institutional punishment has a brutalising impact on the general culture, exacerbating rather than deterring violence. Regarding the relationship between capital punishment and homicide rates, the United Nations concluded that 'The evidence as a whole still gives no positive support to the deterrent hypothesis.'[23] According to polls, the vast majority of criminologists and police chiefs do not believe the death penalty deters violent crime more than imprisonment.[24]

The immorality of the 'double price' paid by prisoners is aggravated by the severity of the punishments they receive. As long as deterrence is believed to be our most powerful lever of influence and, to the extent that more brutal punishments are considered more effective deterrents, there will be pressure to increase the suffering of prisoners. This pressure, founded on morally questionable and factually baseless assumptions, is regularly employed around the world to justify punishments that ought to be regarded as a form of torture. According to the United Nations, torture encompasses:

> any act by which severe pain or suffering, whether physical or mental, is intentionally inflicted on a person for such purposes as obtaining from him or a third person information or a confession, punishing him for an act he or a third person has committed or is suspected of having committed, or intimidating or coercing him . . .[25]

Imagine being taken from your home and locked up for years in a threatening, violent, overcrowded institution – an institution in which people are often beaten, injured, raped or even killed, all the time separated from family and friends, with every aspect of your routine controlled coercively by a group of salaried strangers. The distinction between torture and prevailing forms of criminal punishment breaks down under scrutiny.

Consider the US's 'supermax' prisons in which inmates are kept in solitary confinement for twenty-three hours a day. Prisoners living under such conditions often become mentally ill. They are deprived of any meaningful work, training, exercise or education and are shut off from almost all human contact. Access to a telephone, books, magazines, radio, television – even sunlight and fresh air – are severely restricted or entirely denied. Cells are illuminated at all times.[26] The Committee on International Human Rights argues that this form of confinement 'violates basic human rights' and in many cases 'constitutes torture under international law and cruel and unusual punishment under the US Constitution'.[27] It is estimated that up to 80,000 prisoners are currently living under these conditions.

Criminologists warn of 'the serious psychological harm done to prisoners, and [the] difficulties in coping with the world outside when released, across all security levels and types of institutions'.[28] Amnesty International, Human Rights Watch and the United Nations Committee Against Torture have all condemned the US prison system for its inhumane practices. These include the incarceration of children in adult prisons, abuse of the mentally ill and disabled, the prevalence of rape culture, the shackling of female inmates during childbirth, and the use of electric shocks as a means of controlling prisoners.[29] As Gendreau writes, 'if prison psychologically destroys the inhabitants, then their adjustment to society upon release can only be negative, with one likely consequence being a return to crime'.[30]

The deterrent effect of imposing the 'double price' on lawbreakers is not only overstated but a significant part of the problem. Arguments in its favour are riddled with holes, providing cover for many inhumane, unjust and unjustifiable practices. This cover is strengthened by our instinctive attachment to individual responsibility and the notion of retribution, which permeate the whole practice of punishment, shaping popular attitudes and making it far easier to ignore the grave deficiencies of outmoded penal systems.

Most of us anticipate the likely consequences of our actions, so in some contexts the threat of punishment may dissuade us from a course of action we might otherwise undertake. However, according to recent research, it is primarily the likelihood of getting caught − not the severity of punishment that awaits us − that deters us from doing what we otherwise would do.[31] Once we have detained people who pose a serious threat to society, their suffering (beyond that caused by the removal of their liberty) does not serve the cause of justice and rarely increases the safety of society. In fact, it often makes society more dangerous.

If the justice system were rational, the social impact of harming lawbreakers would not be taken for granted; just like the effectiveness of a new drug, it would be something to be established empirically. The burden of proof would always be on those in favour of inflicting harm to demonstrate its value, and, even then, the benefits to society would have to be balanced against the fundamental right of the individual not to be harmed. Given the humane and effective alternatives to wilfully inflicting suffering on lawbreakers, the logic of deterrence is often hard to justify.

Beyond punishment

One of the most humane prisons in the world is situated on the island of Bastøy in Norway.[32] Every inmate in this open prison is offered high-quality education and training programmes to develop a variety of skills. Prisoners live communally in comfortable homes, six men to a house. Each man has his own room but shares the kitchen and other facilities with the other inmates. A meal a day is provided for the inmates; any other food must be bought from the local supermarket and prepared by the prisoners themselves who receive an allowance of £70 a month and earn roughly £6 a day on a variety of jobs which include growing food, looking after horses, repairing bicycles, doing woodwork, and engaging in different forms of maintenance on the island.

Dotted around Bastøy is a church, a school and a library. In their free time, inmates have the opportunity to engage in leisure activities such as horse riding, fishing and tennis. All the guards are highly qualified, having received three years' training for their post (compared to only six weeks in the UK), and function more like social workers than prison officers. Arne Kvernvik Nilsen, who was in charge of the prison for the five years leading up to 2013, describes his philosophy: 'I give respect to the prisoners who come here and they respond by respecting themselves, each other and this community.' Nilsen believes that, 'We have to respect people's need for revenge, but not use that as a foundation for how we run our prisons. [. . .] Should I be in charge of adding more problems to the prisoner on behalf of the state, making you an even worse threat to larger society because I have treated you badly while you are in my care?'[33] The island houses perpetrators of serious crimes including murder and rape, yet, remarkably, it has the lowest reoffending rates in Europe: 16 per cent compared with a European average of about 70 per cent. And it's one of the cheapest prisons to run in Norway.

Not all Norwegian prisons are as open and comfortable as Bastøy but they all follow a similar philosophy based on the belief that the only punishment the state should inflict is the loss of liberty. The suffering of prisoners is intentionally minimised. There is no death penalty and no life sentencing. The aim is to heal, not harm. And, whatever critics of this philosophy might say, it produces results. Across Norway, reoffending rates may be higher than for Bastøy, but they are still the lowest in Europe at 30 per cent. Across Scandinavia, penal policy is largely left to the experts. Criminologists design policy based on the evidence, and the public have largely been happy to let them do so. Along with Holland and Japan, Norway is a guiding light in the prison sector but there are campaigns in many countries to make prisons more humane.

One of the most effective strategies to stop criminals reoffending has been to provide inmates with the opportunity to study and earn formal qualifications. Where punishment has failed, education is succeeding. A meta-study by the RAND Corporation (sponsored by the US Bureau of Justice Assistance) found that, on average, inmates who participated in correctional education programmes were 43 per cent less likely to reoffend.[34] The former warden of Louisiana's biggest prison has cited figures showing that education is 'one of the few things that work' to keep prisoners from reoffending. At the notorious Folsom State Prison in California, reoffending rates were 55 per cent in the general population but zero for prisoners who had studied for a degree.[35] A 2004 study by the University of California, Los Angeles, found that 'Correctional education is almost twice as cost effective as incarceration' at reducing crime.[36]

Another forward-thinking approach to crime and rehabilitation is 'restorative justice'. It can take various forms, but ideally it brings together victim and perpetrator to engage in a face-to-face, mediated discussion about the crime that took place. Although it can be difficult, many victims of crime have ultimately reported feeling empowered by the process, which is entered into voluntarily. Victims are given the opportunity to explain how the crime has affected their lives, to express their feelings, and ask the questions that haunt them. Offenders have the opportunity to describe the circumstances of the crime and how they have been affected by it. They also have the opportunity to apologise for what they have done and compensate the victim in some way, ranging from community service to financial reparation. Restorative justice has produced astounding results. Numerous studies demonstrate its financial, psychological and crime-reducing value. A seven-year government-funded UK study found that, with serious offences, it reduced reoffending rates by 27 per cent, 'leading to £9 savings for every £1 spent'.[37] It also found that the majority of victims chose to participate in face-to-face meetings when given the opportunity by a trained facilitator, and that 85 per cent reported they were satisfied with the process. In 2007, a meta-study of restorative justice research projects (spanning nineteen years and covering all studies written in English) compiled by criminologists Lawrence W. Sherman and Heather Strang also found clear, positive results.[38] These include reduced reoffending rates, a reduction of victims' post-traumatic stress symptoms, more satisfaction for both victims and offenders than with court justice, a reduced desire for victims to exact violent revenge against their offenders, and significantly reduced costs.

One of the most successful prison projects in the US is the Resolve to Stop the Violence Project (RSVP) introduced in 1997 by the San Francisco County Sheriff's Department. The programme began in a sixty-two-bed jail unit and involved all prisoners. Within the unit itself there were no locked doors. A large central activity area was surrounded by smaller classrooms and meeting rooms. For twelve hours a day, six days a week, it delivered an intensive schedule of activity including art, creative writing, group discussion, academic classes, theatre, role-playing, counselling, and meetings and talks with survivors of violence. Prisoners took part for as long as their sentences permitted, ranging from a few days to more than a year. The results of this experiment were stunning.[39] In-house violence dropped from twenty-four serious incidents a year to zero for the twelve months following the first month of the programme, and reoffending rates for those who spent at least sixteen weeks in the programme were 83 per cent lower than for a comparable group of prisoners outside the programme. And it saved taxpayers about $4 for every $1 spent.

The first form of institutional punishment we encounter is at school. We can be shouted at, detained, suspended and expelled. According to the United States Department of Education, the 2011 to 2012 school year saw 130,000 students expelled from school and 7 million suspensions (one for every seven students).[40] The traditional paradigm of punishment tells us that students who exhibit disruptive, challenging or violent behaviour must be controlled through reward and punishment. Contemporary research tells a different story: traditional approaches to disruptive behaviour often make things worse. Too often, punishments escalate from verbal warnings to expulsion without any behavioural improvement. The logic of deterrence fails and, once expelled, the likelihood of a child ending up in juvenile detention greatly increases.

American clinical child psychologist Dr Ross Greene has pioneered an approach now known as Collaborative & Proactive Solutions (CPS).

It starts with the assumption that kids want to do well. If they're not doing well, it's because they lack the necessary skills. Disruptive children are not simply attention-seeking, manipulative or poorly motivated, they are struggling to meet the demands being made of them. CPS takes seriously the fact that the rules and expectations of the classroom and schoolyard do not bear equally on all. For instance, children with learning disabilities and diagnosed behaviour problems are twice as likely to be suspended and three times more likely to be imprisoned than their peers.[41]

Instead of blaming young people for their disruptive behaviour, Greene urges teachers to try to understand the source of it and work with them to get beyond it. When a student acts in a disruptive or destructive way, he advises taking the following simple steps: find the time to gather information from the child to understand as clearly as possible his or her perspective, share with them your own concerns, then brainstorm with the child in order to arrive at a workable solution to avoid similar behaviour in future. It's a strategy that aims to equip students with the tools to solve their own problems. Key to its success are staff willing to develop new skills themselves and to cultivate strong relationships with students, particularly those with challenging behaviour.

Central School in Maine has implemented a number of Greene's ideas. Before CPS, says Principal Nina D'Aran, 'we spent a lot of time trying to diagnose children by talking to each other . . . Now we're talking to the child and really believing the child when they say what the problems are.'[42] To some, this will sound unrealistic given the demands of modern schooling, but at Central School D'Aran has observed a dramatic change. Disciplinary referrals to her office have dropped by over two-thirds and suspensions have dropped from two a year to zero. She puts it down to 'meeting the child's needs and solving problems instead of controlling behavior'.[43] It's hard work, demanding for both kids and adults, but so far the results suggest it is well worth the effort. Since CPS has been applied in a number of other schools, disciplinary referrals and suspensions have dropped by up to 80 per cent.

Greene's philosophy was developed and tested in psychiatric clinics and state juvenile facilities. In Long Creek Youth Development Center, a correctional facility also in Maine, guards were resistant at first to

CPS. 'Our staff initially thought CPS was just a way to give in to the kids, and a lot of people outside the juvenile system feel they should be punished,' says Rod Bouffard, former Superintendent at the facility. But once it was implemented, the benefits were clear: levels of violence started to drop, there were fewer staff and resident injuries and, when they were let out, kids were far more likely to stay out. Reoffending rates were reduced from 75 per cent in 1999 to 33 per cent in 2012.[44] Indeed, for a number of years they have had some of the lowest re-offending rates in the US.

Prisons like Bastøy, projects like Resolve to Stop the Violence, and approaches like Restorative Justice and Collaborative & Proactive Solutions have transcended the simplistic paradigms of retribution and deterrence in favour of rehabilitation – for both perpetrators and victims. Of course, none of them is perfect: all are part of an ongoing process of experimentation from which better ways of doing things will continue to emerge. However, we already know that these alternatives are more ethical than the current predominant strategies and much more effective.

Root causes

Small details can have a significant impact on moral behaviour. The subconscious effect of a pleasant aroma, a modest rise in the volume of background noise, or rushing to an appointment have all been shown to impact our inclination to be kind to strangers in need.[45] One experiment showed that people who had just found a dime in the coin-return slot of a phone booth were more likely to help when a nearby stranger dropped some papers they were carrying.[46] Finding the coin increased the proportion of those who helped to pick up the papers from 4 per cent to 86 per cent. When people were asked why they had stopped to help, the discovery of the dime was seldom mentioned.

Another study, more salient to the topic of punishment, observed the behaviour of judges.[47] Without their knowledge, eight judges were monitored as they reviewed applications for parole. They spent an average of six minutes on each application, and could spend whole days working through them. Only 35 per cent of applications were approved. The observers took note of the exact time of each decision, as well as the exact time of the judges' three food breaks over the course of the day. What they found was striking: the proportion of approved requests spiked after each food break, with 65 per cent of requests being granted at this time. Over the subsequent two hours, as the judges grew tired and hungry, their rate of approval steadily dropped to roughly zero just before the next meal.

A little science helps to make sense of these results. The nervous system requires more glucose than most other parts of the body. Demanding mental activity uses up a great deal of it, and prolonged mental exertion results in a drop in glucose levels in the blood. This depletion results in a deterioration of performance when carrying out demanding and effortful tasks, as well as a tendency to fall back on automatic behaviour. If an innocuous dime in a phone booth or a mild drop in glucose levels can have such significant, yet unconscious, effects on our behaviour, what influence might the totality of our environment exert over the course of a lifetime?

The most established environmental determinant of violence in a society is income inequality.[48] Less equal societies are more violent.[49] The link between inequality and homicide rates, within and between countries, has been revealed in dozens of independent studies – and the differences are not small. According to the Equality Trust in the UK, there are five-fold differences in murder rates related to inequality between different nations. In fact, higher rates of inequality are associated with a host of social problems: mental illness, child bullying, drug use, teenage pregnancy, divorce, illiteracy and distrust.

James Gilligan sheds light on how some of these factors could conspire to produce particularly violent forms of crime. After years of work with aggressive inmates, he has 'yet to see a serious act of violence that was not provoked by the experience of feeling shamed and humiliated'.[50] For obvious reasons, shame and humiliation tend to be more prevalent in societies with greater inequality, where the race for status is more intense. In these highly competitive environments, argues Gilligan, those at the bottom of the hierarchy struggle to find ways to secure markers of status. Deprived of the education, wealth, care and opportunities enjoyed by others, it becomes incredibly important to them to defend what little status they do enjoy. With other means out of reach, violence often becomes the only way they feel they can do this. The smallest sign of disrespect can provoke the most violent of acts. (This explains why higher education in prisons is so effective at reducing reoffending rates: a degree is a marker of status that serves as an antidote to feelings of shame and humiliation.)

The most horrific individual acts of violence are almost always symptoms of extreme forms of abuse and neglect. In the US, ten times as many people with serious mental illnesses – such as bipolar disorder and schizophrenia – are in prison than in a state hospital.[51] In effect, illness has been criminalised. Having spent over thirty years at the UK criminal bar, and 'rather a lot of time in prisons', Baroness Helena Kennedy QC speaks from experience when she writes:

> For most people, prison is the end of a road paved with deprivation, disadvantage, abuse, discrimination and multiple social problems. Empty lives produce crime . . . The same issues arise repeatedly: appalling family circumstances, histories of neglect, abuse and sexual exploitation, poor health, mental disorders, lack of support, inadequate housing or homelessness, poverty and debt, and little expectation of change . . . It is my idea of hell.[52]

In our society, children subjected to the harshest, most impoverished environments are increasingly being criminalised. Kennedy remarks that 'Ninety per cent of young people in prison have mental health or substance abuse problems. Nearly a quarter have literacy and numeracy skills below those of an average seven-year-old and a significant number have suffered physical and sexual abuse.'[53]

Economic, political and cultural arrangements shape identities, opportunities and, ultimately, behaviour. Harsh punishments aimed at those who have already been brutalised and undermined by these forces only pile injustice upon injustice. If society is not doing what it can to address the root causes of crime – at all levels of the system – the supposedly pragmatic justifications for severe punishment lose all credibility. What right do we have to condemn crime if we do not also condemn the conditions that breed it?

Ultimately, all that separates the criminal and non-criminal is luck. The skewed distribution of 'racial luck' is particularly disturbing. Although black people make up only 12 per cent of the US population, they account for 40 per cent of its prison population. Across the US today, black people are more than six times as likely to be imprisoned than whites, 31 per cent more likely to be pulled over while driving than white drivers, and twice as likely to be killed by a cop (and more likely to be unarmed when killed).[54] Racial prejudice permeates almost every area of American society, greatly diminishing the opportunities available to black people and ethnic minorities. Fifty years after Martin Luther King's 'I have a dream' speech, many of the racial divides in American society persist. A white man with a criminal record is still more likely to be considered for a job than a black man without one.[55] Analysis of US government data by the Pew Research Center shows that 'When it comes to household income and household wealth, the gaps between blacks and whites have widened. On measures such as high school completion and life expectancy, they have narrowed. On other measures, including poverty and homeownership rates, the gaps are roughly the same as they were 40 years ago.'[56]

A similar pattern is to be found among ethnic minorities in the UK, with black people five times more likely to end up in prison.[57] The Equality and Human Rights Commission found that, when officers did not need suspicion of involvement in a crime to stop and search (under section 60 of the Criminal Justice and Public Order Act 1994), black people were thirty-seven times more likely to be targeted. In fact, young black men are more likely to end up in prison than at an elite university.[58] And Inquest, a UK charity that campaigns against deaths in police custody, have found that, since 1990, over 400 people from black communities or ethnic minorities have died while incarcerated or in the custody of the police.[59]

Imprisoning lawbreakers, once the sole responsibility of the state, is now increasingly run for profit by private business – a trend firmly established in the US and garnering support in the UK. In the US, about 10 per cent of prisoners are locked up in privately run institutions. A study from the University of Wisconsin in 2015 found that states with private prisons have higher rates of reoffending and that private prisons are keeping inmates locked up for longer.[60] Given that more prisoners serving longer sentences means more profit, this is a predictable outcome. Today, this $5 billion industry is doing what all big industries do: using a portion of its earnings to lobby governments to rescind regulations and pass laws that will allow them to generate even greater profits. In the case of the prison industry, this means lobbying the government to put more people behind bars. A report from the US National Institute on Money in State Politics shows that, for the 2002 and 2004 election cycles, prison companies donated $3.3 million to political parties. From 2006 to 2008, the nation's largest prison corporation spent $2.7 million on lobbying for stricter laws.[61] The profitability of prisoners does not end there. Inmates' work in private prisons is increasingly contracted out to major corporations for abysmally low wages. In public prisons the wage can be in the region of the minimum wage, but in private prisons it can be as low as 17 cents an hour, or 50 cents in the more generous institutions. Those who refuse to work can be locked up in isolation cells.[62] These practices are beginning to resemble a form of slave labour.

Although the evidence suggests that you cannot be 'tough on crime' without being 'tough on inequality', a shift from the welfare state to the security state has taken place over the last half century. In the UK and US, 'tough on crime, tough on welfare' rhetoric has long been embraced by the major parties. The result has been rapidly rising prison populations and widening social inequality. In the UK, each place in prison costs £75,000 to build and a further £37,000 a year to run (an expense greater than the annual cost of studying at Eton, the elite British school).[63] The annual cost of incarceration in the US is about $63 billion.[64] Criminal justice expenditure in some US states outstrips funding for public education. Over the past couple of decades, California has built roughly one new prison a year, at a cost of $100 million each.[65] Over the same period, it has built only one new public college. Across the US, spending on prisons has risen six times faster than on higher education.[66] Observing the immense costs of an expanding criminal justice system, philosopher Douglas Husak asks: 'Is there no better use for the enormous resources we expend on criminalization and punishment? Money and manpower are diverted from more urgent needs [to] enforce laws that our best theory of criminalization would not justify.'[67]

The vast resources we expend on locking people up could be used to reduce inequality, thereby improving people's lives and eliminating many of the conditions that breed crime. Yet, for decades, politicians have rejected this framing of the problem. President Ronald Reagan asserted: 'we are told that the answer to . . . [crime] is to reduce our poverty. This isn't the answer . . . Government's function is to protect society from the criminal, not the other way around.'[68] Former British Prime Minister John Major warned in 1993 that 'Society needs to condemn a little more and understand a little less'.[69]

The data show that higher rates of material inequality, within and between nations, strongly correlate with larger prison populations. The more unequal a society is, the higher the percentage of people in jail.[70] And people lower down the social hierarchy, with less income and less education, are far more likely to end up in prison.[71] The most unequal societies – led by the US and Singapore with the UK and Israel not too far behind – have, by a wide margin, the largest proportion of their populations behind bars. The most equal countries – Japan, Norway, Finland, Sweden and Denmark – imprison a much lower proportion of their populations. The differences are not small. In the US there are 576 people in prison per 100,000, fourteen times higher than Japan, which has a rate of forty prisoners per 100,000.[72] When US states are compared, the pattern holds, with more unequal states tending to have larger prison populations.

The differences in crime rates can only account for a small part of the variation in the numbers imprisoned across the range of countries. It tends to be ideology that determines how often imprisonment is favoured over non-custodial sentences and how harsh sentencing will be. The UK regularly leads the rest of Western Europe in rates of imprisonment. Since 1990, the number of prisoners in the UK has doubled. But when we compare the UK with a country like the

Netherlands, which has a much lower rate of imprisonment, roughly two-thirds of the difference can be traced to the fact that the Dutch favour lighter non-custodial sentencing and shorter sentences.[73] In fact, in 2015, the Dutch government announced it was to close eight prisons due to a lack of prisoners.[74]

The dramatic increase in rates of imprisonment in the UK can be traced to Michael Howard's assertion in 1992, as Conservative Home Secretary, that 'prison works'. When he made this claim, 45 per cent of adults convicted in the Crown courts were put behind bars; in 2001, the figure had risen to 64 per cent.[75] In what amounted to a continuation of Conservative policy, New Labour's Home Secretary Jack Straw stated that 'Prison doesn't work but we'll make it work'. In 2003, in a special edition of the flagship news programme *Newsnight*, Prime Minister Tony Blair proudly explained that his government had presided over a period in which more people had been sent to prison than ever before.[76] Perhaps this was due, in part, to the fact that between 1997 and 2009 some 4,289 new criminal offences were created, approximately one for every day New Labour were in power.[77]

In the US, the situation is even more extreme. In 1978, roughly 450,000 people were imprisoned; by 2005, the figure had risen to over 2 million.[78] As with the UK, this phenomenal rise was largely down to people being sent to prison rather than being given non-custodial sentences. Today, a quarter of the world's convicts reside in America. In 2004, 360 of these were serving life sentences in California for the heinous crime of shoplifting.[79] The irony of this was not lost on novelist and activist Arundhati Roy, who made the memorable observation that 'the world's "freest" country has the highest number' in prison.[80]

Focusing on rehabilitation and root causes makes sense once we stop thinking of crime as a product of an individual's free agency and view it, instead, as a doctor might view the symptoms of a disease. Although potentially dangerous, violent prisoners are not ultimately responsible for the threat they pose – anyone exposed to the conditions that breed violent crime *could* exhibit similar 'symptoms'. Removing those 'infected' from society, as we would a person with a deadly virus, may be necessary – at least temporarily – but punishing them does nothing to prevent further 'outbreaks'. Instead, it draws resources and attention away from discovering the deeper causes of the outbreak. A more humane and rational approach to crime would focus on eradicating the conditions that produced it, and instead cultivate the empathy, self-control and self-worth that is so bound up with ethical behaviour. To pretend, as legal systems do, that the buck stops with the individual prevents us from tackling the cultural, economic and political causes of violence and criminality.

Double standards

Richard Nixon's 1968 presidential campaign warned of 'the deterioration of respect for the rule of law' and the danger of 'the corrosive doctrine that every citizen possesses an inherent right to decide for himself which laws to obey and when to disobey them', a principle he blamed on civil rights leaders such as Martin Luther King and Malcolm X.[81] Within a few years Nixon was forced to resign in disgrace, facing impeachment over the Watergate scandal. Discussing the events in a 1977 interview with David Frost, he justified his actions with the words: 'When the president does it, that means that it is not illegal.'

Shortly after his resignation, Nixon's successor, Gerald Ford, granted him a presidential pardon. 'I deeply believe in equal justice for all Americans whatever their station or former station,' he insisted, adding that 'a former President of the United States, instead of enjoying equal treatment with any other citizen accused of violating the law, would be cruelly and excessively penalized . . . And the credibility of our free institutions of government would . . . be challenged at home and abroad.'[82] Justifying Ford's actions, Dick Cheney, George W. Bush's Vice President, said at Ford's funeral that 'he was almost alone in understanding that there can be no healing without pardon'[83] – a principle denied to the 7.3 million Americans on probation, behind bars, and on parole.

It's a familiar pattern. The evidence for crimes committed under the recent Bush administration, for instance, is overwhelming, well documented and widely accepted. Few now deny that persistent lawbreaking took place, including the authorisation of torture, imprisonment without trial, the kidnapping and disappearing of detainees, warrantless domestic spying, the destruction of incriminating evidence and an illegal war. In 2014, former top US counter-terrorism official Richard Clarke, who served under the Bush administration before resigning following the 2003 invasion of Iraq, said he believes that Bush and his administration are guilty of war crimes for launching the invasion.[84] Yet, neither George Bush nor his partner in war, Tony Blair, has faced any criminal charges.

As a presidential candidate, Barack Obama passionately declared his support for the rule of law, claiming he was open to investigating and prosecuting Bush-era crimes, but, once elected, his rhetoric quickly changed to support the view that 'we need to look forward as opposed to looking backward' – a principle he has not extended to the 2 million inmates that crowd his nation's prisons, the illegally held captives of Guantanamo Bay, or the whistleblowers Chelsea Manning and Edward Snowden.[85] Obama has blocked every attempt to conduct an investigation into his predecessor's actions.

The 2008 financial crash was caused by fraudulent activity on an incredible scale. This is now widely acknowledged, even by long-time defender of Wall Street, Alan Greenspan, ex-Chairman of the Federal Reserve, who described the financial sector's behaviour as 'just plain fraud'.[86] Their actions have had an unimaginably negative impact on the lives of millions of people but – to date – not a single senior American or British banking executive has been placed behind bars. Instead, those responsible for the crash in the US received over $700 billion of public money with no strings attached; their counterparts in the UK were granted a £1.3 trillion rescue package. Some American states did try to take legal action against the banks, but the Obama administration fought hard against these attempts.[87] A number of banks were found to have lied in court, not once or twice but hundreds of times, yet no bank officials were sent to prison.[88]

The multinational insurance company AIG is a case in point. The same executives who presided over the fraudulent transactions that led to its demise – one that was only averted with taxpayer's money – were soon pocketing millions of dollars in bonuses. In the face of public pressure, Obama claimed there was nothing he could do. Defending his boss, Obama's economic adviser Larry Summers claimed, without a hint of irony, that 'We are a country of law. There are contracts. The government cannot just abrogate contracts.'[89] Later, in 2010, commenting on the $17 million bonus given to Jamie Dimon of JP Morgan Chase and the $9 million bonus paid to Lloyd Blankfein of Goldman Sachs – both banks that were recipients of the billion-dollar bail-out – Obama declared that 'I know both those guys; they are very savvy businessmen' and 'I, like most of the American people, don't begrudge people success or wealth. That is part of the free-market system.'[90] Of course, this had little to do with the 'free market'. These banks would not have survived but for the government bail-out. As many have observed, the financial sector has managed to privatise profits while socialising risk: the rich take home the winnings while the poor are forced to cover the losses.

In the UK in 2014, two RBS bankers who were found guilty of £3 million worth of property fraud walked free after Judge Rebecca Poulet QC decided they had 'suffered' enough already, having 'expressed shame and embarrassment' at what they had done.[91] Matt Taibbi, an American journalist who has spent years exposing the crimes of Wall Street, writes that 'Even in the most abject and horrific cases – such as the scandal surrounding HSBC, which admitted to laundering more than $800m for central and South American drug cartels – no individual ever has to do a day in jail or pay so much as a cent in fines.' Taibbi often asked officials why there were no criminal cases. 'Well, they're not crime crimes,' was an answer one prosecutor gave him. Taibbi continued, 'When I asked another why no one went to jail in the HSBC narco-laundering case, given that our prisons were teeming with people who'd sold small quantities of drugs, he answered: "Have you been to a jail? Those places are dangerous!"'[92]

The truth is that inequality outside the confines of the courtroom eviscerates the equality within it. Steal a car and you end up in jail. Destroy the global economy and you are rewarded with billions of dollars. 'Too big to fail' becomes 'too big to jail'. The reason is clear: banks, along with most large industries, spend millions of dollars lobbying and funding political parties. Roughly 3,000 lobbyists in Washington work on behalf of the financial sector. Since 1997, the banks have spent more than $3.6 billion lobbying the government. Over this period, bank profits have soared. In effect, the money spent on lobbying and campaign funding bought the deregulation that allowed the crisis to occur and, later, the influence to avoid paying for it. Perhaps even more significant is the revolving door between finance and politics. Executives from the financial sector are routinely granted top governmental roles as advisers, regulators and policy-makers while government officials are regularly given top jobs in the banking sector after leaving public office.

The influence we have over the formation of the law, the burden it places upon us, and our ability to defend ourselves from it, depend on the wealth and power we already possess. Large corporations routinely spend millions of dollars on political lobbying, the creation of think tanks, and the funding of political parties to induce governments to pass laws that protect their interests. In court, wealth continues to bring its advantages. It costs money to defend ourselves, and more money buys a better defence. Legal aid can go some way to levelling the playing field but it is often under-funded (particularly in the US), under attack, and is not available for all cases. Those with plenty of money can endure long and costly legal battles and, in some instances, escape criminal charges altogether by settling out of court. A standard strategy of corporations, when dealing with less wealthy opponents, is to offer a small sum by way of compensation and then threaten to engage in an expensive and drawn-out legal battle with an uncertain outcome if the offer is not accepted. Walmart has been accused of paying most of its staff less than $10 an hour, pressurising employees to work overtime for no extra pay and routinely locking them in warehouses overnight. Such treatment has led to at least sixty-three lawsuits in forty-two states, all of which Walmart chose to settle out of court for a tiny fraction of the wages it has saved.[93] Moreover, because the law is complex and difficult to understand, wealth can buy the expert advice necessary to navigate it successfully and, wherever possible, to exploit its loopholes for personal gain – tax-avoidance being an obvious example.

Though laws may apply equally to all in theory, in practice there is little equality. Prohibiting sleeping under public bridges has no impact on the millionaire but to the homeless traveller it could mean hypo-thermia and death. A law against stealing bread places no burden on the affluent but a heavy one on those struggling to feed their children. Some laws explicitly target the most vulnerable people. In Florida, for instance, citizens have been banned from sharing food with the homeless. Arnold S. Abbott, a ninety-year-old advocate for the homeless, defied the law and was arrested and threatened with a $500 fine and sixty days in jail.[94]

The sea of inequality on which the legal system floats makes a mockery of the principle of equal rights before the law. The notion that the law treats all people the same, regardless of race, gender, status or creed, is a much celebrated ideal but, in a society in which the distribution of wealth, power and opportunity are so profoundly unequal, equality before the law is itself unjust. The assumption made by many legal theorists that, with few exceptions, 'the same rules may be applied to all' is a fantasy that becomes less justifiable the more unequal society becomes. This was not lost on the third American president, Thomas Jefferson, who said 'There is nothing more unequal than the equal treatment of unequal people.'[95]

Private law

Who decides what counts as a crime? Who decides which criminals are held accountable? In 2002, three twelve-year-old British children were playing in the street with plastic toy guns. The game abruptly ended when they were surrounded by police patrol cars: the children were arrested, finger-printed, forced to give DNA samples and repri-manded for possessing realistic fake weapons. While in 2015, £5.2 billion worth of arms export licences were approved by the British government for regimes on its own human rights blacklist.[96]

A legal framework functions primarily to advance the interests of those who shape it. It determines the rules of the game according to which everyone must play. Different rules favour different interests. Slaves do not write the laws that oppress them. Colonies do not pass the laws that exploit them. Trade unions do not formulate the laws that criminalise them. The laws defining marriage for most of Western history, which effectively made a wife the property of her husband, were not drafted by women. Those who fought to end slavery, improve working conditions, resist colonialism, expand voting rights, achieve gender and racial equality, stop wars and protect the environment, repeatedly clashed with the law out of necessity, enduring police violence and imprisonment in the process. In each case, the law defended the privileges and prejudices of those with power against the rights and interests of those without it.

Adam Smith, the father of modern economics, observed in 1776 that 'Civil government, so far as it is instituted for the security of property, is in reality instituted for the defence of the rich against the poor, or of those who have some property against those who have none at all.'[97] To the extent that the law is shaped and interpreted by a narrow set of elite interests, it degenerates into a means of defending privilege. In fact, the word 'privilege' originally meant 'private law'. The less accountable a legislative process is, the more law enforcers are reduced to the status of a private army, whose primary role is to serve and protect those already in possession of the privileges that accompany wealth and power. Indeed, many of the police departments in the US originated as patrols to help wealthy landowners capture and punish escaped slaves.

The rights people enjoy today were won by those who were prepared to challenge the 'private law' of their time, acting outside it when necessary. It is to them we owe a debt of thanks for the political freedoms we possess – not to those law-abiding citizens who did nothing to challenge the legally sanctioned slavery, patriarchy, racism, apartheid, child exploitation, torture, imperialism, crippling poverty and disenfranchisement of the past, nor to the police and courts who upheld this legally sanctioned oppression.

Punishment is ultimately about power. When the formulation of the law results from great inequalities of power, its implementation becomes not a neutral act, but a highly partisan one, privileging one set of interests over the rest. Martin Luther King captured the essence of the problem when he asked us, in his 'Letter from Birmingham Jail', never to 'forget that everything Hitler did in Germany was legal'. King himself, like Gandhi and Nelson Mandela, was imprisoned for breaking the law. Mandela was branded a terrorist, not just by the South African government but by the political establishments of the US and UK. And, although he was elevated in popular culture to the status of a modern-day saint after his release from prison in 1990, he remained on the terrorist watch list in the US until 2008.

The 'terrorist' smear continues to be widely used. Canada categorises eco-activism as a form of terrorism and a 'threat to national security'. Those profiting from the destruction of the environment remain undisturbed by the law. In the UK, laws that were passed ostensibly to combat terrorism and anti-social behaviour have been routinely applied to people engaged in legitimate and peaceful protest; spaces in which protests are permitted, specifically those around Parliament, have been heavily restricted; 'stop and search' powers, created under broader anti-terrorism legislation, have been used to harass peaceful demonstrators; advocacy groups, including environmental campaigners and anti-war protesters, have been classed as 'domestic extremists' and infiltrated by undercover policemen who go to extreme lengths (including marrying unsuspecting activists and fathering children with them) to maintain their cover.

In Canada, in 2010, hundreds of thousands of protesters filled the streets of Toronto as part of a peaceful protest against the G20 summit. Halfway through the summit weekend, a senior police commander gave the order to 'take back the streets'. The next thirty-six hours saw a thousand people – from peaceful protesters to journalists, human rights observers and Toronto residents – arrested and detained, a stark illustration of police priorities.[98] Two years later, another instructive example took place in Canada, this time in Quebec. Thousands of students were engaged in protests against the hike in their tuition fees. 'The Maple Spring', as it was dubbed, was met by a concerted clampdown by police, legislators and the courts. Law enforcers used pepper spray, stun grenades and rubber bullets. These draconian measures resulted in new anti-protest laws being passed and over 3,000 arrests in the space of seven months. One of these, a student leader named Gabriel Nadeau-Dubois, was convicted and sentenced for the grave crime of declaring, in a media interview, that he believed student picket lines were a legitimate form of protest.[99]

In the US, the Occupy movement, although a peaceful expression of widely held concerns, resulted in numerous instances of police brutality, human rights violations and mass arrests. And in Puerto Rico, peaceful protests over the last few years have been met with, among other things, toxic chemicals, tear gas, pepper spray, swinging batons, rubber bullets, sting-ball grenades and 'conducted-energy' weapons.[100] These examples are just the tip of the iceberg. Along with the erosion of personal privacy, the criminalisation of whistleblowers, and the broader clampdown on internet freedoms, they appear to be part of a wider trend that threatens our most treasured democratic institutions.

★

The criminal justice system places the cordon of responsibility tightly around the individual. This is a disingenuous way to absolve political and economic systems and to deny the need for real equality beyond the confines of the courtroom. If we judge a person or group to be truly responsible for some deplorable action, we leave no room for a more searching explanation of the deeper causes of that action – and this myopia increases the likelihood of reproducing the confluence of economic, political and cultural forces that created the conditions for it to occur. (In the same way, if we judge a person to be ultimately responsible for an admirable action, our presumed knowledge can blind us to its deeper causes, making it harder to reproduce the kinds of behaviour we *want* to see.)

The responsibility myth has a powerful hold over us: even if we reject it intellectually, it can appear inescapable in practice, in our day-to-day lives. Yet, as we have seen, it gives us a distorted picture of reality. If we accept that people are not truly responsible for what they do, then a prisoner is no more deserving of his sentence than the judge who delivers it to him. The unsavoury truth, as jurist Wendell Holmes understood, is that the law 'bears most hardly on those least prepared for it'.[101]

Today's system of criminal punishment is not a solution to injustice but a symptom of it. Its irrational foundations divert attention away from society's deeper injustices and failings, many of which we will explore in the following chapters. If society was serious about reducing crime it would hold accountable, and attempt to deter, those whose actions and ideologies perpetuate the conditions that breed it: those who fight to preserve and extend enormous inequalities of wealth, power and opportunity. A politician in a suit can do far more harm than any street gang, drug dealer or petty thief.

Crime is a politically determined category that must always be scrutinised. For too long our system of punishment has been the means of reinforcing broader social injustice rather than preventing it. The antidote, at all levels of society, is greater political accountability and equality. Only through the creation of a fairer, more humane society – one that offers dignified opportunities to all – can a criminal justice system ever be truly just.

3

Reward

Every morning, people around the world wake up to another day's work. Across the planet minerals are extracted, machinery operated, goods transported, seeds sown, text typed, houses built, crops farmed, clothes stitched, patients cared for, and children taught. Hours pass and energy is expended. It's a remarkable fact that at the close of each day people are rewarded so unevenly for their contributions. Billions earn less than $2 a day while, at the opposite end of the spectrum, an American hedge-fund manager like David Tepper bags more than $1 million an hour.[1] The result is that the eighty-five richest people on Earth own as much wealth as the poorest half of the world's population, and the richest 1 per cent now own more than the remaining 99 per cent combined.[2]

Disparities in wealth are so pervasive that it takes some effort of imagination to see things afresh, to understand that there is nothing inevitable about poverty or gross inequality in the modern world. There is no immutable law of nature preventing us from sharing things more equitably, so that everyone is fed, clothed, nourished, sheltered and educated. Human choices maintain the current distribution of wealth and human choices can change it.

In pre-capitalist societies, large inequalities in wealth and power were often justified by religious teachings, which claimed that the social and economic hierarchy was ordained by God, so that those with great wealth had a divine right to it. Today's dominant justification for inequality comes not from religion but economics. Ethical considerations play little or no part in the practice and study of modern economics – you will not find a serious discussion of fairness in any standard textbook. The irony of this is striking given that the study of economics evolved as an offshoot of ethics.[3] The father of Western economic thought, Adam Smith, was, after all, a moral philosopher.

The familiar justification for inequality is founded on the principle that people should be rewarded according to the value of their contribution. There is something intuitively compelling about this reasoning: you get what you give. Mainstream (neoclassical) economists tell us that this is precisely what happens in a competitive, free market. The impartial laws of the market determine the value of your contribution and reward you accordingly. If the free market rewards some people hundreds of times more than others, it can only mean the former produce hundreds of times more value than the latter. A worker who adds £50,000 of value to a company is rewarded with £50,000 in wages, so the theory goes. As we will see, this is not actually how people are rewarded but, even if it were, would it be fair?

There are different ways to contribute to the production or provision of something. Suppose we decide to bake a cake: I pay for the ingredients and let you use my kitchen, but you do all the baking. The outcome is a delicious cake but each of us has contributed something quite different. You have put in your time and skills as a chef; I've contributed my money and property. In a market economy, both contributions can generate an income. Some people are rewarded for what they do; others for what they own.

If something we own can be traded in a market, generating an income, economists call it 'capital'.[4] Capital includes land, real estate, industrial equipment and money. The income derived from it can take a number of forms, such as profit, rent, dividends, interest or royalties. But there are glaring problems with the principle of rewarding people according to the capital they own. Most obviously, it allows some people to grow extraordinarily rich without having to do anything at all. After all, wealth generates wealth. Between 1990 and 2010, Liliane Bettencourt, the heiress of L'Oréal, the world's largest cosmetics company, increased her fortune from $2 billion to $25 billion without having to lift a finger (more than ever, investment decisions are made by paid experts).[5]

Our economic system delivers vast rewards to the rich not for what they do, but for what they own. What's more, the greater the fortune, the faster it tends to grow. The largest fortunes can achieve rates of return two or three times larger than those earned by smaller ones (6 or 7 per cent compared with 2 or 3 per cent).[6] Mainstream economists have long assumed that a natural outcome of the market is a reduction in wealth inequality, which ultimately stabilises at an acceptable level, but in reality this depends on the institutions and policies in place. Historical evidence suggests that over time, and left to their own devices, competitive free markets tend to concentrate wealth in fewer and fewer hands. In his 2013 book, *Capital in the Twenty-First Century,* French economist Thomas Piketty provided powerful evidence for this. One of the world's leading researchers into inequality, he argues that unchecked capitalism tends to make the rich richer, producing extremely high levels of inequality.[7] Although this may seem old news to some, it turns mainstream economic thinking on its head and does so with more data than has ever been collected on the subject, covering three centuries and over twenty countries. The lesson from history is clear: we cannot rely on the 'invisible hand' of the market; we must extend the reach of democracy through regulation and taxation.

Vast wealth may take on a life of its own, but how do people come to own it in the first place? One of the main ways is simply by inheriting it. Inheritance is not a peripheral economic issue. In the US, between 1970 and 1980, inherited wealth accounted for 50 to 60 per cent of total wealth – some estimates have put it as high as 80 per cent.[8] Globally, inherited wealth accounts for 60 to 70 per cent of the largest fortunes. Some of these inheritances represent enormous transfers of economic power. The Walton family, for instance, is worth $152 billion.[9]

As capital accumulates, dynasties form and inherited wealth accounts for a larger proportion of total wealth, giving the richest heirs more wealth than the populations of some countries. This is the main reason why ownership of capital is so extremely concentrated. Historically, the wealthiest 10 per cent have always owned more than half of all capital (and sometimes as much as 90 per cent), while the poorest half owned almost nothing.[10] The pattern holds true today. In most European nations, the top 10 per cent own roughly 60 per cent of the wealth, while in the US they own a little over 70 per cent of the wealth. In both cases, the poorest half of the population own less than 5 per cent.[11]

The impact of inheritance is felt over centuries. By tracking rare surnames, researchers in the UK found that, over the last 150 years, the effect of inheritance has consistently overcome political efforts to improve social mobility. The two economists behind the study of January 2015, Professor Gregory Clark and Dr Neil Cummins, summed up their results in simple terms: 'To those who have, more is given.' There was a 'significant correlation between the wealth of families five generations apart'. In other words, 'What your great-great-grandfather was doing is still predictive of what you are doing now.'[12] Today, the descendants of the nineteenth century's upper classes are not only richer, but more likely to live longer, attend Oxford or Cambridge and end up a doctor or lawyer. And there is no sign of any let-up in the power of inheritance to shape the world. The wealth transferred via inheritance from one generation to the next is set to break all records. A report by the Boston College Center on Wealth and Philanthropy predicts that the US is set for the largest inter-generational transfer in history: $59 trillion passed down between 2007 and 2061.[13]

Why should the lottery of birth have such an impact on what people own and the opportunities they enjoy? Being born to wealthy parents is a matter of blind luck. The typical argument made is that those with wealth have the right to do with it as they please, including passing it on to their children. Even if we accept this as a legitimate right, it is certainly not the *only* legitimate right. It ought to be balanced against other rights – most pressingly, the right of all children to enter a world of equal economic opportunity, or, at the very least, one in which they have access to clean water, food, shelter, medicine, education and digni-fied employment. When the two rights conflict, why should the wants of the few outweigh the needs of the many? To the younger generation, equal economic opportunities can mean the difference between health and illness, education and illiteracy, happiness and depression, even life and death. By contrast, reducing great concentrations of economic power by regulating inheritance need not threaten anyone's health, literacy, happiness or existence.[14]

Inheritance isn't the only way to acquire great wealth: much of the world's private property was originally attained through violence and exploitation. Slavery, for instance, rapidly accelerated the accumulation of capital in eighteenth-century Britain. Historian Robin Blackburn writes: 'The thousands of millions of hours of slave toil helped to underpin the global ascendancy of Victorian Britain.'[15] Profits from this exploited labour helped to build many banks (including Barclays), extend vital credit to early industry, modernise British agriculture, finance the experiments of James Watt, and increase economic growth. When a panel of experts attempted to put a figure on the unpaid labour of the slaves who had enriched Britain, they arrived at a figure of £4 trillion.[16] Dr Nick Draper from University College London estimates that as many as 'one-fifth of wealthy Victorian Britons derived all or part of their fortunes from the slave economy'.[17] Adding insult to injury, when slavery was eventually abolished in Britain, 46,000 slave-owners were compensated for their loss of 'property' to the tune of £17 billion in today's money. Their freed slaves did not receive a penny.[18]

What about capital that is secured through talent and hard work – does this entitle an owner to generate unlimited income from it? After a given point, the income generated from capital goes well beyond what is necessary to compensate the owner for any initial effort. As Piketty points out, 'no matter how justified inequalities of wealth may be initially, fortunes can form and perpetuate themselves beyond all reasonable limits and beyond any possible rational justification in terms of social utility. Entrepreneurs thus tend to turn into rentiers, not only with the passing of generations but even within a single lifetime . . .'[19]

The problems go deeper than this, however. Many who reject the idea that we should be able to generate income simply from owning capital still believe that we should be rewarded in accordance with the value of our personal contribution. But how do we measure the value of someone's contribution? In 2010, the world's highest paid footballer earned over £500,000 a week.[20] In the UK, in the same year, a nurse starting in her or his first year earned close to £400 a week.[21] How does the market determine that a footballer's contribution is worth over a thousand times more than the contribution of a nurse?

The mainstream theory of wages defines 'contribution' as the market value of what workers produce as determined by supply and demand, but this value changes with market conditions. If 90 per cent of engineers dropped dead tomorrow, the market value of the skills of the remaining 10 per cent would promptly increase. This would have nothing to do with any change in their efforts or output. Numerous factors beyond our control determine the market value of what we can contribute. Ultimately, as with inheritance, it's just a matter of luck.

Even the 'self-made' rich owe a debt greater than their fortune to those who developed the technologies, institutions, laws and infrastructure that made their enrichment possible. Billionaire Warren Buffett concedes that 'society is responsible' for most of what he has earned. 'If you stick me down in the middle of Bangladesh or Peru or someplace, you'll find out how much this talent is going to produce in the wrong kind of soil. I will be struggling thirty years later. I work in a market system that happens to reward what I do very well – disproportionately well.'[22]

What's more, *what* we can contribute is also a matter of chance. The opportunity to cultivate our innate potential depends on conditions we play no part in creating. For instance, in the US, only 9 per cent of students in elite universities come from the poorer half of the population.[23] Another study released in 2015 by the UK Social Mobility and Child Poverty Commission exploded the myth of a meritocratic society.[24] According to its findings, children from wealthier families with less academic intelligence than their poorer counterparts were nevertheless 35 per cent more likely to end up becoming high earners. Wealthy parents employ a range of strategies to ensure their children end up in 'top jobs' but, whether it's by tapping into powerful personal networks or subsidising unpaid internships, the result is the same: an absence of downward mobility. And, because high-earning jobs are in limited supply, gifted students from less advantaged backgrounds face an uphill struggle to turn their potential into market rewards.

In terms of economic remuneration, talent and hard work mean little if they are not granted the right conditions in which to flourish. Human potential is squandered on an enormous scale because of the extreme inequalities of opportunity that exist in the world. Countless people have perished from preventable diseases, died in senseless wars and starved in avoidable poverty. Billions have been denied the freedom necessary to realise even a fraction of their promise. Many potential Shakespeares and Einsteins, Maya Angelous and Emmy Noethers must have lived and died without ever knowing the wonders of which they were capable.

Just as we should reject the idea that a person deserves large rewards because of inherited wealth, we should not accept that a person deserves large rewards because of their genetic and social inheritance. Influential neoliberal economist Milton Friedman showed up the hypocrisy of rejecting one form of inheritance and not the other by asking, 'Is there any greater ethical justification for the high returns to the individual who inherits from his parents a peculiar voice for which there is a great demand than for the high returns to the individual who inherits property?'[25]

However, there is a distinction to be made between inheriting wealth and inheriting the talent and opportunities to develop it. Becoming rich through inherited wealth requires no effort, whereas becoming rich through inherited talent does. It is not easy to develop talent or to use it to make a valuable contribution. Doctors, lawyers and scientists have to study for years to succeed in their professions; top athletes, artists and musicians must dedicate their lives to cultivating their abilities; and entrepreneurs must often work extremely hard to create successful businesses. But as soon as we bring effort into the equation, we have deviated from the principle of reward according to the market value of contribution. I may dedicate my life to playing tennis but it's clear to anyone who's seen me play that I will never be rewarded for my efforts. Top professionals are ultimately rewarded for what they achieve, not how hard they try.[26]

But would it be fairer to reward people according to effort? We neither choose our innate capacities nor the freedom we're given to develop them; moreover, once these capacities are developed, we do not determine the value the market will assign to them. It all comes down to luck. So, what about the efforts we make? The first thing to say is that working hard is not in itself a virtue. Financial speculators, arms dealers, corporate lobbyists and fossil-fuel executives may work very hard, but they also make the world a worse place to live in for many others.

Some progressive economists have suggested that people should be rewarded in accordance with their *socially useful* efforts. However, the ability to make socially useful efforts is, nevertheless, an ability. It may be more evenly distributed throughout the population than other abilities, but, no matter how hard they try, the very old, the very young, the severely disabled and the sick are often unable to contribute in ways the market recognises or remunerates.[27] Our capacity to be self-disciplined, to persevere, to focus, is just as much a part of our genetic and environmental inheritance as any other capacity. The treatment we receive as children – and whether we are prone to hyper-activity, have trouble maintaining our attention, lack confidence or self-esteem, suffer from severe headaches or depression, and so on – can all impact on our capacity to channel our energies in productive ways. Both the inclination and capacity to work hard reflect the way we are and, for that, we are not responsible. Even remuneration based on socially useful effort, then, fails the test of fairness.[28]

The problem lies with the notion of reward itself. A reward is given in return *for* something. But no concept of reward sits comfortably with our lack of ultimate responsibility.[29] Since we are not truly responsible for what we do, it does not make sense to distribute 'rewards' on the basis of behaviour. It does not make sense to apportion rewards at all. The intuitively compelling notion of 'getting what you give' ignores the fact that what we can give depends on what we get from our genetic and social inheritance. Whichever way we look at it, all paths to wealth, status and success are paved with luck. This fact supercharges calls for increased equality across society.[30]

The hoarding of vast resources – resources that could save countless people and enrich numerous lives – has been normalised and celebrated in our society, but there is no moral justification for it. No path to extreme wealth entitles us to hold on to it – not in a world in which so many fundamental needs go unmet. The idea that we could ever be entitled to vast wealth – that a disproportionate amount of Earth's riches could ever really *belong* to us – is a dangerous fiction, one that has been cultivated to mask naked greed. Great wealth is never deserved. The fact that some people attain it is merely the product of strange institutions, emerging from an odd culture, developed by a flawed species.

For a principle of distribution to satisfy the test of fairness, it has to be based on need. In a world that took a principle of fair distribution seriously, sickness would be reason enough to be treated, hunger would be reason enough to be fed, and homelessness reason enough to be housed. Resources would no longer be distributed according to the arbitrary lotteries of birth and opportunity. Instead, material inequalities would be used as a means of compensating for inequalities in more fundamental domains.[31] For instance, people with disabilities or health problems may need extra resources to enjoy a similar degree of freedom to the non-disabled and physically healthy. Or imagine a society in which everyone is paid the same hourly wage. Some people may choose to work more hours than others and end up with more money. But those who work fewer hours are not necessarily worse off. The well-being accrued from time off work can offset the benefits of financial remuneration. In such cases, the financial inequality that arises is not a problem if the overall balance of well-being, enjoyment and freedom is roughly maintained.

Fairness is not the only important value. There are still trade-offs to be made and other factors to be considered. For instance, as with punishment, perhaps rewards could be used to incentivise people to behave in socially valuable ways (more on this below). Striking the right balance between fairness and other social goals is an ongoing experiment, one that should be directed democratically. But, in order to make informed judgements about these trade-offs, it is essential to dispense with spurious arguments and self-serving fictions. Accusations of the 'undeserving poor' and claims of the 'wealth-creating rich' are baseless attempts to conceal the injustice at the heart of the economic system. Arguments put forward to justify inequality based on notions of desert always have been, and always will be, fundamentally flawed.

A fair day's pay

Rewarding people according to the market value of what they contribute is not fair because the value of our contribution is ultimately determined by forces for which we are not responsible. Whether we inherit a lot of money or property, are free from oppression and prejudice, are well educated, bright, strong, healthy, resourceful or beautiful, is ultimately down to luck.

Yet the idea that we are rewarded according to the market value of our contribution is not just unfair, it's a myth.

Contribution to output is the key idea presented in economic text-books to explain the income people receive for their labour (and capital). 'Marginal Productivity Theory' came to prominence in the nineteenth century and the idea is that under perfectly competitive market conditions, wages for a given worker are driven towards that worker's marginal productivity, that is, the amount of value they add to the company or, put another way, the revenue that would be lost if they left. According to the theory, if you remove one worker from a team and the daily revenue drops from $1000 to $900, then that worker is worth $100 a day.[32]

If workers were paid according to contribution then two workers doing the same job, using the same tools, should earn the same wage. Entry-level jobs in McDonald's restaurants across the globe are similar enough to provide a good way to test this prediction. In fact, just such a study was conducted by economists Orley Ashenfelter and Stepan Jurajda.[33] To avoid problems of currency comparison, the study recorded how many Big Macs an hourly wage could buy in several nations. Although the theory predicts that the wage of all entry-level workers should be able to buy the same number of Big Macs, the actual figures varied significantly. In India an hourly wage bought 0.23 Big Macs compared to 3.04 in Japan, a thirteen-fold increase for producing the same thing. Other studies have found similar disparities. Economist Ha-Joon Chang, for instance, points out that a bus driver in Sweden gets paid about fifty times more than a bus driver in India – and no one believes Swedish bus drivers are fifty times more productive.[34]

Clearly, it is not individual productivity setting the wages. Other factors are at play, one of which is immigration control. If borders were open, large numbers of Indian workers could travel to Sweden and accept a fraction of the wage earned by Swedish drivers, which would still be a significant improvement on their earnings in India. Conceivably, they could replace all Swedish bus drivers since they would be willing to work for so much less. It is the politically determined immigration policies of Sweden – enforced by armed border guards – not a difference in productivity, that allow Swedish bus drivers to earn so much more than their Indian counterparts.

Another factor that influences income is gender. For all the gains feminism has made, men still earn more than women in almost all nations. This disparity exists for a variety of reasons that are not easy to untangle – unequal caring responsibilities, undervaluing work traditionally done by women – but discrimination remains a factor. In the UK, for instance, not only does it take longer in certain sectors for women to be promoted to senior positions, but they are still less likely to receive a bonus in their job, and when they do receive one, it is likely to be significantly lower than one given to a male counterpart.[35]

The popular myth that wages reflect the value of what we contribute is a powerful one, but the briefest examination of who enjoys most of the world's wealth reveals it to be a fiction. Nobel prize-winning economist Joseph Stiglitz makes the point well:

> Few are inventors who have reshaped technology, or scientists who have reshaped our understandings of the laws of nature. Think of Alan Turing, whose genius provided the mathematics underlying the modern computer. Or of Einstein. Or of the discoverers of the laser . . . or John Bardeen, Walter Brattain, and William Shockley, the inventors of transistors. Or of Watson and Crick, who unravelled the mysteries of DNA, upon which rests so much modern medicine. None of them, who made such large contributions to our well-being, are among those most rewarded by our economic system.[36]

If our system genuinely rewarded people according to their contribution, then these individuals, with their rare and historic contributions, would have been among the wealthiest in the world. And what are we to make of the fact that Van Gogh, William Blake, Vermeer and Schubert all died in poverty?

One study focused on expert commentators whose analysis and predictions on economic and political events were in great demand.[37] These people earn good money for offering insights into their field of expertise. Psychologist Philip Tetlock wanted to know how accurate their predictions were, so he asked each participant in his study to rate the probabilities of three outcomes on a given topic covered by their expertise: the continuation of the status quo, more of something (such as economic growth) or less of something. Tetlock gathered data on 80,000 predictions. The results were not flattering. If the experts had simply assigned a probability of one third to each of the three outcomes they would have had more success. In fact, the more in demand (and presumably highly rewarded) a forecaster was, the poorer their predictions turned out to be.

Another study conducted at Duke University looked at the extremely well paid chief financial officers (CFOs) of large corporations.[38] After tracking over 11,000 economic forecasts from CFOs, it found that the correlation between their predictions and what took place was less than zero. In other words, when they said the market would go up, it was slightly more likely to go down. The point is not that these forecasters are stupid (certain things are just too complex to predict reliably) but that the market is rewarding people extremely well for contributions that have no value.

Individuals with strong bargaining power are able to maintain incredibly high wages in the face of significant falls in productivity, corporate CEOs being the obvious example. According to mainstream theory, a CEO's income should be equal to the value they add to their company. Consider the case of Henry (Hank) McKinnell, former CEO of Pfizer, the world's largest research-based pharmaceutical company.[39] From 2001 to 2006, the share price of his company dropped by 46 per cent, yet McKinnell still pocketed $65 million. No one can prove that he did not contribute $65 million worth of value to the company, but neither common sense nor the economics profession provide any reason to suppose that he did. Instead, it is overwhelmingly likely that CEOs like McKinnell exploit their powerful position to extract ever more money from the corporations they manage, even when those businesses perform poorly.

Falls in profit accompanied by executive salary increases are a regular occurrence. It was reported in 2014 that the board of directors at Barclays Bank awarded a 10 per cent rise in bonuses despite a 32 per cent fall in profits.[40] High-level executives are essentially able to set their own pay rates, so unsurprisingly they bear little relation to performance. In 1965, the top CEOs in the US were paid 24 times more than the average production worker; by 2000 this figure had risen to 376 times more.[41] (Over roughly the same period, the median American worker has seen no increase in pay at all.) These CEOs have not become 376 times more productive. Robert Reich writes that 'Anyone who believes CEOs deserve this astronomical pay hasn't been paying attention. The entire stock market has risen to record highs. Most CEOs have done little more than ride the wave.'[42]

The mainstream theory of wages cannot explain what we observe in the world but its problems do not end there.[43] A core assumption of the theory – that an individual's contribution is always measurable and distinct – is seriously flawed. We've seen that the value of our contribution is ultimately down to luck, and that we cannot separate our own contributions from all those, living and dead, whose knowledge, effort, time and skill have richly benefited us. But even if we could separate these things, it would still be extremely difficult – and in many cases impossible – to define and measure the contribution of a single worker. Most work is done in teams, and often a worker's contribution is inextricable from the tools, resources and contributions of others. As Piketty notes, in many cases the 'very notion of "individual marginal productivity" becomes hard to define. In fact, it becomes something close to a pure ideological construct on the basis of which justification for higher status can be elaborated.'[44]

What really determines how income is shared out among those who helped to generate it? The classical economists, from Adam Smith to

David Ricardo, had a simple answer: power. Many factors affect how rewards are divided – talent, education and technology all play a part – but power has always been a decisive factor. Smith was explicit about the importance of bargaining power in determining wages:

> The workmen desire to get as much, the masters to give as little, as possible . . . It is not, however, difficult to foresee which of the two parties must, upon all ordinary occasions, have the advantage in the dispute, and force the other into a compliance with their terms . . . In all such disputes, the masters can hold out much longer [because they are wealthier].[45]

Although, as Smith saw, employers have the upper hand because they are able to 'hold out much longer' in a dispute, workers have tried to level the playing field by banding together in unions and acting collectively. In doing so, they have fought and won many battles: a shorter working day and week, safer working conditions, pensions, as well as laws against child labour, unfair dismissal and corporal punishment at work.

Historically, dividing revenue between those who contribute capital and those who contribute labour has been a source of great conflict. Throughout the Industrial Revolution it was common for labourers to work excruciatingly long hours in dangerous and uncomfortable conditions for a wage that barely sustained their own existence. In nineteenth-century Britain, workers were devoured by a system intent on maximising profits. In parts of Manchester – one of the engines of the Industrial Revolution – conditions were so bad that the life expectancy in some areas was only seventeen years.[46]

The proportion of income that goes to capital has varied over time. Often it's been as much as 25 per cent and sometimes as high as 50 per cent.[47] Of course, the more that goes to the owners of capital, the less the workers receive. If ownership of capital were distributed equally across the population, the split between labour and capital would be unimportant. However, as we've seen, inequalities of capital ownership have always been extreme: today, the wealthiest 10 per cent own somewhere between 80 and 90 per cent of the world's private capital.[48]

For centuries, a concerted effort has been made to prevent workers from unionising effectively. Employers – often working collectively themselves – have used their wealth and influence to harness the might of the state to weaken unions through government legislation, and break up strikes with the coercive power of the police. As early as 1776, Smith saw that big business, the 'merchants and manufacturers' of his time, were 'by far the principal architects' of national policy, shaping the system so that their interests were 'most peculiarly attended to'.[49] By 1800, the British parliament had passed the 'Combination Act', which forbade workers from bargaining collectively for higher wages or to improve their working conditions. Since then, the laws concerning collective action have been regularly contested. The battle for profits and wages continues to rage. Sometimes workers are controlled with violence. For instance, in 2012, thirty-four miners striking for a higher wage were shot dead by South African police at the Marikana platinum plant outside Johannesburg.[50] Sometimes workers are controlled by stealth. In 2014, it came to light that an illegal agreement had been struck between some of the largest tech firms in the world, from Apple to Google, to suppress the wages of hundreds of thousands of their employees.[51] Leaked confidential memos showed how these giants of the tech world agreed not to compete for each other's workers in order to prevent a bidding up of their wages.

The degree of inequality we see in the world is the outcome of policy. It cannot be rectified by trying to make markets look more like the highly abstract models so beloved of neoclassical economists. The growing concentrations of undeserved wealth are not a sign of market failure but a natural outcome of the power dynamics within a market system. In the real world, deregulated markets favour those who own capital. The state has the power to reinforce this advantage or curtail it. There is no value-neutral way to balance the power of workers and corporations: any attempt requires value judgements to be made and most of the time these simply reflect the power balance of competing forces within society.

For decades, many of the world's central banks have pursued policies that objectively favour those who derive income from capital over those who earn income through work. For instance, the form of globalization they have championed has eroded the bargaining power of countless workers by allowing capital to move freely across borders but preventing workers from doing so. The result is that companies hold the trump cards in disputes with workers over pay, as they can threaten to leave if they don't get their way. Ultimately, countries are driven to compete with each other to attract capital by pushing down wages, lowering taxes and reducing regulation. However, if capital lacked mobility and workers were free to cross borders, the dynamic would be reversed: countries would have to compete to attract workers by offering lower taxes, better schools and more attractive working conditions.[52]

Politics, as the classical economists knew, cannot be removed from economics. It will always play a decisive role in setting wages, determining profit margins and sharing out or concentrating wealth. The strength of unions, the level of immigration control, the value of a minimum wage, the degree of corporate regulation and the structure of the tax system are central to any explanation of inequality and wages – and they are inherently political. Power ought to be as central to the theory of income as force is to the theory of motion. In terms of income derived from labour, the imbalance of power in the economy has resulted in a level of inequality in the US that is, according to Piketty, 'probably higher than in any other society, at any time in the past, anywhere in the world'.[53]

When teachers, nurses, doctors, care workers, farmers, artists, street cleaners, bin collectors and builders do a good day's work, society is better off. But much of the work done in societies merely takes money from some and gives it to others without creating any additional value for that society. As Robert Reich puts it, 'High-frequency traders who win by a thousandth of a second can reap a fortune, but society as a whole is no better off.'[54] Although it may boost profits for a few companies, from society's point of view, this kind of work is a waste of talent, effort and training that could have been used in far more valuable ways.

Expending resources on taking a larger share of existing wealth, rather than creating new wealth, is called 'rent seeking': it is an exercise of power. In the 2008 bank bail-out it was the power of the financial sector to shape laws and avoid regulation – not an increased contribution to society – that allowed it to engage in practices that made billions at the expense of ordinary people. Through a range of rent-seeking practices, banks managed to siphon off increasingly large amounts of wealth from the productive economy. These included exploiting buyers' ignorance in order to sell securities that had been designed to fail; taking reckless risks in the knowledge that a government bail-out would be waiting should the gamble fail to pay off; targeting the desperate and uninformed with predatory loans and exploitative credit card practices; and borrowing money from central banks at extremely low interest rates. The financial sector was amply rewarded for its rent-seeking behaviour before the crash and, because of its political influence, continues to be handsomely rewarded *in spite of* it. As union organiser Eugene V. Debs put it, those with 'the power to rob upon a large scale . . . [have] the power to control the government and legalize their robbery'.[55]

How did we end up moving away from Smith's description of wages, which acknowledged the central role of power, to the assertion that wages are determined by contribution instead? Nineteenth-century economist John Bates Clark pioneered today's theory of wages. In doing so, he simply ignored what economists before him had recognised: that it's often impossible to separate one person's contribution from the team in which they work.[56] Clark recognised that Smith's theory of wages had radical political implications, seemingly offering support to the mass of workers demanding higher pay. He believed that a new theory to justify poverty wages was essential to avert revolution. Of the impoverished mass of workers in the nineteenth century, he wrote:

> [T]heir attitude toward other classes – and, therefore, the stability of the social state – depends chiefly on the question, whether the amount that they get, be it large or small, is what they produce . . . The indictment that hangs over society is that of "exploiting labor." "Workmen" it is said, "are regularly robbed of what they produce. This is done within the forms of law, and by the natural working of competition." If this charge were proved, every right-minded man

should become a socialist; and his zeal in transforming the industrial system would then measure and express his sense of justice.[57]

Clark's theory of wages reframed the debate to suggest that it wasn't about power but contribution: that workers *did* in fact receive what they were worth, so they had no cause to demand higher wages. As we have seen, Clark's theory isn't up to the task. It is founded on spurious assumptions and bears little relation to the real world. Power – economic and political – very clearly plays a crucial role in determining wages and the overall distribution of wealth. There is no economic law forcing Walmart to pay its workers starvation wages or demanding that CEOs be paid hundreds of times more than their workers. These are political outcomes. But Clark was right about one thing: power is more vulnerable when it is perceived as illegitimate. Moral justifications, if widely accepted, can appear to rationalise extreme poverty and gross inequality.

Carrots and sticks

Every political and economic system has at its core a conception of human nature. The one underpinning the leading economic models of today assumes you are rational and self-interested with unlimited wants and tastes that do not change. There is, as Amartya Sen observes, 'something quite extraordinary in the fact that economics has . . . evolved in this way, characterizing human motivation in such spectacularly narrow terms'.[58] Extraordinary as it may be, the extreme and growing levels of inequality in our world are often justified with reference to this 'spectacularly narrow' conception of human nature. The argument goes that inequality is necessary to provide the right incentives to increase the overall productivity of the economy. Prevalent assumptions about human nature have led many to conclude that, in order to increase productivity, we should reward what we like and punish what we don't. However, decades of research have turned these intuitions on their head. External 'carrot and stick' incentives often produce the opposite of what their advocates expect.

Behavioural scientists categorise tasks as algorithmic or heuristic.

Algorithmic tasks are formulaic in character and can be completed by following a set of instructions; whereas heuristic tasks are creative, requiring flexibility and imagination. Delivering mail is an algorithmic task: it can be broken down into a series of simple steps, a routine to be repeated day after day. Writing a speech is a heuristic task: there is no manual for doing it correctly; each speech requires novel solutions. Research with both children and adults shows that punishments and rewards are effective motivators when it comes to simple algorithmic tasks, but for creative heuristic tasks, they result in poorer performance. Extrinsic motivations 'crowd out' our intrinsic motivations. They turn play into work and reduce the satisfaction of that work.

The counter-productive nature of rewards has been observed even with toddlers. A series of experiments at the Max Planck Institute in Germany placed a group of twenty-month-old infants in a room where an adult pretended to need help.[59] In the first phase of the experiment, some of the toddlers that tried to help (a majority) were rewarded, while others were not. In the second phase, the helpful infants were given further opportunities to be of assistance to an adult in need. The results showed that the vast majority of the unrewarded group continued to lend a helping hand to the adults (above 80 per cent) but in the rewarded group, a significantly lower proportion continued to help (only about 50 per cent). In other words, material rewards diminished the motivation of the toddlers to carry on helping the adults.

Over the course of numerous experiments, Professor of Psychology Edward L. Deci has found that 'When money is used as an external reward for some activity, the subjects lose intrinsic interest for the activity.'[60] When we are told 'If you do this, I'll give you that' it undermines our autonomy, diminishing the appeal of what had previously been an intrinsically rewarding activity. Although rewards can deliver a short-term boost, the effect soon wears off and often reduces our long-term motivation. According to Deci, we all have an 'inherent tendency to seek out novelty and challenges, to extend and exercise . . . [our] capacities, and to explore, and to learn'.[61] An environment conducive to the full flourishing of these capacities 'should not concentrate on external-control systems such as monetary rewards'. The results of Deci's studies suggest that, to truly motivate people, it's best to empty their minds of financial rewards altogether. This frees them up to engage creatively with the task at hand. Thinking about what we are getting, or what we ought to be getting (perhaps because we are anxious about our financial situation), hampers our creativity.

It has generally been assumed that people are driven predominantly by basic biological needs – hunger, thirst, libido – and the rewards and punishments of their environment. But research on human motivation points to a third crucial drive: 'the innate need to direct our own lives, to learn and create new things, and to do better by ourselves and our world'.[62] Numerous experiments have shown that not only do rewards reduce motivation, they actually hamper our performance. In one famous study, people were asked to solve a problem that required a creative approach. The people who were offered a financial incentive took, on average, 'nearly three and a half minutes *longer*' than those who were offered no financial incentive.[63] A study undertaken for the US Federal Reserve System tested the effect of relatively large rewards on a series of challenging tasks. It found that 'In eight of the nine tasks we examined across the three experiments, higher incentives led to *worse* performance.'[64] Other studies show that this principle also applies to pay-for-performance plans.[65] Speaking of his own professional performance, former chief executive of Shell, Jeroen van der Veer, once declared, 'if I had been paid 50 per cent more, I would not have done it better. If I had been paid 50 per cent less, then I would not have done it worse.'[66]

In light of such research, we need to reassess our assumptions about human nature, work and motivation. For instance, fairness turns out to be an important motivator. Workers who believe they are being paid fairly are more productive. One experiment showed that increasing the wages of workers who felt they were being treated unfairly boosted productivity, while raising the wages of workers who felt they were already being treated fairly had no effect.[67] The implication is that a more equal society would boost overall productivity. It may well be more innovative too. The evidence suggests that the US economy was far more innovative from 1950 to 1970 (when inequality was at a historic low) than it was from 1990 to 2010 (when inequality was growing rapidly).[68]

To change the conditions of work is to change the experience of doing it. Under circumstances that respect human dignity and give us the freedom to pursue our own passions and be led by our own curiosity, work can be a privilege rather than a burden. Even when it places great demands on us, it can have a positive effect on our well-being. If it is meaningful to us, we can enjoy working on the most challenging of tasks. Part of the problem with so much of the work in today's economy is that it is not very meaningful or useful. According to a YouGov poll in 2015, 37 per cent of British workers said their job makes 'no meaningful contribution to the world' (and another 13 per cent said they didn't know).[69] Most jobs are created to enable companies to increase profits, often in ethically questionable ways. High salaries can be viewed as a form of compensation for the absence of real purpose in these jobs. The choice facing many graduates is to work for free as interns in roles they find meaningful or start climbing a ladder they don't really want to be on for a salary. Many others are forced into dull, tiring work for just enough income to survive.

We are all motivated to survive and provide for our loved ones, but other fundamental drives shape our behaviour. Contributing to the lives of others is very rewarding, completing a difficult task can be deeply satisfying, and helping those in need can be profoundly edifying. People give their money, even their blood, to help strangers. Teachers, nurses, artists, scientists, inventors, volunteers and activists do hard and valuable work with modest financial reward or none at all. Every day, people leave highly paid yet unfulfilling jobs to seek work in which they can take pride and pleasure. We forsake higher pay for greater freedom. Developing our minds and bodies, and feeling that we are contributing meaningfully to the world around us, is central to our sense of self-worth and well-being.

A growing body of research suggests that we have evolved to take pleasure from helping others. This pleasure ties communities together in mutually advantageous cooperative relationships. One study found that spending money on others makes us happier than spending money on ourselves.[70] Another study, by psychologists at the University of British Columbia, showed that before the age of two, toddlers 'exhibit greater happiness when giving treats to others than receiving treats themselves'.[71] What's more, 'children are happier after engaging in *costly giving* – forfeiting their own resources – than when giving the same treat at no cost'. Of course, culture can channel and mould these instincts in various ways but the evidence suggests that the desire to work together and help each other is part of what makes us human.

Some degree of inequality may be necessary to motivate people to behave in certain socially valuable ways, but the idea that people do not want to work, that they need to be driven by threats and promises to get anything done, is a misconception.[72] If work enhances our autonomy, if it can be done under dignified conditions, and if we believe it is valuable, most of us welcome it. The Russian scientist and political philosopher Peter Kropotkin held that 'Overwork is repulsive to human nature – not work . . . Work is a physiological necessity, a necessity of spending accumulated bodily energy, a necessity which is health and life itself.'[73]

Of course, not all jobs are equally rewarding. Some tasks carry little or no intrinsic reward and are risky and unpleasant. Today, the most undesirable – though essential – work is largely done by those who are paid the least. A subordinate class of people is obliged to accept these jobs or go hungry. This is a coercive form of motivation based on fear and desperation. Kropotkin writes 'If there is . . . work which is really disagreeable in itself, it is only because our scientific men have never cared to consider the means of rendering it less so. They have always known that there were plenty of starving men who would do it for a few cents a day.'[74] Given our current technological knowledge (and expanding the point to include women), this is truer today than ever before. As Bertrand Russell observed, if we 'had to be tempted to work instead of driven to it, the obvious interest of the community would be to make work pleasant'.[75]

What of the unpleasant work left over? It should either be shared out fairly or carry financial incentives to compensate proportionately for the sacrifice entailed by doing it. Other strategies are coercive and incompatible with a free society. The American historian Howard Zinn writes: 'I worked hard as a college professor, but it was pleasant work compared to the man who came around to clean my office. By what criterion (except that created artificially by our culture) do I need more incentive than he does?'[76]

Incentive-based arguments are often little more than ad hoc justifications for inequality. When examined, they betray a double standard. Cuts to social welfare programmes are justified by the claim they incentivise people out of the 'poverty trap' – as though poverty weren't incentive enough. The reasoning is that if we make poor people poorer by removing their social safety net, they will be forced to go out and find a job or, since many benefit claimants are already in work, a second job. On the other hand, when it comes to discussing incentives for the rich, the opposite reasoning is employed. High salaries for corporate executives are justified as incentivising higher performance, which ends up benefiting the whole of society. The double standard is glaring and ugly. As economist Ha-Joon Chang asks, 'why do we need to make the rich richer to make them work harder but make the poor poorer for the same purpose?'[77]

★

Plato believed that myths to justify inequalities of wealth and power were essential to preserve order in society. He offered the following story: that each citizen was born with a certain kind of metal mixed in with his or her soul. Natural rulers had gold mixed with their soul, their soldiers and assistants had silver, and natural workers had either bronze or iron. According to a divine oracle, if the city were to be ruled by those who lacked gold in their soul, all would be ruined. Later myths, designed to serve a similar purpose, include the divine right of kings, hereditary nobility and the discredited theory of 'trickle down economics'.[78] For millennia, those with power and privilege have used convenient myths to justify their position. Arguably, these myths arise as much to reassure those with wealth as those without it – it's harder to enjoy privileges if you don't believe you deserve them. A sense of entitlement to wealth is nearly as valuable as wealth itself.

In his history of economics, John Kenneth Galbraith writes: 'The explanations and rationalizations of . . . inequality over the centuries have commanded some of the greatest . . . talent of the economics profession. In nearly all of economic history, most people have been poor and a comparative few have been very rich. Accordingly, there has been a compelling need to explain why this is so – and, alas, on frequent occasion, to tell why it *should* be so.'[79] Like their earlier elitist, racist and sexist counterparts, today's justifications of inequality are baseless – yet they provide a veneer of legitimacy to the poverty and oppression around us. They are embedded deeply in the fabric of society, just out of sight, beyond the light of critical scrutiny.

The nineteenth-century English philosopher and father of utilitarianism, Jeremy Bentham, based his moral philosophy on the idea that 'it is the greatest happiness of the greatest number that is the measure of right and wrong'. According to Bentham, the best allocation of resources is one that maximises human well-being. A key assumption he made was that the well-being a person experiences from an additional dollar decreases as that person becomes richer. That is to say, ten additional dollars produce more well-being in someone extremely poor than in someone very rich. The radical implication is that society as a whole becomes better off as material equality increases. We don't have to be utilitarians to see the value of this common-sense insight.

Subjective states like 'well-being' and 'happiness' may be difficult to define and measure, but, as long as large inequalities exist, there is every reason to believe that transferring money from the rich to the poor increases the overall welfare of society. The evidence, in fact, is overwhelming. Many researchers today believe it is possible to collect meaningful data on subjective feelings. Individual self-assessments of well-being are now regarded as an important addition to government statistics, correlating strongly with more objective indicators such as rates of depression and suicide. What the data suggest is that, beyond a certain level of affluence, more money makes no difference to a person's happiness. One analysis of more than 450,000 responses to a daily survey of Americans in 2010 revealed that 'The satiation level beyond which experienced well-being no longer increases was a household income of about $75,000 [roughly £47,000] in high-cost areas (it could be less in areas where the cost of living is lower). The average increase of experienced well-being associated with incomes beyond that level was precisely zero.'[80]

For those who are sceptical about the reliability of 'happiness data', there are more objective indicators. Based on the analysis of extensive data spanning many countries and decades, epidemiologists Kate Pickett and Richard Wilkinson confirm that reducing inequality benefits the whole of society in fundamentally important and sometimes surprising ways:

> In societies where income differences between rich and poor are smaller, the statistics show that community life is stronger and levels of trust are higher. There is also less violence, including lower homicide rates; physical and mental health tends to be better and life expectancy is higher. In fact, most of the problems related to relative deprivation are reduced: prison populations are smaller, teenage birth rates are lower, educational scores tend to be higher, there is less obesity and more social mobility. What is surprising is how big these differences are. Mental illness is three times more common in more unequal countries than in the most equal, obesity rates are twice as high, rates of imprisonment eight times higher, and teenage births increase tenfold.[81]

Humanity has the resources to eradicate starvation, illiteracy, extreme poverty and some of the world's deadliest diseases; it has the means to deepen and expand human freedom for every person on the planet. So why does deprivation and inequality persist? Why do Earth's bountiful resources and humanity's endless creativity serve so few at the expense of so many? Not because the rewards in our society go to those who deserve them, not because it's necessary to incentivise people, and not because it benefits the whole of society. The great imbalance of wealth simply reflects the great imbalance of power.

•

Once we discard the myth of responsibility, the framework of desert that leads us to punish and reward also falls away. We've seen that the distribution of punishment and reward in society cannot be explained in terms of what people deserve. We've also seen that alternative justifications for the outcomes we observe in the world – such as the deterrence argument to justify punishment, and the contribution and incentive arguments to justify extreme inequality – do not stand up to scrutiny.

The distribution of penalties and privileges is ultimately a product of power. Power defines what counts as a crime, who should be punished and how severely. Power shapes the laws which set the rules of the market, strengthening the bargaining hand of some and weakening it for others. The highly skewed distribution of power in our world is central to any explanation of the outcomes we see around us. But how is this unequal distribution maintained? How is it that vast inequalities of wealth and power have survived, even flourished, in the democratic era? Why have people not used the equality of the voting booth to redress the blatant inequalities beyond it?

In Part One we explored the limits on our innate freedom. In Part Two we look at the limits on our political freedom. Numerous social forces vie to shape who we are and influence what we do. Making sense of these methods of control is an important part of changing them. Part Two will take up this challenge.

•

PART TWO

THE ILLUSION OF CONSENT

4

Control

Sitting in a field, you notice an ant struggling to climb a long blade of grass. It falls, and then starts the climb again, diligently persevering until it reaches the top. Why might the ant be doing this? What will it gain? Nothing, actually. Its brain has been modified by a tiny parasite, known as a lancet fluke, that needs to find its way into the stomach of a sheep or cow in order to complete its reproductive cycle. The fluke is manoeuvring the ant into the position where it is most likely to be eaten.[1] It is not conscious of what it is doing (it has no brain of its own); it is simply endowed with features that affect the ant's brain in this way. Similar parasites infect fish and mice, among other species.

Creatures like the fluke control the brains of other organisms directly. Most species exert control by manipulating the signals that reach a brain. The mirror orchid tricks male wasps into delivering their pollen to other flowers by resembling a female wasp. Its deceptive appearance and scent exploit the sexual urges of the male to its own advantage. In fact, the imitation scent is even more intoxicating and alluring than the real thing, leaving male wasps unable to resist doing the orchid's bidding. Other creatures, such as moths, lizards and octopuses, exhibit remarkable powers of camouflage which enable them to deceive predators and prey alike.

In nature, the struggle to survive and the drive to procreate maintain a relentless battle for control. Some species exert control by brute force, others have evolved more subtle strategies. Organisms fight to the death to access the myriad forms of energy locked up around them – in sunlight, plants, flesh and bone. The outcome of this endless struggle determines which creatures gain control over the resources available, including that most valuable resource: other organisms.

Ultimately, all conflicts arise from the desire to control the future. Today's struggles shape what tomorrow will look like. When two aims are incompatible, for one to succeed, the other must fail. The human realm has its own conflicts: the control of slaves by their masters; the persecution of one race by another; the subjugation of women by men; the manipulation of the illiterate by the educated; the exploitation of workers by bosses; and the oppression of poorer nations by richer ones. Like the struggles of other species, human conflict is a battle to determine who gets to do what with the resources available, including that most valuable resource: other people.

We all have visions of the future that we'd like to realise – some grand, some modest – but shaping the future is no easy task. Under our direct and immediate control we have the movement of our limbs and the production of speech, but even these physical and cognitive resources are subject to strict constraints. We can only be so smart and so strong. Our power to act on the world is tightly bounded. One way to transcend our individual limits is cooperation – another is control (and the line between the two is often blurred). If we control not just our own limbs and speech but those of others too, we increase our capacity to bring about the outcomes we desire. The will of a single individual can be channelled through the bodies and minds of many. Alone, a president cannot invade another country, but, positioned at the top of a hierarchy giving him control over a vast army, it becomes possible. Unaided, a media mogul may not be able to sway an election but, as the head of an organisation that directs the activities of hundreds of journalists whose words reach millions of people, it becomes conceivable.

Pyramidal structures concentrate power in the hands of those who sit atop them. This power is always open to abuse. It enables the ideas and priorities of a small number to be imposed on the lives of millions – ideas and priorities that have a strong tendency to include wide-ranging privileges for those doing the imposing. However, the attempt to control people always risks provoking resistance, one born of the power possessed by every one of us: the power to choose. Although we are not ultimately responsible – because we make choices with a brain we didn't choose – we do still make choices. And this power to choose is extremely valuable, the starting point for all the freedom that is available to us.

Choices present an opportunity to those who control them and can pose a threat to those who do not. Unavoidably, they affect the balance of power in society and it is power that determines the future. Just as the power of the river shapes the landscape, the power of choices moulds our social reality. The work we do, the politicians we vote for, the products we buy, the groups we support, the words we say – all of it produces ripples of effects that either reinforce or change the way things are. Every choice becomes part of the chain of causality, transforming the collective reality and altering the course of history. This becomes even clearer when we realise that a choice to do one thing is at the same time a choice *not* to do something else. The choice to work is a choice not to strike. The choice to buy a sports car is a choice not to give that money to charity. The choice to spend billions preparing for war is a choice not to spend that amount on feeding malnourished children. We are condemned to make choices. We cannot avoid taking sides, consciously or otherwise, in the ubiquitous power struggles that characterise our world.

Every choice that is made has two aspects: the situation being faced (the way the world is) and the identity of the chooser (the way the chooser is). In other words, who we are, as well as what we are faced with, determines how we will act at a particular point in time. The decisions we make emerge from the interaction of identity and context. Control of a person's actions can be achieved by shaping either of these elements. Understanding *how* is central to understanding freedom.

Shaping context

Given who we are, we make the choices we do because of the circumstances we find ourselves in. Choices are not made in the abstract; they are made in concrete situations, at particular times, in particular places. These particulars matter. The greater the limits on what we can do, the narrower the range of potential behaviour. Some constraints are imposed by the laws of physics, others by those of society.

The ultimate way to reduce someone's options is to cut short their life. To kill someone is to extinguish their capacity to act on the world. Short of that, the direct application of coercive force, such as imprisonment or physical restraint, dramatically curtails the options available. Threats of physical or emotional punishment can exert control by raising the perceived costs of certain choices. Cultural values can restrict access to many desirable things: a parent can withhold affection, peers can withhold respect, and society at large can deny acceptance and status. Controlling the context of a choice reduces the number and appeal of the options available to a chooser: behaviour is then channelled in the desired direction by shutting off options. While cultural incentives can be powerful, organised coercive force is necessary to close down avenues of action on a large scale.

Modern states expend vast resources on shaping the possibilities and incentives of their populations. Intelligence agencies, police forces and soldiers – along with surveillance cameras, guns and barbed wire – guard the boundaries of 'acceptable' behaviour, changing the risks associated with different courses of action. Laws define what is allowed, and coercive force awaits those who step beyond the paths of compliance. It is in the context of wide-ranging laws, backed by state power, that we make all of our choices.

Without the threat of coercive power, massive inequalities of wealth could not be sustained. The starving will take food if they can, the homeless will occupy empty buildings if they are able, and the sick will obtain treatment if not prevented from doing so. The more concentrated wealth becomes in a society, the more resources must be dedicated to its protection. One way to measure this is to look at the proportion of the national workforce dedicated to maintaining 'security'. This includes police officers, military personnel, prison guards, court officials, but also private security firms and weapons manufacturers. Across nations, a clear pattern can be observed: more unequal nations have a higher proportion of their workforces dedicated to 'guard labour'.[2] Since inequality exploded in the United States, there has been a marked increase in guard labour – in fact, it is a world leader in this respect, boasting 5.2 million workers in the sector in 2011.[3] As a proportion of the total workforce this amounts to four times that of Sweden, a nation with a comparable standard of living. The pattern holds within nations just as it does between them. The most unequal American states have double the amount of guard labour (as a proportion of the workforce) as the most equal ones.[4]

The function of guard labour is to restrict the ways that people can gain access to valuable, often essential, resources – resources under the legal ownership of someone else. Ownership, by definition, reduces the options of other people. The owner of a resource has the power to decide what to do with it. Put another way, to own a resource is to deny the rest of the world the right to use it without permission. It is a relationship between one person (one company, one country) and the rest of humanity – one that is ultimately founded on force.

Centuries of violence have drawn and redrawn national borders, and ownership rights have been transferred to those who wielded the most effective fighting force. Indeed, the modern state was born of war. Given a fairly broad definition, one count estimates that over a thousand wars took place between 1400 and 1984.[5] European monarchies averaged 40 per cent of total expenditure on warfare in the fifteenth century, 27 per cent in the sixteenth, 46 per cent in the seventeenth, and 54 per cent in the eighteenth.[6] In times of war, military costs can exceed 90 per cent of total expenditure. In fact, over the past two centuries, there has not been a single year in which the world has been without military conflict.

From 1500 to the twentieth century, almost every country on Earth came under the direct or indirect control of European colonial powers. Native populations were wiped out or dispossessed of their land. Natural resources were stolen and used to enrich the colonising nations. The last two decades of the nineteenth century saw almost all of Africa conquered and divided up between a handful of European nations. In the blink of an eye, 110 million Africans were turned into subjects.[7]

Nations were conjured out of thin air as territory was demarcated with clean straight lines across the continent. Joseph Conrad called it 'the vilest scramble for loot that ever disfigured the history of human conscience'.[8] Leopold II, King of the Belgians, was a key player in this 'scramble for loot'. For decades he had been obsessed with obtaining a colony for his young country. Belgium 'doesn't exploit the world', he told one of his advisers. 'It's a taste we have got to make her learn.'[9] Though he never set foot on Congolese soil, Leopold took control of a territory seventy-six times larger than Belgium itself with the aim of growing rich on the systematic theft of rubber and ivory. Under his brutal and exploitative rule, at least half the population of his newly created nation perished. According to authoritative estimates, that amounted to roughly 10 million people. It was genocide.[10]

Prior to the First World War, the European powers owned more than three-quarters of the industrial capital in Africa and Asia.[11] During this period, writes Thomas Piketty, 'the rest of the world worked to increase consumption by the colonial powers and at the same time became more and more indebted to those same powers. . . . The advantage of owning things is that one can continue to consume and accumulate without having to work . . . The same was true on an international scale in the age of colonialism.'

Ownership has always been a defining concept of legal frameworks. Laws determine who controls what, what limits exist on that control, and how rights can be transferred. Much ownership can be traced back to acts of violence and subterfuge. Leopold's legal ownership of the Congo began with African chiefs signing treaties in a language they didn't understand and with no idea of what they were giving away. Over the course of history, claims of ownership have been made on all kinds of things, from land, buildings and machinery to water, ideas and even DNA. Claims of ownership have also been made on human beings. The idea that women are a resource to be owned and controlled by men has been deeply embedded in the laws and practices of civilisation for thousands of years. The same is true of slavery. Many millions have lived their lives as the state-enforced legal property of someone else.

In almost every large civilisation, slaves have occupied the lowest tier of a large and complex social hierarchy. Their intelligence, talents and energy were used to bring about outcomes desired by their owners. Just two centuries ago, over three-quarters of humanity were held captive by systems of slavery or serfdom.[12] Traders from Britain shipped close to 1.5 million slaves across the Atlantic, earning for themselves roughly £8 billion in today's money. The conditions of a slave's existence, as historian Adam Hochschild testifies, were abysmal: 'They plant, cultivate, and harvest most of Earth's major crops. They earn no money from their labor. Their work often lasts twelve or fourteen hours a day. Many are subject to cruel whippings or other punishments if they do not work hard enough. They die young.'[13]

Today, the ownership of the talents, energies and time of human beings persists, but takes a very different form. In the past, the control exerted by masters over their slaves was lifelong, coercive and bound by few constraints. Now, control of human labour manifests as highly constrained, temporary forms of consensual ownership: 'employment'. Instead of being sold against our will into indefinite servitude, we rent ourselves out for a fee, for defined purposes and set periods of time (of course, some people are still forced into slavery).

Why do people sell their labour? In the present system, access to basic goods and services – food, shelter, energy, education and healthcare – is increasingly obtainable only in exchange for money. Access to money is closely controlled (a primary function of guard labour). For those that do not inherit wealth, the ways of obtaining this currency are extremely limited. To survive, most people must pass through the tight bottleneck of employment. That money is paid does not change the fact that at the heart of this arrangement is a relationship of control. The employer determines a vision of the future and the employee works to bring it about. Many people are compelled to do this because other paths to meeting their fundamental needs have been closed off or are just too risky to take. In fact, the options available to many people are so limited that those who manage to obtain employment – even dangerous, unsatisfying or low-paid employment – are considered the lucky ones.

Loans are the only other viable source of money for most people. Taking on a debt appears to be a voluntary action, but as pathways to life's indispensable resources are increasingly closed off, it may become unavoidable. The need to borrow money in order to pay for life's fundamental necessities locks people into a relationship of compliance and control. The legal obligation to repay what is borrowed (plus substantial amounts of interest) traps people in a form of indentured labour with respect to the lenders making the loans. The coercive apparatus of the state ensures that failure to make repayments carries heavy penalties, ranging from the repossession of a home to a stretch in prison.

Young people are increasingly burdened by crushing debts. The average US college graduate amasses nearly $30,000 of debt.[14] More and more, parents are co-signing their children's loans, making them liable if their children cannot meet their payments. In one case, parents grieving the death of their daughter Lisa learned that they still had to pay back her student loan worth over $100,000.[15] This was in addition to taking in their daughter's three children. As Lisa's father points out: 'It's just impossible on a pastor's salary raising three kids to pay $2,000 a month on loans.' Today, Americans owe a total of $1.2 trillion in student loans. In the UK, university fees are so high that financial experts estimate that nearly two-thirds of students will never fully pay them off.[16]

The harder it gets for people to meet their basic needs, the more amenable they will be to the demands of a prospective employer, client or creditor. With enough currency in your bank account, the minds and bodies of others – the builder, the artist, the prostitute, the lawyer – are then suddenly at your disposal. Money buys labour power. Some will argue that the poor are still making 'free choices' – after all, no one is holding a gun to their head. But not being able to pay bills, make rent or even eat is as good as a gun to the head for many people, coercing them into agreeing to arrangements of control and compliance: they do so in order to secure their children's education, their parents' health and the roof over their head.

Separated from almost every resource by a price tag, our options expand and contract with our bank balance. Poverty diminishes freedom by reducing the number and appeal of our options. It determines the context of our choices and functions as a remarkably effective mechanism of control.

Shaping identities

Given the circumstances we find ourselves in, we make the choices we do because of who we are. But who we are has already been shaped by our circumstances. From infancy, the conditions created by our natural, built and social environments send us down a particular path of development, one of many permitted by our genetic inheritance. We adopt a way of life through a process of socialisation. This shaping of our identity is unavoidable – every community socialises its young according to dominant ideas about what is valuable or necessary – but socialisation can take many forms. It can enlighten or suppress, empower or tame, control or liberate.[17]

The shaping of a person's identity – their beliefs, values, fears and desires – can be an extremely effective form of control. Coercion based on force alone requires extensive resources. On a large scale and for extended periods of time, it is almost impossible to sustain. It will always provoke resentment and risk rebellion. However, through the shaping of identities, people can be channelled down paths without ever coming into contact with the forces guarding their boundaries. They may even cease to notice these boundaries, and forget the reality of batons and guns, censure and violence awaiting those who veer too close to their edge. As philosopher and revolutionary Rosa Luxemburg is often credited with saying: 'Those who do not move, do not notice their chains.'

Unlike the lancet fluke, humans cannot plant themselves in the brain of another being in order to take control – but they can plant ideas and desires, cultivate habits and values, and instil fears and insecurities, loyalties and beliefs. They can plant them young and from the exalted position of religious, cultural or familial authorities. By the time we have the conceptual tools necessary to question them, the world is already perceived, categorised and interpreted from within the framework of our particular identity.[18] History tells many a tale of people acting against their own interests as a result of such conditioning. Again and again, men and women have upheld ideologies, supported systems and accepted lies that disempower them; over and over, subjugated groups have internalised their oppressor's perspective, accepting as right and proper their subordinate role. The ant sacrifices itself because its brain has been changed by a lancet fluke. The soldier sacrifices himself because his brain has been changed by a belief. Both end up dead.

Social conditioning provides us with a common set of assumptions that colour the way new information is interpreted. From one perspective, a war can look like an act of justice and liberation; from another, an act of theft and murder. To one group, a natural disaster may signify the wrath of God; to another, a symptom of global warming. Within some ideologies, poverty looks like inferiority; within others it looks like exploitation. Dominant narratives tell us what is worth striving for and what can be sacrificed. They tell a story about why things are the way they are, what problems must be addressed, who is to blame, and how the problems should be solved.

Maintaining a highly unequal social order requires the propagation of justifying beliefs and the stamping out of dissent. The domination of Western Europe by the Catholic Church saw not only books burnt but heretics too. According to some scholars, the invention of the printing press in the fifteenth century played a key role in breaking the hold of the Catholic Church and bringing about the Reformation.[19] In part, this was due to the proliferation of different interpretations of the Bible, which cast doubt over the idea that there was one infallible text. Violent suppression of dissenting narratives in the work of scholars, artists or scientists has been a regular occurrence since the first publications. Book-burning and the persecution of scholars goes back at least two thousand years to China's Qin dynasty, when special emphasis was placed on the dangers of non-conformist poets, philosophers and historians.

The battle to control narratives is continuous. Starting in 2011, the Occupy Wall Street movement struggled to highlight the power of 'the 1 per cent', the corruption of the financial industry, and the extreme inequality produced by the present economic system. Leading Republican strategist Frank Luntz conceded that he was 'frightened to death' by the impact of Occupy on the ideas of ordinary Americans.[20] In a bid to neutralise the threat and retake control of the narrative, Luntz tutored Republicans on how to 'talk about Occupy'. He warned against the word 'capitalism', preferring instead either 'economic freedom' or 'free market'. He advised against talking about 'raising taxes on the rich', preferring the phrase 'taking money from hardworking Americans'. He disliked talk of 'bonuses', offering instead the term 'pay for performance'. He discouraged the term 'government spending', recommending the alternative 'government waste'. Most tellingly of all, he advised Republicans to deflect blame for the crisis away from banks and onto government by declaring 'You shouldn't be occupying Wall Street, you should be occupying Washington. You should occupy the White House because it's the policies over the past few years that have created this problem.'

The moulding of beliefs to meet the needs of a political system, although ubiquitous, is most apparent when the reins of power are seized to take society in a radically new direction. Times of revolution are invariably accompanied by attempts to transform the process of socialisation in order to produce the kind of people suitable for the new system. It makes sense: deep social change requires deep shifts in beliefs and values. An oppressive, violent past can leave its scars on whole continents, inhibiting free thought and perpetuating insidious forms of oppression. The decision to change the socialisation process may be motivated by a genuine impulse for greater freedom. On the other hand, it may be little more than a cynical ploy to consolidate power. The twentieth century offers a variety of examples.[21]

When Hitler took power in 1934, significant resources were expended on shaping the beliefs and values of the German population. Censorship was extreme, and the messages conveyed by the media – from films to books – were tightly controlled. Hitler, who devoted three chapters of *Mein Kampf* to the subject of propaganda, was acutely aware of the importance of shaping belief and opinion as a means of control. When the Nazis took power, the German education system was comprehensively revamped so that subjects were approached from within the state's ideological framework. History lessons focused on German military achievements, biology classes taught Aryan superiority and, across the board, Jews were demonised and blamed for the economic hardships Germany had experienced. Outside school, millions of children were signed up to the Hitler Youth by parents keen to appear supportive of the regime. By 1939 the organisation had eight million members.

In spite of their ideological differences, examples of rapid political and social change from the twentieth century share some common features. Whether in Bolshevik Russia, Fascist Italy, Nazi Germany or Communist China, seizure of power was followed by a restructuring of the education system to approach academic subjects from within the confines of the newly adopted ideological framework; teachers who deviated from the prescribed curriculum often faced strict penalties. A violent clampdown on dissenting views was typical. Youth organisations worked with schools to shape the young, and songs, marches and oaths of allegiance were commonplace.

Periods of political upheaval throw into sharp relief the ways in which socialisation is used to meet the demands of a new social system, but every system shapes people to meet its needs, often in ways that tighten centralised control. Collective acceptance of social structures is reinforced through established institutions such as schools, churches, the media and the workplace. If people believe the Queen is ordained by God, they will be more inclined to bend to her will. If people believe they live in a democracy, they will more readily accept their leaders. And if people believe the wealth of the rich is deserved, they will be less likely to ask why they themselves have so little. Cultivating the appearance of legitimacy reduces the risk of protest, rebellion and revolution, and historical narratives are key to establishing legitimacy. Origin stories, whether invoking gods or founding fathers, are used to make sense of life. They serve various functions, including the concealment of uncomfortable realities and inconvenient truths – imperial wars, colonial legacies, mass enslavement and genocidal destruction. As George Orwell put it in *Nineteen Eighty-Four*: 'Who controls the past, controls the future. Who controls the present controls the past.' What we are and therefore what we can be changes with our understanding of what has gone before.

Success, responsibility, ownership, work, normality, equality, freedom – the way we think about such foundational concepts frames reality and guides our choices. Moral concepts exert a particularly powerful force. When deeply internalised, the paths permitted by our moral codes need no armed guards to patrol their boundaries. We reduce our own options, police our own actions, punish our own failings: parents disown their children, patients forego treatment, couples refrain from pre-marital sex, and the young volunteer to kill.

People react strongly if they feel cheated, tricked or manipulated. When economic arrangements are viewed as illegitimate, inefficient or exploitative, they will be contested. One way around this is to obscure and confuse the reality of a coercive relationship, to draw a veil of complexity over it. Those being controlled can then be led into blaming themselves or finding a convenient scapegoat for their predicament. The use of language is important here. Think again of the concept of ownership. We use it to describe a hungry family's relationship to the food on their table, the wealthy businessman's relationship to his factory, the landowner's relationship to thousands of inherited acres, and the pharmaceutical company's relationship to life-saving medicine. The significant moral differences among these relationships are lost beneath the blanket label 'ownership'. As we broaden the scope of our definitions, we erase crucial ethical distinctions, with far-reaching social consequences.

Debt is another example. The repayment of one's debts has long been presented as a moral and social duty. As anthropologist David Graeber points out, 'in Sanskrit, Hebrew, Aramaic, "debt," "guilt," and "sin" are actually the same word'.[22] But taking on debt, for nations as well as individuals, is often an act of desperation. Although economic exchanges give the appearance of parity, they mask injustice when the more powerful party, be they employer or creditor, gets to set the terms of exchange. The fact that a loan has to be taken out to meet extortionate medical bills (the primary cause of bankruptcy in the US) becomes an irrelevant detail. Once the labels 'debtor' and 'creditor' are stamped on the relationship, the moral obligation falls on the debtor to pay back what they have borrowed and that is that. Reducing an obligation to a financial transaction robs it of history and context. Other obligations – of society to its members, of one human being to another, of those with much to those with little – are crowded out. David Graeber writes:

> If history shows anything, it is that there's no better way to justify relations founded on violence, to make such relations seem moral, than by reframing them in the language of debt – above all, because

it immediately makes it seem that it's the victim who's doing something wrong. Mafiosi understand this. So do the commanders of conquering armies. For thousands of years, violent men have been able to tell their victims that those victims owe them something.[23]

In past centuries, European colonialists used debt as a control mechanism to devastating effect.[24] Today it operates as a weapon of what can justly be described as economic imperialism. In the 1970s, as Western banks sought to create investment opportunities for vast sums of money arriving from the world's leading oil-producing nations, they set about trying to convince Third World leaders to take out large loans with interest rates that quickly soared into double digits. This precipitated the Third World debt crisis, giving the Western-dominated IMF (International Monetary Fund) the leverage it needed to take control of the economies of supposedly sovereign nations, cutting vital welfare programmes and public services. Perhaps worst of all, the powerful logic of compound growth meant that the original amount borrowed had to be paid back many times over by the domestic populations who, often ruled by corrupt dictators, played no part in authorising the loans and rarely benefited from them. Since 1970, for instance, the Philippines has borrowed $110 billion, has paid back $125 billion, yet still owes $45 billion.[25]

The spate of foreclosures that followed the 2008 economic crash in the US left many former homeowners blaming themselves.[26] A veil of complexity shrouded the collapse in confusion. In this vacuum of understanding, myths of the industrious rich and the lazy poor prospered, turning economic failure into something shameful for the individual rather than the result of a corrupt, deregulated financial sector and a rigged economic system that was rapidly increasing social inequality. Many victims of the crash channelled their anger inwards or towards their peers rather than towards those whose actions had caused the crisis. The sense of obligation that naturally arises when someone does you a favour has been hijacked by our banking system to place a veneer of legitimacy over what are plainly coercive relationships.

The supposed moral obligation to repay debt – irrespective of the wider context – has trumped far more important obligations. Employing the language of austerity and the rhetoric of 'tough choices', cities and states have been slashing welfare, cutting pensions and dismantling public services, ruining the lives of countless people in the process: children, the disabled, the in-work poor, the mentally ill and the elderly. The claim that we should honour our obligations to billionaires and banks before honouring our obligations to the most vulnerable in society is a thinly veiled attempt to lend moral legitimacy to rampant greed.

In all modern states, a massive infrastructure exists to shape people's identities. From the blackboard to the billboard, the supermarket aisle to the evening news, we are confronted by constant attempts to influence our emotions and priorities. To the extent that this infrastructure defines our thinking, sets the terms of debate and influences our ideas, it exerts a tight grip on our thoughts and actions. It is safe to assume that some of our beliefs, loyalties, biases, habits and values exist simply because they serve the interests of those who have the power to shape them. This has always been how power defends itself. But there are countervailing forces: innate instincts and prior conditioning place limits on how much we can be moulded. Securing our consent, therefore, is not always possible. But short of consent, compliance will do. And the outcome is often the same. People may despise the system under which they live, they may hate the jobs they are forced to do and the conditions under which they must work, they may even long for revolution of one sort or another, but as long as they do not act on these feelings, they do not pose a threat. Upon the obedience of the many, be it secured by inducing fear, ignorance, cynicism or loyalty, rests the power of the few.

★

The distinction between context and identity is useful but the line between the two is irrevocably blurred. The situations we experience shape our identities and our identities determine the choices we make in any given situation.[27] Even violent coercion relies on the shaping of identities. Law enforcers and soldiers under all regimes are subject to psychological conditioning in preparation for their work and the wider culture in every system legitimises – often glorifies – the coercive function they fulfil.

How do these strategies of control impact our power to choose? The answer is that, in almost every case, they don't. As long as our behaviour is the result of what we decide, given our character, values, beliefs and circumstances, the power to choose is preserved. Even when circumstances place extreme limits on our options, or when our identity is the product of indoctrination, we still have choices to make. This is true even when we are physically threatened or restrained. When physically coerced, for instance, we have the choice to resist or comply. If we are physically paralysed, we have the choice to refocus our thoughts. In this sense, at least, we are 'condemned to be free': we cannot escape our ability to choose.

The capacity to choose is fundamental to any meaningful notion of freedom, yet it is only a starting point – necessary but not sufficient. Precisely because it is possessed by anyone with a choice to make, the 'freedom to choose' is extremely limited. Held equally by slaves and slave-owners, it is compatible with the most insidious forms of control. A more profound concept of freedom is needed to answer the deeper question of what qualifies as control and what does not – something that will be developed in Part Three.

Two and a half revolutions: a brief history

The history of our species is bound up with two revolutions of immense significance – the agricultural and the industrial – and the beginnings of a third: the democratic. The agricultural and industrial revolutions transformed the way wealth was produced, distributed and controlled. The democratic revolution threatened to do the same. An understanding of these revolutions sheds light on how control is maintained in the world we see today.

Whether they are armies, state bureaucracies or multinational corporations, large hierarchical structures characterise the modern world, amplifying the dictates of those who control them. Hierarchical social organisation has been around for a long time, but scholarship across numerous fields suggests that for the vast majority of our history we humans lived in small bands of nomadic hunter-gatherers, in highly egalitarian societies, with a substantial degree of gender equality, and no war.[28] Hierarchical structures emerged as a product of specific historical conditions.[29] About ten thousand years ago, in part because of changes in the climate, communities in certain regions began to make the transition from hunting and gathering to farming. This change spread across Asia and Europe from a starting point in the Fertile Crescent of the Middle East. Although it was labour intensive, the domestication of plants and animals enabled more food to be produced than was needed for the community to survive. The emergence of agriculture and the surplus it produced, though small, proved to be a revolutionary step in human history, a precursor to the written word, social stratification, bureaucracy, cities, states and armies – in short, 'civilisation'.

The far-reaching effects of agricultural development manifested themselves over thousands of years, transforming what it meant to be human. The cultivation of grains enabled communities to build permanent homes and live together in villages. Populations expanded, and the surplus allowed some members of the community to dedicate their time to activities unrelated to farming. Divisions of labour were established and hierarchical social structures took hold. Six thousand years ago, the invention of the plough, along with other technological developments, led to an even larger surplus, not just in food but in clothes and raw materials.

Slowly but surely, stratified social structures hardened into rigid hierarchies and gender equality was eroded. The struggle for territory and security, as well as the need for internal social cohesion, gave rise to warrior chiefs and high priests, powerful figures within the community who exerted significant control over the surplus. Inequality was reinforced over the generations as wealth was passed from parents to their children. Elites monopolised new forms of knowledge, taking control of decision-making. Roughly five thousand years ago, certain towns became the world's first cities and soon deep social divisions and centralised government emerged. A military force was required to defend and control the highly unequal distribution of wealth. Power was concentrated in the hands of kings, priests, military leaders and a newly created class of specialists trained in the esoteric arts of writing and book-keeping, both developed to keep records of the many transactions of wealth transfer taking place. Innovations in technology, law, bureaucracy and finance were spurred on by the pressures of warfare and the search by elites for more effective means of governing the surplus. For the next few thousand years, as John Maynard Keynes put it, 'there was no very great change in the standard of life of the average man living in the civilised centres of the earth. Ups and downs certainly. Visitations of plague, famine, and war. Golden intervals. But no progressive, violent change.'[30] Then a few centuries ago, advances in technology and the rapid accumulation of capital set the stage for humanity's second major revolution.

In the fifteenth century, advances in shipbuilding and navigation brought about the first truly global trading network linking Spain, the Netherlands, Portugal, England, Japan, China and India. Key items like spices, silk and wool were sought-after commodities and a form of international currency. Merchants bought cheap and sold dear, moving across continents and amassing great fortunes. Trade in slaves became an integral part of the process as unpaid labour flooded the market with valuable goods. First in England, then across Europe, the system of feudalism, having enjoyed centuries of stability, began to break down. In its place emerged a world of markets, commodities, wage labourers and capitalists.

Under feudalism, the nature, size and distribution of the surplus was relatively clear to all concerned. Peasants could see how much they had produced and how much was taken by the landlord who had contributed no labour to its creation. With the emergence of international trade, open markets and complex financial tools, the scale, diversity and distribution of society's surplus wealth became far harder to comprehend.[31] As divisions of labour became more finely demarcated; as human toil was combined with ever more complex machinery, tightly controlled by a class of managers; and as the role of finance became more central, the processes by which wealth was created were increasingly shrouded in mystery. Adding to the confusion was the fact that labourers were given their share in advance, in the form of wages, before the production process had been completed.[32] Built on a thriving slave trade and an army of impoverished workers living and labouring in deplorable conditions, this system was the source of both immense riches and immense human misery. This was the start of the Industrial Revolution: a second profound change in the way our species produced its surplus.

As merchants grew rich, they eagerly sought opportunities for profitable investment. At the same time, peasants who had been thrown off their land constituted a newly formed workforce desperate for a wage. Technological advances brought these two social groups together in a new kind of workplace: the factory. This system of mass production transformed society at a breakneck pace. Yet the complex world of long-distance trade and volatile markets continued to obfuscate the means by which wealth was created and distributed. The market seemed to have its own economic laws, independent of politicians and the state. In reality, the role of government was central. Its coercive hierarchy determined the rules of the market and stood in the wings ready to defend (and often expand) the growing inequalities of wealth, domestically and internationally. The evolution of the modern state is bound up with the fulfilment of this function. For instance, the need to finance astronomically costly wars played a vital role in shaping core institutions such as efficient tax-collecting bureaucracies, bond markets, stock exchanges and central banks.

Political struggles determine whose interests the governing hierarchy upholds and whose it ignores – what is permitted and what is not. Shifts in power are complex affairs, impacted by technological innovation, cultural change, popular resistance and war. Groups who benefit from these shifts can use the coercive apparatus to modify the 'rules of the game', consolidate their advantage and exert greater influence over the surplus. Social change can be fraught with contradiction, and usually unfolds over long periods of time, but gradually it has produced profound changes in how, and in whose interests, society is organised.

For thousands of years, states were ruled by unaccountable elites. In the age of the Enlightenment, revolutionary energy was unleashed and society transformed. The rise of electoral democracy opened up radical possibilities; it was a chance for the disadvantaged majority to take back control of government, and for the vast productive powers of humanity and the wealth created by them to be freed from the grasp of monarchs, emperors, merchants and industrialists, and placed in the hands of 'the people'. In other words, the rise of democracy threatened to revolutionise – through social rather than technological change – the way wealth was produced, distributed and controlled. At least, that is what many hoped for and, of course, some feared.

The roots of the word 'democracy' – *demos*, meaning 'people' and *kratos*, meaning 'rule' – convey what appears to be a simple concept: rule of the people. But what it really means and how it should actually work has long been debated. Who are 'the people' and what does it mean 'to rule'? Ancient Athens is often held up as the first democratic state, yet, even at its height, only a small minority of men had the right to take part. For the next two millennia, this was the rule rather than the exception. Until the twentieth century, in almost every instance of state-sanctioned electoral democracy, the majority of 'the people' were excluded.

The freedoms that have been fought for and won over the last five centuries have been substantial, paving the way for the creation of today's democracies. In 1500, however, power and privilege was concentrated in the hands of a tiny minority of aristocrats and senior clergy who monopolised access to education, politics and wealth. Notions of individual liberty, privacy, freedom of thought and speech, universal education, rights for working people, equality before the law, representative government and universal suffrage were little more than distant dreams. Making them a reality meant overcoming enormous obstacles: the authority of the Church, the dictatorship of powerful monarchs, and a political culture that upheld institutions of slavery and patriarchy.

Since the first modern campaigns for democratic reform in seventeenth-century England, the transition from aristocracy to democracy has encountered powerful resistance from those who stood to lose power and privilege. As the forces for democratic reform grew over the seventeenth, eighteenth and nineteenth centuries, old power structures sought new ways of maintaining control. An early strategy was simply to prevent those without wealth and property from voting. After the British Reform Act of 1832, only 18 per cent of men (and no women) could vote, and even late into the nineteenth century, the franchise was restricted to freeholders, leaseholders and householders whose property exceeded a certain value. In 1866, responding to plans to extend the right to vote, parliamentarian Lord Salisbury expressed a common concern when he said that granting the working poor the vote would likely lead to the passing of 'laws with respect to taxation and property especially favourable to them, and therefore dangerous to all other classes.'[33]

James Madison, co-author of the US Constitution, saw the role of government as protecting 'the minority of the opulent against the majority'. He claimed that those 'without property, or the hope of acquiring it, cannot be expected to sympathise sufficiently with its rights to be safe depositories of power over them'.[34] The solution, according to Madison, was to keep the power of the government in the hands of those who represent the wealth of the nation. Another Founding Father, John Adams, feared that 'If all were to be decided by a vote of the majority, the eight or nine millions who have no property, would not think of usurping over the rights of the one or two millions who have . . . Debts would be abolished first; taxes laid heavy on the rich . . . and at last a downright equal division of everything be demanded.'[35]

It is no accident that neither the US Constitution nor the Declaration of Independence describes the US as a democracy. In fact, for much of its history, 'democracy' and 'democrat' were terms of abuse. The Canadian political philosopher Francis Dupuis-Déri has shown that major political figures only began to refer to themselves as 'democrats' decades after the American and French Revolutions.[36] Such resistance to democratic reform among elites meant that by 1900 the world still did not have a single country in which all adults could vote.

By the end of the nineteenth century, the elite's fears of public participation in the political process were growing as pressure to extend the franchise increased. These fears were clearly articulated by the influential sociologist Gustave Le Bon in a book entitled *The Crowd* (1895).

Le Bon stressed that the inability of crowds to reason 'prevents them displaying any trace of the critical spirit . . . of discerning truth from error' and claimed that 'the entry of the popular classes into political life . . . is one of the most striking characteristics of our epoch of transition . . . Today the claims of the masses are becoming more and more sharply defined, and amount to nothing less than a determination to utterly destroy society as it now exists . . . The divine right of the masses is about to replace the divine right of kings.'[37]

Historically, the majority of venerated political thinkers have been critical of democracy in both theory and practice. Influenced by the writings of Le Bon, Joseph Schumpeter, one of the twentieth century's leading theorists of democracy, believed that 'democracy does not mean and cannot mean that the people actually rule in any obvious sense of the terms "people" and "rule." Democracy means only that the people have the opportunity of accepting or refusing the men who are to rule them.'[38] Reflecting a common attitude, he saw the public as weak, overly emotional, impulsive and lacking the intellectual capacity to think for themselves about complex issues. Not even education could help: 'people cannot be carried up the ladder' for they are able to discuss complex issues only in 'an infantile way' and are 'incapable of action other than a stampede'.

Power, he believed, should be in the hands of 'governments of experts'. His justification is interesting. Living through the emergence of advertising as a potent social force, he observed the increasing power of advertisers to shape needs, cultivate desires and direct behaviour. For him, this process discredited the notion of an authentic 'popular will'. If public opinion could be shaped by outside forces, it must lack any independent or rational basis. 'If all the people can in the short run be "fooled" step by step into something they do not really want, and if this is not an exceptional case which we could afford to neglect, then no amount of retrospective common sense will alter the fact that in reality they neither raise nor decide issues but that the issues that shape their fate are normally raised and decided for them.'[39]

Well into the twentieth century, these sentiments were still being voiced. In 1934, the head of the American Political Science Association,

Walter J. Shepard, declared that government should be in the hands of 'an aristocracy of intelligence', not directed by 'the ignorant' or 'the uninformed'.[40] This view of the people, held in common by Schumpeter, Le Bon, Weber, Madison and many others, has a lineage reaching back to Plato and Aristotle, both of whom thoroughly distrusted the notion of democracy. Aristotle was concerned with the power democracy would give to the poor, while Plato viewed democracy as rule by the unqualified, and advocated a system of elite rule instead.

The seventeenth-century Scottish philosopher David Hume was fascinated by 'the easiness with which the many are governed by the few'. He found it surprising because 'force is always on the side of the governed' and concluded that government is founded on control of opinion, a principle that 'extends to the most despotic and most military governments, as well as to the most free and most popular'.[41] The claim that force is always on the side of the governed is questionable – certainly in our own time, given the amount of coercive power wielded by modern states – but Hume had a point. The control of public opinion is central to the exercise of power. Preserving domestic inequalities has always required a range of non–violent strategies. From the Pharaohs of Egypt to the Industrial Revolution, writes economist Yanis Varoufakis:

> [T]he rulers' command over the surplus and its uses was based on a combination of their capacity to make compliance seem individually inescapable (indeed, attractive), ingenious divide-and-rule tactics, moral enthusiasm for the maintenance of the status quo (especially among the underprivileged) and the promise of a pre-eminent role in some afterlife. Only very infrequently was it based on brute force.[42]

Where unrestrained force can be used, it lessens the need to control people's beliefs and desires – if you can put a gun to someone's head, it matters less what's going on inside it. It is precisely in societies that combine great disparities of wealth with formal freedom that we should expect to find the most sophisticated forms of control.

As we will see, the threat faced by elites at the start of the twentieth century spawned a subversive solution, one that sought to reinterpret the very meaning of democracy. Modern democracies are founded on the idea that government is legitimised by a mandate – the consent of the governed – but from this principle emerge two conceptions of democracy, for there are two ways to gain the public's consent: one is to modify the government; the other is to modify the public.

The power to choose

The creativity of our species has harnessed more forms of energy, in more complex ways, than any other creatures on the planet. From the domestication of animals and the advent of agriculture to the invention of the steam engine and the nuclear reactor, we have devised ingenious methods for harnessing the power of nature. Technology expanded the power of our species, but it has been techniques of social control that have determined how that power is used. Since the dawn of civilisation, through the shaping of identities and context, extremely skewed distributions of burdens and benefits have been perpetuated. Systems of rule have changed, methods of production have evolved, but coercive hierarchies and deep inequalities have persisted.

Centralised control has always been contested. Until recently, most rulers lacked the means to exert tight control across the vast territories they claimed to govern. Coercive power was dispersed among competing elites, and isolated communities enjoyed considerable political autonomy. There are many cases of communities escaping the reach of centralised power and experimenting with novel forms of self-government. Some were ultimately crushed by force in a relatively short amount of time, but others have survived for thousands of years. The active creation of spaces free from the constraints of centralised power continues today, from the Zapatistas in Mexico and tribes in isolated regions to urban occupations of public and private spaces and virtual communities online.

The many achievements of democratic experiments around the world demonstrate that coercive control is not the only way to coordinate action on a large scale. Mutually beneficial cooperation is the alternative

– working together for a common end, one that benefits all those involved in its creation, in which unity of purpose is preserved by common interest, decisions are reached by dialogue rather than by manipulation or intimidation, and social cohesion is achieved not through carrot-and-stick incentives but by cultivating social values, including a respect for reason, evidence, fairness, equality and democracy. This is an ideal but it has practical value. Ideals orient us. They enable us to evaluate the ongoing experiment that is human society: an experiment in sharing this planet with each other, as families, communities and nations.

In every generation, it is incumbent on those who value freedom to identify its limits and – given our opportunities and talents – work to overcome them. Crucial to being effective in this struggle is an understanding of where power lies. This requires that we look beyond rhetoric and ideology, beyond words laid down in constitutions and legislation, and beyond myths of the market and formal political procedures. It requires that we peel away propaganda, peer behind rituals and lay bare the mechanisms of control that constrain us. It is through understanding control that we understand freedom.

Market democracies are founded on the so-called 'freedom to choose': between competing political parties, products, employers and news sources. But without a careful look at the nature of the choices we face and the way we arrive at our decisions, the experience of making choices can create the illusion that we possess more freedom than we really do. Focusing on the apparent options available to people in the voting booth and the market, while glossing over the way in which people's options and identities are manufactured, conceals the profound imbalances of power at the heart of the system. It conceals entire professions, billions of dollars and increasingly complex technologies dedicated to predicting, understanding and controlling behaviour. It conceals the fact that most of the planet's wealth remains in the hands of a tiny segment of humanity. It conceals a bitter struggle between two competing principles of power: 'one dollar one vote' versus 'one person one vote' – a struggle that continues to shape our world.

The following three chapters examine this wider context. They explore how our political and economic freedoms have been hollowed out while preserving the shell that is the 'freedom to choose'. As we will see, the democratic revolution is far from over. Much of the freedom attributed to the institutional pillars of modern democracies – free elections, free markets and free media – is illusory, compatible as it is with extensive mechanisms of control.

5

Elections

Every few years, millions of people enter small booths set up in local buildings – perhaps a school or town hall. They close the curtain behind them, reach for a pencil and, within the confines of a printed square, mark a cross. The paper is folded and pushed through a narrow slot in a box. Four to five years later they get to repeat the process.

It is primarily the marking of a ballot during the holding of free elections that separates modern democracies from other political systems. Once inside that booth, voters can place their crosses beside any party they choose. It is an act widely hailed as the source of our most cherished political freedoms. And yet, when we place this choice in a larger context, important questions arise: how were the options on the ballot determined? How was the identity – the opinions, loyalties and beliefs – of each voter formed? And, if this liberty is so meaningful, why has voter turnout in most modern democracies been steadily declining?

Manufacturing consent

Democratic reform was not welcomed by the aristocracies and empires of old. The desire of those with power to advance their own interests did not die out as democracies were born. Initially, elites fought the expansion of voting rights, but the growing movement for democratic reform forced a different strategy. As concessions were made, novel methods of control were developed to meet the emerging threat that democracy posed to traditional power structures. These were methods of manipulation rather than coercion.

Technologies of mass communication enable millions of people to be reached with the stroke of a pen or a single broadcast. 'With the emergence of the mass media as a connective tissue of modern life,' observes American historian Stuart Ewen, technology was 'changing the ways that people saw, experienced, and understood the material world and their place within it'.[1] It heralded a revolution in communication and creativity, with huge potential to liberate and educate. But these advances also opened up the possibility of increasing control over the ideas, opinions and values encountered by the public.

Replacing Gustave Le Bon's irrational crowd was, as Gabriel Tarde, a leading social scientist and close friend of Le Bon, put it, the public. Whereas the 'crowd' was viewed as wild and uncontrollable, the 'public' was seen as manageable and educable. 'The crowd may be stampeded into folly or crime by accidental leaders,' wrote social psychologist Edward A. Ross in 1908, but the 'public can receive suggestions only through the columns of its journal, the editor of which is like the chairman of a mass meeting, for no one can be heard without his recognition.'[2]

One of the intellectual pioneers of this 'risk-free' approach to democracy was Walter Lippmann, regarded as the most influential journalist and social critic of his time. Already a confidant of President Woodrow Wilson by the age of twenty-five, he was soon dubbed by Roosevelt 'the most brilliant man of his age'.[3] Lippmann called the practice of managing democracy 'the manufacture of consent'.[4] If Lippmann was the theoretician, then Edward Bernays was the hands-on practitioner. Today Bernays is widely regarded as the father of modern public relations (a term he coined) and, according to some, one of the most influential people of the twentieth century.

The ideas and strategies developed by these men were very much a product of their time. Towards the end of the First World War, they took part in creating the largest propaganda machine the world had ever seen. President Woodrow Wilson had been elected in 1916 on an anti-war platform: 'Peace Without Victory' was his slogan. Nevertheless,

Wilson intended to go to war. The problem he faced was how to deal with the ardent anti-war sentiment in his country; many felt it was simply a 'rich man's war' to recover Wall Street loans. Ewen describes the challenge Wilson faced: 'Sensing that middle-class public opinion was volatile and that a revolt of the masses was possible, a number of noteworthy social analysts began to lobby President Wilson, calling for the establishment of an ideological apparatus that would systematically promote the cause of war.'[5]

One of these analysts was Walter Lippmann. With US involvement in the First World War less than a month away, he advised Wilson to create a government news bureau to make the case that this war would 'make a world that is safe for democracy'. A week after entering the war, Wilson set up the Committee of Public Information (CPI), also known as the Creel Committee. It united the most prominent journalists, artists, advertisers, speakers and intellectuals in the United States with a single ambition: to saturate the perceptual environment with the message that the US had a moral obligation to join the war.

The results were impressive. George Creel, head of the Committee, declared that 'The printed word, the spoken word, motion pictures, the telegraph, the wireless, posters, signboards, and every possible media should be used to drive home the justice of America's cause.'[6] In cinemas around the country, a group known as the Four Minute Men, comprising 75,000 individuals selected by the Committee for their status in the local community and their speaking talents, would stand up between screenings and deliver a rousing, apparently impromptu speech conveying the Committee's central message. Billboards, slogans, adverts of all varieties – drawing on the talents of people who had previously promoted household products – were utilised across the nation. The public were fed fabricated stories of German atrocities and warned of German spies spreading doubts in the minds of the American people. They were asked to fulfil their patriotic duty by alerting the authorities to anyone who was against the war effort. Dissenters were whisked off to jail.

Thousands of 'official war news' press releases were sent to people through the mail. 'Human-interest' features were distributed to capture the attention of those who skipped over the news section of their paper. To target the immigrant population, contact was made with 600 foreign-language papers. The CPI also began publishing its own paper: the *Official Bulletin* had a circulation of 115,000 and targeted public officials, newspapers and other organisations equipped to disseminate information. Hollywood movies, whose plots had been written by the Committee, were soon being filmed by seasoned producers.[7]

Within a few months there was growing war hysteria and a keen hatred of the Germans. By shaping the perceptual environment, a tiny minority had changed the mind of a nation. This was thought-control on a massive scale. The CPI heralded a new age of propaganda (or 'public relations' as it came to be known). At the forefront of these developments were Lippmann and Bernays.

Implicit throughout their work is the idea that public consent is not attained through reasoned, honest discussion but through deception and manipulation. It is worth quoting at length from their writings to demonstrate just how conscious was this attempt to stage-manage democracy. It portrays a very different – and to most people, unfamiliar – conception of democracy, but, as we will see, their strategies and ideas have become commonplace. From think tanks to spin doctors, their legacy pervades our corporate and political life.

Bernays' classic 1928 manual *Propaganda* begins by setting out his vision of a well-functioning democracy:

> The conscious and intelligent manipulation of the organised habits and opinions of the masses is an important element in democratic society. Those who manipulate this unseen mechanism of society constitute an invisible government which is the true ruling power of our country.
>
> We are governed, our minds molded, our tastes formed, our ideas suggested, largely by men we have never heard of.[8]

In a similar vein, Lippmann declared: 'The creation of consent is not a new art. It is a very old one which was supposed to have died out with the appearance of democracy. But it has not died out. It has, in fact, improved enormously in technique . . .'.[9] Harold Lasswell, an American political scientist and perhaps the first analyst of modern propaganda, would write soon after: 'The modern world is busy developing a corps of men who do nothing but study the ways and means of changing minds or binding minds to their convictions . . . more can be won by illusion than coercion.'[10]

Lippman's goal was to ensure the ruling elites could 'live free of the trampling and the roar of the bewildered herd'. He believed the public must be 'put in their place', kept as 'spectators' not genuine participants. In order to keep the public in its place, it is necessary to censor the truth, to redact reality. 'Without some form of censorship, propaganda in the strict sense of the word is impossible . . . Access to the real environment must be limited, before anyone can create a pseudo-environment that he thinks wise or desirable.'[11]

In order to do this, Bernays stressed the importance of an ongoing 'scientific' study of the public, a 'survey of public desires and demands'.[12] With enough data, a publicist can adjust propaganda 'to the mentality of the masses'.[13] What the public want or don't want, desire or detest, fear or hope for can be tracked by focus groups, polls, surveys and market research. Armed with this information, Bernays thought it possible to stimulate the public's fears and hopes to achieve a desired outcome. Symbols – be they a national flag, emotive concept or religious image – play a central role in this process. According to Lippmann, 'The symbol in itself signifies literally no one thing in particular, but it can be associated with almost anything. And because of that it can become the common bond of common feelings, even though those feelings were originally attached to disparate ideas.'[14] Used effectively, the symbol is 'an instrument by which a few can fatten on many, deflect criticism, and seduce men into facing agony for objects they do not understand'.[15] Not only must the 'master of current symbols' use the 'pseudo-environment' to unite disparate groups, he must, argued Bernays, also manufacture public events to direct public attention. These 'stage-managed' moments might include a carefully planned 'spontaneous' photo shoot, a well-worked 'off-the-cuff' sound bite, an orchestrated 'public' protest, or an apparently objective scientific report.

Lippmann repeatedly emphasises the potential for exploiting our limited capacity to make sense of an infinitely complex world. The 'way in which the world is imagined determines at any particular moment what men will do', he writes, but the 'real environment is altogether too big, too complex, and too fleeting for direct acquaintance'. Before we act on the world, 'we have to reconstruct it on a simpler model' in symbolic form.[16] How does a particular symbol take root in the mind of an individual? Lippmann claims that 'It is planted there by another human being whom we recognize as authoritative. If it is planted deeply enough, it may be that later we shall call the person authoritative who waves that symbol at us.'

The rise of the corporation

In his history of public relations, Alex Carey argued that 'The twentieth century has been characterized by three developments of great political importance: the growth of democracy, the growth of corporate power, and the growth of corporate propaganda as a means of protecting corporate power against democracy.'[17] The evidence to support Carey's thesis is overwhelming. The grand scale and conscious intent of twentieth-century corporate propaganda is striking. Any account of modern democracy that excludes it is misleading and incomplete.

Towards the end of the nineteenth century, regulations on corporate mergers and acquisitions were relaxed, leading to a rapid concentration of capital in a small group of 'super corporations'. From 1898 to 1904, almost 2,000 corporations were whittled down to just 157.[18] By the end of the nineteenth century, they had been granted 'corporate personhood' by the courts, winning rights and freedoms that previously had only been possessed by living, breathing people. They were soon to be endowed with a personality. In 1916, following the example of company law in Britain, a US court ruling effectively made it illegal for a corporation to be motivated by anything but profit.[19] To compromise this purpose for the sake of any other considerations – the environment, working conditions or the public interest – would be to act illegally. In 1933, Supreme Court Justice Louis Brandeis compared modern corporations to 'Frankenstein monsters'.[20] Given life by the state, they now threatened to overpower their creators.

Milton Friedman, one of the most influential economists of the twentieth century, defended the view that the corporation's only moral obligation was to maximise corporate profits for stockholders. Executives who prioritised social and environmental goals over profits were, he declared, immoral. The only time such actions are permissible, claimed Friedman, is when they are insincere, that is, when appearing to prioritise the wider social good is merely a means to the end of profit-maximisation. Today, this view of the role of corporations is still supported by the legal framework of most industrialised nations. Legal scholar Joel Bakan explains that the law 'compels executives to prioritize the interests of their companies and shareholders above all others and forbids them from being socially responsible – at least genuinely so'.[21] 'Corporate social responsibility' is tolerated, then, only when it is in the financial interests of the shareholders. Structuring the law in this way only underscores the deeper logic of market competition, which drives competing firms to profit any way they can or perish.

Corporate employees may be decent individuals in their personal lives, but in their institutional roles they are compelled by the goals and priorities of their employer to maximise profit at all costs. This is generally well understood. Jan Kees Vis, Director of Sustainable Agriculture at the multinational corporation Unilever, conceded that the minute he 'adopts a policy that benefits the environment but harms the company' he will lose his job.[22]

A corporation can increase its profits in various ways. Some, such as technological innovation, can benefit us all. But there are many easier ways to increase profits that can, incidentally, cause grave damage: using resources without paying for them; manufacturing unhealthy wants through manipulative advertising; extracting subsidies, tax breaks and bail-outs from the state; and increasing demands on workers while dramatically reducing wages.

The two major threats to corporate profit are market competition and political democracy. No profit-maximising entity truly endorses free-market doctrine for the simple reason that competition harms profits. The corporate support of free enterprise is an opportunistic move – a struggle for power, not principle. Ideally, every corporation prefers to monopolise the market in which it operates and raise entry costs to prohibitive levels, thereby eliminating all competition. Often, this is what happens. Market competition produces winners and losers. Winners then use their gains to consolidate and expand their advantage. They benefit from economies of scale, synergy and larger budgets for advertising, research and political lobbying. Over time, small advantages become magnified and industries become less competitive. In fact, students in business schools are taught how to create barriers to competition in the pursuit of market dominance.

In order to protect citizens and the environment, governments can limit the ways in which businesses can make a profit. So, from the perspective of the corporation, the power of the state poses a persistent threat. Of particular concern is the state's capacity to impose regulation and taxes that eat into profit margins.

But the real threat to profit is not the state (which can be an enormously powerful ally) but the existence of democracy, which can challenge corporate control of the state. Democracy enables people to regulate industry and use their votes to obtain what they cannot afford in the market – healthcare, social housing, education, energy and food – and, in doing so, cordon off parts of the economy from which business might otherwise profit. Consequently, strong incentives and ample means exist for corporations to restrain and control democracy. The goal is to co-opt state power and create an economic environment conducive to their own short-term financial interest. This would be an economy free from democratic interference with minimal regulation and taxation, no legal protection for workers, unions or the environment, coercive support from the state and a host of valuable subsidies.

During the nineteenth century, corporate power was effectively insulated from democratic interference. However, this began to change when, from 1880 to 1920, in Britain and the US, the right to vote was extended from roughly 10 per cent of the population to almost 50 per cent.[23] Men and women from all walks of life were winning the formal right to rule themselves. Meanwhile, widening inequality and worsening poverty were forcing middle-class people to rethink ideological assumptions once widely accepted. Aggravating such conditions were the unaccountable heads of corporations dominating economic life who, writes Ewen, had taken on 'the traits of the despots that eighteenth-century democrats had fought so vigorously to overthrow'.[24]

As long as the right to vote was restricted to those with wealth and property, large corporations could ignore the needs and demands of the disenfranchised masses. At the turn of the century, two factors forced big business to change its attitude: the extension of voting rights and the growing influence of the 'muckraking' press. Investigative journalists were intent on exposing the corruption, exploitation and deceit in business and politics. Exposés bred a growing suspicion of big business among the middle and working classes. A groundswell of working people looked to state regulation as a means of defending their interests and controlling corporate power. The genuine possibility of revolt from working people, along with the extension of the democratic franchise, posed a serious threat to the traditional centres of corporate and state power.[25]

In the US, throughout the 1920s, corporate America fought its corner with considerable success, drawing on the latest social psychological theory and the examples of First World War propaganda. Merger after merger created ever larger and more powerful corporations. By the end of 1929, these giants of industry possessed roughly half the corporate wealth in the country, yet came to be perceived, according to Bernays, as 'friendly giants and not ogres' thanks to the 'deliberate use of propaganda'.[26]

It is no coincidence that this carnival of propaganda ended with the most severe economic crash in history. The illusory bubbles of unlimited growth and perpetual prosperity suddenly burst in October 1929 when $40 billion was lost by stockholders on Wall Street, leading to thousands of American banks shutting down.[27] This had a traumatic impact on American society: 90,000 businesses went bust, one in four workers became unemployed, and 60 per cent of the population found themselves in poverty.[28] It was a period marked by soup kitchens and bread lines. Throughout the early years of the crisis, Washington was dumbfounded. Economic orthodoxy held that the self-correcting mechanisms of the market would kick in imminently, but, as the politicians waited, things only got worse. Ideology was one obstacle, the gold standard another. It tied the amount of currency in circulation to an amount of gold, preventing governments from pumping much-needed money into the economy. President Hoover's decision to cut government spending only exacerbated the situation.

By 1933, American industry had ground to a halt. As the masses suffered and suicide rates soared, captains of industry continued to command exorbitant salaries and bonuses while demanding cuts to social spending for the poor.[29] The head of the NAM (National Association of Manufacturers), John Edgerton, claimed that jobless Americans only had themselves to blame for not practising the 'habits of thrift and conservation'.[30] Such rhetoric fuelled a renewed public anger directed at corporate power.

Traditional unions were severely weakened by the crash, as they often are during recessions. However, the masses of unemployed began to organise, setting the stage for one of the most successful decades for labour organisation in American history. As Franklin D. Roosevelt took office in 1933, the situation had become so volatile that one of his advisers claimed 'that on March 4th we were confronted with a choice between an orderly revolution – a peaceful and rapid departure from the past concepts – and a violent and disorderly overthrow of the whole capitalist structure'.[31] Preferring an 'orderly revolution', FDR planned to institute a system of welfare capitalism in which the government would regulate business and create jobs. One of his first acts was to remove the US from the gold standard. The string of reforms that followed became known as the 'New Deal'. As well as raising the average income by 9 per cent, creating jobs and investment, laws were passed to increase the power of workers and unions. To the corporate world, it was a declaration of war, and NAM was at the forefront of the counter-attack.

Founded in 1895, NAM quickly became the leading business advocacy organisation in the US. In 1913, it was investigated by a committee of the US Congress, which was concerned by its plans to influence legislation by shaping public opinion. The committee concluded that the aspirations of NAM were 'so vast and far-reaching as to excite at once admiration and fear – admiration for the genius that conceived them and fear for the effects which the . . . accomplishment of all these ambitions might have in a government such as ours'.[32]

In response to Roosevelt's New Deal reforms, NAM warned its members that 'Public policies in our democracy are eventually a reflection of public opinion' and that public opinion must be reshaped 'if we are to avoid disaster'.[33] Central to the NAM's programme of 're-education' was a strategy to deal with the threat of the trade unions who had forced Roosevelt's hand, for they were the only societal force that had the potential to challenge big business.

Through collective bargaining and strike action, workers had been able to win higher pay and better working conditions. For decades, the corporate response to strike action had been violence and suppression until, that is, a more sophisticated plan was developed. It became known as the Mohawk Valley formula and was distributed by NAM to all its members in 1936. The strategy was to turn public opinion against strikers by flooding the media and community groups with propaganda, while setting up 'puppet' organisations to condemn industrial action in order to further demoralise strikers. It played heavily on patriotic and religious sentiments, contrasting peace-making owners with trouble-making workers.[34]

James Rand, one of the pioneers of the formula, told the puppet 'Citizen Committee' that had been set up to defend his corporation: 'Two million businessmen have been looking for a formula like this and business has hoped for, dreamed for, and prayed for such an example as you have set.'[35] From this point on, these 'scientific' methods of strike-breaking would be applied to every major strike in the country. In 1939, a committee of the US Senate, established to investigate violations of labour rights, reported that the NAM had 'blanketed the country with a propaganda which in technique has relied upon indirection of meaning, and in presentation of secrecy and deception. Radio speeches, public meetings, news, cartoons, editorials, advertising, motion pictures and many other artifices of propaganda have not, in most instances, disclosed to the public their origin within the Association.'[36]

This tidal wave of corporate propaganda subsided for a period during the Second World War as the country united behind Roosevelt for the war effort, but by early 1945 business picked up where it had left off.

Psychologist Dr Henry C. Link, head of an organisation called 'The Psychological Corporation', announced that a series of large-scale experiments in the 'Techniques of Communicating Ideas' were taking place, sponsored by ten of the country's leading companies. The experiments showed that the most effective way of selling the idea of free enterprise to the public was by associating it with 'Americanism' and by linking New Deal policies to 'un-Americanism'.[37]

The scale of NAM's propaganda went beyond anything that had come before. They had two dominant aims: the first, according to one of its own documents, was to 'link free enterprise in the public consciousness with free speech, free press and free religion as integral parts of democracy'.[38] The second was to build a connection in people's minds between regulation of business and communism. It was an ambitious sell, but proved enormously effective.

In January 1945, with the war almost over, a bill was drafted that would establish the principles of the New Deal firmly in law. It committed the government to a policy of ensuring full employment by investing strategically in the economy.[39] Leading the fight against the bill, NAM argued that it would 'destroy private enterprise' and 'lead to socialism'. Throughout 1945, NAM members, officers and committees spoke directly to the American public via radio for, on average, 3.7 hours a day. Stories about the NAM appeared in newspapers across the country. A series of four full-page advertisements were placed in more than 400 daily and 2,000 weekly newspapers. By the time the bill passed, the NAM had succeeded in significantly diluting its contents.

Contributing to the effort were many other corporate-sponsored organisations. Of particular importance was the US Chamber of Commerce, which in 1946 distributed more than a million copies of the pamphlet 'Communist infiltration in the United States'. In 1947, a complementary pamphlet entitled 'Communists within the Government' was also widely distributed. That same year, the American Advertising Council announced a $100 million programme to 'sell' the American economic system to the American people.[40] Between 1946 and 1950, NAM distributed over 18 million pamphlets.[41]

Daniel Bell, labour editor of *Fortune* magazine, commented on the staggering influence of the opinion-shaping apparatus of big business: 'The Advertising Council alone in 1950 inspired 7 million lines of newspaper advertising stressing free enterprise, 400,000 car cards' and '2,500,000,000 radio impressions'.[42] The combined success of these campaigns culminated in the Labor Management Relations Act, usually known as the Taft-Hartley Act, of 1947 – largely drafted by NAM – which erected tremendous obstacles to workers who wished to organise collectively.[43]

In 1950, *Fortune* magazine reported: 'Many of the countries [sic] largest firms have started extensive programmes to indoctrinate employees.' The programmes were billed as 'Courses in Economic Education' and were designed to increase commitment to the free-enterprise system. In one instance, $6 million was spent by Sears to 'educate' 200,000 employees. Schools and universities were also targeted. Throughout the 1950s, businesses contributed heavily to the education system and, in return, schools faithfully advanced the message of free enterprise.[44] From 1948 to 1965, business gifts to schools rose from $24 million to $280 million a year. According to General Electric, the pay-off for such 'gifts' was improving the 'economic, social, and political climate necessary for the continued existence and progress of competitive free-enterprise'.[45]

Thousands of teachers were invited by America's leading corporations to participate for weeks at a time in educators' conferences, exchange programmes and seminars. During these gatherings, top executives argued vigorously against government intervention in the economy and complained that government welfare destroyed 'initiative and responsibility'.[46] In 1949, the New Jersey State Chamber of Commerce established a bureau to enlist colleges to partake in monthly meetings in which a business leader spoke to the entire student body as well as the faculty. In one year, nineteen business representatives spoke to 48,000 students. NAM ran a similar programme. At its height it was reaching almost 200,000 students and faculty a year.

Spearheaded by Senator Joseph McCarthy, this siege of the public consciousness by corporate propaganda reached a crescendo in the 1950s. Relatively unknown in 1949, McCarthy took a simple but effective approach to politics: accusing any and all of his opponents of having communist sympathies. Given the heightened tensions between the USSR and the US, McCarthy's reckless accusations created a culture of fear and paranoia, ruining many lives and careers in the process. His rise to prominence, the power he seized, and the impact he had was remarkable and shocking. The anti-communist fervour spread by his attacks was to have long-lasting effects on the US political climate. Historian Elizabeth Fones-Wolf writes that, by the end of the 1950s, 'the business community could point to favorable results. Liberal hopes for a fully articulated welfare state had been crushed, while union representation of the labor force had begun its long decline. Meanwhile, the popular image of organised labor shifted from the heroic defenders of the New Deal to just another special interest group.'[47]

The late 1960s ushered in a period of radical social change on both sides of the Atlantic. Powerful movements emerged to fight for civil rights, women's rights, the environment, and consumer and worker protection. The momentum of these movements soon produced legislation that imposed significant constraints on business. In Britain, the years following the war had seen a shift towards socialism. The Labour government of Clement Attlee oversaw the creation of the National Health Service in 1948; the introduction of social security, providing 'cradle to the grave' care for all citizens; and the nationalisation of one-fifth of the British economy. Trade unions constituted a powerful political force, helping to shape government policy and commanding the support of millions of workers. By the late 1960s, the top rate of income tax had hit 75 per cent.

Roosevelt's New Deal helped many but was not extensive enough to end the Great Depression. It took unprecedented investment in war to boost investor confidence and rescue the economy. By the end of the Second World War, the US was the most powerful nation on earth, yet in Washington it was feared that the end of the war could herald a return to economic crisis. Spurred on by this possibility, US policy-makers set about reconstructing the global capitalist system. The lesson had been learned that capitalism could not be managed at the level of the nation state. In 1944, at a conference in Bretton Woods, a plan was drawn up for the post-war economic order. It included the creation of the

International Monetary Fund (IMF), the World Bank, and a system of fixed exchange rates that gave pride of place to the US dollar. With the introduction of the Marshall Plan in 1947, billions of dollars were ploughed into the regeneration of European industry, thereby creating sustainable demand for US manufacturing.

For a while, the new global system worked (at least for some). The 1950s and 1960s would come to be known as the 'golden age of capitalism'. Western Europe and the US enjoyed near full employment, stable economic growth and an unprecedented rise in living standards. To many, this post-war consensus seemed irreversible. Across the political spectrum, parties accepted the need for government and international financial institutions to manage the market. However, this consensus would not last long.

Neoliberalism

Those most empowered by the market have never stopped working to free it from democratic control. Since the 1960s, the ideological vehicle for this task has taken the form of 'neoliberalism'. The term was selected by participants at a French conference in 1928 to discuss the implications of a book called *The Good Society* by Walter Lippmann. Among conference delegates were the economists Friedrich Hayek and Ludvig von Mises, both of whom would become powerful advocates of neoliberal ideology.

At the heart of neoliberal thinking is the belief that the only way to guarantee individual freedom is to protect 'market freedom'. In the 1960s and 70s, the notion of individual freedom resonated widely, appealing to – and in some sense co-opting – the progressive social movements and popular culture of the era. With its emphasis on individual liberty, proponents of neoliberalism were well placed to channel the palpable discontent of the period towards their designated target: the state.

There are two ways to think about neoliberalism. In its theoretical form, it can be viewed as a utopian project in which a combination of strong private property rights, the rule of law and free markets is judged to preserve and protect individual liberty most effectively. In response to the totalitarianism that had spread across Europe under Hitler and Stalin, early neoliberal thinkers saw an urgent need to minimise the power of the state in order to safeguard individual freedom. In its political form, as actually practised, neoliberalism is a convenient means of rationalising and legitimising the advance of corporate interests, regardless of their effect on individual freedom. Although they are fundamentally contradictory, these two conceptions complement each other in some ways. It is the moral and utopian character of neoliberal theory that makes it such a powerful cover for the advancement of business interests.

In promoting the ideology of neoliberalism, think tanks became the source of a powerful form of propaganda aimed not at the public but at society's intellectual and political elites. One of the first and most influential of these groups was the Mont Pelerin Society, set up in 1947 by, among others, Friedrich Hayek and Milton Friedman. For the founding meeting, over forty academics, economists and journalists travelled to the remote Mont Pèlerin in Switzerland for a week of intense discussion about the ailments of civilisation and the urgent need for a remedy. The society maintained that many social and economic problems stemmed from 'a decline of belief in private property and the competitive market' and considered the 'invisible hand' of the market to be the best way to mobilise humanity's basest instincts to serve the greater good. According to Hayek, personal and political freedom were only possible in a society that defended the economic sphere from government meddling.

In their day, the ideas of the Mont Pelerin Society were regarded as ideologically extreme. Hayek wrote at the time, 'Scarcely anybody doubts that we must continue to move towards socialism.'[48] Majority opinion regarded core tenets of neoliberal philosophy as outdated and discredited, blaming them for the 1929 crash and the Great Depression that followed. It was an ideology that stood in direct opposition to the emerging welfare state that was backed by an increasingly powerful labour movement. Social Democratic parties were winning elections throughout Western Europe, and, across the political spectrum, there was a post-war consensus on economic interventionism. For the neoliberals to achieve their aims, all this needed to be overturned.

Neoliberal strategy was founded on the assumption that after 'the more active part of the intellectuals have been converted to a set of beliefs, the process by which these become generally accepted is almost automatic and irresistible'.[49] According to Hayek, this was so because 'the great majority are rarely capable of thinking independently . . . on most questions they accept views which they find ready-made'.[50] Hayek, who saw the battle of ideas as crucial, predicted that it would take at least a generation to overthrow the post-war consensus. He was not wrong.

Many groups in society work to bring about social and political change but, from the outset, the pioneers of neoliberalism had a distinct advantage: their vision of society appealed to wealthy interests – individuals, corporations and foundations – who were willing to provide a steady stream of considerable financial support.[51] As a result, this small society had a huge impact, creating a network of more than 100 free-market think tanks around the world. It helped found the UK's Institute of Economic Affairs (IEA) in 1955. Antony Fisher, its driving force, went on to set up the Atlas Economic Research Foundation whose stated aim was to 'litter the world with free-market think tanks'.[52] Today, Atlas lists on its books 500 free-market think tanks. When Margaret Thatcher came to power in 1979, she elevated the head of the IEA to the House of Lords and wrote in a letter of thanks that 'It was primarily your foundation work which enabled us to rebuild the philosophy upon which our Party succeeded in the past.'[53]

In the US, powerful establishment figures lent their support to the neoliberal cause. Judge Lewis F. Powell advised business lobbies to work together to save the system of free enterprise. In 1971, shaken by the movements of the 1960s, he wrote a secret memo entitled 'Attack on American Free Enterprise System'. It warned business leaders that investing in 'public relations' wasn't enough – 'political power is necessary . . . such power must be assiduously cultivated; and . . . when necessary, it must be used aggressively and with determination'. How was this power to be cultivated? 'Strength lies in organisation, in careful long-range planning and implementation, in consistency of action over an indefinite period of years, in the scale of financing available only through joint effort, and in the political power available through united action and national organisations.'[54] It was such financing through joint effort that allowed neoliberals like Ludvig von Mises, a founding member of the Mont Pelerin Society, to survive in an academic community that viewed his beliefs as outdated and dangerous. His salary at NYU was paid for, not by the university – which regarded his free-market beliefs as extreme – but by wealthy businessmen.[55]

Shortly after writing the memo, Powell was nominated to the Supreme Court by President Nixon. In line with the prescriptions he'd laid out in the memo, corporate America set up the Business Roundtable in 1972. Comprising CEOs of the 200 largest companies in the US, it became the most powerful business lobby in Washington. Its members collectively lay claim to over $6 trillion in annual revenue, and almost a third of the US stock market.[56]

It was widely recognised that the university campus was a crucial ideological battleground. The need to exploit the education system in the 'proper' way was clearly articulated in an unusually frank document published in the 1970s by the Trilateral Commission. The Commission was founded in 1973 at the behest of billionaire David Rockefeller to facilitate global planning among the world's most powerful capitalist democracies. Its early members were drawn from the United States, Western Europe and Japan. Among them were the heads of major corporations and banks, partners in corporate law firms and senators. One of its first major reports was entitled 'The Crisis of Democracy: Report on the Governability of Democracies to the Trilateral Commission' and was written primarily by political scientist Samuel P. Huntington. Alarm was expressed at the rising political engagement of the 1960s, which had spawned rapid social change and a shift in the political landscape of the country. 'Previously passive or unorganised groups in the population' including 'blacks, Indians, Chicanos, white ethnic groups, students, and women . . . now embarked on concerted efforts to establish their claims to opportunities, positions, rewards, and privileges, which they had not considered themselves entitled to before'.[57] It explicitly cites democracy as a threat, arguing that 'the problems of governance in the United States today stem from an excess of democracy' and that '[n]eeded instead, is a greater degree of moderation in democracy'.[58]

The report regarded the education system as '[t]he most important value-producing system in society' and declared that if higher education is geared to raising the cultural level of the population, 'a program is necessary to lower the job expectation of those who receive a college education'.[59] It may be tempting to dismiss this perspective as a fringe element, not representative of mainstream corporate or state priorities, but within two years of the report's publication all the top positions in the US government – the office of President, Vice-President, Secretaries of State, Defense and Treasury – were held by members of the Trilateral Commission. And the Commission's Director had become National Security Advisor.

The 1970s saw the number of corporations with lobbying offices in Washington jump from 100 to more than 500. After the inception of the Business Roundtable, a number of other groups were formed whose goal was to advance the tenets of neoliberalism such as the American Enterprise Institute (AEI) and the Heritage Foundation, each boasting multimillion-dollar annual budgets derived from America's largest corporations. The debt owed by President Reagan to these groups was repaid when he filled more than thirty of his senior administration posts with AEI scholars and officials. Reagan understood well what he owed to Hayek and the neoliberals. He claimed that they had 'played an absolutely essential role in preparing the ground for the resurging conservative movement in America'.[60]

Turning the tide

In the wake of the great Wall Street crash of 1929, British economist John Maynard Keynes argued that markets were inherently unstable, prone to boom and bust, and required careful management by the state to restrict their harmful effects. A consensus emerged after the Second World War that the state should focus on full employment, economic growth and the welfare of its citizens. State power should be used to compensate for, correct, and even replace market processes. These Keynesian policies persisted until the early 1970s, by which time a stalling economy put pressure on governments to seek alternative policies.

The global economic order had been established when the US was running a huge trade surplus with the rest of the world. The financial costs of the Vietnam War, along with increased domestic spending, helped to reverse this relationship, creating a growing budget and trade deficit in the US. The influx of dollars into the world economy threatened to destabilise the fixed exchange rates of the Bretton Woods system. In 1971, President Nixon ended it, triggering a rise in oil prices that raised the cost of production across the world. As inflation rose, economic growth slowed – a pattern that came to be known as 'stagflation'. When the economy contracted briefly in the 1970s, profits dropped and the Keynesian compromise faltered.[61] All these factors conspired to pave the way for a dramatic ideological shift.

It is easy to overstate the problems that occurred during this period. Throughout it, leading capitalist nations maintained growth rates of 2 per cent per capita, higher than would be achieved under the next three decades of neoliberalism.[62] It is true that unemployment on average had risen, but only from 3 to just over 4 per cent, hardly a catastrophe compared with the Great Depression or the economic crash of 2008. Yet, there was enough discontent to create a space for new ideas, and into that space stepped Milton Friedman. He claimed to possess the solution to the problem of rapid inflation: control of the money supply. With neoliberal ideas on the ascendancy, Friedman found a receptive audience across the political spectrum.

Restrictive monetary policy aims to bring down inflation by raising interest rates. (High interest rates mean that fewer loans are taken out, which means that consumers have less money to spend. This reduces inflation.) But high interest rates have another impact: they benefit the rich by maintaining the value of their investments. Other neoliberal prescriptions have similarly convenient benefits. Greater capital mobility, a key free-trade policy, favours the rich because, as Ha-Joon Chang puts it, 'the main source of the ability for the holders of financial assets to reap higher returns than the holders of other (physical and human) assets is their ability to move around their assets more quickly'.[63] This contrasts starkly with the push to increase the market 'flexibility' of labour – a euphemism for greater job insecurity, which serves to weaken the bargaining power of unions. While claiming to be concerned with the sanctity of the free market, neoliberals argued vigorously against labour unions yet were conspicuously silent on the subject of corporate monopolies.

By casting inflation as the bogeyman of economics, and restrictive monetary policy as its saviour, neoliberal economics shifted the focus of policy away from full employment. Reagan summed up the mood when he said 'inflation is as violent as a mugger, as frightening as an armed robber and as deadly as a hit man'.[64] Friedman argued that reducing inflation should be pursued at all costs as it undermined investment and growth. Historically, it is true that hyperinflation has been disastrous for some nations – Germany and Hungary suffered terribly as a result of it – but there is a world of difference between hyperinflation and inflation. Even studies by free-market economists suggest that below 8 to 10 per cent, inflation has no relationship with the economic growth rate of a country. Other studies put the threshold much higher.[65] Nevertheless, the view that the primary goal of economic policy should be the elimination of inflation soon became an economic mantra.

The shift in focus from unemployment to inflation reflected a wider shift in power. Constricting the money supply to curb inflation curtailed demand in the economy as a whole, producing a rapid increase in unemployment and dramatically weakening the bargaining power of trade unions. Under Thatcher, unemployment soared from roughly 1 million to 3.3 million. British economist Alan Budd, Thatcher's one-time chief economic adviser, explains the motivation that drove her policy over this period: 'the 1980s policies of attacking inflation by squeezing the economy and public spending were a cover to bash the workers. Raising unemployment was a very desirable way of reducing the strength of the working class.'[66]

Taken together, these policies – particularly the effects of high interest rates on the economy as a whole – precipitated the most serious economic depression since the Great Depression. By the mid-1980s, notes Galbraith, they had succeeded in taming inflation 'by producing a severe economic slump, a cure not less painful than the condition remedied'.[67] And yet neoliberalism had become the new orthodoxy. Friedman had long understood that 'Only a crisis – actual or perceived – produces real change. When that crisis occurs, the actions that are taken depend on the ideas that are lying around. That, I believe, is our basic function: to develop alternatives to existing policies, to keep them alive and available until the politically impossible becomes politically inevitable.'[68] The ideas that were 'lying around' when Keynesianism appeared to falter were those that had been assiduously cultivated and spread with the help of generous funding from some of the world's largest corporations and wealthiest individuals.

Friedman reached a mass audience when he starred in a television version of his book *Free to Choose* (1980), paid for by a grant from the billionaire Richard Scaife. Further plaudits were secured when the Nobel Prize for Economic Science was awarded in 1974 to Hayek and, two years later, to Friedman. (It should be said that these awards have nothing to do with the original Nobel prizes but were created independently by Sweden's banking elite.) During this period, conservative foundations gave US judges and their families all-expenses-paid breaks to Miami to take part in special courses on the free-market doctrines of Milton Friedman. These courses placed great importance on exempting corporations from regulation. 'By 1980', writes journalist Ben Bagdikian, 'one-fifth of the entire federal judiciary had taken the courses.'[69] With the elections of Reagan and Thatcher, Anglo-American corporations finally had governments ready to fight for their interests. They set about transferring resources and industry into private hands, stripping the unions of their power, reducing the top rate of income tax, and promoting a culture of consumerism and individualism.

A new global economic order had emerged. The US economy, now running a vast trade deficit, depended on a torrent of wealth flooding into Wall Street banks from the rest of the world. Attracted by high interest rates (among other things), profits from leading export nations were sent to Wall Street banks to be invested and loaned out. In 1987, President Reagan replaced the head of the Federal Reserve, Paul Volcker, with Alan Greenspan, a staunch believer in deregulation. Under Greenspan's leadership, the financial industry was freed from 'state interference'. Henceforth, the role of government would be to pick up the pieces when crises inevitably erupted, rather than forestall those crises. The financialisation of the world economy had begun, with America's banks the beating heart of global capitalism.

After the Second World War, the forces of democracy had won a welfare state for the British people – at the heart of which was the National Health Service – and the New Deal had previously won significant gains for the American public. However, by the 1980s, business was no longer on the defensive. It was able to push opposing forces into retreat. 'It took less than six months in 1983', writes political theorist David Harvey, 'to reverse nearly 40 per cent of the decisions made during the 1970s that had been, in the view of business, too favourable to labour.'[70] Highly significant was the unprecedented increase in the national debt under the Reagan administration. It had taken almost a century for the national debt to reach $1 trillion, yet this figure tripled in a single decade unmarked by war or depression, and it was business and the rich who benefited most. The top tax rate was slashed from 78 to 28 per cent.[71]

At the same time, the power of trade unions was dealt a lethal blow on both sides of the Atlantic. In 1981, President Reagan went after thousands of air traffic controllers striking for higher pay and fewer hours. At the height of summer, when demand for air travel was high, Reagan fired over 11,000 air traffic controllers who had refused to comply with his order to return to work. It was a turning point. A similarly defining moment in the UK came with the miners' strike of 1984–5, a year-long battle between the Thatcher government and the miners that resulted in a significant weakening of labour rights.[72] The strike-breaking strategies of the 1930s – a public relations campaign, widespread distortion of the facts, police brutality and the fomenting of discord among the strikers – were all on full display.

Thatcher's ambitions went far deeper than reducing taxes for the rich and weakening trade unions. As she put it, 'Economics are the method; the object is to change the heart and soul.'[73] The change she was trying to bring about was clear: the end of social obligation, the destruction of the idea that we are collectively responsible for each other. She was explicit that 'There is no such thing as society'.[74] It was not the state's job to help the poor, the destitute or the homeless. Opinion polls following the neoliberal revolution suggest that 'the heart and soul' of people have indeed been changed. According to the British Social Attitudes Survey, in the late 1980s almost 60 per cent of people were in favour of raising welfare spending, even if it increased their taxes. Thirty years later, that figure had halved to 30 per cent.[75] This trend accompanied another telling shift: a large increase in meritocratic attitudes. More people were inclined to believe that wealth and success were deserved and the product of hard work, rather than a result of luck.[76]

The British Labour Party had historically been a vehicle for working-class interests, but in the 1990s, rebranded 'New Labour', it turned decisively to neoliberalism. The transition was led by Tony Blair, who was later described by Margaret Thatcher as her 'greatest achievement'. After dropping Labour's historical commitment to public ownership of industry, Blair refused to raise taxes on the rich, repeal Thatcher's anti-union laws or reverse her privatisation of utilities and public services. But he did make a point of cutting corporate tax. In fact, never had so many Labour ministers been drawn from the world of business as when his party took power in 1997.[77] By then, the ballot box offered no real alternative to Thatcherism. The same had long been true in the US. Under President Clinton, the Democratic Party attained and kept power by capitulating to the neoliberal consensus. Indeed, Clinton had been an inspiration to Blair.

At the close of the twentieth century, an economic environment had been engineered in which regulation of business had been reduced to a bare minimum, wealth was increasingly concentrated, and the political spectrum had narrowed and shifted to the right. The virtues of the unregulated free market were extolled by a chorus of government, media and business. Thatcher's triumphant declaration that 'there is no alternative' to neoliberal capitalism was believed by many. So dominant did this paradigm become that commentators, most notably Francis Fukuyama, would soon be declaring the 'end of history'.

One dollar one vote

When democratic power fails to regulate the market to protect the public interest, market power regulates democracy to protect the corporate interest. In the US, a turning point in this battle occurred in 1978 when a court ruling declared that corporations had the same rights as individuals to finance elections. This quickly resulted in the near-complete takeover of the electoral process by major industries.[78] The freedom of corporations to fund US elections was extended in 2010 by the Supreme Court when it judged that freedom of speech applied to corporations just as it did to individuals. The figures paint a clear picture. In 1952, the money spent by all candidates and parties for all federal election campaigns was $140 million. In 2000, it was over $5 billion.[79] In presidential campaigns, American corporations spend hundreds of millions of dollars on their candidates.[80] From 2000 to 2006, the average price of winning a Senate seat increased by 81 per cent from $5.3 million to more than $9.6 million. From 1974 to 1990, 'the cost of a seat in the House of Representatives – the average expense of an election winner – grew from $56,500 to $410,000 and, from 1990 to 2006, it tripled to $1,250,000', even after accounting for inflation.[81] Today, over half of US senators are millionaires.[82]

The priorities of these politicians are plain. In 2013, a study published in *Political Research Quarterly* showed that Senate members primarily represent the views of their richest constituents.[83] A 2014 study from Princeton University reached similar conclusions. According to one of its authors, Martin Gilens, the data shows that 'ordinary citizens have virtually no influence over what their government does in the United States. And economic elites and interest groups, especially those representing business, have a substantial degree of influence.'[84] It found that when 'a majority of citizens disagrees with economic elites and/or with organised interests, they generally lose. Moreover, because of the strong status quo bias built into the US political system, even when fairly large majorities of Americans favour policy change, they generally do not get it.'[85]

The oil industry is a case in point. Large oil companies have always had political influence, but with the arrival of the administration of George W. Bush in 2001, they went from lobbying the government to being the government. In *The Tyranny of Oil*, Antonia Juhasz writes that the 'Bush administration was the prize that Big Oil had been working hard toward for one hundred years'.[86] Bush appointed more than thirty former energy executives, lobbyists and lawyers to top jobs in his administration.[87] The presence of this coterie of powerful insiders did not stop the oil giants from spending big to extend their influence. From 1998 to 2006, ExxonMobil, BP and Chevron spent over $12 million on presidential and congressional elections. However, the real money is spent when elections are over and the policy-making begins. From 1998 to 2006, ExxonMobil spent more than $80 million on lobbying the federal government.

What does this money buy? One study analysed the results of seven different key votes on bills that the oil industry had a clear interest in quashing. Juhasz sums up the findings: 'House and Senate members who voted against these proposals received over four times more oil money than those who voted in the public interest. Overall, the twenty-five members of Congress who took the most oil money between 2000 and 2007 voted for legislation supporting Big Oil on average 86 per cent of the time.'[88]

Banking is another sector with remarkable political influence. From 1998 to 2008, the financial sector spent $1.7 billion on campaign contributions and $3.4 billion lobbying the government.[89] The banks that stood to gain most from deregulation and consolidation were the biggest donors. In April 2009, after the state put together a bail-out worth hundreds of billions of dollars, Senator Richard Durbin noted that 'the banks – hard to believe in a time when we're facing a banking crisis that many of the banks created – are still the most powerful lobby on Capitol Hill. And they frankly own the place.'[90] By October 2009, 1,537 lobbyists had registered to work against financial regulation proposals in Congress. They outnumbered the lobbyists working for stronger regulation by 25 to 1.[91]

It was the ability of Wall Street to place its own people in key government positions that secured their political influence. Goldman Sachs has a particularly impressive record. Bill Clinton's first director of the National Economic Council and second Secretary of the Treasury, Robert Rubin, spent twenty-six years at Goldman Sachs. Bush's last Treasury Secretary, Henry Paulson, was CEO of Goldman Sachs from 1999 to 2006. Gary Gensler and Robert Steel, both Under Secretaries of the Treasury with Clinton and Bush respectively, also came from Goldman Sachs. This employment history helps to clarify why, after the 2008 economic crash, staff at Goldman Sachs enjoyed one of the largest bonus payouts in the firm's history.[92]

The neoliberal consensus is deeply embedded in the British establishment as well. What was once regarded as an extreme position is now largely taken for granted among politicians, journalists and business leaders. It is reproduced and reinforced in a number of ways: through think tanks, a media run by billionaires, corporate lobbying and party funding, and a revolving-door policy that sees members of this elite move seamlessly between government posts, media institutions, corporate boards and think tanks. The flow of personnel through establishment positions serves to consolidate perspectives and strengthen networks. It provides financial and professional incentives to those willing to adopt a neoliberal worldview. In policy terms, this amounts to privatisation, outsourcing of government services, the erosion of the welfare state, dismantling regulation, and lowering taxes on business and the wealthy.[93]

One of the most influential pressure groups in the UK is the Tax Payers' Alliance. It claims to be 'committed to forcing politicians to listen to ordinary taxpayers', yet it is funded by wealthy business people and promotes uncompromising 'free market' policies. Influential neoliberal groups have particularly strong connections with the Conservative Party. A constant flow of personnel between them makes plain their common intent.

The role played by money in politics is most clearly seen in the funding of political parties. The number of donors to a party need not be large – it is the depth of their pockets that counts. In the UK, just 224 donations accounted for almost 40 per cent of the donation income for the three major parties between 2001 and mid 2010. During this time, the Conservatives raised over £45 million of donor income from only fifteen groups in trade, industry and finance.[94] One of their most generous donors is hedge-fund manager Michael Farmer, who, according to the Electoral Reform Society (ERS), has donated over £6.5 million to the party.[95]

When Labour Chancellor Alistair Darling introduced a bankers' bonus tax, he reported that he had 'received lots of calls from lots of bankers . . . they said this was causing them to think long and hard about London'.[96] At the next general election, donations from bankers increased from a quarter to a half of the Conservatives' total income. This was a wise investment. On coming to power, the Conservatives lobbied hard against a financial transaction tax proposed by the European Commission, and when the EU proposed limiting bank bonuses in 2011, the Conservative-led government used over £100,000 of taxpayers' money to mount a challenge in the European Court of Justice.

In 2008, a report by the House of Commons Public Administration Select Committee (PASC) on lobbying concluded that 'there is a genuine issue of concern, widely shared and reflected in measures of public trust, that there is an inside track, largely drawn from the corporate world, who wield privileged access and disproportionate influence . . . [and that] commercial corporations and organisations have an advantage over not-for-profit bodies which is related to the amount of money they are able to bring to bear on the political process'. This privileged access has transformed the state into a source of vast corporate welfare. In one financial year, while harsh austerity was being imposed on some of the most vulnerable in society, the British government gave away – in direct aid, subsidies and tax breaks – £93 billion in corporate welfare, enough to wipe out the entire budget deficit. Aditya Chakrabortty explained in *The Guardian* in July 2015:

> When Richard Branson's Virgin Atlantic took £28m from the
> Welsh government in 2011 to set up a call centre in Swansea, that

was a form of welfare. The German, French and Dutch companies that now run our train services are subsidised by the British public to the tune of hundreds of millions. The £45bn taken by firms in corporate tax benefits is a form of welfare. So is the ultra-low cost insurance scheme the government runs for exporters such as BAE Systems. None of these are labelled corporate welfare, but that's precisely what they are: direct public spending aimed at protecting and supporting businesses.[97]

Part of this vast giveaway is down to taxation, or rather its absence. Leading tax expert and adviser to the Treasury Philip Baker QC puts it plainly: 'I don't think in the last twenty years or so one can say that governments have driven corporation tax policy. It's the large companies that have driven the direction of corporate tax policy.'[98]

Arguably, the most direct and corrosive form of elite influence comes through the revolving door between business and government. This practice involves government officials taking up positions in the private sector and corporate employees being appointed to government posts and departmental boards. A 2011 report written for the research institute Democratic Audit UK by Professor David Beetham of Leeds University found that, between 2006 and 2008, 'no fewer than twenty-eight former ministers had taken up jobs in the private sector. Of these, thirteen were still MPs.' These included seven former health ministers who transferred to positions with private healthcare companies; six former ministers from the Ministry of Defence who found work with defence contractors; and seven former ministers who 'revolved out' into the financial industry.[99]

Of course, the revolving door permits movement in both directions. One study found that Barclays Bank alone had fourteen 'revolving door connections' with government, while ten other banks in the study had more than five each.[100] Consequently, it is no surprise that in 2009 Barclays Bank paid corporation tax at a rate of roughly 1 per cent, or that the UK's four biggest banks are allowed to manage, between them, 1,649 tax haven companies.[101]

Following the 2008 crash, the three official reviews into 'UK banking governance, British offshore financial centres and the UK international financial services' were each chaired by bankers.[102] In order to tackle the growing public health issue of obesity, then Health Secretary Andrew Lansley consulted with representatives from McDonald's, KFC, Mars and PepsiCo, while a group focusing on alcohol abuse was chaired by the chief executive of the Wine and Spirit Trade Association. The list goes on.[103]

So entrenched has the neoliberal consensus become that we find government ministers taking it upon themselves to lobby business to fight for the free market. In 2014, Conservative Chancellor of the Exchequer George Osborne urged an audience of top business people to 'get out there and put the business argument, because there are plenty of pressure groups, plenty of trade unions and plenty of charities and the like, that will put the counter view'. He continued, 'It is, I know, a difficult decision sometimes to put your head above the parapet, but that is the only way we are going to win this argument for an enterprising, business, low-tax economy that delivers . . . a country that is for business, for enterprise, for the free market.'[104]

Professor Beetham concludes his report with the following assessment: 'Instead of popular control we have subordination to an oligarchy of the wealthy and economically powerful. Instead of everyone counting for one, we have the easy purchase of political influence and the well-oiled revolving door between government and the corporate sector.'[105]

Free from democracy

The electoral process has often been compared to a marketplace in which ideas are sold by parties to voters who make their consumption choices in the voting booth. In his compelling study of American democracy, *Golden Rule* (1995), US political scientist Thomas Ferguson argues that we need 'a different account of political systems in which business elites, not voters, play the leading part'. According to Ferguson, most voters possess extremely limited resources as well as insufficient and often inaccurate information. The 'market' for political parties 'is defined by major investors who generally have good and clear reasons for investing to control the state . . . Blocs of major investors define the core of political parties and are responsible for most of the signals the party sends to the electorate.'[106]

Attracting wealthy 'investors' has become a matter of political survival. In 1999, Jim Nicholson, chairman of the Republican Party, wrote to the CEO of pharmaceutical company Bristol-Myers Squibb to request a donation of $250,000, explaining that 'we must keep the lines of communication open if we want to keep passing legislation that will benefit your industry'.[107] There can be no doubt about the motives and expectations of corporations when they donate money to political parties. Legally obliged to maximise their profits, the only way they can justify their political contributions to shareholders is as a financial investment on which a return can be expected. Legal scholar Joel Bakan explains that the money corporations 'spend on the political process is a business expense, an investment in creating a political environment that promotes their profitability and thus helps them survive'.[108]

In August 2015, *The New York Times* revealed that '[f]ewer than 400 of the nation's most affluent families have supplied almost half of the money raised . . . by presidential candidates in both parties'.[109] Where consensus exists among major investors little, if any, debate will be had between major parties. As Ferguson puts it, 'if all major investors happen to share an interest in ignoring issues vital to the electorate, such as social welfare, hours of work, or collective bargaining, so much the worse for the electorate'.[110]

According to a YouGov poll, a majority of voters in Britain – including four out of every ten Conservative voters – support a top rate tax of 75 per cent, but no major party has endorsed such a policy. Another poll showed that 60 per cent of Britons want the minimum wage to be raised to the living wage; 70 per cent support the renationalisation of energy companies; and two-thirds support the renationalisation of Royal Mail and the railways. Before the surprise election of Jeremy Corbyn as leader of the Labour Party in 2015 – a systemic anomaly – these options were rarely discussed in the mainstream and received no support from a major party because they fell beyond the consensus of the political system's major investors.[111] These examples, and count-less others, are evidence of a system in which influence is exerted in proportion to wealth rather than votes. Vast economic inequality yields vast political inequality.

When the term 'free' is used, we need to ask 'free from what?' In the case of the free market, it denotes a market free from democratic control. The logical conclusion to this process is the complete subjugation of national sovereignty to multinational corporate interests. For much of the developing world, this has long been the case. Under the banner of international trade agreements, we are now witnessing the same thing happening in wealthy nations. At the forefront of these developments are deals such as the Transatlantic Trade and Investment Partnership (TTIP), which is intended to unify the regulatory frameworks of the US and European Union. It proposes to enshrine in law the sovereignty of corporate profit over nations and peoples, creating international courts where large corporations can sue governments that – in the process of protecting their citizens – threaten potential profits. The will of democratically elected representatives would be subordinated to the decisions of corporate lawyers acting as judges in secret hearings – no rights of appeal would be granted to those communities affected by these decisions.[112] Precedents for these secretive courts already exist, and many losing governments have already been forced to pay out vast sums in penalties.[113] With the extension of trade deals like these, the power of governments to protect their own citizens, and the power of citizens to protect themselves, will rapidly disappear.

★

The tip of a pencil hovers over a ballot paper. The holder of the pencil can place a cross wherever they please. This is a moment of free democratic participation – a 'free choice'. But this hallowed ritual conceals the fact that our apparently democratic choices have largely been divested of their meaning. The close cooperation, long-term planning and enormous wealth of a small elite have created an environment in which the democratic process is rigged to ensure an outcome favourable to corporate short-term interests and private wealth. The focus of this chapter has been on the US and UK, pioneers of electoral democracy in the twentieth century, but the insights revealed bear on the development and workings of all modern democracies.

While propaganda shapes public opinion, direct pressure is applied on government to restrict the options open to the electorate. These twin strategies constitute a powerful mechanism of control. Like the magician who lets you choose a card, but knows in advance what it will be, corporations have become adept at manufacturing political outcomes. The illusion of freedom is maintained, while the reality of control is concealed. Being tricked may be preferable to being coerced, but to speak of 'freedom of choice' is disingenuous, and to call it democracy is to debase the term.

Political power does not reside in the voting booth. Once a consensus is embedded deeply enough in the minds of politicians and civil servants, there is no real choice on offer in the ballot box. Given the regularity with which politicians break promises, even the narrow range of choices presented is often illusory. As politicians of all stripes are keen to point out, governments are in thrall to corporations who at any time can leave the country, taking wealth and jobs with them if they feel conditions are becoming less favourable.

Marking a ballot takes a second and, once it's done, a typical voter's democratic participation ends until the next election. Yet corporate participation is continuous and on an industrial scale. The work of corporate lobbyists, think tanks and lawyers never ends; the revolving door between industry and government never stops spinning. The 'debts' to big campaign funders do not disappear, and neither does the influence of corporate funding in education and the media. Through numerous channels, vast wealth affords great political advantages to those who possess it, particularly when they work together to advance a common set of interests. It is not the best ideas but the best-funded ideas that win through. This is a politics of bribery, not participation. Yet the exercise of power through market mechanisms appears to be depersonalised, attributed not to individuals or even institutions but to sacred and impartial economic laws to which, we are told, there is no alternative. The enduring dominance of this doctrine is perhaps the greatest achievement of corporate public relations. By far the most powerful actor in the market, the corporation has every incentive to perpetuate the myth that government regulation is coercive, while markets – apparently characterised by voluntarism and cooperation – are not.

Thinkers like Hayek drew a clear lesson from the devastating abuses across Europe under fascist and communist dictatorships: circumscribe state power. The state – with its monopoly on the use of coercive force – is certainly an immense source of concentrated power, but it is not the only one. The world's largest corporations now possess more wealth than many nations. In 2010, the revenue of Walmart was greater than the GDP of all but twenty-three nations, including Denmark, Austria, Greece, Portugal, Israel and Malaysia. ExxonMobil's revenue exceeded the GDP of Finland. In fact, in a list of the top 100 wealthiest economic entities on the planet in 2010, almost half were corporations.[114] In light of these facts, it is nonsense to call for minimal state power in the name of individual liberty, while saying little or nothing of the comparable power of corporations, particularly when they have succeeded so well in co-opting the state and powerful international institutions. After all, a democratic state is, at least in theory, accountable to the people – a private corporation is not.

With its one-sided concern for avoiding concentrations of state power, neoliberal ideology has provided useful cover for big business. Brimming with ideals of freedom, voluntarism, choice and efficiency, it has masked the methodical struggle by corporations to extend and consolidate control. The point is not that the fear of state power is unwarranted, but that it only tells half the story. Concentrations of power, whether state or corporate, are always vulnerable to abuse.

6

Markets

In 1819, the British Parliament, under pressure from a growing labour movement, banned the employment of children younger than nine in cotton factories known for their dangerous working conditions.[1] Older children also saw their working day reduced to a mere twelve-hour shift. The Cotton Mills and Factories Act was highly controversial. Many objected on the grounds that such regulation would undermine the freedom of workers to enter into voluntary, mutually beneficial contracts. If children were willing to work and the factory owners wanted to employ them, what was the problem? Even some parents were against the legislation, fearing that their families would not be able to survive without the extra income.

Today, at least in rich countries, the regulations in place to protect children from exploitation are uncontested, invisible even, because the ethical norms motivating them are widely accepted.[2] The nineteenth-century critics were right about one thing: preventing children from working for twelve hours a day in dangerous conditions is a curtailment of the free market. However, it is justified because the market cannot be trusted to protect the welfare of children, and that is something that most of us believe is extremely important.

Many other restrictions have been placed on today's markets to maintain standards and protect the public. Food must be labelled according to set guidelines, advertisers must adhere to regulations, and many professions require state accreditation to operate legally. We are not free to trade where and when we like: laws prevent disruptive commercial activities in residential areas, and bars, pubs and clubs cannot stay open twenty-four hours a day. We are also not free to sell drugs, weapons or other human beings; and legal decisions, electoral votes, government appointments and university places are not (meant to be) awarded to the highest bidder. 'Before commodities can be bought and sold,' writes economist Raj Patel, 'they have to become objects that people *think* can be bought or sold.'[3] Debates continue around the commodification of healthcare, education and, more recently, the right to pollute. The 'commodity' category is not objective. Its exclusions and inclusions depend on social norms, which by their very nature are in flux.

A completely free market does not exist. As economist Ha-Joon Chang points out, 'Every market has some rules and boundaries that restrict freedom of choice. A market looks free only because we so unconditionally accept its underlying restrictions that we fail to see them.'[4] There are no impartial means of establishing its boundaries. They are constantly contested, often with opposing sides claiming to be on the side of freedom. Decisions about these boundaries and the role of government in the market are political and, ultimately, ethical – advancing some interests at the expense of others. The call for a freer market is a political position like any other, one that happens to shift power from votes to dollars. When some economists argue that a given regulation should not be introduced because it would restrict the 'freedom of the market', they are, as Chang points out, 'merely expressing a political opinion' about whose freedom ought to be prioritised.[5]

Milton Friedman, like many neoliberal thinkers, insisted that 'most arguments against the free market' amount to 'a lack of belief in freedom itself'.[6] He has claimed that, even if capitalism turned out to be less efficient than some other system, he would still advocate it because of its unique capacity to deliver the 'freedom to choose'. Friedman means something quite specific when he speaks of economic freedom. Along with most economists, he does not mean that people should have democratic control over their economic lives, a comfortable standard of living, or even the means to purchase life's essentials. Instead, he views economic freedom as nothing more than the freedom to do what we choose with our person and property.

This definition of freedom harks back to classical liberalism, which claims to have at its core the ideal of individual liberty. Many classical liberals saw this freedom as incompatible with political democracy because they believed the poor majority would use their votes to subvert market outcomes and redistribute wealth, thereby violating the freedom 'to do what one chooses with one's property' – which neoliberals see as 'the most basic of human rights'.[7] According to the doctrine of neoliberalism, economic freedom should be entrusted to 'free markets' just as political freedom is entrusted to 'free elections'.

A market is a social institution whose participants exchange goods and services on terms they find mutually beneficial. Capitalism is a system in which goods are produced privately to be sold at a profit. Adam Smith is widely credited with drawing the world's attention to what appeared to be a remarkable property of markets: exchanges for private gain seemed to be guided by an 'invisible hand' to promote the public interest.[8] The market seemed to harness unbridled selfishness in a way that served the welfare of all. The pursuit of wealth and profit – once associated with sin – was recast as a positive and powerful force. To this day, according to the world's dominant ideology, market processes, when freed from state interference, not only produce, distribute and allocate goods and services efficiently, but preserve and promote individual liberty. As we will see, this is a dangerous fantasy.[9]

Milton Friedman acknowledged that the 'existence of a free market does not of course eliminate the need for government. On the contrary, government is essential both as a forum for determining the "rules of the game" and as an umpire to interpret and enforce the rules decided on.'[10] And so framing debates in terms of those for and against the 'free market' gets us nowhere. Given the need for rules, what matters is the nature of those rules and the outcomes we hope they will produce. Yet the debate is routinely presented as a battle between the miraculous free market and the dangerous interference of an inefficient and coercive state.

An example of this framing was provided by one of the world's most powerful advocates of free-market ideology. From 1987 to 2006, Alan

Greenspan was Chairman of the Federal Reserve, a leading legislator of the world economy.[11] 'I do have an ideology,' Greenspan once said: 'My judgement is that free, competitive markets are by far the unrivalled way to organise economies. We have tried regulation, none meaningfully worked.'[12] Yet, as the global economy imploded in 2008, as a direct consequence of deregulating the financial industry, Greenspan conceded that this way of looking at things may be flawed:

> INTERVIEWER: In other words, you found that your view of the world, your ideology, was not right, it was not working.
> GREENSPAN: Precisely. That is precisely the reason I was shocked, because I had been going for 40 years or more with very considerable evidence that it was working exceptionally well.[13]

Decades of soaring inequality, low growth rates, a steady takeover of the democratic process by private interests and the destruction of the environment hardly seem like a system 'working exceptionally well'. Nevertheless, Greenspan's admission is significant and ought to give pause to those who remain committed to the misleading rhetoric of 'free markets'. It coincided with one of the most dramatic examples in history of state interference in the market, one that the financiers not only did not oppose but insisted on.

When the economy crashed, many speculators who had made enormous losses were bailed out by the state. It seemed that, while they were calling for privatisation throughout the economy and turning whatever they could into commodities, the banks were keen to share one thing with society: risk – more precisely, the immense cost of the risks taken in pursuit of greater profits. In 2008 the US government pledged $200 billion to Fannie Mae and Freddie Mac alone; in the same year, a further $700 billion of taxpayers' money was used to buy up 'toxic assets' with few or no conditions attached.

This extreme violation of free enterprise and the neoliberal 'commitment to competition' was justified on the grounds that leading financial institutions were 'too big to fail', that they would drag the whole financial system down with them. In spite of the fact that this appeared to be capitalism for the poor and socialism for the rich, President Bush claimed it was consistent US policy that 'the federal government should interfere in the market place only when necessary'.[14] But who decides when it is necessary? This is not a technical question but a moral one. The answer we give reflects our values, concerns and priorities. Bush himself implicitly acknowledged that whether the market should be 'free' or not is the wrong question to ask: the real issue is not whether the market should be regulated, but how, to what degree, and in whose interests.

Finders keepers

When freedoms clash, some must take priority over others. In the economy, the mechanism that determines which freedoms are prioritised is the property rights system. Property rights bestow the freedom to control and profit from what is owned. They determine who has decision-making authority over a given commodity. Ownership is necessarily exclusive: as soon as one person owns something, the rest of the world does not. When the Wild West pioneer claimed to own 'newly discovered' land and made it his home, he appropriated resources that had been the preserve of Native Americans for thousands of years.

Neoliberal doctrine claims to oppose state interference and advocate a reduced state, but in order for private property rights to be upheld, state power must restrict the freedom of some at the expense of others. When intellectual property rights are upheld, the right of everyone else to use what has been claimed is curtailed. When natural resources are sold for private profit, the right of everyone else to use them in the public interest is denied. In all cases, the state is waiting in the wings with batons and guns to intervene in defence of private property. There is nothing 'small' or 'non-interventionist' about a capitalist state.

Free-market advocates have little to say about the proper distribution of ownership rights. Friedman argues that it's difficult to favour one set of property rights over another on moral grounds, but that they should be clear-cut to avoid ambiguity. That's largely it.[15] Without criteria for evaluating different distributions of property, Friedman and most of his profession are happy to accept the distribution that history happens to have left to us – a result no doubt welcomed by those already in possession of great wealth, such as the 0.06 per cent of the population who own 50 per cent of the rural land in Britain.[16]

If you trace the history of any commodity, you arrive at a point at which something shared was taken into private ownership. The initial appropriation is beyond the purview of market transactions but necessary to create a market in the first place – you can't sell something unless you first own it. But what does it mean to declare that the ancient resources of nature suddenly belong to someone? Interesting arguments have been put forward to show how this process *could* be justified under certain circumstances (all of which run into difficulties), but they do nothing to justify the *actual* historical origins of private ownership, which are steeped in systematic theft and violence.

The privatisation of land played an important role in creating the conditions necessary for the modern economy. The transition to capitalism required that peasants who lived independently on the land be turned into wage-labourers by a process now called 'enclosure'. Beginning in Britain in the sixteenth century, public land was cut off from local communities, depriving them of any other means of survival. This land had long provided peasants in Britain with the essentials of life: building materials, fuel and food. The right to live off the land ended when private ownership was asserted by decree. Bent on increasing their wealth, prosperous merchants and feudal lords cordoned off fields that until then had been held in common.

The enclosures were strongly resisted by those whose lives depended on shared access to the resources of nature. Large groups of peasants repeatedly attacked them and numerous rebellions took place over the following centuries. Rebels were often executed and thousands died in violent battles. Legislation was passed that resulted in '6 million acres of commonly held lands . . . [being] put into private hands and subsequently hedged and fenced and farmed and herded and hunted for private gain'.[17] The landless peasants lost their livelihoods. Desperate for employment, they were forced to the cities in large numbers. The more peasants that were displaced, the more wages were driven down.

Much of today's private property is the product of coercive intervention by the state on behalf of a wealthy minority. Since the sixteenth century, the assault on the commons in Britain has continued apace. Over the last forty years, two billion people in the Global South have been dispossessed of their ancestral homelands.[18] Large numbers of impoverished people, cut off from resources once held in common, have been forced to trade their labour for low wages and driven into the slums of rapidly expanding cities. There is nothing voluntary about this process. Indeed, it's hard to see the original appropriation and privatisation of commonly owned resources as anything but theft. Economic historian Karl Polanyi saw the enclosures as 'a revolution of the rich against the poor', a process by which the rich 'were literally robbing the poor of their share in the common', a view reflected by popular opinion.[19] These lines from the period capture well popular resentments:

> The law locks up the man or woman
> Who steals the goose off the common
> But leaves the greater villain loose
> Who steals the common from the goose.

> The law demands that we atone
> When we take things we do not own
> But leaves the lords and ladies fine
> Who take things that are yours and mine.

The history of colonialism and imperialism poses further challenges to the legitimacy of property rights today. From the fifteenth century onwards, European nations took control of much of North, Central and South America, large swathes of Asia and, by the twentieth century, most of Africa. Indigenous populations were wiped out or pushed off their land, communities were devastated and resources were appropriated for Western profit. Forests, water systems and farmland were privatised, meaning that native inhabitants often had no choice but to sell their labour in order to survive.

In the nineteenth century, the British Empire led the charge as weaker nations were coerced into opening their borders to British goods and signing trade treaties that advanced British commercial interests. In 1842, the British waged an opium war against China, using military power to smash Chinese trade barriers, obstructing their profits. In 1907, six years before becoming US President, Woodrow Wilson spoke publicly of the need to force open the markets of other nations:

> Since trade ignores national boundaries and the manufacturer insists on having the world as a market, the flag of his nation must follow him, and the doors of the nations which are closed against him must be battered down. Concessions obtained by financiers must be safeguarded by ministers of state, even if the sovereignty of unwilling nations be outraged in the process. Colonies must be obtained or planted, in order that no useful corner of the world may be overlooked or left unused.[20]

There is nothing 'free' about this process. The right of a nation to determine its own policy has been dismissed repeatedly by powerful countries concerned only with advancing their own economic interests. By the start of the twentieth century, colonial powers were using some of the wealth flowing in from their colonies to improve the standard of living at home. This helped to stabilise the political system and avert the risk of revolution.

The means by which rich nations influence economic policies in poorer nations have changed over time, but the goals have not. Instead of military force, rich nations are now more likely to use economic power. In practice, this has meant attaching stringent conditions to foreign aid and loans from international financial institutions. Joseph Stiglitz, former Chief Economist at the World Bank, observed at first hand the process by which rich nations controlled the economies of poorer ones: 'the emerging markets are not forced open under the threat of the use of military might, but through economic power, through the threat of sanctions or the withholding of needed assistance in a time of crisis'.[21] Desperate for financial assistance and foreign markets to buy their goods, poorer nations have little choice but to accept the far-reaching conditions, which often involve curtailing vital health and education spending, and scrapping essential subsidies on food and fuel.

For decades, the IMF and World Bank have imposed rigid constraints, in line with orthodox neoliberal thinking, on governments in the Global South. Privatisation has been pushed through, free trade policies enforced, balanced budgets prioritised and democratically accountable government agencies – central banks, regulatory agencies, and even a tax office – have been turned into 'independent' policy agencies, free from public control. Destroying the autonomy of poorer nations in order to impose neoliberal policies is not just anti-democratic, it's hypocritical. Contrary to prevalent myths espoused by neoliberal economists, free trade is not what made the rich countries rich. Almost all of today's wealthy nations became rich by disregarding the now sacred tenets of free trade. The US and UK, in particular, were the most protectionist nations on Earth when their economies were developing. Only when it was clear that their industries could fare well against international competition did they advocate free trade.[22] Ulysses Grant, US President from 1869 to 1877, understood the path to development:

> For centuries England has relied on protection, has carried it to extremes and has obtained satisfactory results from it. There is no doubt that it is to this system that it owes its present strength. After two centuries, England has found it convenient to adopt free trade because it thinks that protection can no longer offer it anything. Very well then, Gentlemen, my knowledge of my country leads me to believe that within two hundred years, when America has gotten out of protection all that it can offer, it too will adopt free trade.[23]

For almost a century leading up to the First World War, the US maintained the highest import tariffs in the world, hovering at between 40 and 50 per cent.[24] Only when it became the richest country on Earth, able to beat back the global competition, did its trade barriers come down. Even then it continued to subsidise key industries heavily through publicly funded research and development.[25]

The logic of these anti-free-market policies is straightforward: new industries struggle to compete against stronger, more established foreign competition. A developing industry needs time to mature before it can face competition on a global scale.[26] Economic development depends on new industries being subsidised and protected by the state, sometimes for decades at a time. This is known as the 'infant industry argument' and was formalised by Alexander Hamilton, one of the founding fathers of the US. It is this long-term thinking that enabled the rich countries to become rich. During the 1960s and 70s, before the neoliberal consensus had been constructed, developing nations were able to practise various forms of protectionism without being seriously penalised. They grew at twice the rate they would grow under neoliberalism from the 1980s onwards. Even now, as Western nations push poorer ones to drop their trade barriers, they continue to maintain barriers of their own. Throughout Europe and the US, billions are expended each year on agricultural subsidies. The rhetoric of free markets is often just that – rhetoric. When it comes to the crunch, corporations and governments do not let consistency stand in the way of profit.

Today, there is barely a square inch of land or a single branch in a forest that is not owned by someone. Enclosure has moved beyond continents and territories, extending the reach of markets into every corner of our lives. One manifestation of the creep of market logic is in the domain of intellectual property. In what some have dubbed 'an enclosure of the mind', intellectual property rights are being extended to include facets of life that were once considered uncommodifiable. Property rights have been created for algorithms, symbols, words, ideas, seeds and even human genes. What can be owned, bought and sold is always changing and reflects the balance of power in society. The more the boundaries of the market expand into previously protected realms, the more poverty disadvantages the poor. What were once widely viewed as human rights – housing, water, healthcare and education – have gradually been turned into commodities available only to those who can afford them.

In spite of today's distribution of property rights being mired in a history of theft, colonialism, economic intimidation and slavery, we are told their protection is a matter of 'freedom'. Even if we look past their sordid origins and focus only on how wealth is accumulated today (as we did in Chapter 3), we find that it has nothing to do with fairness or justice and bears little relation to socially useful contributions, hard work or sacrifice. Friedman, along with the political establishment, ignores the many exploitative and immoral paths that have led to the present distribution of 'ownership rights' and invites us to accept without question that some people are extremely rich while others are extremely poor. This wilful blindness to gross inequality of wealth contrasts sharply with the importance neoliberals place on equality before the law. Such a selective commitment to equality favours those who enter the market already in possession of privilege and power.

Voluntary choices

Suppose we wipe the slate clean and ignore for a moment the centuries of oppression, dispossession and violence that produced today's global wealth distribution. Would that redeem the neoliberal position on freedom? Friedman makes the case that if every exchange involving labour, goods or money is entered into 'voluntarily', it must be mutually beneficial to those involved, who would otherwise not make the deal. This assumption has two major flaws.

Those who enter into a mutually beneficial transaction are not the only ones affected by it. This is an old problem, and widely acknowledged, at the heart of mainstream economic theory. Yet most economists proceed on the assumption that the effects of transactions on third parties are minimal. If they are wrong about this, the notion that market transactions are characterised by voluntarism cannot be maintained.[27]

The English economist Arthur Pigou pointed out in the 1920s that driving a car generates costs that are not borne by the driver. They are 'external' to the driver and are borne by the rest of society. They include the wear and tear of the road, sound pollution, increased traffic congestion and (we now know) the emission of greenhouse gases. However, Pigou assumed such costs were not significant. Cambridge economist Joan Robinson, a contemporary of Pigou and sharp critic of mainstream orthodoxies, didn't agree: '[t]he distinction that Pigou made between private costs and social costs was presented by him as an exception to the benevolent rule of *laissez-faire*. A moment's thought shows that the exception is the rule and the rule is the exception.'[28] Robinson is not alone in her assessment. 'In reality', write economists Rod Hill and Tony Myatt, 'externalities are pervasive and of great practical importance. Every year, they cost millions of people their lives.'[29] And according to economist Emery K. Hunt, 'externalities are totally pervasive'.[30]

Economist Raj Patel uses McDonald's to illustrate the point.[31] Like all corporations, McDonald's is legally constituted to maximise profits. Its internal decisions are guided by the need to reduce costs and outdo competitors. It drives down the costs of its workers and resources as much as it can and avoids costs entirely wherever possible. If it can emit pollutants such as carbon dioxide without paying for them, it will. Whatever costs the company avoids paying end up becoming externalised, borne by the rest of society. The result is that the price of a McDonald's burger does not reflect its true social cost: the bigger the gap between the price and the social cost, the more profitable the enterprise. How big is this gap for a typical fast-food burger? A report by the Centre for Science and the Environment in India estimated that a typical fast-food burger ought to cost about $200.[32]

One pervasive externality, often overlooked, is the negative psychological effect on society of private consumption. To the extent that material consumption is equated with status, it is a competitive activity for those seeking to maintain or increase their position in the social hierarchy. As Karl Marx put it, 'A house may be large or small; as long as the neighbouring houses are likewise small, it satisfies all social requirement for a residence. But let there arise next to the little house a palace, and the little house shrinks to a hut.'[33] Widespread attempts to increase status with material goods are self-defeating and wasteful. If some people are rapidly buying bigger houses, fancier clothes and flashier cars, other people may well feel that they also have to acquire these goods just to maintain their place in the social hierarchy.

Almost everything produced in the economy makes use of energy from fossil fuels, which release greenhouse gases that accelerate global warming. Nicholas Stern, author of a report commissioned by the British government, *The Stern Review: The Economics of Climate Change*, writes that 'these emissions are externalities and represent the biggest market failure the world has ever seen'.[34] In 2015, a ground-breaking document by the IMF made front pages around the world by revealing that the fossil fuel industry is subsidised by the world's governments to the tune of $10 million a minute![35] Or, if you prefer, $168,000 a second, or $5.3 trillion a year. That sum is greater than the spending on health by all the world's governments combined. These subsidies are largely due to the unpaid costs of pollution – floods, hurricanes, air pollution and droughts – that are routinely dumped on governments. A report by environmental consultancy firm Trucost, which was sponsored by the United Nations Environment Programme Finance Initiative, found that if environmental costs were not externalised, the dirtiest industries would cease to be profitable and would go out of business.[36]

These externalised costs have inflicted severe damage on the Global South. One study estimated the cost of this to be $5 trillion. Most of the damage comes from the consumption and production choices of richer nations. 'The ecological debt of rich countries to poor ones', writes Patel, 'dwarfs the entire third-world debt owed by poor countries to the rich which is only $1.8 trillion.'[37] The externalities of the financial sector are on a similar scale. Deregulating that sector triggered a global financial crisis that cost the world trillions of dollars.[38]

Externalising costs is a form of theft. It is taking something for nothing and leaving others to foot the bill. It is ubiquitous, permeating almost every market exchange. As sea levels rise, as the oceans are acidified, as forests disappear, as workers around the world are prevented from enjoying the profits they help to create, the extent of this theft is becoming increasingly difficult to ignore – and it is vast.

Externalities are not the only factor undermining the 'freedom' of market exchange. Friedman is keen to press home that transactions – assuming both parties are well informed – are agreed upon because they are mutually beneficial.[39] This may be true, but so what? Suppose a gun is pointed at your head and the assailant offers to spare you if you transfer your life savings to him. You accept because it is in your interest to do so – you keep your life and your assailant keeps your money: a mutually beneficial transaction. Was it free? Of course not. You were compelled by circumstances into accepting the terms on offer.

This same principle applies to the labourer who agrees to work twelve hours a day in dangerous conditions for wages that barely keep her alive. She only agrees to do so because she is compelled by an alternative that is even worse. There are many means of coercion more subtle and effective than holding someone at gunpoint.

If a person enters the market owning nothing but their own labour power, and another arrives owning great wealth, seeking to employ someone to further their own interests, the contract the two participants enter into is not free from coercion. Poverty is coercive. The threat of homelessness and hunger is no less real than that of a bullet. It reduces options and forces people to do things they would not otherwise do. As the eighteenth-century journalist Simon Linguet put it, the disempowered masses are compelled by 'the most terrible, the most imperious of masters, that is, need'.[40]

It is in the financial interests of business to keep large sectors of society poor and powerless. Profits rise when workers are compelled by circumstance to accept poverty wages in order to survive. The more desperate people are, the more they can be exploited – in other words, their employer can appropriate a greater portion of the value their labour creates. Centres of production have moved around the globe, but the pattern of desperate people accepting employment on exploitative terms persists. Profit thrives on desperation.

China has become a popular corporate destination, with lax regulation, minimal workers' rights, suppression of trade unions, and masses of impoverished young migrants fresh from the countryside. Take seventeen-year-old Tian Yu.[41] In 2010, she moved from her village to the city of Shenzhen to earn money for her family. She found a job at a Foxconn factory, which churns out parts for iPhones and iPads. She worked in silence on an assembly line for twelve hours a day, six days a week, and slept in a crowded factory dormitory. The working conditions were so unbearable that within a month Tian Yu jumped out of a fourth-floor dormitory window in an attempt to kill herself. That same year saw eighteen other suicide attempts in Foxconn factories. Tian Yu survived but is now paralysed from the waist down. The factory owners responded by putting up nets to prevent any future jumpers reaching the ground.

Bargaining power plays a decisive role in determining how a company's income is divided up among those who contribute to its creation. And, although it is true that in a market no one has to subordinate themselves to anyone else (just like you don't have to hand over your money when a gun is pointed at your head), the fact remains that the rich can survive quite easily without subordinating themselves, while the poor cannot. When disparities in bargaining power between employers and employees are sizeable, buying labour for less than it is worth is an easy way to generate profits, and, without the support of strong unions, the poor invariably have no bargaining power at all. This sits uneasily with neoliberal theories of 'economic freedom'.

That poverty reduces economic freedom has long been ignored or denied by the political right. The argument boils down to definitions. In principle, say neoliberals, those who are very poor have the same freedom to buy a yacht as anyone else; they simply lack the *capability* to do so; in other words, it is not their freedom that is lacking, only their capacity to make use of it. For Hayek, freedom meant 'freedom from coercion, freedom from the arbitrary power of other men, release from the ties which left the individual no choice but obedience to the orders of a superior'. He regarded it as a profound mistake to confuse this form of freedom with 'freedom from necessity, release from compulsion of circumstances'.[42] But is the impoverished worker not destined to obey 'the orders of a superior'? Is the woman driven by her hungry child to sell her body not destined to suffer 'from the arbitrary power of other men'?

How can a person be free to do what they are unable to do? Suppose inmates could buy their way out of prison for a large fee. Would it make sense to say that the poorer inmates, who would be shot for attempting to escape, are as free as the rich inmates sitting in the comfort of their homes? (After all, it is only the capability to pay that is lacking.) To call this freedom is to debase the term. A constraint on our freedom remains a constraint regardless of whether it arises from a lack of money, rights, strength or intelligence. Economists and philosophers can define freedom any way they want, but the restrictions, disadvantages and burdens placed on the poor do not disappear by redefining a term.[43]

The distinction made by Hayek has been accepted by thinkers across the political spectrum. The liberal political philosopher John Rawls, whose *A Theory of Justice* became something of a moral manifesto for liberalism, writes: 'The inability to take advantage of one's rights and opportunities as a result of poverty and ignorance, and a lack of means generally, is sometimes counted among the constraints definitive of liberty. I shall not, however, say this, but rather I shall think of these things as affecting the worth of liberty . . .'[44] Rawls argued that limited capability is just as restrictive and important as limited freedom, but humane as this position may be on its own terms, it concedes valuable ideological ground, allowing market fundamentalists to claim that their primary concern is the protection of individual freedom.

Freedom in a market expands and contracts with spending power.[45] If I try to do something that I cannot pay for, say travel to Brazil, I will be physically prevented from doing so. Poverty restricts options, and those restrictions are enforced by the state through coercive interference. The less money I have, the more I will be subject to this interference. Libertarian philosopher Robert Nozick, author of the influential *Anarchy, State, and Utopia*, argued forcefully against government interference in the market. In the 1970s, he helped lay the philosophical foundations of neoliberalism. His ideas continue to be used to defend the rights of private property and advance increasingly extreme free-market policies.[46] Central to Nozick's analysis is the idea that individual liberty is preserved in the market as long as no one is coerced into an exchange. To justify this he defines freedom in a contrived way: 'Other people's actions may place limits on one's available opportunities. Whether this makes one's resulting action non-voluntary depends upon whether these others had the right to act as they did.'[47] This is an extraordinary claim. When someone is sent to jail for a life sentence, he is deprived of his freedom whether or not we believe that society is within its rights to convict him. Legitimate coercion is still coercion.

When someone living in abject poverty is forced to choose between taking a job they despise or dying of hunger, Nozick tells us the choice is voluntary, and thus free, so long as the actions of others in the economy have been 'legitimate' (of course, this raises the question: who decides which actions are legitimate?). But the legitimacy of other people's actions does not make a person living in abject poverty any less desperate. As philosopher Gerald Cohen argues, if a woman is forced to take the long route around the outside of a field because of a large wall, she is forced to take the long route whether or not the wall has been erected legally. Focusing on the legality of the wall to determine whether she has been forced to take the long route is absurd. To establish whether an economic choice is voluntary or forced, the proper object of our attention should be the available choices, not the behaviour of other market participants.[48]

Market enthusiasts like Nozick and Friedman have proposed and attempted to justify an institutional framework based on a narrow conception of freedom that is rooted in private property rights. Once established, this framework is portrayed as more or less inviolable, whatever outcomes it may produce. Within it, the right of the wealthy to their profits takes precedence over the right of the poor to survive. Economist Amartya Sen explains that enormous human catastrophes can and do unfold without any infringement of private property and free market exchange, as history amply demonstrates. Famines are a prime example. According to Nozick, however, as long as others 'had the right to act as they did', those who die as a result of hunger, thirst or disease have lived and died 'free'.

For Nozick, human suffering can simply be side-stepped: he writes that the question of whether libertarian rights 'are absolute, or whether they may be violated in order to avoid catastrophic moral horror, and if the latter, what the resulting structure might look like, is one I hope largely to avoid'.[49] But what he 'hopes to avoid' is a central question. If his libertarian rights are absolute, then his system is compatible with the worst kinds of human suffering and oppression, and if not, what is left of his theory? Where do we draw the line? How much suffering is necessary to demolish his libertarian principles?

Free-market fundamentalists often claim that freedom of the individual is at the heart of their thinking. In fact, it is not individual freedom but a system of rules that occupies that central position: the experiences and sufferings of real people are routinely ignored. In the name of individual rights, many individuals are disregarded. History is a testament to the dangers of subordinating people to the demands of an abstract, idealised system. To focus exclusively on formal procedures and ignore the conditions of real people, as Nozick and Friedman invite us to do, is to discount the forms of freedom that actually matter to people. For as long as it has dominated the global political scene, this narrow conception of freedom has left billions of people with bleak prospects, meagre opportunities, inadequate resources and insufficient autonomy.

Ownership rights are neither absolute nor inviolable. Property is a social construct, a fiction maintained by legal and cultural institutions that depends for its existence on our collective consent. Property rights can be useful, but when placed beyond question and criticism, they become dangerous. When they are used to oppress and impoverish vast numbers of people, it is the people that should be defended, not the fictions.

Against the backdrop of extreme inequality in our world, we would do well to remember that even when access to resources is not secured through oppressive and exploitative means, it is still ultimately a matter of luck – a product of the lottery of birth and the talents and opportunities it bestows upon us. Nothing we do makes us deserving of a disproportionate share of Earth's bounty.

Producing consumers

'You will be amazed to find how many times in one day people glance at your nails. At each glance a judgement is made . . . Indeed some people make a practice of basing their estimate of a new acquaintance largely upon this one detail.' This advertisement appeared in 1920 in the American magazine *Ladies' Home Journal*.[50] Two years on, an advertisement for Woodbury Soap promised women 'the possession of beautiful skin' so that they might face the world 'proudly – confidently – without fear'. It warned that 'a man expects to find daintiness, charm, refinement in the women he knows . . . And when some unpleasant little detail mars this conception of what a woman should be – nothing quite effaces this conception.'[51] Historian Stuart Ewen describes a booklet from the same era advertising feminine beauty products which 'had on its cover a picture of a highly scrubbed, powdered and decorated nude' and the tag line: 'Your masterpiece – yourself'.[52] This idea of transforming of the individual into a commodity lies at the heart of consumer culture.

Neoliberals are keen to protect our right to do what we want with our person and property but they pay scant attention to the origins of those wants. 'The economist', writes Friedman, 'has little to say about the formation of wants; this is the province of the psychologist.'[53] But the formation of wants is central to the topic of freedom. In the context of pervasive and intrusive attempts to shape our preferences, the idea of 'voluntary' choices becomes hard to sustain. Economic textbooks rarely address the topic, the implicit assumption being that the preferences of consumers are authentic and originate 'from within'. This couldn't be further from the truth, which is why wants are manufactured in every area of our lives. In 2008, advertisers in the US spent almost $1,000 for every American.[54]

Advertising today may be pervasive but it wasn't always so. 'A century or more ago', writes US economist and historian Douglas Dowd, 'most people were not "consumers" in the modern sense; they were wage-earners, and their wages were so low they had no choices to make.'[55] With the dawn of the twentieth century, industrialisation in the world's richest nations changed all that. This technological leap revolutionised production, which happened on a mass scale for the first time in history. Initially, it posed a problem for the free-enterprise system: supply was outstripping demand. To profit from this growing productive capacity, corporations not only had to produce goods, they had to produce consumers to buy the goods, and on an unprecedented scale. To ensure that demand matched productive potential, advertisers helped to develop lifestyles to which consumers were encouraged to aspire. It was no longer enough to dream of meeting one's basic needs; the advertising industry created a grander vision of prosperity to which the public were taught to compare themselves. The 1920s saw an explosion and redefinition of consumption. You could now buy an identity, a way of life, a dream.

Transforming citizens into consumers served a political purpose as well as a financial one. The year 1919 had seen four million workers in the US involved in industrial disputes, a fourfold increase on the previous year.[56] Concerned by the example of Bolshevism in Russia, the threat of revolution in Europe, and a powerful surge of support for socialist and anarchist movements among American workers, industry leaders saw that providing the newly enfranchised masses with a larger stake in the capitalist system could help stabilise the status quo. Strategies to consumerise the worker – that is, to increase wages, extend bank credit and create more leisure time in which to consume – were intended to be an antidote to the anti-capitalist content of the industrial protests. The consumerisation of the worker would be a mission for the public relations industry, which was growing in scale and sophistication. Advertising revenue rocketed from $58 million in 1928 to almost $200 million in 1929. As a writer in one of America's leading advertising trade magazines put it, effective advertising 'helps to keep the masses dissatisfied with their mode of life, discontented with ugly things around them. Satisfied customers are not as profitable as dissatisfied ones.'[57]

Happiness harms profits. The global weight-loss industry is set to hit £220 billion in 2017 and the global cosmetic surgery industry is now worth almost £15 billion.[58] The 'needs' met by these exploding industries have been manufactured by a systematic campaign to distort the self-perception of women (and increasingly of men too). The advertising industry's attack on self-esteem, which began early in the twentieth century, intensified over time. In 1966, half of high school girls classified themselves as fat. Three years on, the figure had shot up to 80 per cent. By 1985, according to one survey, 90 per cent of women classified themselves as overweight.[59]

A report by the American Psychological Association in 2007 found that the sexualisation of women and girls in the media had resulted in a wave of harmful effects: a lack of physical confidence, eating disorders, depression, shame, anxiety and sexual problems in adulthood.[60] In another study, researchers surveying more than 50,000 British children found that these young boys and girls were already very anxious about their appearance. Teenage girls were worst affected. One twelve-year-old told the researchers: 'Sometimes you feel like you can't enjoy yourself unless you are pretty.'[61] In Britain, one in five female students suffers from an eating disorder.[62]

Internationally, skin-lightening cream has become a major industry, with millions of women bleaching their skin on a daily basis to look 'more white'. Bleaching skin carries serious health risks, including blood cancers and cancer of the liver, yet in Nigeria, according to figures from the World Health Organization, 77 per cent of women use this cream. In India, the whitening cream market was valued at $432 million in 2010 and has been growing rapidly ever since.[63]

The idea at the heart of consumerism – that happiness and self-worth increase in line with material possessions – is a lie. Decades of studies have produced robust results confirming that advertising, and the materialism it fosters, is psychologically damaging. The research shows that 'strong materialistic values are associated with a pervasive undermining of people's well-being, from low life satisfaction and happiness, to depression and anxiety, to physical problems such as headaches, and to personality disorders, narcissism, and antisocial behaviour'.[64] Psychologists David Myers and Ed Diener write: 'Even though Americans earn twice as much in today's dollars as they did in 1957, the proportion of those telling surveyors from the National Opinion Research Center that they are "very happy" has declined from 35 to 29 per cent . . . only in the poorest countries, such as Bangladesh and India, is income a good measure of emotional well-being.'[65]

The policies and values that were advanced by President Reagan and Prime Minister Thatcher have been correlated with extremely high rates of mental illness. A UK survey conducted in 2000 showed that '23 per cent of adults have either a neurotic disorder, a psychotic disorder, or were addicted to alcohol or drugs'.[66] A 2014 report found that English children are some of the unhappiest in the Western world. Other research suggests that a million young people in Britain are mentally ill.[67] In the US, 10 per cent of children have moderate or severe difficulties in 'the areas of emotions, concentration, behaviour, or being able to get along with people' and more than half of adults will suffer from some form of mental illness in their lifetime.[68] Of course, the burdens of materialism are not borne equally across society. Women are almost twice as likely as men to suffer depression and anxiety, and poor women up to nine times more likely than wealthy men.[69] Things are different in mainland European nations that practise a more moderate form of capitalism. According to data from the World Health Organization, at the turn of the millennium Spain, Germany, Italy, the Netherlands and France had on average half the rates of mental illness found in the UK, US, Australia and New Zealand.[70] The values promoted by neoliberal society are, it would seem, hazardous to our health.

It is not what we possess that gives us status but what we have relative to those around us – that's the psychology of materialism. One of the key functions of the advertising industry is to induce status anxiety in order to compel us to consume. A study focusing on males in Britain's civil service showed that men in lower status jobs had a death rate three times higher than men in the highest status jobs. The expectation had been that greater responsibility higher up in the social hierarchy would lead to increased stress and worse health outcomes. In fact, the opposite was the case. Further studies with a broader scope confirmed the pattern. Low job status in men and women is related to 'cancers, chronic lung disease, gastrointestinal disease, depression, suicide, sickness, absence from work, [and] back pain'.[71]

Evidence of the health risks of materialism has been mounting over the last few decades, but some have long suspected the connection. Writing in the 1950s, psychoanalyst Erich Fromm argued that materialistic values encourage us to experience ourselves as commodities, resulting in anxiety about our 'saleability'. He characterised a highly materialistic person as 'passive, empty, anxious, isolated . . . [someone] for whom life has no meaning and who is profoundly alienated and bored'. Boredom, he argued, is compensated for by 'compulsive consumption'.[72] This would explain why advertising has become less and less about the product itself and more about the kind of people we could be if we possessed it: sexy, fun, powerful, distinguished and ethical. The 'emptiness' induced by materialism is transformed into its driving force. The dynamism of a consumerist society is maintained by the dissatisfaction it creates.

Mainstream economic models assume consumers have access to perfect information about products. The irony is that corporations do all they can to misinform people whenever public knowledge would threaten profits. According to neuroscientist Kathleen Taylor, the bypassing of reason 'is what a good advertisement aims to achieve'.[73] One way to bypass the intellect is to get to consumers when they are children. In the 1980s, consumer protection laws in the US and UK were designed to give special consideration to the needs and vulnerability of the young, and constraints were placed on advertising aimed at children. In Reagan's first year in office, he repealed these regulations in favour of promoting 'market solutions'. Dr Susan Linn, Professor of Psychiatry at Baker Children's Center, Harvard, observes that 'In trade journals, people talk about cradle to grave brand loyalty. You know if you don't get a child by two or by six you won't have them at all. Or if you get a child by six you'll have them for life. So all of a sudden infants are now fair game.'[74]

Lucy Hughes, director of strategy at one of the world's largest PR companies, Initiative Media, is something of an expert on targeting children with corporate messages. Faced with the charge of manipulating children, she responds: 'Well, is it ethical? I don't know. But our role at Initiative is to move products . . . build that relationship when they're younger, and you've got them as an adult.'[75] Today, $2 billion a year is spent marketing 'junk food' to children. Unsurprisingly, childhood obesity has become a major public health problem. One in every five American children is now overweight. According to Dr Linn, 'The corporate message that children are being implanted with is that buying things will make you happy . . . And in fact the research shows that that's not true.'[76]

From 1992 to 1997, the amount spent on marketing to children doubled. This advertising has been honed by experts to exploit the psychological vulnerabilities of children. The internet has brought with it new ways to reach children without parental mediation. On average, children and teenagers engage with media for almost twice as much time as they spend attending school. Online 'kid marketing' has become a major industry: annually, $15 billion is spent advertising to children both to claim a share of their direct buying power and to harness the spending power of parents, estimated to be over $1 trillion – two hundred times what it was worth forty years ago.[77]

Even babies aren't safe from the profit motive. Along with UNICEF, the World Health Organization (WHO) strongly recommends that babies be breastfed for the first six months of life, and that doing so globally 'could possibly save more than 1 million child lives every year'.[78] Yet infant formula has been marketed internationally as a superior replacement for breastfeeding. The dangers of infant formula are particularly acute in developing nations because of contaminated water. UNICEF places at least part of the blame for this at the door of advertisers' use of highly unethical 'aggressive marketing' which includes the free distribution of infant formula, knowing full well that a lactating mother who uses the sample and stops breastfeeding will cease to lactate, creating a dependency on the formula.

Morals and the market

Inequality has soared since the 1970s. There is a significant and growing body of research into its negative effects on people. One of the most striking findings is the corrosive effect that inequality has on community and social life. High levels of inequality are correlated with low levels of trust and cooperation. Asked if they agreed with the statement 'most people can be trusted', two-thirds of people in Sweden responded positively, but only 10 per cent did so in Portugal. The pattern holds all along the inequality spectrum. The highest levels of trust are to be found in Sweden, Norway, Denmark, Finland and the Netherlands – nations with relatively low levels of inequality – while trust is lowest in Portugal, Singapore, the USA, the UK and Israel – nations with very high levels of inequality.[79]

By normalising greed, less trusting nations are more likely to produce citizens who act selfishly when they expect the benefits to exceed personal costs. Material differences undermine solidarity and community, which is why countries with higher rates of trust and lower rates of inequality also give more to charity. Norway, Sweden, Denmark and the Netherlands are the only nations to meet the UN's target for spending on foreign development (in fact they exceed it). The US and Portugal tend to spend the lowest proportion of their GDP on foreign development.[80]

Psychologists have developed carefully structured games to measure the tendency of individuals to cooperate in different cultures around the world. One of the most famous involves two unacquainted participants, say Emma and Rosa, and a sum of money, say £100. Emma is asked to divide the money into two piles: one to keep, the other to give to Rosa. The money may be divided up in any way but if the proposed division is rejected, neither will get a penny. Obviously, keeping the whole amount comes with a high risk of being rejected by the other player.

What amounts do people settle on? It varies significantly across different societies. Residents from one Indonesian island, whose community placed a high value on cooperation and ritualistic sharing, chose to offer the second participant more than they kept for themselves (on average, a ratio of 43 to 57). The result defied the expectations of mainstream economists who assumed that, being selfish, rational beings, we would all keep as much as possible, offering only what we thought was necessary to ensure the proposal was accepted. After all, it would be rational to accept whatever is offered, because any amount is better than nothing. The islanders were unusual in their generosity, but most people are more generous than they need to be. Commonly, people keep 60 per cent and give away 40 per cent. A strong predictor of generosity was whether people came from a market society in which they were used to making exchanges with strangers.[81] Unsurprisingly, societies that value cooperation produce individuals who are more willing to share.

Another suggestive line of research looked at the effects on behaviour of simply thinking about money. Psychologists have identified a powerful phenomenon called 'priming' which occurs when exposure to a stimulus unconsciously affects a person's response to a subsequent stimulus. In an experiment conducted by Kathleen Vohs, participants were unconsciously primed with images of money. A computer screen saver in one corner of the room showed dollar bills floating in water: just being exposed to this image of money led people to behave more selfishly. They were less willing to help others with their tasks, picked up fewer pencils when another participant dropped them, and showed a stronger preference for being alone.[82]

These findings are a cause for hope. They remind us that the greedy behaviour encouraged in our market societies is, to a large extent, learned, that it is a mistake to equate human nature with the behaviour we witness in capitalist societies. It shows that markets have a bias: they provide skewed incentives which foster competition over cooperation, dissatisfaction over contentment, distrust over community and selfishness over compassion. There are other countervailing influences, of course, but the pressure to accumulate, compete and consume are central features of a capitalist system, and are backed by billions of advertising dollars that exert a profound influence on us all. Economist Samuel Bowles writes:

> The beauty of the market [is that it] works well even if people are indifferent toward one another . . . But that is also the problem. The economy – its markets, work places and other sites – is a gigantic school. . . . We learn to function in these environments, and in doing so become someone we might not have become in a different setting . . . By economizing on valuable traits – feelings of solidarity with others, the ability to empathize, the capacity for complex communication and collective decision making, for example – markets are said to cope with the scarcity of these worthy traits. But in the long run markets contribute to their erosion and even disappearance. What looks like a hard-headed adaptation to the infirmity of human nature may in fact be part of the problem.[83]

Free-market fundamentalists have worked hard to make their politics synonymous with individual liberty; when they succeed, the fight for freedom degenerates into a struggle to protect the rights of property owners. In the words of economic historian Karl Polanyi, writing during the Second World War, 'Free enterprise and private ownership are declared to be essentials of freedom . . . The freedom that regulation creates is denounced as unfreedom; the justice, liberty and welfare it offers are described as a camouflage of slavery.'[84]

In our own time, it has become an article of faith for many that free markets are self-correcting, efficient mechanisms, guided by a benevolent 'invisible hand' to distribute the right goods to the right people in the right proportion. There is, we are reminded, no alternative. But it is worth remembering that a great many societies have never used money, were not based on barter (contrary to the myths perpetuated in economic textbooks), and did not revolve around the pursuit of profit; rather, they fell under what we now call 'gift economies' in which goods and services are freely given without agreement about any future repayment. For most of human history, markets did not exist.

The last thirty years have seen a grand experiment in deregulated markets and corporate control, and the results are in: extreme inequality, economic instability, exploited workers, unhappy consumers, mass unemployment, the erosion of democracy, and environmental disaster. The conclusion is unavoidable: the claim that free markets promote freedom is false. The market is a social mechanism that can do some things well but fails horribly at others. It must be tamed and directed democratically to ensure it pulls us in a direction *most* of us want to go. Markets are enormously powerful but, as Stiglitz puts it, 'they have no inherent moral character'.[85] Like a wild animal, the market has the power to drag us in many directions. Guided by short-term interests, it is dragging us over an environmental and social precipice. The neoliberal fantasy of a free-market utopia is a dangerous distraction from the real-world dynamics of politics and control.

Many dictatorships have supported free markets, while many democracies have pursued a different ideal of freedom with higher taxes, extensive regulation and public ownership. The case of Chile under the military dictatorship of Augusto Pinochet is revealing. A violent military coup brought Pinochet to power, deposing the democratically elected socialist president, Salvador Allende. Friedman and his students played an influential role in the economic affairs of Chile, advising Pinochet to tear apart the programme of socialist reforms the people had voted for and set about creating a textbook neoliberal economy. As instructed, Pinochet dissolved the rights of labour unions, opened capital markets, privatised social security, cut welfare and sold off state-controlled industries. Wages dropped and economic inequality shot up.

While following the advice of Friedman and others, Pinochet ruled a repressive regime that murdered thousands of its citizens, imprisoning and torturing tens of thousands more. It is thought that over 200,000 Chileans were driven into exile. Despite this, Friedrich Hayek, regarded by many as a champion of liberty, believed that 'personal freedom was much greater under Pinochet than it had been under Allende'.[86] Although it had taken the murder of thousands of trade unionists, he praised the 'Chilean miracle' for having broken 'trade union privileges of any kind'. In fact, he favoured what to many will be a contradiction in terms, 'a liberal dictatorship rather than . . . a democratic government devoid of liberalism'.[87] Hayek's allegiances were clear: when political freedom clashed with property rights, he prioritised the latter. Although the values behind the neoliberal project remain unchanged, the language used to pursue them has now been modified. Modern neoliberals do not openly oppose democracy; instead they attempt to discredit the competence of the state itself, arguing that true freedom lies not in a free functioning democracy but in a free functioning market.

It took centuries of struggle to expand the freedom of the masses through the establishment of a democratic system in which every adult can vote. The rights and services secured by democratic participation have improved people's lives in countless ways and undeniably expanded our freedom. But the vehicle through which voters express their preferences – the government – is routinely depicted as the primary threat to individual freedom. The real path to liberty, we are told, is through the transfer of power away from the voting booth and into the market, from the principle of 'one person one vote' to 'one dollar one vote'.

Every year, malaria kills over a million people, debilitating many millions more, but more research money is spent on treatments for baldness than this deadly disease.[88] The market cannot register a need unless it is backed by money. It is blind to the hunger of the poor, deaf to the cries of the sick, yet it creates whole industries to meet the trivial demands of the rich. The vote was fought for to give people without wealth – women, the unemployed, the working class – the means to secure for themselves the rights and services that would expand their freedom but which were denied to them in the marketplace. But for too long the power of the market has neutralised the power of the vote.

★

Freedom may lie at the heart of justifications for the free market, but the freedom being defended is not what most people associate with the word. It is a freedom compatible with crippling poverty and exploitation, authoritarian control and systematic manipulation. It was born of theft and spread through war. It has been skilfully deployed to justify corporate independence from popular control. Twisted out of shape by neoliberal theory, the lofty ideal of liberty has been used by corporations to co-opt state power and erode human rights. Releasing this ideal from the distorting grip of free markets is an urgent priority for those seeking to create a freer society.

Where we draw the boundaries of the market is not a technical question. Economists have no more right to answer it than you or I. If we believe a poor child has the same right to proper medical treatment, parental love and education as a rich child, we are rejecting market logic. If we believe a prisoner should not be able to pay for a nicer cell, we are rejecting market logic. If we believe a house fire should be put out whether or not the home-owners have paid for the privilege, we are rejecting market logic. If we believe people should have access to clean air, clean water and healthy food, however much money they possess, we are rejecting market logic. If we believe poor families have as much right as rich families not to have toxic waste dumped near their home, we are rejecting market logic. If we believe genes, people, academic qualifications, elections, judges, organs, children and friendship should not be owned, bought and sold, we are rejecting market logic.

The *market* does not care about the starving or the sick. It does not care about fairness and justice. It does not care about how hard people work or how kind they are. But *people* do care about these things, and that's what ultimately matters.

7

Media

We spend more time with television, newspapers, magazines, websites, computer games, radios, BlackBerrys, iPods and iPhones than we do in bed. Britons and Americans frequently gaze at digital screens for at least eight and a half hours a day.[1] These media saturate our daily experience, exposing us to a world of words, sounds and images brought to us by large corporations. This world constitutes an alternative reality in which many of us spend much of our lives. Yet it is artificial.

What we see when we pick up a newspaper, turn on the news or flick through a magazine is the outcome of a process of selection and filtering. Every day, media professionals decide which facts and perspectives will reach the public and which will not. What they select depends on agendas set by editors, executives and owners. The content of the curriculum in a classroom in 1930s Germany differed radically from one in Churchill's Britain or from Mao's China. Similarly, the information conveyed in the 1930s by *Pravda* differed sharply from that in *The New York Times* or Germany's *Der Stürmer*. Selections and omissions reflect the values, priorities and goals of those with the power to do the selecting.

Impartiality, so often taken for granted, is unattainable. It is impossible to present information objectively, neutrally or impartially. The journalist, teacher or speaker must make use of some selection criteria, and the topics that are covered, the angle and the carefully chosen words reveal his or her values and priorities. Every media system necessarily privileges some ideas, perspectives and facts over others. The important question is, which forces guide this process and whose interests do they serve?

The power of voters is dependent on what they know. Information is the oxygen of democracy: its health depends on the quality of the ideas and facts circulating through society. If voters can be systematically misled, they can be systematically manipulated. In a totalitarian society, the media is an extension of the government. Everyone expected the Soviet Union's leading newspaper to serve the interests of the state. But in today's capitalist democracies, the media still represent a vast concentration of unaccountable political power. The interests they serve are protected by the enduring and powerful myth that, in a market, the media are free.

When the media became 'free'

The traditional account of press history in Britain goes like this: in the nineteenth century the heroic battle by the press to rid themselves of burdensome taxes finally resulted in victory. Only then did a truly independent press, free of state regulation, emerge.[2] According to this account, a new influx of profits from advertising rescued the press from financial dependence on government. From then on, the media was regulated by market forces alone. It was free. But this is just half the story. It appears plausible only if we ignore the inherent bias of market forces. A closer look shows, as media historian James Curran explains, that this period 'did not inaugurate a new era of press freedom . . . it introduced a new system of press censorship more effective than anything that had gone before'.[3] Market forces would succeed in shaping media output to serve elite interests where legal repression had failed.

In the first half of the nineteenth century, Britain had a thriving radical press that reached a large working-class audience. It presented a picture of the world that resounded with the lives and experience of working people and reflected and reinforced the belief that social change could be achieved through the organised action of workers. It was considered a major threat by the ruling elites who tried repeatedly to suppress it. British MP Dr Philimore summed up a sentiment shared by many of his contemporaries when he warned the House of Commons that 'Those infamous publications . . . inflame passions and awaken their selfishness, contrasting their present conditions with what they contend to be their future condition.'[4]

The initial strategy of control used laws against seditious and blasphemous libel, which was defined in extremely general terms and functioned as a useful tool of censorship. But as judicial reform gradually empowered juries rather than judges, court cases often did not go the government's way. The strategy also gave the radical press great publicity. Its circulation was on the rise. Something more had to be done.[5]

The government's response to this 'crisis' was a new strategy focused on increasing the cost of publishing by imposing taxes. This was meant to price out poorer readers and, as Lord Castlereagh explained to the House of Commons, ensure that 'persons exercising the power of the press should be men of some respectability and property'.[6] But although these taxes were doubled between 1789 and 1815, this heavy-handed approach also failed. The working-class readership adapted impressively to the increased prices. Each week, people pooled resources to buy a radical paper. Unions and other collectives also purchased them. The surprising result was an increase in circulation of the popular press as it became a collective activity.

The threat posed to elite interests by the popular press was certainly real. It published radical ideas, facts and perspectives that did not appear in any of the 'respectable' papers and played a central role in building and maintaining support for working-class organisations. It provided labourers with a new framework with which to make sense of their lives, cultivating an empowering self-image that elevated workers to the 'only productive and useful section of the community' in sharp contrast to 'parasitic' elites who were portrayed as profiting from exploitation.

By the mid-nineteenth century, it had become clear that neither libel law nor taxation had stamped out the influence of the radical papers, and a new debate began. Most traditionalists called for tougher regulation and enforcement, but a growing number of the establishment favoured a different approach. They wanted to abolish press taxes to incentivise wealthy men to produce cheap papers that would undercut the radical press and act as an ideological weapon against trade unionism. It was argued that free trade and the abolition of these taxes would, as the president of one lobby group put it, create 'a cheap press in the hands of men of good moral character, of respectability, and of capital' who would gain access 'to the minds of the working classes'.[7]

As history testifies, once the taxes were repealed, the economic might of the rich in a free market succeeded in crushing the radical press. The second half of the nineteenth century did not see the creation of a single daily radical paper. In place of the popular working-class press, a new local daily press came into existence, just as the reformers had hoped, including the *Daily Mail* in 1896 and the *Daily Mirror* in 1903. It was a new era for the British media.

Who owns the media?

Who has the resources to set up and run a newspaper, TV station, publishing house or film company? Today, hardly anyone has. In 1837, the cost of establishing a British newspaper was less than £1,000. By 1918, this had increased to over £2 million.[8] The explosion in start-up costs was due to the creation of new technologies for printing newspapers, which only those with vast wealth could afford. By the 1980s, *Today* and *Sunday Today* were launched with an initial outlay of £22.5 million, *The Independent* with £21 million and the *London Daily News* with an outlay of well over £30 million.[9] If only the very rich can afford to set up large-scale media outlets, then it will inevitably become the priorities of the very rich that will shape media output. To see how important ownership is, imagine what the news would look like if all our media institutions were run by communists instead of capitalists.

The right of those who own the media to set the political tone of their output is taken for granted in an industry where the notion of 'public service' is considered by many to be old-fashioned romanticism.[10] Max Hastings, former editor of *The Daily Telegraph*, was clear that he 'never really believed in the notion of editorial independence' and thought the paper's owner, Conrad Black, was 'richly entitled to take a view when he owns the newspaper'.[11] Today, the *Telegraph* is owned by the Barclay brothers. According to deputy editor, Benedict Brogan, it is 'utter madness . . . to stand up and say the guy who owns the train set has no say over the train set'. As he points out, 'It would be defying the truth about newspapers throughout the ages. What is the point of owning a newspaper if you can't take an interest in what the newspaper is up to?'[12] Andrew Neil, former editor of the *Sunday Times,* owned by perhaps the most powerful media mogul of all, reports that his former boss, Rupert Murdoch, 'expects his papers to stand broadly for what he believes: a combination of right-wing Republicanism from America mixed with undiluted Thatcherism from Britain'.[13] He described Murdoch as 'an interventionist proprietor who expected to get his way'.

The value of newspapers to their owners is not measured solely in terms of profit. Many national newspapers have made large losses for decades at a time. They are maintained because they serve a valuable political function. A media outlet gives enormous political power to its owners and their allies. It can shape culture, mould public opinion and promote its own values. Favoured viewpoints can be highlighted, and opposing perspectives ridiculed or simply ignored. Newspapers and television networks can set national and international agendas and perhaps even sway elections. They need not reflect public opinion. In the 2010 general election in the UK, just 36 per cent of voters supported the right-wing Conservative Party, compared with 71 per cent of newspapers (by circulation). This mismatch has held true for decades.[14]

Because the media are so powerful, political leaders actively seek their support. When Alastair Campbell, Tony Blair's Director of Communications, was asked about New Labour's historic 1997 electoral victory, he replied: 'without doubt, the biggest turning point . . . was when *The Sun* came out in support of us'.[15] So cosy was Blair's relationship with Rupert Murdoch that, after his premiership ended, he became godfather to one of Murdoch's children. Murdoch's influence since then has not waned. In a fourteen-month period under the Conservative-led Coalition government, ministers averaged a meeting a week with News International editors, executives or owners.[16]

Not only is ownership of the media limited to the super rich, it is also highly concentrated. In 1983, fifty corporations owned the majority of the media in the US; in 2012 the number had dwindled to six. Six companies control the content of almost all the newspapers, magazines, television, books, music, films, news websites and radio consumed in the US, as well as a large proportion of media consumed globally. Things are not much better in the UK where, in 2014, just three groups controlled 70 per cent of Britain's newspapers.[17] As a result of the many mergers and takeovers that have taken place, those who own the media are also big players in other sectors like oil, transport, mining, construction, engineering, finance and the leisure industries. Already in 1977, the UK Royal Commission on the Press concluded: 'Rather than saying the press has other business interests, it would be truer to argue that the press has become a subsidiary of other industries.'[18] Conflicts of interest inevitably arise. In 1991, as the American network NBC reported on the Gulf War, it was owned by General Electric which had designed, manufactured or supplied almost every weapons system being used by the US army.[19] Today, media corporations share many members of their board of directors with other large corporations in banking, energy, pharmaceuticals and technology.

More important than concentration of ownership is the commonality of experience, education, background, social class and interests that link those who own, run and work in media organisations. Graduates from Oxford and Cambridge make up less than 1 per cent of the population as a whole but account for 47 per cent of newspaper columnists.[20] A study by the Sutton Trust showed that while only 7 per cent of the population go to private schools, over half of Britain's top journalists received a private education.[21] Almost all new entrants into journalism must possess an expensive degree and work unpaid for, on average, seven weeks as an intern before receiving a wage. This has made it far harder for working-class people to get a foothold on even the lowest rungs of this profession.

In today's markets, with vast wealth concentrated in few hands, those who can afford to set up or buy an existing large-scale media organisation are usually billionaires. This is the first form of bias that emerges from a 'free market' in media. As with any commodity, privatisation empowers those with private wealth. It has turned information into a commodity to be bought, sold, distorted, disseminated and withheld. Predictably, this arrangement shapes media content in ways that serve the interests of those who already possess great power. Rather than being a neutral tool of social enlightenment, exposing truths and informing the public, the media have become a weapon of social control.

Who holds the purse strings?

The media were once funded primarily by sales revenue but this has not been the case for a long time. In nineteenth-century Britain, after the press taxes were repealed, the price of advertising fell dramatically and investment in advertising shot up, allowing the price of newspapers to be cut by 75 per cent over two decades.[22] Spending on advertising steadily increased throughout the second half of the nineteenth century, reaching an estimated £20 million in 1907.[23] With the growing dependence on advertising revenue, advertisers acquired the power to decide which papers would survive in a competitive market, spelling doom for the radical press for two reasons – one ideological, the other commercial.

The ideological reason was that corporate advertisers favoured papers that supported their interests. More significant, however, were commercial considerations. Working-class readers had limited disposable income to spend on advertised goods so advertisers tended to avoid papers with poorer readers.[24] 'Some of the most widely circulated journals in the Empire', wrote the head of one leading ad agency in 1856, 'are the worst to advertise in. Their readers are not purchasers, and any money thrown upon them is so much thrown away.'[25] Many working-class papers collapsed due to lack of advertising revenue. This was the fate of the *Daily Herald*, which enjoyed a circulation of 4.7 million – double the combined readership of *The Times*, *Financial Times* and *The Guardian*.[26] For the popular press, the alternative to liquidation was to adjust their content to attract wealthier readers and, with them, more advertising. A number of progressive papers took this route, moderating their politics in the process, and increasingly reflecting the concerns and views of more affluent audiences.

An interesting test case for the influence of advertising occurred in Britain during the Second World War. In 1940, newsprint was rationed to make efficient use of scarce resources. Two years later, new regulations were introduced that limited the amount of space allocated to press advertising. Once again, the majority of revenue generated by newspapers came from sales instead of advertising. This was an important shift. Corporations could no longer be so picky about where they placed their ads. With limited advertising space, progressive papers found they could again afford to appeal to low-income readers. The ideological shift to the left that followed paved the way for social democracy in post-war Britain. It helped to bring about the welfare reforms introduced after the war and a landslide victory for the Labour Party in 1945. In 1942 the Beveridge Report, a relatively obscure official document which the Minister of Information had hoped would be published discreetly and which outlined many of the reforms later implemented by the Attlee government, received banner headlines and was hailed as 'the Magna Carta for the toiling masses in Britain' by a rejuvenated popular press. The report was an ambitious manifesto of social reform, proposing a National Health Service, a full employment policy, and social security. It was so well publicised that Cecil King, owner of Mirror Group Newspapers, noted that 'The volume of press support is so great that it seems to be assumed in the House that it will be politically impossible to drop the Report.'[27] The groundbreaking reforms that followed owed much to this renaissance of the radical press.

When newsprint rationing was phased out, the economic environment of the British press reverted to what it had been prior to the war. Advertisers were elevated to a de facto licensing authority and their ideological and commercial considerations began to exert a powerful influence once again. As one advertiser put it, 'I'm not going to keep a newspaper which, the first time I get a strike, will back the strikers.'[28]

The experience of influential US magazine the *New Yorker* provides another useful case study. For a number of years it sold more advertising pages than any other magazine. That changed on 15 July 1967 when it carried an extended article on how the village of Ben Suc in Vietnam had been burned to the ground by US troops. This critical account of the event broke with the dominant narrative of American benevolence and success in Vietnam. It marked an editorial shift. From then on, the *New Yorker* spoke out against the invasion. Although the publication of anti-war articles failed to dent its circulation, the composition of its readership changed as it began to attract younger readers with less disposable income. The response of advertisers was decisive. Advertising revenue dropped by 40 per cent and net profits fell by two-thirds, while the circulation of the magazine remained constant.[29]

For well over a century, what has mattered most is the amount of advertising revenue a paper makes, not the number of copies it sells. Its market is not shaped by the choices of consumers but by those of advertisers. The primary product is not the news but the public. They are sold by media institutions to advertisers who pay good money for their attention. This is equally true of television networks, radio stations, websites and magazines.

The price an advertiser pays for a television ad is determined by the size of the expected audience. As media historian Jean Seaton writes, 'advertisers regard programmes merely as the means by which audiences are delivered to them. These are the realities which help to determine what kinds of programmes are made, when they are shown and who sees them.'[30] An obvious pressure arising from these constraints is to produce programmes with mass appeal or that deliver particularly sought-after consumer groups such as women or young people. As Condé Nast, founder of *Vanity Fair, Glamour, Vogue, Mademoiselle* and *House & Garden*, put it, the aim is 'to bait the editorial pages in such a way to lift out of all the millions of Americans just the hundred thousand cultivated persons who can buy these quality goods'.[31]

Using their privileged position, advertisers are able to influence the material that appears around their adverts, favouring content that puts people in a buying mood. Light-hearted, superficial output is more likely to maximise the effectiveness of an advert promoting a pair of shoes than, say, a documentary about the exploitation of child workers in the Asian sweatshops that made them. Stories of substance can make adverts seem trivial, unimportant, perhaps even offensive by comparison, and, regardless of the importance of a story to the public interest, that is unacceptable to those holding the purse strings.

In the 1960s, the consumer goods corporation Procter & Gamble made the following demands on media outlets that carried its adverts:

'There will be no material on any programmes which could in any way further the concept of business as cold, ruthless and lacking all sentiment or spiritual motivation. If a businessman is cast in the role of villain, it must be made clear that he is not typical but is as much despised by his fellow businessman as he is by other members of society.'[32] Any attacks on 'the American way of life' were to be rebutted 'completely and convincingly' later in the same broadcast.

Before cigarette commercials were banned in 1970, the Brown & Williamson Tobacco Corporation in the US demanded that, in programmes carrying tobacco advertising, 'Tobacco products should not be used in a derogatory or harmful way. And no reference or gesture of disgust, dissatisfaction or distaste be made in connection with them . . . no cigarette should be used as a prop to depict an undesirable character.'[33] Media watchdog Fairness and Accuracy in Reporting (FAIR) have described how major advertisers BP and Morgan Stanley issued directives demanding that their ads be pulled from any edition of a publication that included potentially 'objectionable' content.[34] Examples abound.

It is easy to underestimate the influence of advertisers on the media in a 'free market', exerted as it is behind the scenes. To see the true depth of their impact on our world, a historical perspective is necessary. The papers that exist today are those that survived the marketisation of the media and the culling of the progressive press that took place in the nineteenth and early twentieth centuries due to the choices made by advertisers. Their legacy is impossible to measure with any precision, but it is likely that today's ideological landscape would look very different had they not taken the reins.[35]

Advertising generates a distinct bias in favour of corporate interests and arises naturally in a profit-driven market system. Globally, almost $570 billion was spent by advertisers in 2015.[36] Roughly $195 billion came from the US. In the UK, what are regarded as the most progressive broadsheet newspapers – The Guardian, The Observer and The Independent – have long secured 75 per cent of their revenue from advertising.[37] The loss of advertising revenue is a persistent threat, a point recognised by the BBC's Andrew Marr: 'the biggest question is whether advertising limits and reshapes the news agenda. It does, of course. It's hard to make the sums add up when you are kicking the people who write the cheques.'[38]

Where do they get their news?

In a market system, businesses must sell their products at a competitive price to survive. Media corporations are under pressure to keep production costs down and this impacts the process of 'collecting' enough news to fill the papers and airwaves each day. In a competitive market, journalists are pushed towards established and easily accessible news sources. The most obvious examples are government departments and large corporations, both of which have the multimillion-dollar budgets necessary to meet the demands of news organisations by providing a steady stream of speeches, reports, press releases, photo opportunities and press conferences. They go out of their way to make things easy for news organisations. 'In effect,' as analysts of the media Edward Herman and Noam Chomsky put it, 'the large bureaucracies of the powerful subsidise the mass media, and gain special access by their contribution to reducing the media's costs of acquiring the raw materials of, and producing, news.'[39]

As budgets have been slashed and competition has grown, dependence on a restricted set of news sources has steadily increased. Most of our news now comes from just two sources: press releases supplied by governments and corporations, and 'wire services', like Reuters and Associated Press. A study by media researchers at Cardiff University focusing on the most prestigious newspapers in the UK – *The Times, The Guardian, The Independent* and *The Daily Telegraph* – found that 60 per cent of the print stories consisted 'wholly or mainly of wire copy and/or PR material, and a further 20 per cent contained clear elements of wire copy and/or PR' to which some material had been added.[40] Only 12 per cent of the stories were generated by the reporters themselves, and only one in a hundred wire stories carried by these papers cited the source.

The decline of advertising revenue and the overall tightening of budgets meant that, in 2005, the average time available for journalists to research, check and write their stories in the UK's most prestigious papers had been reduced to a third of its 1985 level. Many other countries have followed the same trend. *Columbia Journalism Review* found that more than half the stories in one edition of the *Wall Street Journal* 'were based solely on press releases' reprinted 'almost verbatim or in paraphrase'.[41]

Two wire agencies, Associated Press (AP) and Reuters, provide the majority of the international news, pictures and video for the media. The selections made by these two agencies – the stories, angles, quotes and pictures – reach over 1 billion people. They define what is news for a large part of humanity.[42] The Press Association (PA) supplies much of the UK media with its daily facts, quotes and stories. Jonathan Grun, its former editor, characterised its role in the following terms: 'What we do is report what people say and accurately . . . Our role is attributable journalism . . . What is important is in quote marks.'[43] Whether or not the account that exists between these quote marks contains any truth at all is simply not their business. If a leader declares he is starting a war to 'spread democracy', it gets repeated millions of times around the world as 'news', and those who repeat it are called journalists when, in effect, they are merely acting as megaphones for powerful voices.

Nick Robinson, former political editor of ITV News, wrote of the run-up to the Iraq War: 'I and many of my colleagues were bombarded with complaints that we were acting as mouthpieces for Mr Blair . . . I always replied in the same way. It was my job to report what those in power were doing or thinking . . . That is all someone in my sort of job can do.'[44] This way of thinking about journalistic responsibility is fairly standard. On 22 December 2005, BBC defence correspondent Paul Wood reported that, 'The coalition came to Iraq in the first place to bring democracy and human rights.' When Helen Boaden, director of BBC News, was challenged to justify this statement, she responded: 'Paul Wood's analysis of the underlying motivation of the coalition is borne out by many speeches and remarks made by both Mr Bush and Mr Blair.'[45] Of course, this was true, but the problem with Boaden's response – and the wider attitude it represents – is that these are precisely the sources the media should be scrutinising. When world leaders claim to be taking their countries into war for freedom and democracy, the claim itself does not count as evidence. Noble rhetoric accompanies the launch of all wars. Sometimes politicians lie. Presenting the unsupported claims of the powerful as fact is not journalism, it's propaganda.

So much vital information – about the West's backing of Saddam in the 1980s, the errors and misrepresentation of intelligence on his non-existent weapons of mass destruction, not to mention one hundred years of foreign policy explicitly aimed at gaining control of Iraq's oil fields – was largely, if not completely, omitted at a time when it mattered most – when millions of lives were under threat in the lead-up to the 2003 invasion.

A serious investigative report might take months of research, eating into already limited resources, so why not simply repeat the 'news' other people give you? As investigative journalist Nick Davies points out, media organisations all over the world have suffered from 'cuts in staff coupled with increases in output, less time to find stories and less time to check them, the collapse of old supply lines, the rise of PR and wire agencies as an inherently inadequate substitute, less and less input being repackaged for more and more outlets'.[46] This favours those that, like the Pentagon with its $4.7 billion PR budget and large corporations with their own multimillion-dollar PR budgets, have the resources to provide 'news' for 'free'. Their privileged position as providers of content allows government and business to manage the media, setting the agenda to suit their purposes. That's bad news for democracy.

Who scares the media?

Media organisations may receive negative responses to some of their output in the form of letters, phone calls, petitions, lawsuits, speeches and other modes of complaint and punitive action.[47] The media are reluctant to upset those forces in society that have the power to hit back. But who has the resources to really make their anger felt? Whose responses are likely to have the most influence? Few forces have more power to make themselves heard than governments and large corporations.

The bias towards powerful sources has even been enshrined in law. The UK Defamation Act 1952, for example, has long protected journalists from being sued for libel if they can show their story is based on an official statement 'by or on behalf of any government, officer of state, local authority or chief officer of police'. Updates to the Act have expanded this list, but the bias remains. The domain of libel law is broad, concerning any story that can seriously harm the reputation of its subject. In practice, libel law primarily provides protection for the wealthy because it is extremely expensive to sue, and libel suits are not covered by legal aid. According to Davies, 'it is common practice for a newspaper lawyer, confronted with a potentially libellous story, to ask the reporter: "Does this chap have money?"'[48]

A critical or threatening response from a powerful source can intimidate even the largest media organisation. This was well illustrated when the UK government rounded on Andrew Gilligan and the BBC for claiming it had 'sexed up' the now infamous 'dodgy dossier' which claimed Iraq was able to deploy biological weapons within forty-five minutes. The government's crusade resulted in the resignation of the BBC's Chairman, Director-General, and Gilligan himself. The formal inquiry, conducted by Lord Hutton, concluded in 2004 that Gilligan's story was 'unfounded'. Even if this were true (which remains contestable), the stories put out by journalists that followed the government line on Iraqi weapons of mass destruction also turned out to be 'unfounded'. But the failure of those journalists met neither rebuke nor penalty. Following the official line, even when unsupported by evidence, is a form of self-protection.

Any serious criticism of those in power is a risky affair, demanding courage, time and resources.[49] One way to insure against such criticism is to give roughly equal time to opposing views, thereby leaving it up to the audience to make their own judgement. Reasonable as this sounds, it is a dangerously flawed approach. For decades there has been overwhelming scientific evidence warning us that carbon emissions are heating up the planet. Yet, in the name of 'balance', journalists have continually given over precious airtime and column inches to climate change denial. A study by Max and Jules Boykoff found that, between 1988 and 2002, over 50 per cent of media stories in the US focusing on climate change gave equal time to discredited denials.[50] A study by the US Union of Concerned Scientists found that when it comes to the topic of climate change, Fox News is scientifically inaccurate 93 per cent of the time and the *Wall Street Journal*'s opinion pages are misleading 81 per cent of the time.[51]

The same form of misleading neutrality occurred when scientists tried to warn that smoking was linked to lung cancer. Journalists juxtaposed this scientific consensus with contrary claims from the tobacco industry. For many years, tobacco companies were, without exception, the top advertisers in the US, ruthlessly using their clout to penalise publications that produced anything resembling bad publicity, namely the truth.

Of particular concern is the inconsistency with which the principle of balance is applied. When a voice is critical of power, it is 'balanced' by a contrary viewpoint, but when power speaks, opinion is often presented as fact without opposition. No counter-balancing opinion was given when politicians claimed they 'came to Iraq in the first place to bring democracy and human rights'. On the rare occasions when the opposing claim – that the UK went to Iraq to appease the US, consolidate NATO's influence in the Middle East and maintain access to oil in the region – was expressed, a balancing voice from an official source was always to be heard. BBC guidelines declare a 'commitment to impartiality', requiring that journalists 'strive to reflect a wide range of opinion and explore a range and conflict of views so that no significant strand of thought is knowingly unreflected or under represented'. Yet as Baghdad fell to the invasion, condemned as illegal by many scholars, Andrew Marr, who once stated 'When I joined the BBC, my Organs of Opinion were formally removed', offered the following analysis live on the BBC: '[Blair] said that they would be able to take Baghdad without a bloodbath, and that in the end the Iraqis would be celebrating. And on both of those points he has been proved conclusively right. And it would be entirely ungracious, even for his critics, not to acknowledge that tonight he stands as a larger man and a stronger prime minister as a result.'[52]

A report by Cardiff University in 2003 found that the BBC 'displayed the most "pro-war" agenda of any broadcaster' in the UK during the Iraq invasion. Over the first three weeks of the conflict, the BBC had the highest proportion of coalition military and government sources, was less likely than Sky, ITV or *Channel 4 News* to use independent sources, placed least emphasis on Iraqi casualties, and was least likely to report on Iraqi opposition to the invasion.[53] Leading up to the Iraq invasion, the Stop the War Coalition was the most important organiser of anti-war rallies and marches and played a leading role in organising Britain's largest ever march. Yet, prior to the invasion, the press officer for Stop the War had 'been invited to appear on every TV channel except the BBC'.[54]

Donahue was a show on MSNBC hosted by Phil Donahue from 2002 to 2003. Despite having the highest ratings of any show on that network, it was cancelled on 25 February 2003 in the lead-up to the Iraq War. A leaked NBC memo described how the show presented a 'difficult public face for NBC in a time of war . . . He [Donahue] seems to delight in presenting guests who are anti-war, anti-Bush and sceptical of the administration's motives.'[55] In conversation with Bill Moyers, Donahue told how he could 'have the supporters of the President [appear on the show] alone. And they would say why this war is important. You couldn't have a dissenter alone . . . Our producers were instructed to feature two conservatives for every liberal.'[56]

Fear of retribution creates a culture of conformity. If lone journalists stray beyond the expectations of conformity, there can be significant repercussions. In May 2003, Pulitzer prize-winning journalist Chris Hedges, a war correspondent at *The New York Times*, delivered a commencement address at Rockford College in which he spoke out against the invasion: '[W]e are embarking on an occupation that, if history is any guide, will be as damaging to our souls as it will be to our prestige and power, and security.'[57] The newspaper responded with a written reprimand for 'public remarks that could undermine public trust in the paper's impartiality'.[58] Hedges had strayed from the safe perspective and was being punished for not being 'impartial'. Believing that he would be fired for expressing his beliefs, and not wanting to be censored, he decided to leave the paper soon after.

Every journalist knows that access to influential sources can make a career. American journalist Amy Goodman calls this the 'access of evil', explaining that the most successful reporters do well because 'they're trading truth for access, they're not asking the tough questions so they can get access to the most powerful people, get that quote, and the way they get it is by lobbing soft-ball questions'.[59] Journalists who buck this trend face being cut off from powerful sources. Goodman recounts her own experience when President Clinton called up her talk show on election day in 2000, hoping to generate support for the Democratic candidate, Al Gore. Her questions included: 'What do you say to people who feel that the two parties are bought by corporations, and [. . .] that their vote doesn't make a difference?', and 'The past two UN heads of the programme in Iraq have quit, calling the US/UN policy "genocidal". What is your response to that?'[60] Towards the end of the interview, Clinton chastised Goodman for asking questions in a 'hostile, combative, and even disrespectful tone'. After the interview, she received a furious call from the White House press office claiming she had broken 'the ground rules for the interview'.[61]

Dan Rather, one of the leading journalists in the US, told Larry King in 2003: 'Look, I'm an American. I never tried to kid anybody that I'm some internationalist or something. And when my country is at war, I want my country to win, whatever the definition of win may be. Now, I can't and don't argue that that is coverage without prejudice. About that I am prejudiced.'[62] Of course, this form of prejudice comes without professional penalty. It is safe because it benefits those already in power.

On the rare occasions that the press pose a serious threat to centres of power, the response is explicit attempts at censorship – and not just by government. In 2003, the closing of ranks in preparation for war was widespread in the media on both sides of the Atlantic. In May 2008, Katie Couric, CBS news anchor, told of how, as a host of NBC's *Today* programme, she had felt pressure from 'the corporations who own where we work and from the government itself to really squash any kind of dissent or any kind of questioning of [the Iraq War]'.[63] In 2003, Jessica Yellin, then a reporter for MSNBC, said that journalists had been 'under enormous pressure from corporate executives, frankly, to make sure that this was a war presented in a way that was consistent with the patriotic fervour in the nation'.[64]

The most influential justification for the 2003 invasion was that Iraq possessed weapons of mass destruction. One British paper, *The Observer*, had the opportunity to publish powerful proof that this claim was false. In autumn 2002, roughly six months before the start of the Iraq War, Ed Vulliamy, one of the paper's leading reporters, talked with Mel Goodman, a former CIA analyst who retained high security clearance and regular contact with his former colleagues. Goodman told Vulliamy that, contrary to everything being said by the British and American governments, the CIA were reporting that Saddam Hussein had no weapons of mass destruction.[65] Goodman was willing to go on record as a named source. At a time when Britain and the US were doing everything they could to persuade the public to go to war on these grounds, this was an incredible scoop of international importance, yet *The Observer* refused to publish the story. Vulliamy submitted seven versions of his article – each one was rejected by his editors. The paper's position, as laid down by its editor Roger Alton, was that: 'We've got to stand shoulder to shoulder with the Americans.'[66]

When the media fails to censor itself, the state is prepared to step in. Recent examples include the treatment of whistleblowers Edward Snowden and Chelsea (formerly Bradley) Manning. Snowden, with Glenn Greenwald and *The Guardian*, released a stash of secret files showing the vast scale and scope of the NSA's global surveillance programme. Soon after, *The Guardian's* editor, Alan Rusbridger, was contacted by senior officials from the British government 'claiming to represent the views of the prime minister' and demanding the destruction of all the files they were working from. Undeterred, his paper continued to publish the documents, redacted to protect the lives of servicemen as well as national security secrets. A month later, reports Rusbridger, 'I received a phone call from the centre of government telling me: "You've had your fun. Now we want the stuff back." There followed further meetings with shadowy Whitehall figures. The demand was the same: hand the Snowden material back or destroy it.'[67]

The Guardian's refusal to back down culminated in a bizarre scene on Saturday, 20 July 2013, in the basement of its London offices. An editor and a computer expert from the paper were forced by technicians from Government Communications Headquarters (GCHQ) to destroy the hard drives on which the encrypted NSA files had been stored. (The files had, of course, been copied and stored elsewhere, making the act little more than one of intimidation.) Even after this coercive stunt, pressure to silence the story continued. In October 2013, Prime Minister David Cameron threatened to stop newspapers publishing Snowden's revelations, declaring that 'If they don't demonstrate some social responsibility it will be very difficult for government to stand back and not to act.'[68] Rusbridger would later be hauled up in front of the Home Affairs Select Committee and asked by the committee's chair, Keith Vaz MP: 'Do you love this country?'[69]

A case study: cuts

On 17 October 2010, British Chancellor of the Exchequer George Osborne told the nation it had been 'on the brink of bankruptcy'. Four days later he revealed his rescue plan: £80 billion of government cuts. No country had ever volunteered such extreme austerity. The claim that there was an urgent need for deep cuts was part of a growing political consensus held together by a simple story: Britain was in an 'economic mess' thanks to the previous Labour government's overspending and the economic priority had to be elimination of the deficit and reduction of the debt. Government spending on everything from unemployment benefit to disability living allowance would need to be slashed. It was going to be painful, but collective sacrifices had to be made.

Though the story had the virtue of simplicity, it was wrong on every count. According to Cameron and Osborne, bringing the debt – the total amount of money owed as a result of government borrowing – under control was 'the most urgent task' facing the Coalition. However, most economists disagreed and some had published a letter in *The Guardian* to provide some perspective: 'History shows, first, that British public debt is not high by the standards of the last 200 years. It is rather low in comparison to the second half of the 18th century, the first three-quarters of the 19th century, and most of the inter-war and post-

Second World War era in the 20th century. It is also low in the context of the developed world.'[70] In 2010, the national debt was 57 per cent of GDP, lower than Italy, France, Germany, Japan, and the US. At the end of the Second World War – when the British government created the National Health Service, the welfare state, national pensions, a motorway network and council housing – government debt stood at 238 per cent of GDP.[71] In other words, when Osborne became Chancellor, public debt was not a pressing issue.

Then there's the deficit – the difference between the amount a government spends and the amount it raises through taxes. The Coalition's austerity narrative blamed the rising deficit on Labour's spending, but much of the rise could be explained by the global recession itself, not the unremarkable spending of the previous government. An economic downturn automatically increases dependency on social benefits and reduces tax revenue because people lose their jobs, wages drop and less tax is collected, all of which naturally increases the budget deficit. The recession was a global phenomenon, far beyond the control of the Labour government. Despite this fact, a banking crisis that had its origins in the irresponsible and illegal behaviour of the private sector was repackaged as a crisis of government finance.

When the Coalition came to power, neither history nor mainstream economic theory provided any support for the claim that cuts were the only way to reduce the deficit. Cutting spending in a recession has been tried many times and – without exception – failed.[72] For instance, in the aftermath of the First World War, the US, Britain, Sweden, Germany, Japan and France all adopted austerity policies with devastating impacts on their economies. President Herbert Hoover's austerity response to the 1929 economic crash was followed by the Great Depression.

The historical failure of austerity as a response to economic crises resulted in a widespread consensus among academic economists that, since recessions are caused by a reduction in demand (and when there is no room to offset cuts by reducing interest rates), cutting spending only makes the situation worse. The textbook response to economic downturns, as any student of the subject knows, is to increase spending. By spending more in the short term, a government can reduce public debt faster because smart spending creates jobs, increases tax revenues and releases more people more quickly from dependency on the state.

However, as governments began to embrace austerity, a handful of economists produced research telling them exactly what they wanted to hear.[73] It was seized on by politicians and journalists alike to justify the unorthodox remedy. This research was ultimately discredited: questionable assumptions, dubious procedures and outright mistakes were exposed.[74] As time passed, what little academic support for austerity existed, fell away. At the start of the Coalition's time in power, twenty prominent economists sent a letter to the *Sunday Times* urging Osborne to eliminate the budget deficit over the next five years. The letter was gratefully acknowledged by the Chancellor. Two years later, as the UK suffered a double-dip recession and Osborne was forced to borrow billions more than he had planned, the same group were asked if they stood by their initial advice. Only one out of the original twenty said they did: many were now in favour of ending austerity and increasing public spending.[75]

By 2013, the economies of countries that had imposed severe spending cuts were experiencing slower growth than those that had increased their spending.[76] The IMF, though it had recommended austerity in 2010, in effect conceded it had made a mistake by underestimating the damage of cutting government spending in a weak economy. Its own figures showed that austerity consistently undermined growth. Economist Paul Krugman observed that 'since the global turn to austerity in 2010, every country that introduced significant austerity has seen its economy suffer, with the depth of the suffering closely related to the harshness of the austerity'.[77] According to Simon Wren-Lewis, Professor of Economic Policy at Oxford University, the cost of austerity in delaying the UK economic recovery is about £100 billion. He points out that 'If any other government department had wasted that amount, there would be a huge outcry from the media . . . [which] continues to misrepresent economic ideas even though it has access to academic expertise.' A government campaigning for re-election with that kind of performance, he continues, 'should be trying to avoid talking about its economic record at all costs'. In fact, the opposite was the case.[78] In the lead-up to the 2015 election, David Cameron boasted that austerity had rescued the economy and created jobs. This was a deception that only 15 per cent of economists agreed with.[79] Simon Wren-Lewis explains why:

> To see how absurd this claim is, imagine that a government on a whim decided to close down half the economy for a year. That would be a crazy thing to do, and with only half as much produced, everyone would be much poorer. However, a year later when that half of the economy started up again, economic growth would be around 100 per cent. The government could claim that this miraculous recovery vindicated its decision to close half the economy down the previous year. That would be absurd, but it is a pretty good analogy to claiming that the recovery of 2013 vindicated the austerity of 2010.[80]

In fact, the recovery only began once austerity policies were relaxed two years into the Coalition's term. The original plan had been to eliminate the deficit in the first five years, but by 2012 – with no hint of a recovery, lower tax revenues than expected, and waning academic support – Osborne quietly backtracked. From then on, there was much less deficit reduction. The predictable result was that in 2013 the economy began to improve, three years later than it should have done. Of course, the recovery did not benefit everyone equally: real wages had fallen by 10 per cent, while top earners increased their share of the wealth.[81] The majority of new jobs created were low-paid, lacked security and left people without enough paid hours. In 2015, inflation-adjusted GDP per capita was still lower than it had been before the crisis.[82] On top of this, overall government debt had soared. In his first budget, Osborne claimed to have 'set the course for a balanced budget and falling national debt by the end of this Parliament'.[83] Yet his economic plan had increased the national debt by 80 per cent in just five years. In fact, Osborne borrowed more in five years than his predecessor did during a whole decade.[84]

Even if we accept that reducing the government deficit was an immediate priority, there was more than one way to do it. Osborne opted for a strategy that harmed the most vulnerable, creating a cost-of-living crisis in the world's seventh richest country. He forced a million people to rely on food banks, stripped disabled people of essential financial support and cut benefits to the low-paid and unemployed. Many people have died because of these policies. One study looked at the impact of the newly introduced Work Capability Assessment, designed to reassess the eligibility of disabled people for out-of-work benefits with the stated aim of getting more people 'back to work' so as to reduce the welfare bill. This programme, which declared many sick and severely disabled people 'fit for work', was associated with a significant increase in suicides, mental health problems and the prescription of anti-depressant drugs.[85] In 2011, Mervyn King, then Governor of the Bank of England, summed the situation up when he said 'The price of this financial crisis is being borne by people who absolutely did not cause it' and 'I'm surprised that the degree of public anger has not been greater than it has.'[86]

The deficit could have been reduced by placing the burden on the wealthiest instead of the poorest. Rather than cuts to public services, the British government could have raised taxes on the wealthiest individuals and corporations; introduced a financial transaction tax (the so-called Robin Hood tax); eliminated tax loopholes that benefit the top earners; and ensured that corporations paid the full value for using national resources. 'These revenue raisers would not only make for a more efficient economy' writes Joseph Stiglitz, they would 'substantially reduce the deficit [and] also inequality.'[87] But the rich did not bear the burden of reducing the deficit. Instead, the Conservatives cut the top rate of tax – a policy so unpopular that even the majority of their own voters were against it.[88]

If austerity is bad economics, why did business leaders and politicians support it? The simple answer is ideology. It is an article of faith for neoliberals that the state must shrink, welfare and social security must be cut, and everything from healthcare to prisons must be privatised. The focus on deficit reduction provided a convenient cover to lay waste to the welfare state. Speaking candidly at the Lord Mayor's Banquet in 2013, David Cameron revealed that spending cuts were ultimately about 'building a leaner, more efficient state . . . Not just now, but permanently.'[89] In addition, the austerity narrative also heightens the political bargaining power of business. As Krugman puts it, 'Business leaders love the idea that the health of the economy depends on confidence, which in turn – or so they argue – requires making them happy.'[90]

As soon as the financial crisis hit, the case against austerity was overwhelming. Given that the most vulnerable people in society were set to be punished for the failings of the financial sector, a free media in a functioning democracy would have torn the government's austerity fairytale to shreds. This didn't happen. In response to the Coalition's plan, the *Financial Times* claimed 'There are alternatives to UK austerity, just not good ones.'[91] Instead of challenging the need for cuts in the lead-up to the government's Comprehensive Spending Review in October 2010, the BBC, Sky and ITV asked their viewers and listeners where they should fall. *The Daily Telegraph* celebrated George Osborne's budget, calling it 'fair and progressive', one of 'authority and intelligence'.[92]

In interviews with government ministers, the assumption that cuts were needed went unchallenged. The BBC's John Humphrys prefaced a question to the Liberal Democrat leader Nick Clegg with 'We know you need to make cuts, but . . .'.[93] On BBC TV, Andrew Marr conceded to George Osborne 'You clearly need to make the savings, the cuts . . .'.[94] On *Channel 4 News*, Jon Snow grilled Labour leader Ed Miliband after he left out a section in his speech on the deficit, asking 'How could you not mention paying off this appalling deficit? Surely it is the most important issue of all. It is the essence of our economic crisis.'[95]

On 1 April 2015, the Centre for Macroeconomics at University College London had just published a survey showing that the vast majority of economists disagreed that austerity had boosted growth or employment. On the same day *The Daily Telegraph* emblazoned its front page with a letter from a hundred businessmen expressing their enthusiastic support for austerity. Although a survey conducted by the *Financial Times* found that less than 20 per cent of economists believed that the beginnings of a recovery in 2013 were due to austerity measures, it still declared in September that: 'Osborne wins the battle on austerity' – a claim repeated across the media.[96]

Research by Julien Mercille at University College Dublin examined the coverage of austerity after the 2010 election, looking at four leading national papers – *The Daily Telegraph*, *The Times*, the *Financial Times* and *The Guardian*. Mercille found a clear pro-austerity bias (*The Guardian* being the exception).[97] Of 347 articles, only 21 per cent showed any opposition to austerity. When *The Guardian* is removed from the sample, the figure drops to 13 per cent. Another way of demonstrating press bias is to examine which 'experts' were invited to comment on the cuts. Almost all of them were bankers, economists and politicians. Only 1 per cent came from a trade union.

The preference for establishment sources is the norm. Cardiff University lecturer Mike Berry conducted a study into the impartiality of the BBC and found that 'across all programming, business represent-atives received substantially more airtime on BBC network news . . . than they did on either ITV . . . or *Channel 4 News*'.[98] On the BBC's *News at Six*, the year the crisis hit, business representatives outnumbered labour union representatives by more than five to one. This ratio rose to nineteen to one in 2012. Another study focused on BBC Radio 4's *Today* programme for the six weeks following the collapse of Lehman Brothers in 2008. The study found that the expert sources invited on were 'almost completely dominated by stockbrokers, investment bankers, hedge-fund managers and other City voices'. Thus the sector that had created the crisis 'were given almost monopoly status to frame the debate' to the complete exclusion of voices questioning the legitimacy, scale and value of the financial sector.[99]

Of course, there were notable exceptions across the media. A number of high-profile journalists and economists did their best to voice oppo-sition to Osborne's cuts. But a look at public opinion over the period shows how influential the austerity narrative had become. In June 2009, a poll by *The Daily Telegraph* found that three-quarters of voters believed the cuts were necessary.[100] Initially, there was some opposition to the way cuts were being made but, according to the YouGov polls tracking public opinion, this opposition steadily declined over the next few years. As this decline occurred, the proportion of people who believed the cuts were 'too slow', doubled.[101] The most popular cuts were often those that targeted the most vulnerable: the disabled, the unemployed and those receiving housing benefit. By 2014, an ICM poll showed that the public, by a wide margin, trusted the Conservatives more – the party of austerity – 'to manage the economy properly'.[102]

Throughout this period, immigrants, criminals and welfare claimants were offered up by much of the press as scapegoats upon whom the public were invited to heap blame for the failing economy. An Ipsos MORI 2013 survey for the Royal Statistical Society and King's College London compared public opinion on issues such as benefit fraud, crime and immigration.[103] The public believed 24 per cent of welfare was claimed fraudulently – the actual figure is 0.7 per cent. Almost a third of respondents believed that more welfare goes to the unemployed than to pensioners. The reality is that fifteen times more is spent on pensions. The majority believed that crime was rising – in fact, the figures show it had dropped significantly. A majority thought that 31 per cent of the population were recent immigrants; the actual figure is 13 per cent. In each case, public perceptions mirrored the carefully constructed media narrative that deflected criticism from the Coalition's failing experiment with austerity.

Throughout the Coalition's time in government, the Labour Party did not oppose austerity. Under the leadership of Ed Miliband, Labour was committed to 'austerity-lite': cuts were needed, they claimed, but not quite as many or quite as fast as the Tories were planning. After losing the 2015 election, Miliband resigned, and the only anti-austerity candidate on the ballot, outsider Jeremy Corbyn, surged to victory on a wave of popular support, earning the largest mandate ever won by a party leader. The media onslaught that followed was remarkable. As subsequent research has shown, the British press 'systematically undermined' Corbyn 'with a barrage of overwhelmingly negative coverage'. Analysing nearly 500 pieces across eight national newspapers, the Media Reform Coalition found that, in Corbyn's first week as leader, for every positive article there were more than four times as many that were openly hostile or expressed animosity or ridicule.[104] News articles, which are meant to be more balanced, demonstrated more bias than comment pieces or editorials, with 61 per cent judged to be negative.

The 'impartial' BBC mirrored this pattern. When asked if he was 'shocked' at the way the BBC 'rubbish Jeremy Corbyn', former BBC political editor Nick Robinson – one-time president of the Oxford University Conservative Association – replied 'Yes' and said that he had written to colleagues expressing his grievances.[105]

The experience of austerity in the UK has been relatively mild compared to nations like Portugal, Spain and, worst of all, Greece. They have suffered particularly badly under the austerity fever that swept the eurozone after the financial crash. But not every country took the path of swingeing spending cuts. As the austerity narrative amplified across Europe, Iceland showed that another way was possible. It is an interesting story that has been largely ignored by the press. An effective media would have drawn on this test case to challenge the prevailing narrative.

According to *The Economist*, 'Iceland's banking collapse is the biggest, relative to the size of an economy, that any country has ever suffered.'[106] Its financial industry imploded, the stock market fell by 90 per cent, and investments worth many times the output of the nation were wiped out in a single week. Desperate for money, the government turned to the IMF for $2.1 billion in loans. The loans came with conditions: the government would have to slash public spending and use half its income to repay investors who had lost money on their private investments. In effect, Iceland's taxpayers were being asked to foot the bill for the bad investment decisions of its banking elite.

On the back of riots and protests, the Icelandic president granted the people a referendum. Nine out of ten voters said 'no' to paying off bankers' debts and instead demanded increased investment in their fragile economy. Taking this on board, the government rejected the IMF conditions, allowed its banks to default, imposed urgent capital controls and raised spending on public welfare. Universal education and healthcare were protected, social security was strengthened for those most in need, and many people had their mortgage debts written off. As for the bankers, the worst offenders were prosecuted and sent to prison. In other words, Iceland ignored every principle in the financial industry's rulebook.

The stock markets reacted negatively to the vote, and Iceland was widely condemned. Yet, by 2012, this tiny country was outperforming the US and many European nations with an economy growing by 3 per cent a year and with unemployment levels falling below 5 per cent. Iceland went further and adopted a new crowd-sourced national constitution to safeguard its future. By 2015, even the IMF had to admit that Iceland had achieved economic recovery 'without compromising its welfare model'.[107] In fact, it became the first crisis-struck European nation to top its pre-crisis peak of economic output and is close to repaying many of the debts it owed to other nations. In response to the question, 'What is the reason for Iceland's recovery?', President Ólafur Ragnar Grímsson famously answered: 'We were wise enough not to follow the traditional prevailing orthodoxies of the Western financial world in the last 30 years. We introduced currency controls, we let the banks fail, we provided support for the poor, and we didn't introduce austerity measures like you're seeing in Europe.'[108]

Manufacturing compliance

The forces that shape media output combine to create a structural bias which favours the selection of information and perspectives that are supportive of elite interests, state and corporate. This does not rely on any kind of internal conspiracy. The forces that shape media output arise organically as a result of deregulated market competition.

Edward S. Herman and Noam Chomsky made the argument in the 1980s in their book, *Manufacturing Consent*. They identified a number of filters held in place by the market through which 'reality' must pass before it reaches the public. These filters include ownership, advertising, elite news sources and flak. They acknowledge that these filters do not function perfectly, so dissident views will find their way, periodically, into the mainstream. Many good journalists exist, and it is by no means true that all news organisations hold the same views or are equally subservient to power. But the point is that wider systemic forces tilt the playing field in favour of elite interests.

Herman and Chomsky argue that tolerance of limited dissent within the mainstream plays an important propaganda role: it helps to maintain the illusion of a free media, making the pseudo-environment it generates more credible. Instead of total conformity, they predict that furious debate will rage regularly in the mainstream but only take place within narrow parameters set by elite opinion. This gives the appearance of an obstinate and critical media while conveniently sidelining dissident opinion and issues of serious importance. In spite of heated internal debate on many issues, the press share a common framework of assumptions and pressures. It is this framework that imposes ideological boundaries, excluding certain sources, ideas and perspectives.

This analysis accounts for both the systematic bias in the media and the fact that many journalists believe they are free to perform their duties with integrity and honesty. Like any business, the hierarchical structure of media firms gives owners the power to hire and promote employees at their discretion. If owners select editors and journalists with similar backgrounds to themselves who reflect their political views – which is to be expected – journalists are unlikely to feel that their independence is compromised by the interference of proprietors. This point was concisely illustrated in a classic exchange between Chomsky and Andrew Marr in a rare programme on the BBC that explored the workings of the media:

> MARR: What I don't get is that all of this suggests . . . people like
> me are self-censoring.
> CHOMSKY: I don't say you're self-censoring. I'm sure you believe
> everything you're saying. But what I'm saying is, if you believed
> something different you wouldn't be sitting where you're sitting.[109]

Commercial criteria for decision-making is not politically neutral. What is commonly downplayed as commercial bias is, in fact, political bias. The market is a political construct that gives greater weight to the wishes of those with greater wealth. Nowhere is this truer than in the media. The impact of this bias on society is substantial.

As psychologist Daniel Kahneman reports, numerous experiments show that a 'reliable way to make people believe in falsehoods is frequent repetition, because familiarity is not easily distinguished from truth. Authoritarian institutions and marketers have always known this fact.'[110]

An intriguing experiment led by the psychologist Robert Zajonc demonstrates the point.[111] Over a period of weeks, an 'ad-like box' appeared on the front page of student newspapers at two different universities: the University of Michigan and Michigan State University. The box contained 'one of the following Turkish (or Turkish-sounding) words: *kadirga, saricik, biwonjni, nansoma*, and *iktitaf*'. Some words were shown only once while others appeared up to twenty-five separate times. The words that were presented most often in one of the university papers were the least frequent in the other. After the ads stopped running, a questionnaire was sent out asking students whether they thought each word meant something 'good' or something 'bad'. The results were clear: words that had appeared more often were rated more favourably, even though most students would have made no sense of any of them. 'The finding', writes Kahneman, 'has been confirmed in many experiments, using Chinese ideographs, faces, and randomly shaped polygons.'[112] This tendency to respond favourably to what is familiar has been routinely exploited in the design of messages and symbols that crowd our perceptual environment. It matters, for instance, that according to a study published at the end of 2015, billionaire Donald Trump received twenty-three times as much network coverage as self-described socialist Bernie Sanders, even though they were receiving similar levels of public support in their respective leadership campaigns.[113]

To understand the influence of the media, it is necessary to bear in mind that we are continuously forming new thoughts about the world. Situations change and circumstances shift, so, as events unfold, we depend heavily on the media to update our mental maps. In particular, we depend on journalists to do what we lack the time, opportunity and expertise to do: to discover truth and expose lies. On matters of economics, politics, war and science, we depend on the work of media professionals to tell us what's going on. To most people, the austerity narrative sounded plausible enough, so they accepted it, even though it was against their interests to do so. In 2003, almost half the American public believed that Saddam Hussein's regime was 'directly involved in planning, financing, or carrying out the terrorist attacks of September 11th, 2001' – even though journalists and politicians were well aware that he had no involvement in the terrorist attacks of 9/11.[114] Our vulnerability to repetition may explain why 48 per cent of US citizens thought there were links between al-Qaeda and Iraq, 22 per cent believed that weapons of mass destruction had been discovered in Iraq, and 25 per cent believed that world public opinion supported the US invasion of Iraq.[115] Sixty per cent of respondents had at least one of these misperceptions. Viewers of Murdoch's Fox News were the most misinformed, with 80 per cent subscribing to one of these erroneous statements.

The future of the media is bound up with the development of the internet. In many ways, the web has already empowered the marginalised, revolutionised journalism and advanced freedom of speech. But it has proven to be a double-edged sword, for it has become the most powerful form of surveillance the world has ever seen – a means of tracking behaviour and eroding privacy without precedent. It also enables people to easily partake in virtual communities and access sources of information that mirror their prejudices, whatever they happen to be. In other words, the World Wide Web can preserve ignorance as much as promote knowledge. In the war of ideas and the conflict between market and democratic logic, the internet is itself a key battlefield. Few examples illustrate these contradictions as well as the story of WikiLeaks. This non-profit, online organisation has released millions of classified documents from anonymous sources into the public domain. A number of these revelatory documents hit the front pages of leading papers around the world. From censorship and surveillance to the concealment of torture and civilian deaths in Iraq and Afghanistan, to details about secretive trade deals, the leaks have revealed corruption and illegality by governments, corporations and the military. This gave rise to a powerful backlash against WikiLeaks which exposed the tight control states and corporations are able to exert online.

After its 2010 release of government cables, WikiLeaks was attacked on numerous fronts. In support of state power, the giants of the online world quickly closed ranks. Amazon prevented WikiLeaks from using its servers, so that, without a viable alternative, the site temporarily collapsed. PayPal, MasterCard, Visa and Bank of America cut ties with the site, blocking donations to the organisation; Apple banned a WikiLeaks app from its stores; and a number of governments called for the banning of the site. This was all despite the fact that no charges had been filed against WikiLeaks and no one associated with the site had been convicted of any crime. Since then, WikiLeaks staff have been detained, searched, interrogated and denied access to legal counsel at border crossings. WikiLeaks itself has been labelled a terrorist organisation and some, including politicians and journalists, have called for the extra-judicial assassination of its founder, Julian Assange.[116]

The overt censorship of WikiLeaks, and the ongoing criminalisation of whistleblowers, is symptomatic of the wider struggle for transparency, free speech and freedom of information. The story of WikiLeaks highlights the timidity of many mainstream media outlets in the face of state and corporate pressure, but it also shows the need for well-funded journalism. The rise of 'citizen journalism' has been a democratising force, turning anyone with a smartphone into a potential on-the-ground journalist with a global audience. It has played a vital role in the movements of the last decade, from Occupy to the Arab Spring to Black Lives Matter, showing events through the eyes of people whose perspectives would otherwise be ignored. When power is abused and rights are violated, it is now possible that 'the whole world will be watching'. Production, research and distribution costs have also been slashed, and it is easier now to connect with other journalists around the globe than ever before. But a problem remains: who has the resources to fund serious investigative journalism? Citizen journalism is no substitute. It takes time, money and often legal support to engage in the sorts of investigations that can truly expose the facts that the powerful do their best to conceal. WikiLeaks has shown that releasing information into the public domain is not enough. It took collaboration with some of the world's leading news outlets, with their paid, professional journalists, to comb through the millions of released documents, analyse them, redact them and write the stories that would capture the public's imagination.

Online media may be largely free and easy to access, but the decline of print journalism has serious consequences. Almost all original reporting is done by newspapers. According to Alex S. Jones, formerly of Harvard's John F. Kennedy School of Government, 85 per cent (other sources have put it as high as 95 per cent) of all professionally reported news originates in daily newspapers.[117] Dr Chris Paterson of Leeds University found that by 2006 the most popular online news websites – all controlled by leading press and broadcasting organisations – reproduced over 50 per cent of their published content from the top three wire agencies: AP, Reuters and Agences France-Presse.[118] Dr Paterson concludes: 'A few original producers of content provide the lion's share of the international news for those aggregators despite the audacious pretence of source diversity which each promotes.'

The advertising upon which traditional media has depended for over a century is moving online too. In the US, advertising revenue for daily newspapers dropped from $20 billion in 2000 to $5 billion in 2011. As rapidly as print media revenues are imploding, a new media empire is being built on the fibre-optic skeleton of the World Wide Web. In 2014, the world's top twenty online news sites mirrored the dominant brands so familiar in the offline world: Fox News, *The New York Times*, the *Daily Mail*, CNN, *The Wall Street Journal*, *The Guardian*, BBC News, *Forbes* and *Time*, alongside online giants Yahoo! and Google. There are notable exceptions acting as beacons of light in the online world. Viewer-funded news organisations have emerged – for instance the Real News Network and Democracy Now! – that provide valuable independent journalism. Yet in their book *Power Without Responsibility*, about the evolution of the media, Jean Seaton and James Curran concluded that 'the imbalance of power and resources in the offline world structure the online world'.[119]

Technology opens up new possibilities, but the way it is used always depends on the balance of power in society. The same battles between elites and the radical press that were taking place in nineteenth-century Britain continue today. They are battles to control the flow of facts and ideas through society, battles to shape beliefs, values and behaviour. Legislation to 'police the internet' and commercialise its content – the Stop Online Piracy Act (SOPA), the Cyber Intelligence Sharing and Protection Act (CISPA) and the Anti-Counterfeiting Trade Agreement (ACTA) – have so far been vigorously resisted, but the intent of governments to restrict internet freedom is clear, and corporate attempts to privatise every aspect of this cyber reality are unrelenting. Just as in the offline world, whether the web is used to inform, manipulate, control or liberate ultimately depends on how vigorously people fight the encroachments of state and corporate power.

★

The countless events that occur around the globe remain shrouded in darkness, beyond our awareness and understanding. In order to shine a spotlight on this hidden landscape, we depend on the information that reaches us through the media. This information plays a crucial role in the formation of our beliefs and biases, shaping our perceptions of success, beauty, government, war, activism, police, freedom and democracy. It frames debates, reinforcing some beliefs while challenging others, and, perhaps most importantly, it shapes our perception of each other.

The press writes the first draft of history. It is not the only source for historians but it is one of the most important. The picture of history we inherit, painted to a considerable degree by the original accounts laid down in newspapers of the time, informs our generational memory. If an event is ignored by the press of its time – the corruption of an official, the torture of a prisoner, the starvation of a family – it may well lie beyond the reach of humanity's consciousness thereafter.

In this age of telecommunications, the media direct the thoughts of billions of people. They have vast potential to emancipate, and yet in the hands of the market have become tools of oppression and misinformation wielded by the powerful. They do not always succeed in manufacturing consent, but simply creating the appearance of support for this war or that policy can be enough to give powerful institutions a licence to act. The appearance of widespread support gives the impression that no viable alternatives exist, inducing hopelessness and apathy. Where consent is not possible, compliance will do.

At the heart of the debate on media is the issue of free speech. Although we all have the same right to speak, we do not all have the same freedom to be heard. That freedom is monopolised by the few who own, fund and subsidise our media. It is a freedom that comes with a hefty price tag.

•

Our choices shape the future. What we choose emerges from who we are and the options we face. To control a person's identity or context, therefore, is to influence the decisions they make. This control constrains freedom and concentrates power.

For a long time, power has been highly concentrated in the hands of privileged elites who have controlled society's surplus wealth. The struggle for democracy was meant to change this. Equality of power in the voting booth was meant to overcome inequalities of power in the market. It looked for a time as if this was happening, but the introduction of elections was just the start of a long battle between two principles: one person one vote and one dollar one vote.

Multinational corporations, the giants of the market, joined forces to fund think tanks, universities, political campaigns, lobbyists, public relations, lawsuits, media outlets and journalism. Democratic options narrowed and political beliefs were moulded. The freedom of the market compromised the freedom of elections and media. Although many valuable gains were won through the ballot, democracies were weakened by these sustained attacks. Slowly but surely, corporate freedoms expanded and inequalities widened. With the rise of neoliberalism, the logic of the market overwhelmed the logic of democracy. Instead of free elections, markets and media, what emerged were corporate elections, markets and media.

In Part One, we looked at inherent limits; in Part Two we looked at political limits. In the final part, we move from constraints on freedom to creating freedom.

•

PART THREE

THE FIGHT FOR
OUR FREEDOM

8

Creativity

Two people arrive at a laboratory in a prestigious university. They've volunteered to take part in a psychological study to examine the effects of punishment on memory and learning. The scientist greets them and explains how the experiment will be run. One volunteer is designated the 'teacher', the other, the 'learner'. The teacher is placed in front of an electric-shock generator with a series of switches rising from 15 to 450 volts. Next door, the learner is strapped into a chair, hooked up to a generator, and given a series of word pairs to memorise. The teacher is instructed to inflict increasingly severe electric shocks each time the learner forgets a word.

The experiment begins. A few questions in, the learner makes an error and is given his first shock. It's a small one: 15 volts. With each subsequent error the intensity of the shock increases: 30 volts, 60 volts, 105 volts. The learner starts to complain but the experiment goes on: 120 volts, 135 volts, 165 volts. The learner protests vehemently but is ignored. At 195 volts he lets out an agonised scream and yells: 'Let me out of here! My heart's bothering me! You have no right to keep me here.' The teacher is rattled, unsure what to do next. He hesitates and looks to the scientist for guidance. 'Please continue,' says the man in the white coat. 'You accept full responsibility?' asks the teacher. 'The responsibility is mine,' responds the scientist. The teacher nervously pulls the next switch . . .

This is the classic obedience experiment first conducted by the psychologist Stanley Milgram in the 1960s.[1] The memorisation tasks were just a cover to see how members of the public would respond when asked by an authority figure to electrocute a complete stranger. The volunteer 'teacher' didn't know it but the 'learner' was actually an actor and only pretending to receive the shocks. Prior to the experiment, a group of psychiatrists had predicted that just one in a thousand 'teachers' would continue to the 'fatal' 450-volt switch.[2] Although most of the participants experienced high levels of stress, roughly two-thirds of them pulled every one of thirty shock switches, continuing until the researcher stopped the experiment.

The experiment has been repeated many times, in different countries. The average proportion of participants prepared to inflict potentially fatal voltages is over 60 per cent.[3] What's remarkable about these results is that they were achieved without any threat of penalty or punishment. Participants were even told that they could keep their fee for taking part whether or not they completed their task. In no sense were they threatened, coerced or bribed. The key finding was just how susceptible we are to authority and, more generally, context. As psychologist Thomas Blass put it, 'often it is not the kind of person we are that determines how we act, but rather the kind of situation we find ourselves in'.[4]

The initial motivation for Milgram's study was to understand how so many German citizens could have participated in the horrors of the Holocaust, horrors that 'could only have been carried out on a massive scale if a very large number of people obeyed orders'. The reaction to the study from students around the US was illuminating. Milgram recalls: 'I faced young men who were aghast at the behaviour of experimental subjects and proclaimed they would never behave in such a way, but who, in a matter of months, were brought into the military and performed without compunction actions that made shocking the victim seem pallid.'[5]

Once inducted into the hierarchical structure of an army, a man or woman becomes an instrument to be wielded by their superiors, to be remotely controlled by people they will probably never meet. Within such a structure, a benevolent individual can be turned into a killing machine. In the My Lai massacre of 1968, US soldiers murdered between 350 and 500 unarmed Vietnamese civilians. One soldier, who was later interviewed on CBS News, described how he was ordered to kill men, women, children, even babies: 'he told me to start shooting. So I started shooting.' Asked why he had obeyed, he replied: 'I felt like I was ordered to do it, and it seemed like . . . at the time I felt like I was doing the right thing . . .'[6]

According to Milgram, 'The essence of obedience consists in the fact that a person comes to view himself as the instrument for carrying out another person's wishes.'[7] Obedience transfers power from those following instructions to those giving them. On a large scale, this creates vast concentrations of power – in the form of states, armies and corporations. Total obedience reduces the status of a person's autonomy to that of a machine: goals are determined externally, requiring no further thought or reflection. When an ideology is established deeply enough or an authority is considered legitimate enough, following orders, conforming to the dictates of a system and meeting expectations all appear to be neutral acts. The political theorist Hannah Arendt, a Jewish woman who escaped Nazi Germany, observed: 'The sad truth is that most evil is done by people who never make up their minds to be good or evil.'[8]

Obedience and conformity are often confused with neutrality. This confusion arises when the wider justification for a task – be it national security or just putting bread on the table – is so deeply embedded, so ingrained, that attention is focused solely on getting the job done. Milgram's experiment showed that most participants were influenced by what they perceived to be the wider context of the experiment – the pursuit of scientific truth in a prestigious university. Once the authority of the experimenter had been accepted, and the values motivating the experiment internalised, participants were 'freed up' to focus on narrower tasks. They became 'so absorbed in the narrow technical aspects of the task that [they lost] sight of its broader consequences'.[9] Such myopia makes tasks look technical and therefore value-free, but technique only comes into play once the aims have been established. We can only question these aims and their merit when we step back and look at the big picture. The appearance of neutrality requires the obliteration of context.

The worst crimes – war, genocide, slavery, the subjugation of women, the destruction of nature – are made possible by mechanisms of control that induce obedience on a mass scale. Few acts are as politically significant as obeying orders and conforming to expectations; political neutrality is unattainable. Despite this, neutrality is generally assumed to be a marker of fairness preferable to bias. However, what counts is the nature of a bias, not bias itself. A truly neutral being does not care if children eat or starve, nor if the environment is preserved or destroyed. A truly neutral being does not care about anything at all.

At the heart of a relationship based on obedience is an imbalance of power expressed as a division of labour between setting goals and working to bring them about. Milgram showed that, even without any threat of punishment or penalty, an authority figure can compel people to make choices they do not want to make. Using authority to compel is one of many ways to exert control. Whether by manipulating identities or context, all forms of control undermine freedom by inhibiting our capacity to discover what we value and obstructing our pursuit of it – the concept of value is the starting point of freedom. What makes us free is not the power to choose, but the power to turn our choices into expressions of our own values, our lives into testaments to our own visions. We expand our freedom when we transform the power to choose into the power to create, when we identify the things that matter to us and dedicate ourselves to them. This is 'creative freedom'.

We may not be ultimately responsible for who we are or what we do, but we still have choices to make. Our actions have consequences in the world and, not being neutral creatures, we favour some of these consequences over others. The identity bequeathed to us by fate has needs and desires: we attach great importance to certain people, experiences and outcomes. We find some things beautiful, others repugnant; some inspiring, others depressing. The way the world is matters to us. Central to what we value are principles that underlie judgements about what things are worth living and struggling for. These principles reflect conceptions of the good, the right and the beautiful. They constitute answers to life's profound questions about meaning and purpose.

Discovering what we truly value is not easy. Inexperience, ignorance and flawed reasoning routinely prevent us from finding out what really matters to us. For thousands of years and across many cultures, the blood of men, women and children was spilled to placate imagined gods. The belief driving this violence – that deities need appeasing in order for things to go well – had no basis in fact, but countless innocents perished. Beliefs reflect what we think the world is like. Values, on the other hand, reflect what we think it should be like. On the turbulent seas of life, we depend on our beliefs to act as a compass for our values – to signal, in any situation, the direction of travel. When they are false, they lead us astray, often preventing us from realising our goals. People take wrong turnings, vote against their interests, buy the wrong product, pick the wrong career, marry the wrong person.

With better understanding, we could make better choices and avoid many mistakes. You and I may be searching for the same goal, but differ radically in the means we employ to attain it. I may believe the path to happiness is fame; you may believe it is fortune. These beliefs will send us down different paths, but, if we find ourselves miserable and unsatisfied, we can reconsider our beliefs and the values based on them. We might even ask questions about our ultimate goal – why, for instance, we are striving to attain happiness rather than, say, justice, peace, knowledge or meaning? We might ask what we even mean by these terms. Answers to such questions are not set, nor should they be.

The value we place on things – love, work, nature, fame, family and fortune – is profoundly affected by our conditioning. When we question that conditioning, our thoughts about what is worthwhile and important can change, sometimes radically. Eyes can be opened to dimensions of value previously unseen. Moral codes evolve. Aesthetic tastes alter. Political views refine. Personal ambitions shift. Much of the challenge is to balance our competing values, to make judgements about the relative importance of different people, projects, desires and principles. There is no formula for this, no final answer. Perhaps the important thing is not to stop asking the question, to take time to scrutinise our reasons for living as we do instead of sleepwalking along paths laid down by convention and habit.

We can pursue many valuable goals with our choices: a nourishing relationship, personal fitness, professional success, artistic achievement, political transformation. We can create objects, ideas and technologies of great utility and beauty. We can enhance the well-being of those around us, support them in their endeavours, listen when they need someone to talk to. Whatever we do, the lives we lead send ripples of effects into the world – some we are aware of, many we are not – that reverberate through the choices of others long after we are gone.

Creating what we value is not just about changing the external world, but finding new ways to experience and respond to it. An experience is itself a creation. As we change ourselves, we transform how we perceive. A rich inner life, a powerful imagination, a good sense of humour, a reservoir of peace and equanimity are powerful creative tools. They allow meaning to be found in suffering, beauty in sadness, peace in chaos.[10]

Our capacity to identify and create what we value depends on the resources at our disposal. They determine what we are capable of doing in a given situation, constraining our ability to discover, create and experience what we value most.[11] Through economic and political impoverishment, we can be denied access to external resources: land, minerals, forests, animals and oceans; the dazzling products of civilisation, its science, technology and art; and the intelligence, talents and energy of other people. Similarly, through emotional, social and nutritional deprivation, we can be denied access to physical and psychological resources: strength, stamina, patience, perseverance, confidence and imagination. The care we receive, the early relationships we establish, the suffering we endure, as well as the genes we inherit, shape who we are and equip us with particular attitudes, qualities and abilities – tools with which we can create or obstacles we have to overcome.

An artist may dedicate a lifetime to refining her concept of beauty and mastering the technique to bring it into existence, but there is no more important canvas than the world around us. Our choices mark it every day, shaping ourselves, society and the planet. With the flicker of consciousness that interrupts an eternity of non-existence, we can do valuable things with our power to choose. The more inspiring our vision, the more meaning we will take from participating in its creation.

Rules and values

Thirty-two pieces, sixty-four squares, a universe bounded by rules and values: the game of chess begins from a position of perfect equality. Strict rules govern how each piece may move, making some more valuable than others. The choices players make emerge from their understanding of the options available. There are many strategies to consider – controlling the centre of the board, maintaining a strong pawn structure – but the game is guided by one overriding goal, an ultimate purpose built into the fabric of this artificial universe: to checkmate the opponent's king.

Games are a useful metaphor for the many domains of our lives and how we find value within them. Each has its own set of rules that determine which actions are permitted, who the players are, and the aims of the activity. Whether studying at school, toiling in the workplace, praying at a temple, or fighting on the battlefield, we pursue established goals within existing rules and conventions. Society is made up of many overlapping 'games'. The process of socialisation thrusts us into different arenas, each with its own rules, expectations and values. The obedience experiment was such a game – its ostensible aim was to attain knowledge about memory and learning; the experimenter established the rules and the participants were assigned roles to play.

There is a distinction to be made between observing rules and obeying them. To live by rules that serve our values – or at least do not clash with them – is not obedience. Barring exceptional circumstances, it is in everyone's interests to keep to a particular side of the road while driving. Collectively, living by rules can be a form of mutually beneficial cooperation. On the other hand, we are often obliged to obey rules that conflict with our values because the price of not doing so is too high, or because we have been taught to defer to an authority. Whether or not following a rule is an act of obedience depends on our perspective. Deferring to someone with greater experience and expertise – a parent, a doctor, a teacher – might help us achieve our goals, at least in the short term. However, that is for us to decide. There may be good reasons to defy an authority figure. As our understanding increases, our perception of who has legitimate authority, in what contexts, and to what extent, changes. The question is not whether we should follow rules, but which rules we should follow and when.

Play a game long enough and you will change to meet its challenges. Depending on the wider context, this can be a privilege or a punishment. In pursuit of technical mastery, the pianist may dedicate years to retraining her brain. In pursuit of compassion, a monk may dedicate a lifetime to meditation. In each case, the task of changing body and mind can be seen as a deep expression of creative freedom. In many contexts, however, the physical and mental changes people undergo arise from an absence of freedom rather than an expression of it. The process of socialisation normalises such changes and conceals the true social function of the games we play. As every anthropologist knows, the deeper purpose of a belief or ritual is often hidden from those whose lives are shaped by it. George Orwell put it succinctly, 'To see what is in front of one's nose needs a constant struggle.'[12]

When there are powerful incentives to play a game that conflicts with our own rules and values – as citizens or professionals – one response is simply to ignore the clash. We are remarkably adept at compartmentalising. At church, the young believer is taught that 'it is easier for a camel to go through the eye of a needle than for a rich man to enter the kingdom of God'. In business school she is told that, by the virtues of 'avarice and usury'[13], we shall 'benefit our fellow men most if we are guided solely by the striving for gain'.[14] Economists tell her greed is good, the Bible that it's bad. Which game should she play?

Such dilemmas arise all the time. Our friend may truly believe in the wisdom of 'thou shalt not kill', yet perceive no contradiction when she cheers the troops or supports the death penalty. Psychologists use the term 'schemas' to refer to the different patterns of thought and behaviour that are triggered by specific contexts: on speaking to your boss, playing with your child or meeting a stranger. You may spend your days devising more effective ways to market fast food to children and still be a caring friend or parent. You may shoot civilians on command, but abhor violence in the home. Neuroscientist Kathleen Taylor writes that 'officials at the Nazi death camps were able to activate schemas concerned with duty

. . . while watching children go to the gas chambers, and then go home, activate their fond parent schemas, and cuddle their own children.'[15] The ease with which we enter a different arena, switch to a new schema and obey a different set of rules shields us from the glaring inconsistencies in our lives.

Ignorance keeps us bound to schemas that with greater understanding we would reject. Fear ties us to schemas that we detest. Seeing through the illusory divisions in our lives is central to being consistent in the goals we pursue. The more context we seek for our actions, the more we understand our impact on the world. The different roles we play – consumer, businessman, student, soldier, voter, parent, employee, patriot, worshipper or professional – obscure the fact that, in the end, each of us is a human being whose every choice is an act of creation, a mark on ourselves, a mark on history. When they are not in harmony, their impact is undermined.

It takes resolve and ingenuity to preserve core values, to be the person we want to be, particularly under oppressive conditions. In his account of Nazi concentration camps, holocaust survivor and psychoanalyst Viktor Frankl writes:

> We who lived in concentration camps can remember the men who walked through the huts comforting others, giving away their last piece of bread. They may have been few in number, but they offer sufficient proof that everything can be taken from a man but one thing: the last of human freedoms – to choose one's attitude in any given set of circumstances, to choose one's own way.
>
> And there were always choices to make. Every day, every hour, offered the opportunity to make a decision, a decision which determined whether you would or would not submit to those powers which threatened to rob you of your very self, your inner freedom; which determined whether or not you would become the plaything of circumstance, renouncing freedom and dignity to become molded into the form of a typical inmate. [. . .] Such men are not only in concentration camps. Everywhere man is confronted with fate, with the chance of achieving something through his own suffering.[16]

Systems of rules exist at all levels of society, each one exerting pressure on us to think and behave in certain ways. To resist being bent out of shape by the force of circumstance, we rely on the cultivation of inner resources such as imagination, equanimity, patience, humour, reason and empathy. Rather than yield to oppressive rules, the brave and resourceful individual may choose to bend them where possible and break them when necessary. The daring CEO might place people before profit, the principled politician might cherish integrity over promotion, the maverick teacher might put learning before grades, the idealistic student might prioritise activism over exams – but subverting dominant values often carries heavy costs, particularly for those with little power.

As the quality of our options reduces, we have to make greater and greater sacrifices, and the capacity to pursue diverse goals diminishes. We are forced to prioritise certain values and goals, and relinquish others. Inevitably we abandon things of importance – a moral framework, time with people we love, our dignity, our health. These are hard choices to make. We may well live to regret them.

The 'pieces' of society are not reset each time a child is born. Each of us must play the position we inherit. For those who find themselves in a weak position, individual sacrifice is the typical response. This may have the appearance of rational behaviour – each person pursuing what they believe they value most, given dwindling options – but fails to address the root of the problem: the game that everyone is being forced to play. Individual sacrifice begins to look irrational when we observe millions of people in a similar position – working harder, earning less, losing more. It looks irrational because collectively this group often has the power to change the game being played, as history amply demonstrates. Students can organise to end tuition fees. Communities can save hospitals, cap rents and cancel debt. Workers can win higher wages, better conditions and more rights. When people join together and make strategic sacrifices collectively, they can do more than accept the options presented to them: they can create new ones. Instead of making the best of unjust rules, they can tear up the rulebook.

Rather than conform to the expectations of a patriarchal society, suffragettes like Emmeline Pankhurst, Sylvia Pankhurst and Emily Davison fought to change it. Instead of accepting the limits placed on them, they challenged them head-on. Through demonstrations, window-smashing, arson and hunger strikes they showed that they were willing to endure severe penalties – including death in Emily Davison's case – in order to change the rules of the game they were expected to play. In a world where domestic and sexual violence affects 35 per cent of women, their struggle continues today and it involves more than changing laws and institutions; it involves changing the cultural values that perpetuate male entitlement and privilege.[17]

Rosa Parks defied the rules of society in 1955 when, sitting on a bus, she refused to give up her seat to a white man. She was convicted for violating the segregation laws in her state. Black community leaders – including Martin Luther King Jr. – responded by organising a bus boycott, which helped to spark the American Civil Rights Movement. A year after Parks' arrest, a year in which she was forced out of her job, the US Supreme Court ruled that segregation on buses was unconstitutional. People had refused to play along, organised collectively, and rewritten the rules of the game.

Individuals like Rosa Parks and Emily Davison have become cultural symbols, embodying the ideal of the struggle for freedom, but such courageous acts are not rare. For every icon there have been countless others who chose to defy rules and conventions, in countless ways and contexts, often risking safety and security in the process, to defend and express their core values.

Games within games coexist, responding and adapting to each other, competing for space, resources and autonomy across society. As a game captures more of our time and energy, it controls more of our behaviour and establishes powerful incentives to keep us playing. For centuries, religious fundamentalists have fought to expand the scope of their holy books, pointing to the absolute authority of God. For decades, market fundamentalists have worked to expand their influence, pointing to the benign power of the invisible hand. Each one wishes to impose their logic over new domains: from education, healthcare and housing to politics, employment and art.

Large-scale attempts to overthrow competing value systems and impose new rules can take many forms, from the formation of empires and colonies to the establishment of structural adjustment programmes and far-reaching trade deals. When rules and values become dominant, they can appear immutable, and the behaviour that results from them can seem natural and inevitable. A totalising system imposes a single overarching game on society. It subordinates and constrains freedom by defining what we must become in order to succeed and survive. Every attempt to expand the scope of a game faces resistance. The democratic spirit of secularism was an attempt to curb the power of dogmatic religious institutions. The creation of the welfare state was an attempt to limit the reach of the amoral market. Preventing a single game subsuming the rest has been an essential part of guarding the freedom to decide upon and pursue our own values.

Power struggles take two forms: the struggle to succeed according to the values of a particular game and the struggle to decide which game is being played. There are countless overlapping value systems in the world, but one system has come to dominate the rest. It is a 'game' that organises human activity like no other, rewriting laws and legislation, shifting priorities, shaping identities and infiltrating every area of our lives. We call it 'capitalism'.

The profit game

Vast amounts of currency circulate the globe, leaving behind a trail of human labour that changes the face of our planet. The contours of today's society are the remnants of yesterday's flows. Ensuring that at least a few drops of this vast torrent of wealth find their way into our possession is a matter of life and death. Human activity is driven by the countless exchanges of money that take place every second of every day. The question is, what drives this circulation?

Large state and corporate hierarchies control most of this wealth, but they function within a wider system that imposes certain restrictions. Although powerful, those individuals who direct financial flows often have very little independence. The power they possess is little more than the power to advance an agenda set by the logic of the system in which they operate. This logic overpowers the wishes of any individual. It produces a clear imperative that lies at the heart of the global system of capitalism: invest money for a profit.

Profit is what drives the flow of money. From the construction site to the coffee shop, the TV show to the ice-cream van, the high street bank to the Apple store, human activity is organised around its pursuit. Banks, hedge funds, governments, NGOs, universities – everyone is caught up in the game of sending money in search of more money. Most people simply use money to meet their basic needs. Unlike wealthy investors, their money does not 'work for them' – they work for it. That said, anyone with a bank account is engaged in the process of investment. Most of the time, and often without our knowledge, the deposits in our savings accounts are crossing borders and setting people to work on vast projects around the world.

The profit motive has three major components: market competition, political power and social status. First, in competitive markets, businesses are driven to reinvest and expand to survive. Second, money confers power. The more wealth a person controls, the greater their capacity to determine the future. For those who wish to increase their power, amassing ever greater fortunes through reinvestment is extremely appealing, particularly when competing with others doing the same. Third, in a culture that measures achievement in terms of wealth, the pursuit of greater profits becomes the pursuit of higher status. From having the right iPhone in the classroom to the right investment port-folio in the boardroom, money measures success.

Profits can be generated in numerous ways – extending loans at interest, selling products for more than they cost to produce, charging rent on land and property – but ultimately they go to those with the most extensive ownership rights. Some ways of generating profit can benefit society, but there are many ways that cause great harm, and they are often the easiest: lowering wages, lobbying for deregulation, exter-nalising costs. If lobbying and bribing the government to change laws is cheaper than cleaning up waste, the path to greater profit for a wealthy corporation producing vast amounts of pollution is clear, and it's not one that benefits the majority.

Increasingly, profits are generated by gambling on asset prices, an exercise that serves no one but the investor, while destabilising the whole system. As prices are pushed up by bidding, they lose any connection to the real economy, producing economic instability. When crisis hits, the political power that money buys pushes the resulting costs onto the wider population, evidenced by the wave of austerity imposed across Europe since the 2008 financial crash. Political power can be used in all sorts of ways to rig the system to increase profits: it can privatise national assets for a fraction of their value, crush unions, tear down national barriers to wealth flows, dodge taxes, repeal costly regulations, impose debilitating conditions on international loans, facilitate the exploitation of cheap labour at home and abroad, and so on. In the process of creating and exploiting profitable opportunities, the power of concentrated wealth reorganises human society to reduce and eliminate the obstacles it encounters. Unfortunately, these obstacles include the effectiveness of democratic structures, the integrity of Earth's life support systems, the rights of workers and the health and happiness of citizens. All are sacrificed on the altar of short-term profit.

Even the huge potential of technology to liberate has been squandered. Philosopher Edward Skidelsky writes: 'We now have machinery sufficient to free the affluent world from drudgery [and provide food, education and healthcare to the less affluent world]. It is only our failure of political organisation and of ethical imagination that holds us back.'[18] The reason is clear: the 'rules of the game' dictate that the first purpose of technology is to increase profit, not feed and educate the world, improve the lives of human beings, or reduce the time people spend working. The uses to which technology is put depend on effective demand. If states wish to spend their wealth on expanding the military or spying more effectively on their citizens, vast resources are available to do so. The aims of research and development are determined by those with the pockets deep enough to fund them.

The game of capitalism requires certain kinds of player. Reorganising society for profit requires the moulding of identities – beliefs, values and habits. As early as 1776, Adam Smith wrote in The Wealth of Nations that 'It is not from the benevolence of the butcher, the brewer, or the baker, that we expect our dinner, but from their regard to their own interest. We address ourselves, not to their humanity but to their self-love, and never talk to them of our own necessities but of their advantages.'[19] Fast forward to the twentieth century and the world's leading economist John Maynard Keynes declares that 'Capitalism is the astounding belief that the most wickedest of men will do the most wickedest of things for the greatest good of everyone.'[20] Astounding this belief may be, but Keynes subscribed to it. Speculating about the future economic prospects of society, he concluded with great optimism that capitalism would ultimately make everyone rich. But, he cautioned, in order to reach that point, 'we must pretend to ourselves and to everyone that fair is foul and foul is fair; for foul is useful and fair is not. Avarice and usury and precaution must be our gods for a little longer still. For only they can lead us out of the tunnel of economic necessity into daylight.'[21]

The reference to gods is revealing. As many have observed, the doctrines of the market are not so different from those of religion. Instead of belief in a powerful, unseen god, faith is placed in a powerful 'invisible hand'. And just as God has all of our best interests at heart, so the invisible hand can be trusted to produce the best outcomes for all. Sacred scripture provides the only way to salvation whereas economic orthodoxy provides the only way to prosperity. But whereas compassion, forgiveness and love are part of the moral code of the world's religions, capitalism is characterised by precisely the opposite: greed, selfishness and avarice. As Friedrich Hayek put it, 'We will benefit our fellow men most if we are guided solely by the striving for gain.'[22] According to this modern faith, 'the road to heaven', as E. F. Schumacher puts it, 'is paved with bad intentions'.[23]

Capitalism has imposed its value system on the world more success-fully than any empire, ideology or religion. The global market, writes David Graeber, is 'the single greatest and most monolithic system of measurement ever created, a totalizing system that would subordinate everything – every object, every piece of land, every human capacity or relationship – on the planet to a single standard of value.'[24] Like all dominant value systems, it is based on a conception of human nature, in this case one that assumes individuals know what they want and are attempting to get as much of it as possible for the least amount of effort. When someone donates to a charity, they do so not to help but to make them feel good about themselves. In attempting to maximise their pleasure, they make a calculation: the value given (in pounds) should be at most the value received (in positive feelings); to give more would be irrational. Even if we accept this strange, one-dimensional way of looking at things, it leaves untouched the more interesting question of why helping others makes us feel good in the first place. What does it say about our nature that it makes us feel good to help people we've never even met?

The attempt to reduce the plurality of life's incommensurable values to one unit of measurement is based on the assumption that all people are selfishly chasing some abstract yet quantifiable notion of 'pleasure', and that the value of all goods is reducible to pounds, dollars, euros or yen. The value of a human life and the beauty of a sunset, then, can be quantified in terms of tins of beans and chocolate bars. This may sound far-fetched but such calculations inform important government policies.

The Natural Capital Committee, set up by the British government, quite literally aimed to quantify the value of nature's aesthetic beauty in pounds and pence. It claimed that the aesthetic value of protecting fresh-water ecosystems would be worth £700 million.[25] In 2011, the Department of Environment stated that if we protect our parks and greens they will enhance our well-being to the tune of £290 per household per year in 2060. When broken down, this figure includes spaces in which 'our culture finds its roots', 'shared social value' derived from 'a sense of purpose' and the maintenance of 'strong and inclusive communities'. From this they 'calculate' the very precise but completely meaningless figure of £290 per household per year. The language is telling: not nature but 'natural capital', not ecological processes but 'ecological services', not hills and mountains but 'green infrastructure'. Governments aren't the only culprits. The World Wildlife Fund recently put a monetary value on the world's oceans: $24 trillion. Economic logic dictates that if we could make more money from destroying the oceans, it would be inefficient not to do so.[26]

There's a reason these absurdities are taken seriously. The monetisation of value has become so widespread that unless a value can be articulated in pounds and dollars it is simply ignored. Viewing the world through the distorting lens of markets blinds us to the value of anything without a dollar sign attached to it. This conception of value takes life's diversity, squashes it, cuts it up and lays it, deformed beyond recognition, at the altar of our revered currency. The market has a long tradition of subsuming the sacred, stamping price tags on the priceless. In medieval times, even spiritual purity was turned into a commodity that could be bought and sold. Sin could be cancelled out by purchasing an 'indulgence' from a senior churchman – a ticket to heaven.

Rather than being a means to an end, the economy has become an end in itself. Instead of serving the great kaleidoscope of shared and incommensurable values that bring colour and meaning to our lives, we are forced to serve the monolith of profit – anything else is heresy. In this game, the ultimate measure of success is economic growth, which has long been the primary criterion against which government policy is judged. The incessant process of reinvestment for a return places enormous pressure on the system itself to expand into new spaces – physical, social and intellectual. This logic drove the brutal enclosure movements of medieval Europe, the colonisation of the Global South, and now drives the commodification and privatisation of the natural world and social services. When growth stalls, it is called a crisis as last year's profits have nowhere to go. Demand drops, unemployment increases and the value of accumulated wealth risks being devalued or destroyed. (Asset values dropped by more than $50 trillion after the 2008 economic crash.[27])

The pioneers of neoliberalism – who sought to establish a deregulated form of capitalism – saw concentrated state power as the greatest threat to freedom. They feared what they called 'collectivism', defined by Hayek as a system in which 'the whole of society and all its resources' are organised for a 'unitary end'.[28] What the end was didn't matter. Hitler's Germany, Stalin's Russia and Mao's China all qualified as collectivist societies because they subordinated the will of individuals to a singular vision of society. However, Hayek's critique also applies to capitalist societies, under which everything is organised for a unitary end: profit – the goal to which all competing values are subordinated.

According to Hayek, a man in a collectivist state must 'be prepared actively to break every moral rule he has ever known if this seems necessary to achieve the end set for him'.[29] We see the same pressures on today's workers and professionals. People are paid to achieve their employer's goals, not their own. In order to advance the goals of exploitative and environmentally destructive corporations, many construction workers, miners, engineers, lawyers, accountants, advertisers, public relations experts, journalists, security personnel and politicians must be willing to subordinate their own moral codes. Legal scholar Joel Bakan writes that 'whatever may be our human inclinations, motivation, feelings, and beliefs, when we enter the corporation's world we become operatives for its imperatives, subsuming our own personal values to its institutional demands'.[30]

Hayek tells us that the 'most effective way of making everybody serve the single system of ends towards which the collective social plan is directed is to make everybody believe in those ends'.[31] He warns that in a collectivist society 'the whole apparatus for spreading knowledge, the schools and the press, wireless and cinema, will be used exclusively to spread those views which, whether true or false, will strengthen the belief in the rightness of the decisions taken by the authority'.[32] Yet, as we have seen, the logic of the market produces its own consistent bias, which distorts and omits truth to serve corporate and establishment interests. Throughout the twentieth century, the 'apparatus for spreading knowledge' was commandeered by wealthy interests to strengthen belief in the free enterprise system and weaken the influence of democracy. Hayek bemoans the absence of 'science for science's sake, art for art's sake' in a collectivist society, but in a market nothing is produced for its own sake – all is for profit.[33] Market logic turns everything into a commodity whose value is measured in monetary terms – science and art included. Instead of wealth being a means to further knowledge and beauty, it is the other way around.

Hayek tells us there is no limit to what a citizen in a collectivist society is expected to do, 'no act which his conscience must prevent him from committing' when 'his superiors order him'.[34] But obedience to centralised authority is a fact of life in any unaccountable hierarchical society, whether it is dominated by large corporations, state bureaucracies, political parties or the military. Elsewhere, Hayek tells us that when 'you admit that the individual is merely a means to serve the ends of the higher entity called society or the nation, most of those features of totalitarian regimes which horrify us follow of necessity'.[35] But within a capitalist system, the worker is explicitly reduced to a means of generating profit. Without democratic safeguards, they are paid as little as possible, obliged to work in dangerous conditions with minimal rights and job security, often to the point of early death or suicide in parts of the world where life is cheap. This exploitative control wears the mask of consent, but the possibility of meaningful consent is destroyed by great imbalances of bargaining power between contracting parties. Formal contracts merely paper over the coercive force of circumstance that pervades any society with great inequalities. The insatiable appetite for profit has driven hundreds of thousands of people to suicide, left many millions to die of preventable diseases, increased inequality, shifted welfare from the poor to the rich, driven nations into lucrative wars, and is now jeopardising the conditions for life on Earth.

Struggles take place every day at all levels of society to determine which games will expand and which will contract, whose power will grow and whose will diminish. Many of these struggles – for affordable housing, a living wage, universal healthcare, free education, racial equality, a sustainable economy, greater democracy and an end to war – are different fronts in the same battle against the impact of capitalism on people and planet. The values, rules and players of this game make it an unjust, undemocratic, unsustainable way to organise society and incompatible with the demands of freedom. However, like any game, it is just a construct, an illusion preserved by our collective belief. It can be changed.[36]

Changing the game

Michelangelo worked miracles with his blocks of stone, within a tradition of classical sculpture. Van Gogh touched millions with paintings that would have been considered a failure in Michelangelo's time. A clear pattern can be discerned from the way artistic forms evolve: again and again painters, poets, actors, singers, dancers, composers and writers have sought to escape the fetters of convention, to push back the boundaries and break the rules. In the process, creativity has been unleashed and culture enriched. There's a parallel, too, in science. Dominant paradigms direct investigation and define modes of thinking, yet beyond a certain point they become obstacles to understanding. Copernican astronomy gave way to Galilean astronomy. Newtonian mechanics gave way to Einsteinian relativity. In the pursuit of knowledge, aims and methods have to be refined or redefined.

Not only do values compel us to reinvent our disciplines, they sometimes oblige us to transcend them completely. Mark Twain became a key anti-imperialist organiser protesting against the American war in the Philippines. He stepped out of the category of 'author' to challenge the injustices he explored in his novels. Climate scientist James Hansen has been arrested six times on protests against the ecocidal policies of his government: he went beyond the role of 'scientist' to try and preserve the life-sustaining conditions that his research told him were being destroyed. His work as a scientist clarified the problem, but the solution, as he saw it, was political.

Rules mark out what we can do; values tell us what we should do. Yet values are what count. Rules are created, bent, ignored and rewritten to advance values, not the other way around. Across the political spectrum, politicians, journalists and businessmen claim to favour freedom, yet so many people have so little of it. As a species, do we really want to continue being bound by the imperatives of profit and growth? When the things we most care about are being destroyed by the games we're forced to play, it is time to change the game.

The call to do just that is growing in volume as more voices join together in a chorus of popular resistance against many aspects of the global system of capitalism. In 2015, Pope Francis surprised many by describing the unfettered pursuit of money as 'the dung of the devil', continuing: 'let us not be afraid to say it: we want change, real change, structural change . . .' He accused today's system of imposing a 'mentality of profit at any price, with no concern for social exclusion or the destruction of nature' and told his audience that this was intolerable for people and 'Mother Earth' herself.[37] Strong words from the spiritual leader of 1.2 billion people.

The Catholic Church itself remains a powerful institution, but its scope and influence has been dramatically curtailed. The over-arching dominance of its value system had to be overcome to create the space for art, science and democracy to flourish. We need to achieve a transformation of similar scope regarding the rules and values of capitalism. The pursuit of profit must be curtailed and tamed, its reductive value system rejected, and people and planet protected from its voracious appetite. The specifics are up for discussion but the need for profound transformation is beyond serious doubt.

Tucked away behind every critique of a social system is a conception of human nature. To be human is to be subject to mental and physical constraints. The way we think about these constraints determines the way we think about freedom. Without intrinsic limits, there is no reason to favour one set of conditions over another for the development of a human being. If we greeted the world as 'blank slates' and all our needs and values were programmed from the outside, there would be no moral argument against raising some people to be happy slaves and others to be happy slave-owners. And there would be no moral argument against capitalism.

Bertrand Russell advised that we regard 'a child as a gardener regards a young tree, i.e. as something with a certain intrinsic nature, which will develop into an admirable form given proper soil and air and light'.[38] Like a young tree, we require certain things from our environment in order to flourish. Denied the proper material and social conditions, our physical, emotional and intellectual potential will not be realised. From a combination of instinct and research about human nature we develop ideas about what people have reason to value and what kind of society is desirable. A society cannot avoid making decisions about what constitutes a dignified and meaningful life. These decisions justify its socialisation process and institutional arrangements.

To make freedom an organising principle of society is to recognise the importance of being able to determine for ourselves what it means to live well, to see this capacity as an integral form of human flourishing. Many have claimed that capitalism does just that, that the free market enables people to consume what they desire, work where they want, and pursue what they value – but this is to ignore the impact of inequality on the distribution of power, the profound imperfections of markets, and the greedy, selfish and materialistic values it fosters.

It may not be possible to prove that creative freedom is an inherent part of human flourishing, but it is a claim that resonates deeply and finds powerful support in the extraordinary sacrifices people make in its pursuit and defence. Humans have been manipulated, deceived and coerced, yet the desire for freedom has never been extinguished. As Solomon Northup, whose memoir inspired the Oscar-winning film *Twelve Years a Slave*, describes, the instinct for freedom runs deep:

> Let them know the *heart* of the poor slave – learn his secret thoughts
> – thoughts he dare not utter in the hearing of the white man; let
> them sit by him in the silent watches of the night – converse with
> him in trustful confidence of 'life, liberty, and the pursuit of happy-
> ness,' and they will find that ninety-nine out of every hundred are
> intelligent enough to understand their situation and to cherish in
> their bosoms the love of freedom, as passionately as themselves.[39]

Vast concentrations of power pose a threat to all conceptions of human flourishing, however they may be defined. A society that took freedom seriously would recognise this danger and attempt to share out resources – internal and external – so as to undermine centralised authority and control. But there has always been resistance to sharing out the resources on which freedom depends.[40] Advocates of capitalism have argued that 'freedom breeds inequality', that you cannot have the former without the latter.[41] But the vast inequalities in society have been produced and maintained by power – violence, theft and oppression – not 'freedom'. Protecting the wealth of a few by sacrificing the fundamental freedoms of many does not serve the cause of liberty. A high degree of economic and political equality is a necessary precondition for a free and democratic society, not a threat to it. Without such equality, power becomes too concentrated and the contracts that pervade society cannot be considered genuinely consensual, meaning that coercion is a ubiquitous feature of the system. If freedom is to flourish, the way wealth is produced, distributed and controlled must be transformed. If democracy is to prosper, the power of private capital must be overcome.

In his twenty-one-minute inaugural speech of 2005, George W. Bush used the words 'liberty' or 'freedom', on average, every thirty seconds. Freedom is a banner that has been wrapped tightly around the machinery of capitalism – a call trumpeted at every election, an ideal employed to justify violent dispossession, military invasion, tax cuts for the rich, and welfare cuts for the poor. Yet the problem lies not with freedom but with how it has been appropriated to justify its opposite. If we want freedom to be more than empty rhetoric, if we want it to be a core principle around which society is organised, we will have to create it.[42]

History gives us cause for hope. Courageous attempts to experiment with new ways of organising society light up our past. It's worth remembering that as well as slaves fighting bravely for – and winning – their own freedom, many people questioned the power structures of their day and fought for the freedom of slaves they had never met and never would. Historian Adam Hochschild writes 'For fifty years, activists in England worked to end slavery in the British Empire. None of them gained a penny by doing so, and their eventual success meant a huge loss to the imperial economy.'[43] This was one of the first times in history that 'a large number of people became outraged, and stayed outraged for many years, over someone *else's* rights. And most startling of all, the rights of people of another color, on another continent.'[44]

The abolitionists raised the political and moral consciousness of enough people to change the rules of their society. By redefining what was acceptable, they built a movement powerful enough to make the unthinkable inevitable. A similar task faces all those who value freedom today. The moral and political consciousness of society once again needs to be raised; a unifying, compelling, inspiring vision again needs to be articulated – and the ideal of freedom needs to be at its core.

Every social system is an experiment to be revised and renewed by each generation. A vision of society gives us a direction to move in, not a blueprint of our destination. To abolish slavery it was not necessary to believe that society would be perfect as a result, nor was it necessary for abolitionists to agree on what a truly free society would be like.[45] Today, the barriers to creative freedom are so pervasive and obstructive, and the distribution of wealth and power so skewed, that the case for rapid transformation is as overwhelming as it has ever been.

The remaining chapters examine this transformation through four lenses: knowledge, power, survival and empathy. Each chapter illuminates important aspects of the aims, nature and tensions of this multifaceted struggle for change, shedding light on the conditions that need to be established if creative freedom is to flourish.

★

Under the brutal conditions of life in a concentration camp, Viktor Frankl saw the importance of holding onto a sense of purpose, of finding value in one's life. He described how, when a feeling of point-lessness set in, many prisoners gave up on life altogether. According to Frankl, the most powerful human drive is 'not to gain pleasure or to avoid pain but rather to see a meaning in his life'.[46] This meaning is to be found in 'the striving and struggling for a worthwhile goal, a freely chosen task'.[47] Even in the most oppressive of contexts, he believed, it is possible to find such tasks.

Meaning is found by caring about the future and our role in creating it. But to care deeply about something or someone is to open ourselves to the frustration and suffering that comes when things do not go as we had hoped – we are vulnerable to what we value. The urge to turn away from what we cherish can be overwhelming at times. It is tempting to respond to failure and loss by denigrating what is most meaningful and precious to us, to numb our feelings and deaden our sensitivity. But the pursuit of freedom challenges us to rescue our humanity in the face of brutality, to reopen our hearts in the face of loss, and hold on to our ideals in the face of injustice. Historian and activist Howard Zinn offers these words of advice:

> To be hopeful in bad times is not just foolishly romantic. It is based on the fact that human history is a history not only of cruelty, but also of compassion, sacrifice, courage, kindness.
>
> What we choose to emphasize in this complex history will determine our lives. If we see only the worst, it destroys our capacity to do something. If we remember those times and places – and there are so many – where people have behaved magnificently, this gives us the energy to act, and at least the possibility of sending this spinning top of a world in a different direction.
>
> And if we do act, in however small a way, we don't have to wait for some grand utopian future. The future is an infinite succession of presents, and to live *now* as we think human beings should live, in defiance of all that is bad around us, is itself a marvelous victory.[48]

A free society creates free people, but it takes free people to create a free society. To break the stalemate, we need to make the most of the freedom we have to establish the conditions for creative freedom to flourish. The chains of obedience running up and down society have no end. Some people are far richer than others; some occupy positions of great power, but all are subject to the logic of a system they do not control. We need to break out of this logic, stray from the pathways along which we are channelled by current institutions. We owe much of the freedom we enjoy today to people who did just that, people who, against all the odds, used their choices to serve a vision of the future they found meaningful and inspiring – one that included our own liberty. We incur a debt to all those who played a part in creating the conditions that made possible the freedom we have – labourers, mothers, fathers, friends, politicians, soldiers, teachers, slaves, artists, writers, activists. The greater our freedom, the greater our debt. The abolition of slavery, the expansion of democracy, the decolonisation of the Global South, the rights of women, people of colour, and LGBTIQ groups – all these victories and many more were won through the cumulative creativity of countless people, most of whose names we will never learn. Freedom is a gift, one to cherish, develop, protect, and – if we are to repay our debt – pass on.

In this struggle for freedom the stakes could not be higher. The decisions we make today may be the difference between the survival of our species and its destruction. Through action and inaction, we all play our part. In the face of greed, cruelty, exploitation and violence, the choice is clear: compliance or creativity. When institutions fail to protect our freedoms, it is left to the solidarity of people to safeguard liberty, a solidarity that crosses the many social, racial and political boundaries we are taught to observe. Rationalisations for inaction are pervasive – from denial of problems to cynicism about solutions – and they need to be overcome.

The task of creating freedom might be daunting but it is not hopeless. If it sometimes seems that way, it is worth recalling Zinn's message: 'to live now as we think human beings should live, in defiance of all that is bad around us, is itself a marvelous victory'. This idea captures the essence of the creative spirit. If we focus on doing the best we can to create what is worthwhile, we can continue in the face of setbacks and apparent failures, because we judge our success not just by what we achieve but by the sincerity of the attempt to achieve it. That, in itself, is a beautiful victory, a wonderful manifestation of the impulse to be free. It's a valuable victory too, sending ripples far and wide, revealing rich and beautiful dimensions of life that we so often forget. Music, paintings and stories can do this, but so can acts of courage, generosity and compassion. Such behaviour uplifts and inspires, interrupting and subverting our routines and expectations, challenging us to imagine something better and reminding us of the extraordinary potential within us all.

9

Knowledge

Elections are won and lost, wars declared and averted, revolutions triggered and suppressed, all on the basis of beliefs we carry around in our heads. The struggle for power has always been bound up with the struggle to control the flow of ideas, facts, perspectives and narratives through society. Each mind is a battleground of competing forces, the frontline of the fight to determine the future. Control thrives on ignorance. Freedom thrives on knowledge.

The particulars of our birth largely determine who we become and the representations of reality we construct in our minds. Our environment channels our vast potential into a particular identity. How we end up speaking, thinking, feeling and acting owes much to the examples, opportunities and ideas to which we are exposed. From childhood until the day we die we are subject to a steady stream of influences – familial, corporate, state, school, religious, cultural – working to shape our habits, beliefs, assumptions, ideals and aims: our picture of reality. The goals that appear valuable to us, and the best route to achieving them, emerge from the confluence of these and other forces.

Standing between reality and our understanding of the world is the arbitrary process by which our identity is formed. If we are not to be misled by the mental constructs we inherit, we have to question them. This is easier said than done. Anyone setting out to understand themselves and society – why it is the way it is and how it could be different

– faces obstacles at every turn, many of which exist precisely to mislead and misdirect. By the time we've developed the capacity to begin questioning our identity, much of who we are has already been established. The emotional loyalties we develop towards our family, friends and community are entangled with the ideas they pass on to us. To question effectively we need to place a higher value on the elusive ideal of truth than on loyalties to nation, religion, race, culture or ideology – in short, to our inherited identity. We need to be able to cultivate enough doubt and uncertainty to look at our beliefs – our definitions of success, failure, love, family, good and bad, right and wrong – with scepticism. Faith in every authority, expert and tradition needs to be put on hold long enough to be interrogated. As our mental faculties mature and strengthen, the challenge is to focus them not just on ideas that clash with our inherited identity but on the very process that generated it.

Adam Smith argued that we should put ourselves in the shoes of an 'impartial spectator' and examine our beliefs and behaviour 'as we imagine any other fair and impartial spectator would examine [them]'.

> We can never survey our own sentiments and motives, we can never form any judgement concerning them; unless we remove ourselves, as it were, from our own natural station, and endeavour to view them as at a distance from us. But we can do this in no other way than by endeavouring to view them with the eyes of other people, or as other people are likely to view them.[1]

To view our lives from different angles and different perspectives requires a flexible imagination. As Hannah Arendt puts it, 'To think with an enlarged mentality means that one trains one's imagination to go visiting.'[2] Imagining how things look from different perspectives helps loosen the arbitrary ties to an identity that leads us to speak of 'my beliefs', 'my country', 'my race', 'my party', 'my president', at least long enough to question them. Most of us inherit ready-made belief systems that attempt to justify action in the world on a large scale and in the long term, describing – even defining – aspects of reality.[3] Each is a framework for interpreting reality, a lens through which to view the world. But why limit ourselves to one perspective? Smith challenges us to make use of what may be a uniquely human capacity: to think about our own thoughts and develop ideas about our own desires. This enables us to reflect on our conflicting impulses and identify with or distance ourselves from them. He encourages us to commit to a method rather than a conclusion, a way of establishing truth rather than any particular version of it.

The attempt to view ourselves from different perspectives is an important counter-balance to the subjectivity of experience. My needs command my attention and motivate my behaviour in a way that yours do not. Subjecting my reasons to critical scrutiny from diverse perspectives is a powerful way to transcend this inherent bias. It is an integral part of moral development. Imagining things from many perspectives opens up windows on to forms of value that we would not otherwise have considered. It is how we can begin to root our beliefs and values in something less arbitrary than the lottery of birth.

Freedom is often seen as an escape from restrictions, but the question is not whether we'll be restricted, but by what. The constraint of reality is unlike any other because it exists whether or not we acknowledge it. No amount of belief in my ability to fly will save me if I jump off a cliff. To commit unequivocally to a system of belief is to render it impervious to reality. The more divorced from reality our beliefs are, the more vulnerable we become. There is no single correct way to represent the world. Like a map, our mental constructs are always simplifications of reality, abstractions that pick out certain features, isolating and distinguishing them from others, and representing them in a symbolic form. Whatever our ultimate goals, we depend on our cognitive maps to navigate towards them. As we learn more about ourselves and society, the appeal of destinations can change, as well as the routes to them.[4] An inaccurate map makes it difficult to get where we want to go. Misleading beliefs – about politics, climate change, capitalism, success, human nature, happiness, responsibility, or simply the speed of a car as we cross the road – distort our perceptions and blind us to the consequences of our actions.

On a larger scale, the 'maps' of reality passed from one generation to the next set a course for the whole of society. Just as they can liberate, they can imprison or lead astray. In general, the capacity to shape reality expands as our beliefs conform to it. But the obstacles to knowledge and the barriers to questioning are varied and powerful, ranging from innate psychological biases and the trappings of language to the many attempts to mislead and confuse that saturate our perceptual environment. Overcoming these obstacles is a lifelong challenge. The better we understand them, the better our chances of success.

The illusion of knowledge

Eyelids part and reality rushes in. Vast and complex machinery rapidly transforms the billions of photons streaming through our eyes into what we take to be an effortlessly faithful account of the outside world. Of course, what we see is not the actual world but a mental representation of it. Information is collected through our senses and interpreted by the brain to construct an experience. When you see a rose, light of a particular wavelength hits the cones in your retinas and the neural circuitry connected to them produces an experience of 'redness'. It feels as if you are passively viewing a flower but the experience is being actively constructed by your brain. An organism with a different brain could perceive the same rose as blue, green, yellow or some colour never experienced by you.

The price of perception is subjectivity. Look at the image below:

Most people perceive a triangular pattern. We can't help but connect the dots with straight lines. Why do we connect them with straight lines rather than, say, curved lines to make a circle? Why do we connect them at all?

When you hear the sounds of a foreign language, the unfamiliar words seem to flow into each other without any perceptible gaps, but in your mother tongue you hear words, spaces between words and sentences. This does not happen because in your language there are pauses between the words, but because when you recognise a word your brain inserts a gap. Just as our brains can easily discern a face from random scribbles, they can make out words from a stream of sounds.

The relationship between perception and knowledge has occupied thinkers for millennia. In trying to establish a foundation for certain knowledge, the French philosopher René Descartes hypothesised the existence of an 'evil demon' – a being 'as clever and deceitful as he is powerful' – who was dedicated to misleading Descartes himself. Faced with such a formidable adversary, Descartes wondered if he could be certain about anything. If all his perceptions could be fabricated and distorted, how could he trust his beliefs about the world? A modern twist on this idea formed the central conceit of the *Matrix* films in which the story's protagonist discovers that his world, every aspect and every experience, has existed only as part of an elaborate computer-generated reality. All his life he had believed he was free, though his body had lain motionless in a pod within a vast structure connecting millions of human brains to the virtual reality of which he was a part.

These scenarios highlight the impossibility of certainty by showing that all we ever experience directly are subjective representations, rather than reality itself. But the limits on our cognitive powers do not end there.[5] Not only are there restraints on what we can know, there are strict limits to what we can think. It is clear that some ideas are inconceivable to a cat or dog. What they can understand is bound by their biological potential. No cat or dog can solve problems of trigonometry, compose a symphony or discover the structure of the atom. Nevertheless, there are plenty of problems that cats and dogs can solve. The maps of reality they possess correspond to reality in ways that enable them to navigate the world well enough to have a reasonable likelihood of meeting their short-term needs. The human brain is a biological structure with its own scope and limits. It stands to reason that there are truths that fall beyond its cognitive reach, things that we are unable to comprehend. Noam Chomsky distinguishes between two kinds of ignorance: problems and mysteries. Problems have solutions that we can comprehend, mysteries do not. Although we lack the means of establishing with precision the boundary between mysteries and problems, we have every reason to suppose it exists. The brain is a biological organ. It did not evolve to understand every facet of the universe. The only reality amenable to our direct, undiluted perception is our own subjective experience.

Uncertainty about the reality behind our perceptions is inescapable but that uncertainty is extremely valuable, for curiosity is deadened by the illusion of knowledge. Answers are preceded by questions, and a question is not asked if the answer is presumed known. When we walk through an unfamiliar place in the dark, our instinctive, physiological response is an increased state of alertness – our senses become heightened, the pupils in our eyes dilate, and we feel our way carefully, straining to make sense of the surroundings, our ears attuned to the slightest sound. Though subjective, our perceptions are not arbitrary. Millions of years of trial and error directed by natural selection have led to increased levels of attentiveness to our immediate environment when we find ourselves in an uncertain state. This response to uncertainty can be harnessed in our pursuit of knowledge.

John Maynard Keynes was once criticised in Parliament for changing his mind on an important issue. He's alleged to have replied: 'When the facts change, I change my mind. What do you do, sir?' We act today in the knowledge that tomorrow may teach us something that will invalidate our reason for action. Unfortunately, in the realms of religion and politics, it's often seen as a sign of strength to commit unwaveringly to a system of belief, even when it contradicts the facts. Many religious groups are explicit on this point: belief without evidence is virtuous. For thousands of years, questioning has been condemned as blasphemous and heretical, punishable by torture and death. But the chain of events leading to a discovery will not be set in motion unless we first admit that we do not yet possess the knowledge we seek.[6] We need to accept and even welcome the uncertainty that comes with not-knowing if we're to continue making breakthroughs.[7] Humility and uncertainty pave the path to knowledge, not arrogance, complacency or faith that we already hold the answers.

The illusion of knowledge is a persistent obstacle to its pursuit. As Mark Twain is reputed to have said: 'It's easier to fool people than to convince them that they have been fooled.' It takes effort to face uncertainty and doubt. The automatic mind continuously generates suggestions: impressions, intuitions, feelings. Questioning is a process of 'unbelieving' what has been accepted. Knowledge is the prize, but it's the end result of a long process. Epiphanies, discoveries, moments of inspiration are nearly always preceded by long periods of uncertainty. If they prove too uncomfortable, we give up and cling to easy answers instead. The eminent physicist Richard Feynman believed that the essence of the scientific approach – doubt and uncertainty – has much to teach wider society:

> The scientist has a lot of experience with ignorance and doubt and uncertainty, and this experience is of very great importance, I think. [. . .] We have found it of paramount importance that in order to progress we must recognize our ignorance and leave room for doubt. Scientific knowledge is a body of statements of varying degrees of certainty – some most unsure, some nearly sure, but none *absolutely* certain. Now we scientists are used to this, and we take it for granted that it is perfectly consistent to be unsure, that it is possible to live and *not* know. But I don't know whether everyone realizes this is true. [. . .] Our freedom to doubt was born out of a struggle against authority in the early days of science. [. . .] Our responsibility is to do what we can, learn what we can, improve the solutions, and pass them on. It is our responsibility to leave the people of the future a free hand. In the impetuous youth of humanity, we can make grave errors that can stunt our growth for a long time. This we will do if we say we have the answers now, so young

and ignorant as we are. If we suppress all discussion, all criticism, proclaiming 'This is the answer, my friends; man is saved!' we will doom humanity for a long time to the chains of authority, confined to the limits of our present imagination. It has been done so many times before. It is our responsibility as scientists, knowing the great progress which comes from a satisfactory philosophy of ignorance, the great progress which is the fruit of freedom of thought, to proclaim the value of this freedom; to teach how doubt is not to be feared but welcomed and discussed; and to demand this freedom as our duty to all coming generations.[8]

The dramatic acceleration of scientific knowledge over the last four centuries is testament to the power of accepting uncertainty and seeking evidence. Doubt invites experimentation. Einstein's prediction that light is deflected by gravity was rejected by almost every authority before it was borne out by observation. Yet, as he is reported to have said, 'No amount of experimentation can ever prove me right; a single experiment can prove me wrong.'[9] Even the best of minds can be proved wrong. Many expert opinions on biology, medicine, physics and chemistry that were held just two hundred years ago seem incredibly outdated today, some of them appear even ridiculous.

To subject our beliefs to experiment is to begin a dialogue with reality. The more precisely we word our questions, the more informative the response will be. Becoming receptive to reality, attempting to engage with it, may require an elaborate and costly experiment (e.g. particle physics at CERN) or be as simple as looking both ways before crossing the road. Ultimately, the demands of a problem dictate the form of our approach. A set approach to problem-solving presumes a sufficient level of understanding about the nature of the problems being solved. This is often warranted but the cutting edge of any discipline deals with problems not yet understood. Over-confidence in a particular method can be counterproductive in the long run. Pursuing truth within the strictures of a methodology risks the complacency that comes with routine. The best method is one that can evolve and adapt.[10]

Tricks of the mind

We attain knowledge by observing the world carefully from a fixed perspective, but we raise our level of objectivity only when we take into account our relation to the world. To develop an understanding of this relationship, it is useful to explore our psychological biases – some of them innate, others the products of our particular experiences. This approach enables us to view our activities and values as we might those of a different species or culture. In doing so, we transform the familiar into the strange, the mundane into the intriguing. We begin to place cultural norms and instinctive responses in the wider context of evolution, history, geography and politics.

We are all engaged in a struggle with the past: to understand, interpret, learn from and accept it. Our capacity to trust, empathise, give and receive affection, form intimate relationships and attain happiness is deeply affected by our early experiences. Formative relationships provide us with templates for later life that can be hard to shake off, even when they are no longer useful. Gender stereotypes place great pressure on us to behave, think, love and work according to prevailing norms, making it hard to develop aspects of ourselves that do not conform to societal expectations. Past conditioning leaves us with a psychological lens through which we perceive and experience the world. We should not forget its existence, that it is one of many, or that we can refocus it. Learning about the impact of our conditioning can be uncomfortable – 'objective' certainties may turn out to be subjective distortions – but failing to question our conditioning can blind us to untapped possibilities in ourselves, others and life itself.

Numerous findings in experimental psychology reveal that most of what the mind does is automatic, beyond conscious control, requiring little or no effort. This complex machinery functions behind an impregnable veil that renders it inaccessible to the conscious mind.[11] When we interpret facial expressions or tone of voice, assess whether one object is nearer than another, answer the question 2 + 2 = ?, flinch at a loud sound, descend a staircase or catch a ball, we do so without having to think about it. Some actions are so automatic they're involuntary. You can't help but distinguish an angry face from a joyful one. You can't help but understand this sentence.

Psychologists have identified a number of mechanisms that predispose us to cling to the views we happen to hold. Confirmation bias is a tendency to privilege information that confirms our beliefs over information that challenges them, so we are drawn to media, people and institutions that reinforce our worldview. We're more likely to believe that a statement is true if we've heard it before, creating a default bias in favour of familiar thoughts and beliefs. We also have a tendency to like or dislike everything about something, be it a person, an idea, a sports team or a nation. This is known as the 'halo effect'. It arises because we're predisposed to create coherent narratives automatically from whatever information we possess. Experimental psychologist Solomon Asch demonstrated the halo effect by asking people to consider descriptions of two people: Alan is intelligent, industrious, impulsive, critical, stubborn and envious. Colin is envious, stubborn, critical, impulsive, industrious and intelligent. Most people feel more favourably towards Alan, even though the traits listed are the same for both men. The first items colour the way we interpret what comes after.

Not all thinking is automatic, however. Some tasks require a lot of conscious focus: memorising a speech, doing mental arithmetic, focusing on one person's voice in a crowded room, filling out a tax form, maintaining a faster walking pace than normal, attempting to communicate in a second language, and so on. Attention is a precious resource. When we focus on one thing, our thinking in other areas becomes more automatic. For instance, when you're trying to hold a shopping list in your short-term memory, you're more likely to resort to superficial judgements, employ racial and gender stereotypes, and believe outrageous statements. Consciously directed thinking takes effort.

The broader lesson is that the workings of the mind generate systematic biases. A particularly problematic tendency of the brain is the habit of jumping to conclusions on limited evidence. This bias means we rarely allow for the possibility that we lack the right information to make a sound judgement. We focus on what we already know, ignore the gaps in our understanding, and fail to ask what evidence would be required to arrive at an informed opinion. The tendency to behave as if 'what we see is all there is', as Daniel Kahneman puts it, makes us susceptible to the effects of framing. Compare how you'd feel if your cardiologist told you that the surgery you needed gave you a 90 per cent chance of surviving with being told that it gave you a 10 per cent chance of dying. The information provided by the statements is equivalent; our emotional response to them is not.

The conscious self can steer the unconscious machinery of the brain, set it tasks, establish goals and determine agendas. It takes mental effort but we can utilise the vast resources of our automatic brain to discover and create what we value. By questioning and reflecting on our internal 'software', we can reprogramme it; we can change ourselves in ways that serve our conception of what is valuable, beautiful and worthwhile. This capacity is central to the pursuit of creative freedom.

Ethologists observing animals in their natural habitat have observed how automatic behaviour in the animal kingdom can be manipulated. Psychologist Robert Cialdini writes that '[i]t is almost as if the patterns were recorded on tapes within the animals. When a situation calls for courtship, a courtship tape gets played; when a situation calls for mothering, a maternal behavior tape gets played.'[12] This pre-recorded behaviour is often triggered by a single specific feature of the environment. To save on brain power, male robins on the lookout for rivals have developed a shortcut: they simply look for red feathers. This has become a trigger for aggressive territorial behaviour. Experiments have shown that a stuffed robin without red feathers provokes no reaction from a male robin, whereas an isolated clump of red feathers triggers violent aggression.[13] Are we so different? We have long been primed to react to religious symbols, national flags and corporate logos.

Our brains are not able to identify and analyse every aspect of every person, event and situation we encounter, so we often classify and react to a few key features. To make sense of the overwhelming quantity of information we are exposed to, we collect distinct phenomena with common properties under generic symbols. 'Yes, every snowflake is unique,' writes Steven Pinker, 'and no category

249

will do complete justice to every one of its members. But intelligence depends on lumping together things that share properties, so that we are not flabbergasted by every new thing we encounter.'[14] However, it is also a mark of intelligence to understand the limited nature of our abstractions. Imagine watching sped-up footage of a decomposing pear on the ground. It changes colour and collapses in on itself until it becomes one with the soil. When two weeks are compressed into thirty seconds, you cease to see a thing – labelled 'pear' – and perceive a process instead. The boundaries of 'pear', 'air' and 'soil' begin to fade. The stability of the nouns we learn is imposed on a world forever in flux.

A conceptual label makes distinctions to help us comprehend the world. The danger is that, as we render the world more manageable, we lose sight of it. It is easy to learn the label, far harder to understand the reality to which it refers. The more general and encompassing a label, the more subtlety and complexity it conceals. We may know that the label 'Second World War' refers to a conflict that began in 1939 and ended in 1945, involving many countries from Hitler's Germany to Churchill's Britain. We may even have read some books describing in detail certain aspects of it – key battles, weaponry, death tolls and so on – but no matter what dates and figures we can reel off, we'll never come close to comprehending the total reality it denotes, which involved countless places, people, struggles, ideas, emotions, stories, tragedies and relationships.

Huge gaps in our knowledge appear to vanish when we name them. The danger of the symbol lies in its ability to discourage thought by providing simplistic shortcuts to beliefs and judgements. This makes them a useful tool of control. Patriotic feelings and religious devotion are skilfully deployed in the cause of war by leaders wrapped in flags, claiming to be God's representatives. Much effort is dedicated to imbuing symbols with powerful emotions. It begins in childhood and continues throughout the process of socialisation. David Spritzler, a twelve-year-old student at Boston Latin School, faced disciplinary action when he refused to recite the following words: 'I pledge allegiance to the flag of the United States of America and to the republic for which it stands:

one nation under God, indivisible, with liberty and justice for all.' According to Spritzler, the pledge is a 'hypocritical exhortation to patriotism' and an attempt to bind 'the oppressed and the oppressors. You have people who drive nice cars, live in nice houses and don't worry about money. Then you have the poor people, living in bad neighbourhoods and going to bad schools. Somehow the Pledge makes it seem that everybody's equal when that's not happening.'[15] The wording of the pledge is significant. It's not to the ideals themselves that allegiance is pledged by the children who recite these words but to a symbol they've been told represents these ideals. This focus is important. The pledge conflates what is valuable − liberty and justice − with a rectangular pattern of colours and shapes − a trigger, like the red feathers so provocative to the male robin. Once people are committed emotionally to a symbol, they're primed to follow it even as it leads them away from the high ideals they believe it represents. Respect for what we believe the label represents can cause us to endorse contradictory ideas and actions without proper scrutiny.

What is a nation? What is a flag? When we ask such questions, all sorts of useful ambiguities rise to the surface. A nation is a fiction maintained by collective belief and a coercive force − it is too large, too complex, with far too many people and far too much history to be captured by our mental conceptions. A flag conceals this complexity. It fosters the illusion of continuity, identity and moral purpose by hiding all the contradictions, internal struggles and hypocrisies. An over-reliance on conceptual shortcuts fosters automatic responses − flag equals liberty, economic growth equals progress − which are vulnerable to manipulation.

Freedom and justice have no nationality, gender or religion. To follow the ideals we cherish, we need to free them from any labels, symbols or entities that claim to represent them. Patriotism is one example but the same holds for many of the ideological and religious labels we adopt. Racism, sexism, homophobia and other forms of irrational prejudice are maintained in part by the power of symbols to conjure up the illusion of knowledge. To reduce a person to a label denoting their skin colour, place of birth, religion, sexuality or gender makes it easy to ignore all that we are ignorant of regarding that person. The ease with which we do this enables us to project our prejudices onto those we label. History shows us that for a group of people to treat another inhumanely they must place them in a separate conceptual category through the use of derogatory, dehumanising labels.

The labels we place on ourselves – liberal, socialist, environmentalist, Christian, Muslim, atheist – can mean different things to different people. Even the same person at different times in their life can have very different views about what a familiar label represents. The categories in which we place ourselves often confuse rather than enlighten, making it easy for others to dismiss our views without having to engage with them. If we seek knowledge and clear communication, we have to peel away the labels that deflect attention from matters of substance and try to be precise about what it is we think. This is more demanding than professing adherence to an ideology or religion, and is not always convenient, but it has the advantage of encouraging clarity and exposing gaps in our own understanding.

Beliefs with benefits

At the age of thirteen, Josh Stieber, horrified by the attacks on the World Trade Center, vowed to join the US Army to fight for the noble ideals of freedom and democracy around the world. He was true to his word. In 2007, after graduating from high school, he enlisted, was sent to Iraq and spent over a year on the ground. However, changed by his experiences, he later applied for – and was eventually granted – conscientious objector status. Talking about his personal journey, he describes the conditioning he received:

> I grew up very religiously and very patriotic . . . I only wanted to hear things that I wanted to hear and only things that I thought would make my country look better and make my beliefs look better, and I wasn't very interested in understanding other perspectives. And the vision I had of my country was that, you know, we were going all throughout the world doing . . . all this great stuff and helping people in need . . . [A]fter 9/11 I was obviously affected

252

. . . and wanted to protect the people that I cared about, and, from everyone I trusted, was told that the military would be a good way to do that . . .[16]

Stieber explains that his patriotism was closely tied to his religious beliefs: 'in a government class that I was in at this religious high school, we read a book called *The Faith of George W. Bush*. And people like that were held up as, you know . . . people that are fighting for God's will here on Earth. So religion was very interwoven with a sense of nation-alism.'[17] Doubts about the path he had chosen began to surface during army boot camp. 'Training was very desensitizing. We screamed slogans like, "Kill them all, let God sort them out." We watched videos with bombs being dropped on Middle Eastern villages with rock and roll music in the background. People really started to celebrate death and destruction, and that definitely didn't match up to what I'd expected.' He and his friends were taught to march to the following chant: 'I went down to the market where all the women shop; I pulled out my machete and I begin to chop. I went down to the park where all the children play; I pulled out my machine gun and I begin to spray.'[18]

Confronted with the reality of war, Stieber's doubts grew stronger. The ideals he held dear clashed with the reality of military action. He recalls that, as violence in his province escalated, 'our battalion commanders gave the order that every time a bomb went off, we were entitled to open fire on whoever was standing around. The way I interpreted that was that we were told to out-terrorize the terrorists. That was really troubling for me . . .'[19] It wasn't long before Stieber found himself in the aftermath of an explosion, but he refused to shoot unarmed civilians. His actions were criticised by his superiors and he was fired as a gunner, becoming a radio operator instead.

At the base, a couple of shops sold bootleg DVDs to the soldiers. He ended up watching the film *Gandhi* and was introduced to a new philosophy of struggle that resonated with the moral ideals that had motivated him to fight in the first place. Inspired by the non-violent methods of Gandhi, he decided that he'd rather go to military jail than continue as he was. 'This inward reality that I had started to explore and that had started to bring meaning back into my life – preserving that became more important than preserving my external reality.'[20]

To stay true to his core values, Stieber had to redraw his internal map of reality. He had to re-evaluate the labels he'd learned and question the games he had been taught to play, expose their inconsistencies and begin the process of determining his own values and the rules that best expressed them. This brought him into direct conflict with his fellow soldiers, superiors, and even his own family. Yet by confronting the contradictions between his beliefs and actions, he learned more about what really mattered to him and how to protect it.

Stieber's story stands out because challenging such a deeply ingrained worldview is rare and difficult. Yale University's Cultural Cognition Project has demonstrated just how adept we are at ignoring evidence and selectively picking facts to confirm views held in common with the cultural group we identify with. One study looked at attitudes towards climate change. Dan Kahan and colleagues found that the facts of climate science were accepted or rejected according to pre-existing worldviews. Contrary to expectations, this effect became stronger with greater scientific literacy. In other words, those who better understood the implications of the science for their value system were more likely to respond in accordance with their worldviews. Kahan reports:

> When told the solution to global warming is increased antipollution measures, persons of individualistic and hierarchic worldviews become less willing to . . . [believe] information suggesting that global warming exists, is caused by humans, and poses significant societal dangers. Persons with such outlooks are more willing to . . . [believe] the same information when told the solution to global warming is increased reliance on nuclear power generation.[21]

Kahan and his colleagues found that differences in these basic values exert more influence over the perception of climate change than any other individual attribute: gender, race, education, income or even party affiliation. To challenge the worldview of our cultural group risks losing valued friendships, a sense of belonging and the privileges that come with membership. This creates a bias in favour of deploying or disregarding facts according to their usefulness in defending values to which we are already committed. Kahan argues that we have a strong bias against information that threatens our 'preferred vision of a good society'.[22] The danger is that citizens 'experience scientific debates as contests between warring cultural factions – and . . . pick sides accordingly'.[23]

In a 2016 national survey published in the journal *Science*, US researchers investigating how climate change was being taught in schools discovered some surprising trends. Only a minority of teachers were aware that the vast majority of scientists agreed climate change was caused by humans (the figure is about 97 per cent) and, true to the findings of Kahan and his colleagues, those teachers who identified with small government and free markets were 'least likely to be aware of or accept the scientific consensus'.[24]

When we fear the implications of our own values in light of an honest appraisal of the facts, a common response is to deceive ourselves. In order to justify his lifestyle, an eighteenth-century plantation owner needed to believe slaves were sub-human because his own value system would have told him that enslaving people of equal status was wrong. The need to dehumanise reveals an appreciation of the importance of human dignity. The denial of climate facts in order to protect a worldview that champions deregulation and small government also implicitly recognises that if a choice has to be made between protecting profit and protecting the environment, the latter is more important. Contesting the facts is often proof of shared fundamental values. Self-deception is a mechanism by which we avoid the discomfort of perceiving the clash of core values, beliefs and perceived interests. It does not settle the question of what we truly value; it merely postpones having to ask it. Like the man who ignores the symptoms of his disease to avoid confronting an uncomfortable truth, it is a disempowering response, one that reduces our creative freedom.

We adopt and defend beliefs for many reasons that have nothing to do with their accuracy. As the writer Upton Sinclair observed, 'It is difficult to get a man to understand something when his salary depends upon his not understanding it.'[25] Yet, perceptions of self-interest are often flawed. It is easy to be lazy, callous and ungenerous, but to learn what it means to act in our own interest, to be truly selfish, is one of life's great challenges: it requires that we know what we really value and how to dedicate ourselves to it. The hordes of deeply unhappy, dissatisfied, disillusioned people in the world – including many with wealth, fame and power – are a testament to this challenge. In life, the default outcome is not that we act in our self-interest but that we change ourselves to meet the needs of the games we are taught to play.

It is a mistake to conflate power with freedom or happiness. Relationships of control systematically stunt the emotional and psychological development of oppressors as well as the oppressed. In this sense, the liberation of oppressors is bound up with the liberation of those they oppress. It would be misleading to conceive of, say, feminism as a movement only to liberate women. As Rebecca Solnit writes:

> Women's liberation has often been portrayed as a movement intent on encroaching upon or taking power and privilege away from men, as though in some dismal zero-sum game, only one gender at a time could be free and powerful. But we are free together or slaves together. Surely, the mindset of those who think they need to win, to dominate, to punish, to reign supreme must be terrible and far from free, and giving up this unachievable pursuit would be liberatory.[26]

Systems of male privilege impose oppressive stereotypes on men as well as women, and these can distort and constrain the identities and lives of men. Prominent models of masculinity that, for instance, discourage men from sharing their feelings or appearing weak and vulnerable may help to explain why rates of male suicide are between three and seven times higher than female suicide across the world, and why, in the UK in 2015, suicide was the biggest cause of death for men under the age of 45.[27] By granting men power over women, patriarchy robs both of the freedom to define their own identity, to cultivate their diverse capacities, to benefit from each other's flourishing. In countless ways, our artistic, intellectual, emotional, and moral lives are enriched, not threatened, by the liberation of others.

The truth may set us free, but it can also strip us of any sense of entitlement to advantages we have become accustomed to and drive a wedge between us and the cultural groups to which we belong. Privilege is a persistent obstacle to knowledge, a comfortable cage in which we insulate ourselves from reality. It gives no special insight into what makes life valuable or meaningful, but it does give us a reason to postpone finding out. The extra comfort, status and pleasure it affords threaten to hook those accustomed to it to a lifestyle that neglects other fundamental needs and crowds out other dimensions of value.

Even with the best of intentions, it is hard to perceive the truth of our privilege and the ways we facilitate the oppression of others. Studies show that of those people who believe racial prejudice is wrong, many harbour unconscious racist attitudes that reflect prevalent social stereotypes. A programme at Stanford University called Recruitment to Expand Diversity and Excellence found that about three out of four 'whites and Asians demonstrated an implicit bias in favor of whites compared to blacks'.[28] These hidden biases can have a significant impact on behaviour. One study showed that, as the implicit racial bias of white medical residents increased, their treatment of black patients worsened: they were less likely to administer life-saving drugs and more likely to recommend unnecessary surgeries.[29]

All privilege is built on accident and injustice.[30] Unravelling the intricate dynamics of power, privilege and prejudice takes commitment and humility. It is a lifelong journey. No one gets it right all the time, and understanding one form of oppression is no guarantee of understanding another. It takes persistent effort to dispel the alluring myth that one's advantages are somehow deserved. It is a myth that returns again and again in countless ways to justify the unjustifiable. The myth has long been strengthened by acts of charity in which the privileged come to see themselves as saviours of the oppressed, failing to recognise that the system which grants them undeserved privilege condemns the oppressed to undeserved oppression. The pioneering Brazilian educator Paulo Freire, who worked closely with the impoverished peasants of

Brazil, observed that 'True generosity consists precisely in fighting to destroy the causes which nourish false charity.'[31] Another convenient rationalisation is that we are apolitical – impartial, neutral, objective; dispassionately observing reality rather than actively creating it; contemplating the struggles of humanity rather than taking part in them. This attitude is often fostered by educational institutions and reinforced by professional norms, but the pretence of neutrality only hides conformity to dominant power structures. No life is politically neutral.

To be the people we wish to be, we have to battle against the forces of habit, ignorance, fear and unwanted desire. Before we can challenge an oppressive map of reality, we have to free ourselves from its grasp. Internalised oppression is ubiquitous, manifesting in many ways and to varying degrees. Over a century ago, the sociologist, historian and civil rights activist W. E. B. Du Bois described the 'double-consciousness' of black Americans, 'this sense of always looking at one's self through the eyes of others, of measuring one's soul by the tape of a world that looks on in amused contempt and pity'.[32] To varying degrees, this holds for all those who fall beyond the narrow conception of normality established by society.

The process of questioning and reasoning forces us to make hard choices. It exposes inconsistencies and contradictions, casting doubt over convenient beliefs. As Bertrand Russell writes:

> [People] fear thought as they fear nothing else on earth – more than ruin, more even than death. Thought is subversive and revolutionary, destructive and terrible, thought is merciless to privilege, established institutions, and comfortable habits; thought is anarchic and lawless, indifferent to authority, careless of the well-tried wisdom of the ages. Thought looks into the pit of hell and is not afraid . . .[33]

In striving to advance our freedom, it's not so much ignorance that impedes our progress but ignorance of ignorance. All worldviews are flawed, but some are more receptive to evidence than others. When the process of questioning, reasoning and seeking evidence is highly valued by a cultural group, adjusting opinions and priorities in light of compelling discoveries can feel like a confirmation of an identity rather than a threat to it. The scientist who discards a long held, cherished theory in light of new evidence can draw strength from the fact that her identity as a scientist – a 'seeker of knowledge' – has been vindicated by her willingness to submit to the evidence. Nevertheless, even among scientists, questioning old ideas is not easy. The physicist Max Planck once said: 'Science advances one funeral at a time.'

As Josh Stieber's story demonstrates, it can often take a crisis to overcome the inertia of existence and the grip of cultural conditioning. Interestingly, psychologists have found that most people who suffer trauma experience a profound sense of personal growth after the event.[34] This can take the form of improved relationships, increased empathy, a renewed appreciation of life, an openness to new possibilities or a greater sense of personal strength. The most accepted explanation for such transformations comes from the psychologists Richard Tedeschi and Lawrence Calhoun, who coined the term 'post-traumatic growth'.[35] They argue that a traumatic event has the power to challenge core beliefs and assumptions about who we are and what is of value, shocking us out of complacency and shattering the foundations of our worldview. Destruction precedes creativity. Marie Forgeard, a psychologist at Harvard Medical School, argues: 'We're forced to reconsider things we took for granted, and we're forced to think about new things.'[36] It's a challenging and difficult process to go through, but, alongside grief and loss, immensely positive change can occur. These findings do not suggest that trauma is necessary or sufficient to engage in serious questioning but they do show the benefits of casting doubt over our maps of reality, reconsidering what makes life valuable and reimagining the kind of life we want to lead.

The distortions of power

Just months before the housing bubble burst in 2007, Jean-Philippe Cotis, Chief Economist at the OECD, declared, 'Our central forecast remains quite benign'.[37] He was not alone in his assessment. Remarkably, the mainstream of the economics profession – neoclassical economics

– failed to predict the seismic financial quake that began towards the end of 2007. Some economists did make impressively accurate predictions, forecasting a real estate crisis, warning of a severe recession caused by the financial sector, and explaining the mechanisms by which this would take place. They even gave a timeframe within which it would occur and publicly declared their concerns. However, none of them came from the neoclassical school and their warnings fell on deaf ears, or worse, were derided.[38] Given that a crucial test of a theory is its predictive power, this was a very public failure for the mainstream of the profession, yet perhaps it was unsurprising when we consider that the forecasting models being used de-emphasised, or omitted entirely, important features of the economy employed by heterodox economists, including credit, banks, securitisation and income distribution.

There are many schools of economic thought – Marxist, feminist, institutional, ecological, post-Keynesian, classical, Austrian, development, to name a few. Each conceptualises the subject in different ways, in part because they are grounded in different ethical and political values, but university courses in economics tend to focus almost exclusively on the neoclassical school. In its cruder formulations, neoclassical economics has a clear free-market bias. Unfortunately, as economist Robert Prasch notes, 'market fundamentalism remains the perspective of virtually every introductory economics textbook'.[39] Students are not exposed to many of the theory's crucial caveats and qualifications unless they take on postgraduate study. Most never make it that far and graduate from college believing in a caricature of just one school of economic thought.[40] Thomas Piketty's critique of his profession is damning: 'To put it bluntly, the discipline of economics has yet to get over its childish passion for mathematics and for purely theoretical and often highly ideological speculation, at the expense of historical research and collaboration with the other social sciences.'[41]

The failure of mainstream economics to predict or deal with the financial crash has not yet resulted in the rewriting of textbooks but it has helped to galvanise a growing movement of economics students who are calling for an overhaul of how their subject is taught. Protest groups spanning thirty countries are now demanding radical change to their courses. It is worth quoting their manifesto at length:

> The lack of intellectual diversity does not only restrain education and research. It limits our ability to contend with the multi-dimensional challenges of the 21st century – from financial stability to food security and climate change. The real world should be brought back into the classroom, as well as debate and a pluralism of theories and methods. This will help renew the discipline and ultimately create a space in which solutions to society's problems can be generated . . .
>
> [E]conomics is often presented as a unified body of knowledge. Admittedly, the dominant tradition has internal variations. Yet, it is only one way of doing economics and of looking at the real world. Such uniformity is unheard of in other fields; nobody would take seriously a degree program in psychology that focuses only on Freudianism, or a politics program that focuses only on state socialism. An inclusive and comprehensive economics education should promote balanced exposure to a variety of theoretical perspectives, from the commonly taught neoclassically-based approaches to the largely excluded classical, post-Keynesian, institutional, ecological, feminist, Marxist and Austrian traditions – among others. Most economics students graduate without ever encountering such diverse perspectives in the classroom . . .
>
> [And] students should be systematically exposed to the history of economic thought and to the classical literature on economics as well as to economic history . . .
>
> Economics is a social science; complex economic phenomena can seldom be understood if presented in a vacuum, removed from their sociological, political, and historical contexts. To properly discuss economic policy, students should understand the broader social impacts and moral implications of economic decisions.[42]

This battle is important; few subjects have as much influence on our world. Economic theory shapes our thinking on wealth distribution, markets, unions, taxes, the role of government and even human nature, but the subject has been politically compromised. One way to highlight the bias of the subject in its prevailing form is to look at the impact on those who are taught it. Numerous studies show that an education in neoclassical economics reduces cooperation, generosity and ethical behaviour. One study found that it 'was associated with more positive attitudes towards greed and towards one's own greedy behaviour', and students who had taken at least three economics courses were more likely than peers to regard greed as 'good', 'correct' or 'moral'.[43] Israeli researchers found that third-year economics students rated honesty, loyalty and helpfulness as significantly less important than first-year students.[44] Another study that looked at how the political views of students changed over time found that 10 per cent of first-year economics students regarded themselves as conservative whereas by the fifth year the number had risen to 23 per cent. This mirrored a significant drop in the number of those who described themselves as 'radical', a percentage which fell from 13 per cent in their first year to 1 per cent five years on.[45] It has even been found that economics professors in the US give less money to charity than professors of philosophy, psychology, history, sociology, physics, chemistry, biology, anthropology or literature.[46]

The neoclassical approach, in studying individual choices, accepts as given the distribution of wealth and power so that the focus tends to be on what can be achieved within prevailing social structures. This marginalises solutions to problems that involve systemic change.[47] This is not politically neutral. Nor is it neutral to present economics as a value-free science, to promote endless economic growth in a world of finite resources, to foster selfishness and greed in those who study the subject, to focus on abstract mathematical modelling at the expense of understanding history or real world economies, or to equate 'economics' with a single school of thought when many other sophisticated schools exist. Ideological bias is pervasive and highly convenient for those who wish to defend the vast inequalities of our present system and the power of private capital.

The battles surrounding the framing, teaching and practice of economics are a microcosm of the wider political struggle to control ideas and information. As we question the foundations of our identity and the forces that shaped it, we have to contend with the webs of deceit and secrecy that have been spun throughout our society. The interests and goals of the powerful exert a selection pressure on ideas, facts and values, filtering out some and amplifying others. We see this in prevailing historical narratives. Just as mainstream economics privileges one theoretical perspective to the exclusion of others, history is overwhelmingly seen through the eyes of kings and queens, military leaders, prime ministers and presidents. Generations of children have heard the heroic story of Christopher Columbus – a brave explorer whose voyages led to the 'discovery' of the Americas. With few exceptions, the perspective of the Arawaks, who warmly greeted Columbus to their shores – viewed by the sixteenth-century Spanish state as 'natural slaves' created by God to serve their conquerors – has been omitted. Columbus's legacy of genocide, slavery, torture and theft has, for many, been airbrushed out of existence.

Flattering myths about the past buy legitimacy in the present. A YouGov poll in 2016 showed that more Britons were proud of their nation's colonial legacy than regretted it.[48] This is unsurprising considering that the crimes of the British Empire are unknown to most people. There certainly has been no shortage of historians or political leaders ready to declare that the nation should be proud of its imperial past.[49] That the empire is responsible for the deaths of tens of millions of people, that it reaped huge profits from the slave trade, locked up hundreds of thousands in concentration camps (including many children), massacred civilians and is guilty of systematic brutality, torture and theft is not part of the nation's consciousness. These crimes are omitted from the national curriculum, but their suppression goes far beyond school textbooks. In 2012, it was revealed that the British government had destroyed thousands of documents detailing the mistreatment of colonial subjects, and that those papers not destroyed had been hidden for fifty years in a Foreign Office archive, contravening the legal obligation for them to be transferred into the public domain.[50] Instructions had been given in 1961 by Ian Macleod, Secretary of State for the Colonies, that post-colonial governments should be denied any material that 'might embarrass Her Majesty's government' or 'members of the police, military forces, public servants or others, e.g. police informers' or that might 'be used unethically by ministers in the successor government'.[51]

Careful scholarship has revealed that, behind the official myth of British benevolence, there is indeed much to 'embarrass Her Majesty's government'. In 2006, a book called *Imperial Reckoning: The Untold Story of Britain's Gulag in Kenya,* by Harvard professor Caroline Elkins, won the Pulitzer Prize for General Non-fiction. It detailed Britain's crimes in the suppression of the Kikuyu's Mau Mau revolt in 1950s Kenya. After a decade of research, Elkins found that the official account – still repeated by many journalists and historians – was highly sanitised and false on numerous counts. The official line was that 80,000 people had been detained in camps by British authorities. In fact, almost 1.5 million people were held in camps and fortified villages, where thousands were beaten to death and well over 100,000 people, including many children, died from malnutrition and disease. Those who were detained were forced into slave labour. Disobedient individuals were murdered in front of other inmates to set an example. Many were subjected to interrogation and horrific forms of torture, including castration with pliers and being burned alive. The brutal rape of male and female prisoners by their guards, sometimes with knives or broken glass, was also practised. These crimes, Elkins found, were backed by senior government figures.[52]

State control of public perception continues to be a vital part of achieving foreign policy goals. When the UK's Ministry of Defence temporarily rebranded its state propaganda from 'psychological operations' to 'information support', the House of Commons Defence Committee stated that 'the concept has changed little from the traditional objective of influencing the perceptions of selected audiences'.[53] The aim remained to 'mobilise and sustain support for a particular policy and interpretation of events'. As one former intelligence officer declared, the purpose of MI6's psychological warfare section is 'massaging public opinion into accepting controversial foreign policy decisions'.[54] A Ministry of Defence paper concurred with this position when it suggested that 'we need to be aware of the ways in which public attitudes might shape and constrain military activity . . . public support will be vital to the conduct of military interventions'.[55] In December 2003, another official report argued that future military operations should 'place greater emphasis on information and media operations, which are critical to success'.[56] It also observed that the tactic of embedding journalists with the US–British military had been successful, the analysis showing that 90 per cent of the reporting done by embedded correspondents 'was either positive or neutral'.[57] In 2015, it was announced that the army was setting up a new unit to expand its 'psychological operations'. Historian Mark Curtis writes that 'Government propaganda towards the British public is a permanent aspect of major operations, especially military interventions, in every British foreign policy I have looked at.'[58]

Omission and concealment are effective forms of deceit, but outright fabrications are sometimes required to construct the desired narrative. The 2003 invasion of Iraq was justified with a deception about weapons of mass destruction that was perpetuated by US and UK leaders and repeated, most of the time uncritically, by the mainstream media. The deception had been cultivated for over a decade. According to Scott Ritter, a former chief UN weapons inspector, MI6 had 'institutionalised a process of "cherry picking" intelligence produced by the UN inspections in Iraq that skewed UK intelligence about Iraqi WMD towards a pre-ordained outcome that was more in line with British government policy than it was reflective of ground truth'.[59] Pulitzer prize-winning investigative journalist Seymour Hersh cites a former US intelligence officer as saying 'the Brits wanted to plant stories in England and elsewhere'. They were fed dozens of unverified intelligence reports from a supportive member of the UN weapons inspection team to spread throughout the media, but 'it was intelligence that was crap, and that we couldn't move on'.[60] Such planting of fabricated stories in the domestic and international press by state intelligence services is routine practice.

The 1991 invasion of Iraq, led by the US with support from the UK, was accompanied by a story about Iraqi forces removing Kuwaiti babies from incubators and leaving them to die. This shocking accusation, apparently from an anonymous eyewitness, was widely disseminated by politicians and the media, yet, once the tale had served its purpose, it was exposed as a fiction. The supposed eyewitness was a young girl called Nayirah, the daughter of the Kuwaiti ambassador. Her testimony was traced to a meeting of the Congressional Human Rights Caucus, stage-managed by the vice-president of American firm Hill & Knowlton, one of the world's largest PR companies, which also happened to be on the payroll of the Kuwaiti royal family in exile.[61] A few decades before that, in August 1964, the American public was told by President Johnson of an unprovoked attack on a US destroyer in the Gulf of Tonkin. This invention served to whip up public support and establishment approval for a full-scale war with North Vietnam. It often takes the courage of individual whistleblowers to lift the lid on persistent lying. Daniel Ellsberg's release of the Pentagon Papers in 1971 demonstrated, as described by *The New York Times*, 'that the Johnson Administration had systematically lied, not only to the public but also to Congress, about a subject of transcendent national interest and significance'.[62]

Government transparency is a vital part of a functioning democracy, which is why policies of concealment are so common. Negotiations around far-reaching trade deals, for instance, often take place in secrecy. In August 2015, during the negotiations for the highly controversial Transatlantic Trade and Investment Partnership (TTIP) – an agreement that threatens to undermine the sovereignty of democratically elected governments by granting excessive rights to corporations – the European Commission introduced a rule that meant politicians could only view the text in a secure 'reading room'. Electronic transmission of the text was limited to prevent leaks to the public. In stark contrast, *The Guardian* reported in 2015 that the EU has granted ExxonMobil privileged access to 'negotiating strategies' that were 'considered too sensitive to be released to the European public' and that one oil refinery association had been asked 'for "concrete input" on the text of an energy chapter for the negotiations, as part of the EU's bid to write unfettered imports of US crude oil and gas into the trade deal'.[63]

You don't need to suppress facts if they haven't yet been uncovered. In 2016, the Conservative government blocked moves for an impact assessment of its proposed cuts to the Employment and Support Allowance (ESA), an essential benefit for disabled people. Research by the Disability Benefits Consortium found that the benefit was already so low that many who receive it struggle to heat their homes and stay healthy, with some unable to afford enough food to eat. Yet an understanding of the impact of reducing this meagre benefit was not welcomed by those making the proposals. Calls for this assessment by the Labour opposition, the House of Lords and civil society were ignored, and the cuts were pushed through. When you know the answer will undermine your agenda, why allow the question to be asked? In 2016, Chancellor George Osborne scrapped an official 'distributional' analysis designed to reveal how much money his budgets take from the poor and give to the rich.[64] The simple act of failing to keep records is a way of obscuring public understanding. It's remarkable, for instance, that there is no comprehensive database in the US that tracks the number of civilians killed by police and corrections officers. The situation is improving, but it has taken years of pressure.

When we consider the revelations leaked by Edward Snowden, exposing the vast global surveillance powers of the NSA, a broader pattern can be discerned: while public access to state information is under attack, state access to private information is increasing. In 2013, the Conservative Party deleted a decade of speeches from its website, a number of which contained commitments and promises it had made to the electorate. Ironically, one of these speeches had Conservative leader David Cameron extolling the democratising virtues of the internet by making 'more information available to more people'. In another deleted speech from 2007, George Osborne declared: 'We need to harness the internet to help us become more accountable, more transparent and more accessible – and so bridge the gap between government and governed.'[65] According to *The Guardian*, 'In a remarkable step the party has also blocked access to the Internet Archive's Wayback Machine, a US-based library that captures web pages for future generations, using a software robot that directs search engines not to access the pages.'[66] After attempting to wipe clean their own online history, the Conservative government proposed a bill in 2016 to extend the powers of police to access private web histories and to hack into smartphones.[67]

The evolution of dominant economic ideas, political ideologies and historical narratives is the outcome of struggle. Trying to make sense of the world without factoring in the distorting force of concentrated power is like trying to understand the movements of galaxies without taking into account the gravitational distortions of concentrated matter. The trajectory of a falling apple and the orbit of a moon are both manifestations of this invisible, far-reaching force. Similarly, a vast array of social phenomena, on scales large and small – from the content of economics textbooks to advertising billboards, from historical narratives to the evening news – can only be properly understood by taking into account the systematic distorting effects of those who control society's resources, which are invariably states and corporations.

Even the practice of science is not immune to these corrupting effects. Private pharmaceutical companies routinely hold back the results of their own studies, placing profit before patients. Roughly half of all clinical trials, involving hundreds of thousands of participants, have never been publicly reported. As physician Ben Goldacre explains:

> Nobody can give you a fully informed view on the benefits of any treatment . . . because the results of clinical trials are being routinely and legally withheld from doctors, researchers and patients . . . This undermines our ability to make informed decisions on everything from surgical techniques to drugs and devices. Unsurprisingly, trials with positive results are twice as likely to be published as those with negative results, so the evidence we do see is potentially biased . . . Information isn't just passively left unpublished: it is actively withheld when requested by researchers.[68]

The upshot is that independent researchers are unable to verify claims about safety and effectiveness that 'Big Pharma' makes about its products. A campaign to change this, spearheaded by Goldacre and comprising a number of groups, including the *British Medical Journal* and the Centre for Evidence-based Medicine, has met with corporate resistance. Drug companies have 'mobilised' a number of patient groups to lobby on their behalf against any laws that would force them to publish the results of their trials. When facts threaten profits, they are marginalised, denied and distorted. As we will see in Chapter 11, even the dissemination of scientific discoveries, vital for the survival of much of humanity, has been undermined and obfuscated for decades by corporations intent on protecting their short-term profit.

There is no shortage of valuable information, but when it challenges the dominant ideologies of those who wield wealth and power, it struggles to permeate the public consciousness. Like the invisible force of gravity, concentrated power warps our perceptual environment. Our perceptions may not be manipulated by Descartes' evil demon, but they are subject to numerous social forces intent on censoring, framing and fabricating information.

It takes persistent and collective effort to compensate for these effects. The output of the media needs to be scrutinised in the wider context of market competition, corporate advertising and the interests of billionaire owners. The content of a school curriculum needs to be considered in the wider context of state priorities, prevailing ideologies and commercial pressures. The work of academics and scientists has to be evaluated in the wider context of the structure and funding of universities and think tanks, and the nature of professional incentives that permeate these institutions.

The practice of questioning, seeking evidence, establishing reliable sources and honing the capacity to reason effectively has always been a part of the fight for freedom, but no one can do it alone. Every discovery, insight and creation emerges from a vast web of relationships stretching far and wide, across time and space. The ability to make use of this rich tapestry of knowledge and experience is closely tied to the privileges we enjoy. In a world of misdirection, in which opportunities are so unevenly distributed, it is vital to build movements that develop and popularise an understanding of who possesses power, the mechanisms by which they hold onto it, how this power can be overcome, and the alternative ways in which it could be distributed – to join the dots between disparate consequences and common causes, and provide illuminating context for the steady unfolding of history. No movement or group will get it right all the time, truth can never be monopolised, but if people do not work together to compensate for the distortions of power, they will be systematically misled.

Each generation is trained to fulfil functions within the machinery of the present system, not to fundamentally change it. Movements for freedom work to disrupt this process and to challenge how we think and what we believe is possible. From independent journalism, art and social media to community organising, civil disobedience and protest, a range of possibilities exist to mount a powerful challenge to established narratives and ideas. Of central importance is the peeling away of the excluding jargon in which so many important questions are wrapped. By framing moral challenges as technical problems, people are discouraged from participating in the vital discussions that affect their lives. Ha-Joon Chang argues that today's economists fulfil the function of the priesthood in medieval Europe: 'In the old days, they refused to translate the Bible, so unless you knew Latin you couldn't read it. Today, unless you are good at maths and statistics, you cannot penetrate the economic literature.'[69] In each case, power is insulated from scrutiny and criticism.

Before the failings of society can be addressed, they need to be recognised, their causes identified and their solutions understood. Central to a politics of freedom is the sharing of knowledge and the exposing of lies. It includes attempts to encourage, inspire and sometimes shock others into seeing the world in new ways. Those groups who encounter the most prejudice wield the least power, so their perspectives are systematically marginalised. It has always taken a great deal of effort, creativity and courage to compel society to see itself from critical viewpoints, through the eyes of those it is failing.[70] Movements for freedom demand that we try to look at the world through many eyes, and in doing so expose the hypocrisies and injustices concealed by self-serving narratives and ideologies.

★

Beliefs about the future are not bound by reality in the same way as those about the past. Although all maps of reality should aim to inform, maps of the future should also aim to inspire. They can fill us with the energy and hope to create something better. If we don't believe in the possibility of a better future, we won't make the effort to create it. Maps of the present need to highlight the most pressing problems of society: the absence of genuine democracy, the power of capital, the injustice of inequality, the systematic oppression of marginalised groups, the systemic bias of the media, and the urgent threat of climate change. If a movement that can overcome the power of private capital is to take root, it has to unite around a common vision for change, one that can counter the claim that 'there is no alternative'. When the next crisis hits and old certainties appear to crumble, this vision needs to command enough support to be transformed into reality.

There are those who are called 'realists' because their map of the future deviates little from the conventional maps of the present. By contrast, those who imagine something different are often labelled 'dreamers'. History teaches us that it has always taken 'dreamers' to improve things. It took bold imaginations to abolish slavery, spread democracy, win rights for women, gay people and people of colour, and to expand our moral, artistic and scientific horizons. If the evolution of human culture is to continue, our collective imagination must travel far beyond the limits of present experience.

10

Power

While India starved, her crops fed the English. This was the Great
Famine of 1876–8, which by some estimates took over 10 million lives.[1]
Throughout the famine, Viceroy Lord Lytton oversaw the export to
England of a record 6.4 million hundredweight of wheat. The celebrated
railroads built by the British were used to export vast quantities of grain
from drought-stricken regions to centrally located stores for hoarding
and protection. Grain prices soared as hunger struck. By late 1877, as
historian Mike Davis describes, 'social order was preserved only by
terror. When desperate women and their hungry children, for example,
attempted to steal from gardens or glean grain from fields, they were
"branded, tortured, had their noses cut off, and were sometimes killed".'[2]

Lytton was a free-marketeer who believed in the sanctity of private
trade. As millions died of hunger-related illnesses, he argued against
government intervention. He dismissed as 'humanitarian hysterics' the
concerns of those who were troubled by his policies.[3] Typically, the
victims were blamed for their plight. Senior British officials branded
starving peasants as idle, criminal and incapable of following orders.
Once the crop failure had passed, the military sought to obtain all
unpaid taxes and debts from the decimated peasantry. Behind the actions
of Lytton and others was a cold calculation summed up by the famine
commission of 1878–80: 'The doctrine that in time of famine the poor
are entitled to demand relief . . . would probably lead to the doctrine

that they are entitled to relief at all times . . . which we cannot contemplate without serious apprehension.'[4]

A similar crime had been committed in Ireland during the Great Hunger of the 1840s: the Irish died as Irish-grown food was exported to England. And the justification was the same: the workings of the market should not be interfered with. In both cases, millions starved not because there wasn't enough food but because there wasn't enough democracy. This is the rule, not the exception. No major famine has ever occurred in a political democracy, even in those democracies that are extremely poor and suffer periodic food shortages. In every instance we know of, the decisive cause of major famine has not been the lack of food (though shortages play a part), but a lack of control over the supply by those who subsequently starved. India suffered numerous famines under British rule right up to Independence (the Bengal famine started in 1943), after which they 'disappeared suddenly with the establishment of a multiparty democracy and a free press'.[5] The historical record has shown that even limited democratic accountability makes a big difference. Pioneering economist Amartya Sen writes:

> Famines have occurred in ancient kingdoms and contemporary authoritarian societies . . . modern technocratic dictatorships, in colonial economies run by imperialists from the north and in newly independent countries of the south run by despotic national leaders or by intolerant single parties. But they have never materialized in any country that is independent, that goes to elections regularly, that has opposition parties to voice criticisms and that permits newspapers to report freely and question the wisdom of government policies without extensive censorship.[6]

By contrast, authoritarian rule has a long history of famines, whether in Ireland and India under British rule, the Soviet Union, China, Cambodia, Ethiopia, Somalia or North Korea. It's a grim history. Between 30 and 60 million people perished during avoidable famines in the last quarter of the nineteenth century alone.[7] In the twentieth century, more than 70 million people died in avoidable famines.[8] In almost every case, people could have been fed from surpluses kept elsewhere in the nation, empire or region. What causes people to starve is not weather patterns but commodity markets, price speculation, authoritarian institutions and international indifference.

Although millions died because of his decision to export grain, Lytton's own calorific intake went unaffected. We can only wonder how long his commitment to the 'free market' would have lasted if he had been the one starving. Without the freedom to influence the decisions that affect our lives, we are extremely vulnerable. Options can be drastically reduced by those who control the conditions of our existence, opening the way for the most severe forms of oppression.

Self-defence, self-development

Few would deny that hoarding and exporting grain during a famine is immoral. However, the hoarding and exporting of wealth occurs on a daily basis across the globe. Trillions of dollars rest in international tax havens while billions of people go without clean water, a nutritious diet, life-saving medicine or basic liberties. The same economic and political forces that determine who survives a famine are at work every moment of every day deciding who eats or starves, who's imprisoned or free, who lives or dies. These are the forces that buried hundreds of textile workers beneath an eight-storey factory in Rana Plaza, Bangladesh, drove tens of thousands of Indian farmers to suicide, and condemn hundreds of thousands of African children to die each year from malaria. They push a million people to food banks in the UK, and drag one in three children into poverty in the US.

Whenever there is a significant imbalance of power between groups, the weaker is vulnerable to the whims of the stronger. As the balance improves in favour of the disempowered group, so does the quality of their options – all else being equal – and with it the ability to identify and pursue what they value. This is why people have fought for centuries to decentralise power by establishing and extending democratic forms of decision-making. While these may vary over time and place depending on culture, scale, experience and immediate goals, they are linked by the simple conviction that people have the right to manage their own lives.

It has become commonplace to define democracy quite narrowly. Political scientist Samuel Huntington offers a typical summation: 'Elections, open, free, and fair, are the essence of democracy, the inescapable sine qua non.'[9] But the way modern elections work is just one manifestation of the democratic impulse, and one that most of the time fails to empower people. Democracy demands more: conditions that allow people to pursue a deeper understanding of themselves and their world, and institutions that provide the options to participate meaningfully in the decisions that affect their lives.

Democratic structures have emerged all over the world at different times and places, from African and Indian villages to pirate ships and peasant communities, from Ancient Greece to seventh-century Japan, and from the Zapatistas in Mexico and workers' councils in Venezuela to the Global Justice Movement and the Occupy movement. These experiments offer valuable insights into how people can solve common social problems in a participatory way. Democracy is not a peculiarly Western invention. Nor is it a single set of institutions. Experiments with democracy are driven by the desire to scale-up creative freedom and harmonise the process of identifying and creating valuable outcomes among large numbers of people. Process must be balanced against outcomes. To coordinate the wishes of large numbers of people in an efficient and effective way requires planning and experimentation. Creating a political vehicle that can be steered by many without stalling or crashing is an engineering challenge. Different vehicles suit different tasks and scales. Some will be more hierarchical than others – the challenge is to make them all truly accountable to the people they serve.

As we have seen, most political thinkers have been critical of democracy. Even using the narrow definition of 'majority voting', they argue that people lack the capacity to rule themselves. Again and again, the public have been dismissed as too lazy, stupid and emotional to manage their own lives. One of the twentieth century's leading political scientists, Harold Lasswell, asked that we recognise the 'ignorance and stupidity of the masses' and not succumb to 'democratic dogmatisms about men being the best judges of their own interests'.[10]

Along with Walter Lippmann, Plato and many others, Lasswell advocated a system in which only a special class of experts is entitled to rule. They assume that the challenges of government are primarily technical – Plato spoke of the 'royal science' of government – and conveniently ignore the conflicts of interest that exist at the heart of political life. The notion that the ends of government are obvious to all and that the means of achieving those ends are all that require the attention of rulers flies in the face of history. Decision-makers routinely make value judgements about whose interests are to be advanced, at what cost and at whose expense. These are not technical decisions.[11] Values, freedoms, and rights inevitably conflict. When they do, privileging some over others is unavoidable.

Those who consider themselves most qualified – Lippmann's 'specialised class' – must in practice subordinate themselves to those already in control. Whether in Communist China, Nazi Germany or capitalist America, highly trained technocrats have always conformed to the prevailing ideology, however destructive it may be. This is the natural outcome of a hierarchical system that lacks genuine accountability. Why else – if not to advance their own agenda – would those at the top of a hierarchy confer power on those below? The levers of power are reserved not for the most able or wise but for those willing to rule on behalf of the powerful.

Critics of democracy highlight genuine difficulties, but the alternatives they propose do not avoid these difficulties – they exacerbate them. The need for a ruling elite is based on a pessimistic view of the moral and intellectual resources of ordinary people. Even if we accept this view, why should we believe that a special class of individuals with purer hearts and clearer minds exists or could be created? It is 'foolish and irrelevant', writes Robert Dahl, 'to contrast an idealized portrait of rule by a wise and virtuous elite with a mobocracy disguised as democracy, as Plato did and many enemies of democracy have done since his time'.[12]

The elitist vision is a form of utopian thinking that selectively ignores the failings of human beings. Whatever we think of the arguments against democracy, the arguments in favour of elite rule do not stand up to scrutiny. Democracy is not founded on an assumption of equal competence. It's a hard-headed recognition of the limitations of human beings and the tendency, as Lord Acton observed, of power to corrupt and absolute power to corrupt absolutely.

Even if we could find a benevolent elite to rule wisely over its people, there are at least two good reasons to prefer a democratic decision-making structure. First, people perish whereas decision-making structures do not. There is no guarantee that the next generation of leaders will be able or willing to maintain benevolent rule. Second, people are shaped by the options available. The act of participating in the creation of our future is an empowering experience, even if we make mistakes. Freedom to fail is part of the process of learning how to fulfil our creative potential. We learn to speak, write, run and climb through experience, and so it is for the exercise of freedom. For our creative potential to mature, we must first have the opportunity to exercise it. Democracy is both a form of self-defence and self-development.

The outcomes of a democratic process vary significantly according to the competence and wisdom of those involved. Ignorance, gullibility and complacency – individual or collective – can lead to outcomes that conflict with our deepest values. Critics of democracy are right to warn against the rule of the unqualified. It is crucial to have effective mechanisms for collecting and disseminating expert knowledge. Criminologists have a lot to teach us about our penal system. Climatologists have a lot to teach us about climate change. Epidemiologists have a lot to teach us about public health.

These ideas overlap with what's known as 'deliberative democracy'. A meaningful democratic process goes beyond simply recording fixed preferences; it involves a process of deliberation that allows participants to improve their understanding of issues in pursuit of an informed opinion, rather than just giving people a vote. Why assume that people enter the political arena already knowing exactly what they want or how best to achieve it? Our ideas and values evolve as we interact with people who have different views, experiences and expertise. A commitment to reason is more than a commitment to use our intelligence to advance our interests: it's an attempt to understand. This brings us back to Adam Smith's impartial spectator. An ongoing public discussion gives all involved the opportunity to appreciate new perspectives and transform private preferences into positions that stand up to scrutiny.

To achieve this, there have to be deep cultural shifts, along with a profound transformation of media and education. We not only need equal rights to cast votes, but equal enjoyment of the conditions necessary for effective, meaningful and informed participation. To meet these requirements, there has to be a high degree of economic equality. People and institutions are two sides of the democratic process.

The transition from autocratic monarchies and religious rule to political democracies has been fraught with contradictions. There is nothing preordained or absolute about the degree of democracy that we see around us. Our political and economic structures have been around for the blink of an eye. The boundaries of democracy are continually being contested; they can recede or expand. To assess the level of democracy in a country, it is not enough to establish whether elections take place: we need to know how much power people have.

Once, it was considered radical to speak of the democratic participation of the poor, women and people with darker skin. The extension of the democratic franchise was won by those who could see beyond the prejudices of their time and imagine something better. However, many progressives fought against certain forms of oppression while being blind to, or even upholding, other forms of it. The power of emperors and monarchs was denounced as illegitimate by many leading Enlightenment thinkers who saw nothing wrong with the rule of men over women. In the eighteenth century, Mary Wollstonecraft was scorned by contemporaries for suggesting that for society to escape from tyranny, not only must 'the divine right of kings' be contested, but the 'divine right of husbands'.[13]

To enhance our creative freedom, we need to free ourselves from the influence of arbitrary authority and coercive power wherever they are found. We have to peel away the prejudices of our own time and ask who has power, who does not, and why there is an imbalance. Today, many large and unaccountable concentrations of power remain immune to popular control. Private ownership of the world's resources by a tiny minority of individuals and corporations exerts a vice-like grip over much of humanity. People cannot control their lives if they cannot control the resources on which their lives depend.

We can safely assume that in any system in which a tiny percentage of the population possesses disproportionate wealth, they also possess a disproportionate influence over the decisions that enable them to acquire and hold onto that wealth. Wealth is used to influence political outcomes. The problem is not so much the methods themselves – lobbying, public relations, media pressure, party funding – but the fact that they are controlled by a small minority whose resources allow them to do what most people cannot. In order to combat the subversion of democratic ideals, two things must be done. The first is to significantly reduce the level of inequality within and between nations. The principle of one-dollar-one-vote would cease to threaten the functioning of democracy if everyone had roughly the same amount of money. The second is to make systemic changes that reduce the impact of money on decision-making. These approaches are complementary.

When discussing alternatives, people often raise the question of viability. It's a valid concern but often conceals a problematic assumption: that the current system is doing fine. The world's climate scientists have been telling us for decades that this system is destroying the environment. Moreover, given that it's also impoverishing billions, disempowering the majority and concentrating the world's power and wealth in the hands of a few, it's safe to say that it fails the viability test. The question, then, is not whether we should change, but how. Arriving at a fair distribution of creative freedom across society is the challenge faced by our democratic institutions.

Every institutional arrangement is part of an ongoing social experiment, the outcomes of which must be critically assessed if we're to learn from mistakes and improve on past efforts. This book is not the place to look in depth at alternative systems. Nevertheless, to awaken the imagination and free it from the confines of limited experience, let's explore some ideas that extend democratic principles into areas that have so far remained largely impervious.

Democratising education

There is little freedom for students in most schools. The combination of dress codes, rigid syllabi, set lessons, constant examination, hours of passive listening and an absence of internal democracy mean that schooldays are, typically, characterised by tight control. Study is geared to exams, which grants great power to those who set them and little autonomy to those who take them. The sheer quantity of disconnected units of information leaves students struggling to keep up. Careful attention to a syllabus is rewarded over careful attention to one's curiosity. Regurgitation of facts is rewarded over originality, passionate engagement or independent thought. These arrangements prepare students for a society in which they have little say over the decisions that affect their lives: long hours of hard work on externally set problems is good preparation for professional obedience.

In a genuinely democratic society, educational institutions would exemplify the principle of participation and equality. Decision-making and organisational procedures would empower students, parents and teachers and, if equality of opportunity was taken seriously, a pupil's education would have no relation to the wealth of his or her parents. This may sound utopian and unworkable but compelling examples already exist. In Finland, a child begins schooling at seven with no pressure to do any academic work before then. Their entire education up to and including university is free (including school meals) and private schools are prohibited. There are neither league tables nor school inspections nor uniforms, and homework is minimal. Students have a say in designing their own timetables, are not segregated from other children according to ability, and don't take a national exam before the age of eighteen.[14] The government determines the curriculum but teachers have the freedom to teach subjects as they see fit, experimenting with different approaches and methods. For older students, a move away from subject-specific lessons is currently under way.[15] Instead of dividing the school day into traditional subjects, some lessons now focus on particular topics, such as the European Union, which bring together elements of politics, economics, geography and languages. As well as this holistic approach to knowledge, there is also an increasing emphasis on collaborative learning, with students working in smaller groups to solve problems together rather than on their own.

The Finnish system is built around a strong commitment to equality, in which children and teachers have high levels of autonomy. According to the Programme for International Student Assessment (PISA), which ranks students around the world, the results are impressive. Finland has repeatedly been one of the world's highest scoring countries, at times claiming top place in Science, and second place in Maths and English. The achievement gap between the weakest and strongest students is the smallest in the world, and, according to their ambassador, the Finns are 'the world's most active readers'.[16]

Elsewhere, experiments in democratic and egalitarian education have yielded similarly encouraging results. The educational model known as Escuela Nueva originated in Colombia but has since spread around the globe. It places great emphasis on making the curriculum relevant to the lives of students, encouraging self-directed learning, the fostering of democratic values, and the promotion of dialogue, cooperation and action over passive listening and competition. David L. Kirp, Professor of Public Policy at the University of California, observed at first hand that, 'Escuela Nueva turns the schoolhouse into a laboratory for democracy. Rather than being run as a mini-dictatorship, with the principal as its unquestioned leader, the school operates as a self-governing community, where teachers, parents and students have a real say in how it is run.'[17] Numerous studies have demonstrated that the model tends to outperform conventional schools academically, while also promoting higher levels of self-esteem, participation and cooperation.[18]

We cannot separate a system of education from the society it functions to serve. The needs and predominant values of a society determine the aims and methods of its schooling. If we change the way we educate without changing the needs of society, a conflict will arise. A democratic education requires a society receptive to the sorts of individuals that it would produce. In the Foreword to Paulo Freire's text *Pedagogy of the Oppressed*, Richard Shaull describes two main paths an education can take:

There is no such thing as a *neutral* educational process. Education either functions as an instrument which is used to facilitate the integration of the younger generation into the logic of the present system and bring about conformity to it, *or* it becomes 'the practice of freedom', the means by which men and women deal critically and creatively with reality and discover how to participate in the transformation of their world.[19]

The selection and omission of facts and perspectives is unavoidable in the process of teaching. The beliefs and values held dear by a teacher – or whoever has the power to design the curriculum – dictate the material that is presented, the emphasis, and the perspective offered. The way to transcend this inherent bias is to acknowledge it, to communicate the problem of bias explicitly to students by highlighting the power imbalance of the teacher/student dynamic and, in doing so, encourage them to question the educational process: its aims, methods and content. Exploring the process of identity formation is an important part of this. Throughout history, the power to shape identities has been used to advance the interests of those with the power to do the shaping. Studying critically these mechanisms of control can go a long way towards undermining their power.

To acknowledge a bias we have to be clear about our values, about what has led us to frame the subject as we have and select the information that we transmit. Howard Zinn once wrote: 'in a world where children are still not safe from starvation or bombs, should not the historian thrust himself and his writing into history, on behalf of goals in which he deeply believes? Are we historians not humans first, and scholars because of that? . . . my point is not to approach historical data with preconceived answers, but with preconceived questions. I assume accuracy is a prerequisite, but that history is not praiseworthy for having merely achieved that.'[20] In the same way, an education is not praiseworthy for having merely imparted information and skills.

Education is a means of passing valuable lessons from one generation to the next. It is not enough to transmit technical expertise – that is merely training. A democratic education has to grapple with the core questions of power, control and freedom. The stability of democracy depends on a process of socialisation that cultivates the tools for its protection and evolution. These concerns ought to inform the way reality is divided up into subjects for study. Alongside the traditional disciplines – physics, maths, literature – why not include 'War and Peace', 'Identity Formation', 'Empathy and Dehumanisation', 'Climate Change and Survival', 'Equality and Oppression'? In a class on War and Peace, students might investigate the methods different governments have used to persuade, cajole and manipulate people into supporting war. They might look at the economic incentives of military action – how it serves certain interests in society while sacrificing others – as well as the ethics of international intervention and the wider objectives of foreign policy. Through historical case studies students might explore the role of the media in securing public consent and learn about those who campaigned for peace: their reasons for doing so, the methods they used, and the successes and failures they enjoyed and endured. By reading literature, biography and poetry they could analyse, debate and discuss accounts of soldiers – from training to the battlefield to integrating back into society. To engage with the world in this way, students would have to acquaint themselves with, and perceive the links between, numerous areas – history, politics, economics, philosophy, psychology, media and literature – all with a distinct goal in mind, a bias stated from the outset: to understand the obstacles to peace so as to overcome them more effectively.

The innately political character of whatever is studied should be identified, discussed and periodically returned to. For instance, it ought to be explained from the outset that history can be used as both a weapon of oppression and a tool of liberation, and that what we understand about the past shapes our thinking about the present and the future. Fostering this awareness – perhaps through a critical study of textbooks, old and new – is more valuable than any particular historical fact or event. Too often, where students should see connections they are taught to see only disciplinary boundaries. Severing connections between subjects, rather than building them, leads to confusion. A confused populace is a vulnerable populace, one unable to identify the source of their woes or effect change. The ubiquitous evils of poverty, exploitation, racism and war are rooted in a number of causal factors ranging from the psychological, political and economic, to the historical, philosophical and sociological. To understand such problems, let alone solve them, requires a holistic approach – one that is precluded by a curriculum emphasising strict specialisation, one that isolates rather than connects its subjects. Specialists are needed in every society, but a nation of people who know a lot about very little will struggle to function as a democracy.

Everyone stands to benefit from being able to participate effectively in the political decisions that impact them. As things stand, most students pass through the education system without serious engagement with – often without a single lesson in – capitalism, inequality, social control, activism or democracy. These are foundational subjects for an under-standing of power. The millions of children studying topics that will never be of any use to them are testament to a system that welcomes political confusion and apathy – a system that obscures the world, rather than reveals it.

If independence of thought is the mark of a good education, it cannot be the role of the educator to decide on the ultimate goal of those they educate. If the inevitable political bias of education favours democ-racy and freedom it will seek to create an environment in which students develop the tools to direct their own education, an environment that nourishes their curiosity, hones their critical faculties, gives them the confidence to follow syllabuses of their own making and the hunger to ask – and seek answers to – their own questions. These are invaluable traits to foster if people are to engage creatively with the world around them. To cultivate the capacity to question, reason and seek evidence is the opposite of control – it is the transmission of a method, not a conclusion. When reason is promoted as a means of staying in touch with reality, the hope is that reality dictates where it leads, not a state, religion or any other centralised authority.

The philosopher John Dewey wrote that democracy 'cannot go forward unless the intelligence of the mass of people is educated to understand the social realities of their own time'.[21] A democratic education provides people with the tools to defend and expand what is of value. The threats of war, oppression and exploitation are forever present. Freedom-preserving institutions that curb concentrated power require a questioning, informed, organised and confident population to safeguard them. The more susceptible people are to manipulation, the less secure everyone's freedom becomes. A politically literate citizenry is the antidote to the dangers of centralised authority and control. The artist Ricardo Levins Morales sums it up: 'If you give me a fish you have fed me for a day. If you teach me to fish then you have fed me until the river is contaminated or the shoreline seized for development. But if you teach me to organize then whatever the challenge I can join together with my peers and we will fashion our own solution.'

Democratising the workplace

During the Spanish Civil War, a priest named Don José María Arizmendiarrieta narrowly escaped execution by Franco's forces. In 1943, he went on to establish a school for working-class boys. Before then, the educational record in that region had been dismal, not a single working-class youth from Mondragón had ever attended a university. Guided by this visionary priest, the students set up a number of cooperatives, starting with a factory in 1956 that made small cookers and stoves. Two years later they founded another to make machine tools. A year on, they established a bank to provide investment and expertise to existing cooperatives wanting to expand and new cooperatives trying to get off the ground. As the cooperatives spread, supporting structures were added to the growing network, including a technical university, a social security organisation, research institutes and a series of consumer outlets. In 1991, the network formalised its association by creating the Mondragon Corporación Cooperativa. In recent years, it has boasted 83,000 employees, 9,000 students, global sales of over 12 billion euros, and assets totalling 35 billion euros. It is the world's largest cooperative.

At the heart of the Mondragon structure is the individual worker-owned cooperative. These send representatives to councils, which coordinate activity at higher levels of the organisation. The system of governance combines direct democracy in general assemblies with representational democracy at councils. The workforce elects managers, and big decisions – about profits and production – are taken by a board of directors representing the members or by a general assembly of worker-owners. In 2007, the top 365 US companies gifted their chief executives rewards well over 500 times the average wage of their employees. In Mondragon, the highest paid managers are paid a salary just eight times that of the lowest paid worker.[22]

Each cooperative donates a portion of its profits to a solidarity investment fund which enables Mondragon's more profitable cooperatives to subsidise those that might temporarily be in difficulty. Since the economic crash that started in late 2007, Mondragon has been severely tested. Spain has struggled through a double-dip recession, with extreme austerity and unemployment levels hovering at 25 per cent. But the cooperative has withstood these pressures remarkably well, as it has many times before, maintaining its workforce with minimal lay-offs. 'When times are bad,' says one of the early founders, 'we cut wage costs by deciding it among ourselves.' Members of the cooperative also get to vote on executive pay, holiday time and other work issues.[23]

Mondragon has its problems but it is a remarkable indication of what is possible. It is an appealing alternative to the traditional corporate structure in which people have little say over the aims, conditions and availability of their work. In the dominant corporate structure, shareholders vote on a one-share-one-vote basis to select a board of directors. The board are almost never drawn from the ranks of the workforce, yet have the power to decide what commodities to produce, how and where they are made, and which managers and workers to hire. Crucially, they also decide how to distribute the profits. They are legally obliged to represent the interests of the owners of the corporation: the shareholders.

If democracy is something we value, why is it excluded from the institutions to which we devote so much of our lives? Why should workers not be able to participate in the decisions that impact them? Why should those who create profit not decide how it is spent? Why must the democratic rights of the citizen be left behind on entering the workplace? There are no good answers to these questions. There never have been. This is why attempts to bring democracy into the workplace have never gone away.

In some instances, workers have taken over management of the workplace. This is a step in the right direction but it is a rather small one, because the typical function of managers is to implement the plan created by the directors. Nevertheless, worker self-management is preferable because it allows workers to control more effectively the modes and pacing of the work they do. Elsewhere, workers have taken over ownership of the enterprise. At annual elections they vote on who the board of directors will be (they are rarely able to vote for themselves). This is an important change but still leaves the most important decisions in the hands of a board that excludes the workers. Although the shareholders are regarded as the owners in today's corporations, a great deal of power rests with the board members who make the crucial decisions, including how much of the profits are distributed as dividends to shareholders.

The key decisions in most enterprises are taken by the directors, not the shareholders, so in a truly democratic workplace each worker is an equal member of the board and major decisions are arrived at democratically by the principle of one-person-one-vote. Economist Richard Wolff calls such workplaces 'Workers' Self-Directed Enterprises' (WSDE).[24] Workers can hire managers, but they also possess the power to set their wages and fire them. Not surprisingly, in practice this leads to far smaller wage differences.

Workers may also rotate certain roles so that no one occupies the role of manager for too long. Even within a democratic one-person-one-vote structure, imbalances of power can emerge from traditional divisions of labour. Over time, if a handful of people monopolise managerial roles, they will acquire skills, knowledge and confidence that may result in a disproportionate influence over discussions, debates and ultimately decisions. This can undermine the democratic structure of the whole enterprise if a rift opens up between managers and other workers.

There are other advantages to job rotation. When the same tasks are performed repeatedly over a period of years, there is little opportunity to develop new abilities. Adam Smith's *Wealth of Nations* may have recognised the advantages of specialisation for productive efficiency, but he was not blind to its downsides, warning that specialisation could produce workers 'as stupid and ignorant as it is possible for a human creature to become'.[25] Job rotation gives people the chance to discover what they enjoy doing (and what they dislike), what they're good at, and gives them the chance to learn new things. The arrangements vary from institution to institution, but this way of working has already been implemented with great success, from independent publishing houses to giant firms generating billions a year in revenue. A particularly successful example is W. L. Gore & Associates, maker of Gore-Tex apparel, one of the 200 largest privately held US companies, with 10,000 worker-owners, and sales of $3 billion in 2012.[26]

Gore is an ESOP, a company that offers all employees an Employee Stock Ownership Plan, a direct stake in the success of the firm. It has been voted one of the best places to work in the UK, Germany, France, Korea, Sweden and Italy for several years in a row. This may have something to do with the fact that there are no bosses, formal titles or traditional hierarchies. A worker may lead one task this week and follow someone else on a different task next week. Teams are largely formed organically when people are attracted to a project led by an individual they are happy to work with. This flexibility has produced a remarkable record of innovation. It is not a perfect example of a democratic workplace but it is a good illustration of a more empowering way of doing things.

Share-ownership schemes cover roughly a quarter of all British employees. In the US, eight million employees are part of Employee Stock Ownership Plans. However, share and stock ownership often provide no real participation in decision-making so they do not advance workplace democracy. Interestingly, research has shown that only when they are combined with increased democratic decision-making do these schemes result in substantially higher levels of productivity, in some cases over 50 per cent.[27] Globally, 800 million people are part of a cooperative, according to some estimates. Clearly, numerous experiments in worker democracies already exist. Few go far enough, but a broad foundation has been laid.

Democratising the workplace leads to different criteria for decision-making. In undemocratic workplaces, labour-saving technology is almost always used either to produce more goods or the same amount of goods with fewer workers in order to increase profits. The old promise that technology would lead to more leisure time has not come to pass. It doesn't have to be this way. Gains in productivity could shorten the working day, week and year. In North America and Europe, labour productivity has typically increased by about 2 per cent a year. Economist Dan O'Neill writes, 'Assuming that labor productivity continues to increase at this rate, we could have a four-day workweek in twelve years, a three-day week in twenty-five years, and so on, with no decrease in incomes.'[28] By reducing working hours at the same rate as labour productivity increases we can work less while earning, spending and consuming what we already do. There is nothing special about the number of hours people currently work. It is arbitrary and varies from country to country. We grow up seeing our parents leave for work and return a set number of hours later, so it is taken as normal – familiar enough to escape our critical scrutiny.

Some countries have already pursued policies to convert increased labour productivity into fewer working hours. In the Netherlands, unions and employers signed an agreement in the 1980s to reduce unemployment by sharing work. This policy, along with others that encourage more flexibility and security for workers, has led to the Netherlands achieving the lowest number of working hours among high-income countries: 1,377 per year compared with 1,647 in the UK and 1,778 in the US. This amounts to roughly ten fewer working weeks for the average Dutch person than the average American. (In 2009, the Netherlands had under 4 per cent unemployment compared with 10.9 per cent in the US.[29])

At every stage in the extension of the democratic franchise, people have argued that democratic governance and the inclusion of the 'unqualified' and 'unpropertied' masses would lead to chaos. Similar arguments arise in discussions about workplace democracy. A look at the evidence lays these concerns to rest. Mondragon is not an isolated example. Numerous studies show that productivity in firms where there is worker participation in management is, on average, equal to, if not higher, than traditional corporate structures.[30] Further evidence suggests that control over our working lives is good for our health. One study in Britain concluded that having control at work was the most important single factor explaining differences in death rates between senior and junior civil servants working in the same government offices.[31]

Why reject political tyrannies while accepting them at work? Democratising the workplace is an essential step towards expanding and deepening democracy in general.

Democratising politics

The problems created by money in politics have worsened over time. If we're to address climate change, reduce inequality and create a fairer society, getting money out of politics is an urgent priority. American legal scholar Bruce Ackerman has proposed a simple solution:[32] grant every citizen a bank card — a 'democracy card', say — which is credited with $50 each year by the state. The card can only be used to fund a candidate or a political party. After accepting this funding, politicians would not be allowed to take money from any other source. Given the vast pool of funding locked up in these cards, a powerful incentive exists to forgo corporate donations. If these incentives prove too weak, the government could declare the cards the only legal source of funding. Erik Olin Wright takes the idea further, arguing that the democracy card should be able to fund other forms of political action such as lobbying, activism, campaigns and social movements.[33] The proposals have a number of caveats designed to overcome potential difficulties that I won't discuss here, but a mechanism of this sort would clearly erode the influence of private wealth on political outcomes.

The media also hold great sway over political outcomes. A similar idea has been put forward to democratise funding of the press. Robert McChesney argues that journalism is a public good because it is central to maintaining a free and democratic society. The market can't provide the quantity and quality of original journalism that a free society needs, so a non-market solution is needed to rescue journalism from its rapid decline. Why not give every adult a 'citizen news voucher', worth $200, to be donated to any non-profit news medium of his or her choice? McChesney explains, 'This funding mechanism would apply to any nonprofit medium that does exclusively media content. The medium could not be part of a larger organisation that has any nonmedia operations. Everything the medium produces would have to be made available immediately by publication on the Internet, free to all. It would not be covered by copyright and would enter the public domain.'[34]

We can tinker with the details but the overall strategy is promising. It could plausibly rejuvenate news journalism and, by extension, electoral democracy. It is a proposal that could overcome, or at least mitigate, the deficiencies that have plagued traditional media for over a century: ownership by the super rich, dependency on advertising for survival, over-reliance on powerful news sources to cut costs, and a fear of offending those with the means to hit back.

Removing money from politics is one way of rescuing elections; another is to reduce inequality and its impacts more generally so that power in society is more equally distributed. There are many ways to do this. We need to create a more progressive taxation system, one that closes the loopholes through which so many billions pass. Taxation, as Thomas Piketty writes, 'is preeminently a political and philosophical issue . . . Without taxes, society has no common destiny, and collective action is impossible.'[35]

In the decades leading up to the Thatcher and Reagan years, the UK and US had some of the most progressive taxation systems on the planet. But as neoliberal ideas took hold, the top rate of income tax rapidly plummeted from roughly 85 per cent to 35 per cent. There is no good economic reason for this. For instance, the evidence suggests that in the US a top rate of 80 per cent on incomes over $500,000 would not harm economic growth at all, while significantly reducing inequality.[36]

The difference between the tax that should be paid and the tax that is actually paid is known as the 'tax gap'. In the UK, a leading study in 2014 put this at £119 billion – an amount that would eliminate the government deficit overnight.[37] This figure is likely to rise as staff numbers at HMRC, the institution responsible for collecting tax in the UK, have been cut by almost 50 per cent over the last decade.[38]

Financial transparency is essential to taxation. Banks in tax havens maintain a lot of secrecy, making it far harder to track and tax wealth across borders. Tax havens enabled Walmart to report $1.3 billion profits in Luxembourg from 2010 to 2013, where it has not a single store, in order to benefit from a tax rate of less than 1 per cent.[39] Tax haven expert Nicholas Shaxson writes: 'In 2011, Google shuffled four-fifths of its profits through a subsidiary in the tax haven of Bermuda, cutting its worldwide tax rate in half and its tax rate in some countries to nearly zero.'[40] Google CEO Eric Schmidt did not deny this. In fact, he claimed to be 'very proud of the structure that we set up . . . it's called capitalism'.[41]

At the end of 2010, $21 trillion of unreported financial wealth was locked away in these havens. As one study showed, 'if the income from this wealth was charged to tax in the countries where those rich individuals were resident or derived their wealth, the additional tax revenue available to fund public services and investment around the world would range between $190 and $280 billion annually'.[42] This is just one form of tax loss. There are a number of others. Globally, as much as $3 trillion a year may be lost to illegal evasion of tax.[43]

According to Piketty, the best way to respond to rising concentrations of wealth is a progressive global tax on capital. He acknowledges that the level of international coordination it would require makes it politically difficult to implement but suggests it could be introduced regionally. The annual tax would only need to be a few percentage points to raise significant revenue and it would apply only to the top few per cent of the population. Those who owned less than a million euros wouldn't be taxed at all; fortunes between one and five million euros would be taxed at 1 per cent, and anything above that at 2 per cent. 'If applied to all member states of the European Union, such a tax . . . [while only affecting] about 2.5 per cent of the population . . . [would] bring in revenues equivalent to 2 per cent of Europe's GDP.'[44] This would be about 300 billion euros a year.

Increased tax revenue is urgently needed to fund social programmes and reduce inequality. Even in the richest countries, the need for social spending is immense – to reduce university fees, to increase the supply of affordable housing, defend adequate pensions and provide universal healthcare. To close the gap between rich and poor, there is also great need for a living wage, caped incomes, comprehensive child support, stricter inheritance laws, and increased investment in deprived areas.

Passing laws to strengthen unions is another powerful way to reduce inequality and curtail corporate power. One study that focused on the UK, the US, Australia, Canada, Germany, Japan and Sweden during the 1980s and 1990s concluded that the single most important factor bearing on levels of inequality was union membership. As membership has dropped, inequality has increased.[45] Across the EU, union agreements cover the wages of about 62 per cent of employees. In France, the figure is 98 per cent; in the UK, it's 29 per cent (one of the lowest in Europe).[46]

Union membership in the US peaked in the 1950s but has since dropped to roughly 15 per cent. At the same time, the amount of tax paid by corporations has also dropped substantially. In 1945, corporate tax accounted for 35 per cent of federal receipts; by 2003, it was 7 per cent.[47] The diminishing tax rate on the super wealthy is also significant. In 2007, the average tax rate on the wealthiest 400 households in the US was, in effect, 16.6 per cent, lower than the 20.4 per cent for taxpayers in general. In fact, the 400 top households each received, on average, a $30 billion gift in 2008 and a $45 billion gift in 2007 when capital gains tax was reduced.[48]

Would the public support efforts to reduce inequality? Polls suggest they would. Despite decades of propaganda, and even though most people vastly underestimate the level of inequality in society, two-thirds of Americans believe the distribution of income should be more equal, and 56 per cent of Britons favour a more equal distribution, even if it reduces the overall amount of wealth.[49]

Democratising ownership

Should market logic decide who has access to healthcare, food, water, energy and education? As neoliberalism took hold in the 1980s, existing state-run services were increasingly dismissed as wasteful. Decades of privatisation since then have increased inequality while concentrating economic decision-making in fewer and fewer hands. The result is a system that works for short-term private interests keen to extract wealth rather than create it. When we regard access to a resource as a fundamental right, we cannot leave its allocation to the whims of the market.

Decades of ideological attacks on public services ignore much of the evidence. Globally, the strategy of ignoring the 'private good, public bad' mantra of free-market ideology has proved essential for economic development in the world's richest nations, as well as a number of the most successful developing countries. The last hundred years provides numerous examples of successful state-run and state-sponsored enterprises. In fact, over the last two centuries there has been a strong correlation between rapid economic development and state assistance; examples are to be found in the US, the UK, France, Finland, Germany, Sweden, Austria, Italy, Norway, Brazil, Taiwan, South Korea, Japan, Singapore and China. These nations have endorsed many forms of direct state interference in the market, including protectionist measures to develop key industries. Referring to the golden era of capitalism – the decades following the Second World War – Amartya Sen observed, 'It is remarkable that if we look at the sizable developing countries, the fast growing and otherwise high-performing countries have all had governments that have been directly and actively involved in the planning of economic and social performance . . . their respective successes are directly linked to deliberation and design, rather than being just the results of uncoordinated profit seeking or atomistic pursuit of self-interest.'[50] Even billionaire Bill Gates conceded in 2015 that 'Since World War Two, US-government R&D has defined the state of the art in almost every area.' He regards private sector investment as 'in general inept'.[51]

Nationalised services have been an important and sometimes remarkably successful alternative to the market. The persistent claim that privatisation always leads to increased efficiency is comprehensively rebutted by the facts. It has long been known, for instance, that markets often fail to deliver good quality, affordable healthcare. The combination of high costs and uncertainty about the care people will need tends to produce insurance-based systems when healthcare is privatised. Now, the primary objective of insurance companies is to generate profits. This can be done in two ways: by increasing revenue or cutting costs. In *The Body Economic*, epidemiologists David Stuckler and Sanjay Basu show how this creates perverse incentives 'to sign up the healthiest people who need the least amount of care, and purge from their ranks the sickest people who need the most care'.[52] This is known as the inverse care law: sick people cost insurance companies money; healthy people do not.

The principle was clearly demonstrated during the recent recession, when the profits of American healthcare companies hit record highs. In 2009, the top five health insurance companies increased their profits by an impressive 56 per cent, despite the fact that 2.9 million Americans lost their health insurance that year.[53] Stuckler and Basu explain that as companies were losing people from their books, 'they were paying out less for patient care, making more money in the process . . . the rich got richer and the sick got sicker'.[54] Angela Braly, CEO of the health insurance company WellPoint Inc., drew a clear lesson from the bump in profits: 'we will not sacrifice profitability for membership'.[55] In other words, those who benefit most from private healthcare are not the patients, many of whom cannot afford insurance, but the providers: drug companies, insurance companies and hospital corporations. The British National Health Service has long achieved superior or comparable outcomes to its US privatised equivalent, and at roughly half the cost.[56] Even in Cuba, a nation that spends a fraction of what the US does on healthcare, men enjoy a higher life expectancy than in the US, and the life expectancy for women is almost the same.[57]

The UK railways were privatised in the 1990s, but more public money is spent subsidising them today than was spent running them when they were owned by the nation. And the increase is not small: before privatisation, £2.4 billion was spent annually by the UK taxpayer; today the figure has risen to over £5 billion.[58] Over the same period, passenger fares have increased significantly. A study in 2012 showed that over a billion pounds of taxpayers' money could be saved if the railways were to be renationalised.[59]

The impact of the profit motive on the UK energy industry has also been disastrous. Between 2007 and 2013, the profits of the 'Big Six' energy companies increased tenfold.[60] Over this period, 24,000 elderly people died each winter because they couldn't afford to heat their homes properly.[61] Millions more have had to choose between heating and eating. Official findings show that most people have been paying hundreds of pounds more a year for gas and electricity than they would have if the industries had not been privatised.[62]

The 'Big Six' companies have become so unpopular that 68 per cent of the population want them renationalised.[63] The establishment has so far ignored them. Ironically, a big chunk of the UK energy sector *is* run by state-owned companies – they just happen to be foreign. As Andrew Cumbers writes, 'it could be argued that Chinese, French, Norwegian and Russian governments – through their state-owned corporations – have collectively far more control over UK strategic energy interests than any British political actor'.[64]

Democratisation of industry doesn't have to mean nationalisation. State control centralises power and, in certain cases, fails to meet people's needs. Democratic ownership can take other forms, combining a mix of grass-roots cooperatives, city councils and state support. The green community energy revolution, gaining rapid momentum around the world, is a powerful example. Denmark has been a world leader, focusing primarily on wind power. It went from complete dependence on foreign oil and gas in the 1970s to total self-sufficiency in 2000, with a renewables sector accounting for almost a third of its electricity needs. In doing so, it created 20,000 jobs, and now accounts for roughly half the global wind turbine market.[65] The path taken by Denmark was founded on a commitment to decentralised collective ownership. There was also an important role for the state to play in subsidising the process and compelling energy providers to buy a certain amount of renewable energy each year.

Germany is another example. Across the country private energy is being taken back into public hands. In some areas, energy companies have been bought back by the state. Elsewhere, local communities are investing in their own renewable power sources. The state has played its part by guaranteeing these providers priority access to the energy grid and a set price, both of which significantly reduce the risk for small renewable suppliers. Farmers, local groups and cooperatives own about half the renewable energy facilities. Localised control means that the revenues generated can be invested back into the community. By scaling-up the solar panel industry, they reduced production costs, making the technology more viable in poorer countries. Green energy sources have been growing much faster than fossil fuels, becoming much cheaper as fossil fuels get more expensive. This remarkable transition has already created 400,000 jobs and, in 2014, Germany generated a record 28 per cent of its electricity from renewables. Similar trends have been taking place in other industries.

Perhaps land is the most fundamental resource of all. Owners decide how land is used and whether it will serve the common good or be used to turn a profit in ways that harm community life and the balance of nature. Scotland has one of the highest concentrations of private ownership in Europe. Just 432 people – 0.008 per cent of the population – own half of its private land. Yet interesting changes are taking place. Scottish communities are taking back control. It's the beginning of a long process, but the early signs show why it's such an important transition. Half a million acres of land are now owned by local communities.[66] Some have used their land to service their energy needs, grow food or plant forests; and many are using it for new housing. Under this ownership model, profits generated are reinvested into the community for future sustainable development. The Scottish government is assisting the process with a fund set up to help communities buy back local land.

Democratising industry is really about questioning who controls humanity's vital resources. In the private sector, the sole criterion for making decisions is short-term profit. This provides little incentive for private companies to build affordable and sustainable housing, tackle climate change, maintain infrastructure, construct hospitals and take on many other socially valuable tasks. When resources are privatised, urgent priorities are often ignored. Energy companies reaping large and immediate profits from oil, gas, coal and nuclear are not inclined to commit to long-term investment in green energy. All governments can do to influence corporate priorities is to provide massive financial incentives to invest in socially beneficial ways. This has been wasteful and ineffective. The choice is not between profit-maximising corporations on the one hand and a centralised state bureaucracy on the other. The most democratic alternative is decentralised public ownership, of which many examples are emerging around the world to meet the challenges in farming, renewable energy, water and other sectors.

Under capitalism, a powerful pressure exists to broaden the scope of the market through an endless process of commodification. As Derek Wall writes, 'Wherever you live, there will, if you dig deep enough, have been a struggle between commoners and the monopolising state or market for control.'[67] To counter this pressure we need to not only resist privatisation but challenge the notion of ownership itself. We need to find ways to 'defend, extend and deepen the commons'.[68] When a resource is part of the commons, it provides open and shared access to all potential users, bypassing the market and the state. There is no pay wall and no profit to be made. This can take a myriad of forms, and numerous examples exist that demonstrate the value of common ownership, from the sharing of fisheries, farmland and forests to open source programming and websites like Wikipedia. Democratising resources is ultimately about changing the way we relate to each other and the natural world. It is about picking apart ideas of 'property' and 'commodity' – what they mean, when they are useful – and finding effective ways to share more equally the things we all need to survive and thrive.

Democratising money

Who has the power to create money? Most people assume it is either the government or the central bank on the government's behalf. In fact, most money has been created by private banks, by corporations like Barclays, HSBC and Lloyds. They do it by granting loans. If you borrow £50,000 from your high street bank to start a small business, £50,000 will appear in your account. The bank makes a note of what it has given you (its liability) and what you owe them (its asset). Where did the £50,000 come from? Nowhere. It was created from nothing. It would be illegal for you or me to do this, but banks can do it because of a system that allows them to make loans far in excess of their deposits. Banks lend money they don't have, bringing it into existence by typing some numbers into a database.

Most people don't realise this is how it works (even students of economics, policy-makers, and those who work in the financial industry), but it's a fact and widely acknowledged by central banks around the world. It's unfamiliar because it's rarely taught in universities (the dominant neoclassical models of economics largely ignore banks, debt and money). Economics students learn that banks are little more than intermediaries, moving money around the economy to where it will be of most use.

IMF economist Michael Kumhof, who spent five years managing a branch of Barclays Bank, was unequivocal: 'The key function of banks is money creation, not intermediation. And if you tell that to a mainstream economist, that's already provocative, even though it's one hundred per cent correct.'[69] Lord Adair Turner, former Chairman of the UK Financial Services Authority and Senior Fellow at the Institute for New Economic Thinking, was equally candid: 'Banks do not, as too many textbooks still suggest, take deposits of existing money from savers and lend it out to borrowers: they create credit and money ex nihilo – extending a loan to the borrower and simultaneously crediting the borrower's money account.'[70] Paul Tucker, former Deputy Governor of the Bank of England and member of the Monetary Policy Committee, wrote: 'Banks extend credit by simply increasing the borrowing customer's current account . . . That is, banks extend credit [make loans] by creating money.'[71] And Mervyn King, former Governor of the Bank of England, revealed: 'When banks extend loans to their customers, they create money by crediting their customers' accounts.'[72]

In the UK, just 3 per cent of the money in existence was created by the Bank of England and the Royal Mint; the rest came from private banks. The only real constraint on the amount they create, according to Kumhof, 'is their own expectation of how profitable loans will be and whether they risk endangering their solvency'.[73] Why have governments allowed this to happen? In nineteenth-century Britain, efforts to prevent banks from creating money culminated in the Bank Charter Act 1844, which was intended to return the control of the money supply to the state. Fatefully, it only outlawed the creation of printed money and did not include bank deposits.[74] At the time, this wasn't a problem since cash was used for most transactions, but that's no longer the case: today, over 99 per cent of payments (by value) are made electronically.

If everyone with deposits in a particular bank decided to withdraw them on the same day, most people would get nothing. This is known as a bank run and it occurs when people lose faith in the bank's ability to pay back what has been deposited. Banks only hold in reserve a tiny proportion of deposits and reserve requirements have become increasingly lenient. On 31 January 2007, banks held just £12.50 of real money for every £1,000 shown in their customers' accounts, a total reserve of 1.25 per cent.[75]

There are serious problems with private money creation. First, the power to create money comes with a great financial benefit called 'seigniorage'. It costs a few pence to create a £10 note but, once created, it can be exchanged for £10 worth of goods. For every coin or bank-note it creates, a central bank makes a very large profit (close to 100 per cent). In the UK, the profits on creating paper money were almost £18 billion between 2000 and 2009.[76] That's just paper money, making up 3 per cent of the supply. The profits from the remaining 97 per cent go to private banks. Over the last decade, UK private banks have created over a trillion pounds. The profit from this comes from the interest they charge on it, which amounts to billions of pounds. Economist Herman Daly asks, 'Why should the public pay interest to the private banking sector to provide a medium of exchange that the government can provide at little or no cost? Why should seigniorage (profit to the issuer of fiat money) go largely to the private sector rather than entirely to the government (the commonwealth)?'[77]

There's also the important question of where new money is allocated. In the UK, roughly 85 per cent of the nation's current account funds are held by just five banks: HSBC, Barclays, Santander, RBS and Lloyds.

In the five years that preceded the financial crash, the loans approved by the banks came to £2.9 trillion. Over the same five years, the government spent only £2.1 trillion, that is, the banks had more 'spending power' over this period than the government.[78] A bank's 'spending power' comes from its ability to choose which sectors of the economy will receive loans. As profit-seeking corporations, their first priority is not to benefit society but to maximise returns. From 2000 to 2007, roughly 40 per cent went to property, 37 per cent went into financial markets, and just 13 per cent went into businesses. The rest went into credit cards and personal loans. The outcome, as we know, was devastating: inflated house prices and the neglect of investment that society desperately needs in green energy, healthcare, the construction of affordable housing and the maintenance of failing infrastructure. The lack of transparency also means that people depositing their money in banks have no idea where it's being invested. In fact, once our money is deposited, it no longer legally belongs to us.[79]

Allowing private banks to create money by making loans inevitably mires the whole of society in debt. Every pound created by private banks is also, by definition, a pound of debt which has to be repaid with interest. In the UK, £100 billion to £200 billion is paid to banks as interest each year. This amounts to an enormous, unnecessary, transfer of wealth from public pockets to private banks.[80] Debt bubbles burst at some point; loans become unpayable and people default. This leads to bank runs, bankruptcy and massive instability in the economy at great human cost, as we've seen since the financial crisis. Lord Turner recognised this in 2012 when, as Chair of the Financial Services Authority, he commented: 'The financial crisis . . . occurred because we failed to constrain the financial system's creation of private credit and money.'[81]

It is clear that private banks effectively create money, that few constraints exist to control how much they create or where they spend it, and that this arrangement has negative effects on society. Some economists think that significantly increasing regulation of the banks, while separating retail banking from investment banking, would be enough to make private banks accountable. Others disagree, proposing a more radical solution. A number advocate the 'Chicago Plan', which was devised in response to the 1929 Wall Street crash. At the time, it was supported by leading economists including Irving Fisher, Henry Simons and Frank Knight. Even Milton Friedman later advocated something similar. There have been various attempts to update the Chicago Plan. An influential IMF working paper of 2012, entitled 'The Chicago Plan Revisited', champions an overhaul of the monetary system that would prevent banks creating money.[82] It argues that if the plan is implemented, it could have wide-ranging benefits for the whole of society.[83]

The UK-based think tank Positive Money has also published detailed proposals for updating the Chicago Plan for today's economy. They argue that private banks create too much money in good times, inflating economic bubbles in the process, and not enough money during recessions, when it's desperately needed. They propose removing the power to create money from banks, and placing it solely in the hands of a democratically accountable body – a Money Creation Committee. Decisions about how much money to create would be separated from decisions about where it should be spent. The process would be completely transparent and the committee accountable to a cross-party parliamentary group. The success of this proposal largely depends on the competency and accountability of the committee, which would create money from nothing and place it in an account that only the government could access. This would be debt-free money that the government could spend in the economy any way it pleased. The priorities for investing it would be established democratically so that resources could be channelled to where they were most needed.

At the level of personal banking, there would be two kinds of account: an investment account that earned interest and a current account that would simply store the money.[84] When depositing your money, you would have to decide whether you want it saved or invested. If saved, the bank would hold onto it and you'd receive no interest. To receive interest, you would need to transfer money into an investment account. The bank would be required to tell you where it plans to invest your money, giving you the chance to opt out if you found it unethical.[85] The price of receiving interest would be the shared risk of losing your investment.

There's no way to know in advance all the consequences, welcome or otherwise, of making such far-reaching changes to a complex system. But certain things are clear: the current banking system is not fit for purpose. It is undemocratic, leads to economic boom and bust with disastrous effects for society, and grants huge power to profit-seeking corporations that have no scruples about what they do with the trillions of pounds under their control. Economic growth is being fuelled once again by unsustainable borrowing, much of it being ploughed into the housing market. In 2016, Britons are set to spend £40 billion more than they earn. The Office for Budget Responsibility (OBR) has predicted that the nation's household debt-to-income ratio will reach 163 per cent by 2021. This is almost the level that preceded the 2008 economic crash.[86]

There's another problem with the way money is controlled in the present system: central bank independence. A popular argument is that central banks should be independent from government to prevent politicians from managing policy in their own short-term interests rather than the long-term interest of the economy. As a result, central banks have been insulated from political pressure. For instance, the Federal Reserve is independent in the sense that 'its monetary policy decisions do not have to be approved by the President or anyone else in the executive or legislative branches of government'.[87]

There are two difficulties with this reasoning. First, it can be applied to many government functions. Incumbent parties can lower taxes or inflate budgets for short-term advantage at long-term cost, so why not simply make all these decisions the responsibility of independent institutions? Such reasoning would simply lead to more and more decision-making slipping beyond the reach of popular control, thereby undermining what little democracy already exists. The second problem is more fundamental. The decisions taken by a central bank are not just technical, they are political – different policies serve different interests.[88]

As Ha-Joon Chang writes, the 'flip side of the argument that central bankers can take good decisions only because their jobs do not depend on making the electorate happy is that they can pursue policies that hurt the majority of people with impunity – especially if they are told not to worry about anything other than the rate of inflation'.[89] It's well understood, he continues, that central bankers 'tend to listen very closely to the view of the financial sector and implement policies that help it, if necessary at the cost of the manufacturing industry or wage-earners'.[90]

Recent scholarship supports this conclusion. In his 2013 study, *Bankers, Bureaucrats, and Central Bank Politics – The Myth of Neutrality*, Christopher Adolph shows how central bankers are often driven by narrow professional ambitions, implementing policies that will please potential future employers, while sacrificing the public interest.[91] For instance, the Federal Reserve lends large amounts of money to big banks at interest rates that, especially during a crisis, fall far below the market rate, sometimes close to zero. This amounts to a massive giveaway of free cash. If a bank borrows at an interest rate close to zero and then uses that money to buy a government bond yielding say 3 per cent, it makes a 3 per cent profit for doing nothing. Joseph Stiglitz explains: 'they can lend to triple A-rated firms, prime customers, at much higher interest rates. If they can lend at 10 per cent, then the government's willingness to lend them a trillion dollars at close to zero interest is a $100 billion a year gift.' Stiglitz's own time in government offers a window on how things work.

> The bankers try to veto anyone who does not share their belief. I saw this first hand during the Clinton administration, when potential names for the Fed were floated . . . If any of the potential nominees deviated from the party line that markets are self-regulating and that the banks could manage their own risk there arose a hue and cry so great that the name wouldn't be put forward or, if it was put forward, that it wouldn't be approved.[92]

The result of this influence is a central banking system independent from voters but in thrall to private banks. The record shows that the financial sector exerts significant control over central banks with dire consequences for the rest of society. A central bank cannot be impartial. Its policies benefit some groups at the expense of others. The risks of politicians interfering in monetary policy for short-term political gain are real, but if a central bank is to favour the majority rather than a privileged minority it must be democratically accountable and immune to private sector pressure.

Internationally, things only get worse. The design of the IMF and World Bank reflects the power balance that existed between nations at the time of their creation at the end of the Second World War. It is a one-dollar-one-vote system: richer nations cast more votes. Within the IMF, the US, the UK, Canada, Japan, Russia, France, Germany and Italy together possess 49 per cent of the vote. Averaged across the four main agencies of the World Bank, the figure is 48 per cent. The reality is worse than these numbers suggest. According to the founding constitution of both institutions, any major decision requires an 85 per cent majority. The US alone has 17 per cent of the vote in the IMF and 18 per cent in the World Bank, enabling it to veto any major resolution proposed by any other country – even if the rest of the world supports it. In addition, the senior positions have always been occupied by Americans and Europeans, and both institutions are located in Washington DC. The predictable outcome is a system that reflects the interests of the rich nations.

The World Trade Organization (WTO) is not much better. It determines the rules that govern international trade, constraining the sovereignty of nations in far-reaching ways. On the surface, it appears to be democratic. Every member nation gets one vote. In reality, most of the poorer nations only get to exercise their vote once the key decisions have already been made by the rich nations. The WTO agenda is set informally in what are known as 'Green Room' meetings involving the US, Canada, the European Union and Japan. By the time formal trade talks begin, poor nations can only vote against their proposals. Even this is no simple matter. Voting against the proposals of rich nations may lead to penalties such as the withdrawal of foreign aid or a curtailment of export markets.

Democratising money – determining how it's created, who benefits from its creation, where it is invested and on what terms – is an urgent priority. Some thinkers have attempted the daunting task of combining several institutional changes into a fully fledged model of a new economic system.[93] Over three decades, David Schweickart has developed a model he has called 'Economic Democracy'.[94] Its three main pillars are work-place democracy, a competitive market and democratic control of investment – a radical alternative to the way banks and investment currently work. Most wealth is concentrated in the hands of a relatively small number of private individuals. As Schweickart writes:

> Because it is theirs, they can do with it whatever they want. They can invest it anywhere and in anything they choose, or not invest it at all if profit prospects are dim. But this freedom, when coupled with recently enhanced transfer capabilities (both money and goods move faster than ever before), gives capital a mobility that now generates economic and political insecurity around the globe. Financial markets now rule, however 'democratic' political systems purport to be, and this rule is often capricious, often destructive.[95]

The power to determine where money is invested enables the steering of finite resources and vast numbers of people towards certain activities and away from others. In Schweickart's model, workers have almost complete democratic control over the decisions that affect them but they don't own any capital – in the form of land, buildings or equipment. This belongs to society and is rented out to worker-owned businesses. The revenue generated from this becomes part of a national investment fund under democratic public control. These funds find their way back into society first according to a principle of fairness and then, in order to promote efficiency, subject to competitive forces. The principle of fairness specifies that the investment received by a given region be proportional to the size of its population, reducing regional inequalities over time.[96] Once the money reaches a community, the efficiency principle kicks in: the amount a regional local bank receives is 'determined by the size and number of firms serviced by the bank, by its prior success at making economically sound grants, and by its success in creating new employment'.[97] In fact, society could impose whatever criteria on the process it wanted – though sustainability ought to be a top priority. These public banks give grants, not loans, and their employees are paid out of tax revenue 'according to a formula linking income to the bank's success in making profit-enhancing grants and creating employment'.[98] If there are not enough worthy investment opportunities in a given region, the excess funds are sent back to the centre to be reallocated to where they are needed. Although the banks themselves are not profit-maximising institutions, they are nevertheless incentivised to invest in enterprises that demonstrate socially useful, profitable potential. This is only a thumbnail sketch of the proposal but it is enough to appreciate the many shades, permutations and possibilities that exist between unregulated markets and centralised state control.[99]

Democratising power

We have been told that there are two ways of organising an industrialised society: capitalism (more accurately 'state capitalism') and communism (more accurately 'state socialism'). The story goes that since state socialism failed in 1989, state capitalism has been the only alternative. This narrative is familiar and enticingly simple but it blinds us to the great wealth of human experience and imagination at our disposal. An array of alternatives exists, each balancing power in different ways. New permutations of democracy are arising all the time. More efficient, humane and sustainable ways of arranging society are possible.

This chapter has sketched out some ways to deepen and extend democracy. These ideas are just the tip of the iceberg, but they dispel the myth that no alternatives exist. Once change begins, there is no end point. It is an open-ended process of creativity and experimentation. We cannot know in advance where it will lead. Perhaps one day humanity will evolve beyond the idea of nation states and centralised government altogether. But in the present, the real challenge is not to discover better ways of doing things but to overcome the powerful obstacles we face in implementing those discoveries. Democracy is an ongoing experiment, but the right to conduct this experiment is something for which we need continually to fight. The future of our world depends on both the outcome and nature of this fight.

Three main sources of power shape society: economic, state and social. Economic power is derived from control of wealth, state power from control of coercive power, and social power from collective action. Every large, modern, social system is a hybrid combining these forms of power in different proportions. Our immediate task is to use social power, the power of people working together, to deepen democratic control over the state and use the state to overcome concentrated economic power. If the principle of one-dollar-one-vote is to give way to one-person-one-vote, citizens need to find ways to exert their influence outside the impoverished and compromised channels of 'democratic' representation, channels that now embody the logic of the market. This is a profound challenge, the solution to which will have to be arrived at collectively through the diverse and complementary efforts of us all. It is the countless actions of people across society, from different backgrounds, in different jobs, at different ages – some actions public, others private – that together create a swell of momentum to move society in a new direction. There are no defined boundaries to such a movement.

Voting is one of the tools we possess to bring about change. Even when the differences between leading parties are small, as they have been for decades, they can have significant effects on people's lives. Casting a vote for the lesser of two evils can therefore be a worthwhile act. At critical moments, when the hold of major parties is broken or radical politics wins mass support within an established party, electoral victory can be pivotal. Generating enough support for these alternatives to gain power – be it Podemos in Spain or Jeremy Corbyn's Labour Party in the UK – then becomes an organisational priority.

There is no way to achieve systemic change without democratising the state. Electoral victory is a crucial step in that direction, but under the present system it is extremely difficult for radical parties to implement their policies. Immediate constraints include pre-existing international trade deals, membership of entities like the European Union, a corporate-owned media, a reticent civil service, corporate power, and censure and aggression from foreign nations. Facing such challenges, progressive political parties need the movements that give rise to them to hold them to account and counteract the inevitable pressures that so often derail their plans. The real work of politics gets done between elections in the building of networks, communities and movements, and the changing of cultural narratives through public debate, the media, education and art. A strong, durable movement is rooted in the bonds of friendship, trust, solidarity and respect – bonds that nourish and replenish those who form them. Building a movement is a process of reimagining and rebuilding community, a creative refutation of Margaret Thatcher's claim that there is no such thing as society. Movements force change, not leaders, though leaders can play an essential role in galvanising and unifying them.

The point of gaining access to the levers of power is to deepen democracy across society, to change the game being played, and to alleviate – not just temporarily – the pressures on those forced to play it. To achieve this, we have to overcome the true opposition: capital. As long as the vast majority of wealth is controlled by a tiny proportion of humanity, democracy will struggle to be little more than a pleasant mask worn by an ugly system. Given the international reach of capital, solidarity across countries is vital if democratic forces are to prevail. Transforming the words of a manifesto into reality involves the creative involvement of many people.

The tale of Syriza in Greece points to the battles to come. This democratically elected party swept to power on a relatively mild anti-austerity platform but found itself on a collision course with the power of international capital. Would the issues of debt, finance and investment be settled in the name of people or profit? The result was unequivocal. Even after a national referendum in which the Greek people emphatically rejected the crippling terms of the deal being imposed by the European Union and IMF, Greece was compelled to submit to the will of its creditors. As an entire nation was brought to heel, there was little doubt where the real power lay. But this was one battle, fought by a small country, against unfavourable odds. Next time could be different.

II

Survival

As the twenty-first century began, the UN assembled over a thousand scientists to compile a 'Millennium Ecosystem Assessment'. It found that 'human actions are depleting Earth's natural capital, putting such strain on the environment that the ability of the planet's ecosystems to sustain future generations can no longer be taken for granted'.[1] Since then, the strain has steadily increased. We are eroding our life-support systems at an incredible rate through the release of vast amounts of greenhouse gases and agricultural chemicals into rivers, oceans, land and atmosphere.

The conditions for our survival are impacted by at least nine planetary processes: climate change, biodiversity loss, nitrogen and phosphorus cycles, stratospheric ozone depletion, ocean acidification, global freshwater use, changes in land use, atmospheric aerosol loading and chemical pollution. There is a limit to how far humanity can safely disrupt these processes – exceeding just one of them risks calamitous effects on a global scale. According to a pioneering study by the Stockholm Resilience Centre, we have already exceeded four of them: climate change, biodiversity loss, land-system change and the phosphorus and nitrogen cycles.[2]

Climate change is perhaps the most pressing environmental issue of our time. In a report in 2014, the Intergovernmental Panel on Climate Change (IPCC) concluded that 'Human influence on the climate system is clear, and recent anthropogenic emissions of greenhouse gases are the highest in history.'[3] It states with 95 per cent certainty that most of the observed increase in global average temperatures is due to greenhouse gas emissions, generated primarily from fossil fuel use. It goes on to say that continued emissions will cause 'long-lasting changes in all components of the climate system, increasing the likelihood of severe, pervasive and irreversible impacts for people and ecosystems'.[4]

The situation is rapidly spiralling out of control because temperatures have increased enough to set in motion feedback loops that accelerate the warming of the climate. One such effect is the melting of Arctic ice. Shiny white ice acts as a mirror, reflecting the sun's rays back into space. As it melts, large areas of the Earth's surface are transformed from a white mirror into a dull blue ocean that absorbs the sun's rays, thereby accelerating global warming, which speeds up the melting of Arctic ice, and so on. Another process that is triggered by high temperatures is the release into the atmosphere of large quantities of methane that have long been locked away beneath frozen subsoil. Methane is a powerful heat-trapping gas, far more so than carbon dioxide. Its release into the atmosphere rapidly accelerates global warming. Before the century's end, 100 billion tons of methane could be released, increasing temperatures at a rate equivalent to 270 years of carbon dioxide at current emission levels.[5] That would be disastrous. In 2013, Jason Box, a glaciologist with a reputation for being more outspoken than most in his profession, stated that, due to these effects, a rise in sea levels of 21 metres over the next few centuries is probably already 'baked into the system'.[6]

Not only are we pumping more carbon into the atmosphere, we're reducing the capacity of our forests to remove it. We've already destroyed roughly half the earth's mature tropical forests.[7] Estimates vary, but around 13 million hectares of forest are destroyed each year at present.[8] If we continue at this rate, no tropical forests will be left by the end of the century. Deforestation exacerbates and accelerates global warming because forests act as carbon sinks, absorbing carbon dioxide from the atmosphere. Some estimates put the percentage of greenhouse gas emissions caused by deforestation at 15 per cent.[9] Destroying forests also destroys wildlife. Close to 80 per cent of the world's species live in rainforests. Rapid deforestation is causing the extinction of numerous species at rates of between a hundred and a thousand times the normal background rate.[10] Some scientists believe this process poses a greater threat than climate change to humanity's chances of a prosperous future.

In 2015, it was reported that a scientific model supported by the British Foreign Office was producing sobering warnings about future food shortages. According to Dr Aled Jones, Director of Anglia Ruskin University's Global Sustainability Institute, the model shows that by 2040, 'based on plausible climate trends, and a total failure to change course, the global food supply system would face catastrophic losses, and an unprecedented epidemic of food riots. In this scenario, global society essentially collapses as food production falls permanently short of consumption.'[11]

The development of our species has taken place in a world whose atmosphere contained about 275 parts per million (ppm) of carbon dioxide. This helped trap enough heat to create a climate warm enough for human survival. At 275 ppm, carbon dioxide helps rather than hinders, but the amount of carbon dioxide in the atmosphere has shot up since the beginning of the Industrial Revolution just over two centuries ago. That revolution was driven by the extraction of large quantities of fossil fuel – coal, gas and oil – from beneath the Earth's crust. Today, almost everything we do relies on consuming energy obtained from the burning of fossil fuels. The daily activities of our economy are heavily dependent on this energy source.

By 2015, carbon dioxide in the atmosphere had risen to 400 ppm. Most climate scientists agree that we need to reduce that number to no more than 350ppm, yet it's rising by roughly 2 ppm a year.[12] Although we still have fuel to burn, we have run out of atmosphere into which we can safely dump the carbon released by fossil fuel use. Concentrations of carbon dioxide are higher now than they have been at any point during the last 800,000 years, and possibly much further back than that.[13] As more carbon accumulates in the atmosphere, more heat is trapped and the average global temperature rises.

Since the Industrial Revolution, the average global temperature has risen by about 1 °C (one degree Celsius).[14] The Copenhagen Accord of 2009 agreed that humanity should not exceed a 2 °C increase in global temperatures – so we're already halfway to reaching that threshold. For a while, staying below 2 °C was the target around which most climate discussions revolved. It was viewed as the point beyond which the risks become unacceptably high, but many scientists argued this limit was set far too high. Leading climatologist James Hansen called it a 'prescription for long-term disaster'.[15] At 2 °C each year, 1.5 billion people will be exposed to heatwaves, the same number will endure 'water stress', and 30 million will be affected by flooding. Many species and ecosystems will die out, catastrophic droughts will become increasingly common in parts of Africa, and sea levels will rise by over half a metre, leading to some low lying island-states being wiped out.[16] Since 2009, spurred on by these sobering predictions, developing nations, campaigners from around the world, and over a hundred Small Island Developing States, have fought to place a new temperature threshold of 1.5 °C at the heart of the debate.

There is disagreement over which numbers to use for carbon 'budgets'. Various factors are at play: the level of risk we are willing to accept, the latest science about how much warming will be caused by a given amount of carbon, the latest assessment (which changes frequently) of proven fossil fuel reserves, and how optimistic we are about geo-engineering solutions. Whatever numbers we use, the indisputable truth, as climate expert Duncan Clark points out, is that 'there's far more fossil fuel than we can burn, and the more of it that we take out of the ground, the greater the risk of an irreversible climate catastrophe'.[17]

According to Professor Kevin Anderson, a leading climate scientist based at the University of Manchester, the budgets reported in the media are generally far too optimistic, grounded in speculative and outdated assumptions. These include the view that large amounts of carbon 'can be removed from the atmosphere in the coming decades' by as yet undeveloped forms of technology, and that global emissions peaked in 2010 even though the latest data refute this. It might be more politically palatable to present optimistic scenarios, compatible as they are with economic growth, but, according to Anderson, they are ultimately a result of scientists 'censoring their own research' to 'conform to today's political economic hegemony'.[18]

> In plain language, the complete set of 400 IPCC scenarios for a 50% or better chance of 2°C assume either an ability to travel back in time or the successful and large-scale uptake of speculative negative emission technologies. A significant proportion of the scenarios are dependent on both 'time travel *and* geo-engineering'.[19]

Analysis of the IPCC's figures reveals some sobering facts. Based on current emission levels, we have until 2021 before the chance of staying below 1.5 °C drops below 66 per cent.[20] Meeting the 1.5 °C target already looks implausible. Even if we accept coin-flip odds to stay below 2 °C, the challenge is daunting. The 2 °C target comes with a larger carbon budget – over two decades – but drastic action is required right away to make the changes we need in that time. Climate negotiations take for granted that we will wait until 2020 to start reducing emissions. In this case, to stay below 2 °C we need global cuts in emissions of around 3 to 4 per cent a year for decades to come (some estimates put the figures at 5 to 6 per cent).[21] Such projections assume that all countries will share the burden of emission cuts equally, but, if rich countries are expected to take a larger share of the burden (on account of their historical responsibility for releasing the majority of carbon and their relative affluence), we are looking at cuts of 10 per cent a year in wealthy nations without delay.[22] Kevin Anderson and Alice Bows argue that achieving these drastic cuts will require 'radical and immediate de-growth strategies in the US, EU and other wealthy nations'.[23] Cuts on this scale are without precedent, and challenging the growth mantra, let alone planning for de-growth, is nothing short of heresy in mainstream economics.

If no changes are made, we could be on course for a temperature increase of 4 °C or more.[24] Already, glaciers – the source of drinking water for hundreds of millions of people – are melting fast. Drought is becoming increasingly common; mosquitoes are spreading to new areas, bringing with them deadly diseases; sea levels have begun to rise, and may have risen several metres by the end of the century, submerging many of the world's cities and islands; flooding and forest fires have become increasingly extreme and more common in certain areas, and oceans are absorbing ever larger amounts of carbon dioxide, which increases their acidity and threatens marine life, including coral reefs.[25]

'We have five minutes before midnight,' warned Rajendra Pachauri, then chair of the UN's Intergovernmental Panel on Climate Change, before the publication of the 5th IPCC report in 2013. 'We cannot isolate ourselves from anything that happens in any part of this planet . . . It will affect all of us in some way.'[26] Pachauri believes there is still hope if we can chart a new course that increases energy security, reduces pollution and improves health, while also offering new job opportunities. However, a number of scientists believe that we are already locked into an extremely dangerous rise in global temperatures, whatever measures we take. Given the severity of the situation, we cannot afford to ignore the bleaker scenarios that our models tell us are possible. We need to prepare for the worst while doing all we can, as fast as we can, to prevent it.

What needs to happen?

Known reserves of oil, gas and coal contain roughly 3,000 billion tonnes of carbon dioxide.[27] Depending on the risks we are willing to take, that amounts to between seven and twelve times more fossil fuel than we can safely use if we wish to stay below 1.5 °C. Even with the inadequate 2 °C target – and a 66 per cent chance of staying below it – the reserves are still well over three times what we can use. Predictions are continually being refined and updated as new research emerges, but the bottom line is clear: we must keep the vast majority of fossil fuels underground (over 80 per cent according to most climate scientists). The less we use, the less temperatures will rise.

This is easier said than done. The world's fossil fuel reserves are owned by corporations and governments. In 2011, these reserves were estimated to be worth $27 trillion.[28] Market evaluations change but, barring a miraculous advance in technology, if we are to stay within a safe carbon budget we will need to write off many trillions of dollars' worth of fuel. Opposition to doing this is one of the greatest obstacles to addressing climate change. In a system driven by the pursuit of profit, even survival is of secondary importance. This is madness, but the resistance is real and has to be overcome if we are to stave off disaster.

Carbon emissions have been soaring for two centuries. With the exception of the years since the 2008 economic crisis, nothing we have done at the global level has reduced this rate of growth. For the past 150 years, increases in energy efficiency and the utilisation of new forms of energy have accelerated the release of carbon emissions, increasing our dependence on fossil fuel use rather than reducing it.[29] The only reliable way to keep that fuel in the ground is to agree internationally to a legally binding, absolute carbon limit. Various mechanisms could achieve this – that's not the difficult part – but so far the global response has failed spectacularly to agree on such a limit.[30]

To date, the global response to climate change has been abysmal. Countries with the biggest fuel reserves – the US, Canada, Australia, China, India, the Middle Eastern nations – have been the most resistant to striking a deal. The Kyoto Protocol, adopted in 1997 to come into effect in 2005, committed the advanced economies to a 5 per cent reduction in greenhouse gas emissions from 1990 levels to be achieved by 2010. This target was not nearly ambitious enough, but even these modest reductions were not made. Global carbon emissions were 61 per cent higher in 2013 than they were in 1990 when negotiations began.[31]

In 2009, the world's leaders met in Copenhagen to discuss solutions to the problem of climate change. Though hopes were raised in the lead-up, the meeting itself was a grand disappointment. One study showed that if you took every pledge made by every government at the conference and added them all together, it would still produce almost a 4 °C rise in temperatures.[32] At the end of 2015, governments came together again in Paris. It was the twenty-first meeting of its kind and, as with all prior meetings, it failed to deliver. It sounded good: two hundred countries signed off on a deal to keep global temperatures 'well below' 2 °C and recognised the importance of a 1.5 °C limit. UN Secretary-General Ban Ki-moon called this 'a monumental triumph for people and planet'.[33] The shift in rhetoric was significant, representing a step in the right direction, but words are cheap. In spite of the celebratory headlines and self-congratulatory speeches that followed the summit, the deal failed to meet even the minimal demands of science and justice. James Hansen called it a 'fraud'. According to Asad Rehman of Friends of the Earth, 'The iceberg has struck, the ship is going down and the band is still playing to warm applause.'

Not only are there no legally binding emission targets in the agreement, but even if the promises made by every single country were kept, we could still be looking at an increase in warming of well over 3 °C.[34] There was no mention in the agreement of the need to keep fossil fuels in the ground or of 'decarbonisation'. In fact, the words 'coal', 'oil' and 'gas' do not appear at all. No mention was made of the 'polluter pays' principle. No new money was promised to developing nations to help them move beyond a fossil fuel economy. The most vulnerable nations were not given the right to seek reparations for the damage that has been and will be inflicted on them by climate change. Emissions from planes and shipping – which are rapidly rising – were not included in the deal. And almost nothing was said about climate refugees – a problem that will only grow more serious over time, quite possibly resulting in hundreds of millions of people being forced to flee their home nations.

The text is premised on the unstated assumption that we will develop technologies able to take vast amounts of carbon out of the atmosphere at some future date. In effect, the agreement gives nations the green light to overshoot their already risky carbon budgets as long as they commit to making amends later on. As Kevin Anderson points out, without these highly speculative technologies, 'the 1.5 °C target is simply not achievable' and 'there is only a slim chance' of staying below 2 °C. The first problem with hanging our hopes on a would-be technological fix is that it increases the likelihood of setting in motion feedback effects that will be impossible to halt and that will rapidly increase global temperatures. The second problem is that research into the viability of these technologies does not give cause for optimism.[35]

One study, released shortly before the agreement was concluded, conducted a large overview of 'negative emission technologies' and concluded that reliance on them was 'extremely risky'.[36] Authored by forty scientists, the study found that every technology, when scaled up to the level necessary to make an impact on the concentrations of carbon in the atmosphere, came with huge financial and natural cost. The numbers do not add up. For instance, it looked at the popular idea of bioenergy combined with carbon capture and storage (BECCS), which would involve planting vast numbers of trees and plants, burning them to generate energy, and then capturing the carbon released for underground storage for millennia. The technology to do this on a large scale does not yet exist but, even if it did, it would require land between one and three times the area of India to remove enough carbon from the atmosphere to have an impact. Geo-engineering solutions remain dangerous fantasies that reveal a greater willingness to gamble with the survival of our species than to challenge the logic of capitalism.

There is another way. The necessary technology already exists to switch the entire global energy system to renewables, and do so relatively quickly. Mark Z. Jacobson, a Professor of Civil and Environmental Engineering at Stanford University, and Mark A. Delucchi of the University of California, co-authored a pioneering study in 2009 that showed 'how 100 per cent of the world's energy, for all purposes, could be supplied by wind, water and solar resources, by as early as 2030'.[37] Jacobson acknowledges that it would require effort and ambition 'comparable to the Apollo moon project or constructing the interstate highway system' but he has no doubt it is possible with available technologies. 'We really need to just decide collectively that this is the direction we want to head as a society.'[38] In 2015 they updated their work, demonstrating in impressive detail how 139 countries could meet all their energy needs with wind, solar and water-power technologies, and create over 50 million jobs in the process.[39]

Other reports have arrived at similar conclusions. One such study commissioned by the Inter-American Development Bank (IDB) found that Latin America and the Caribbean's renewable energy potential is large enough to cover their anticipated electricity needs for 2050 twenty-two times over.[40] Having undergone a rapid energy revolution, Uruguay is already supplying 95 per cent of its electricity from renewable sources.[41] Detailed blueprints have been outlined for a number of regions showing how cost-effective renewable energy could completely replace or come very close to replacing fossil fuels within the next twenty to thirty years.

If technology isn't the issue, perhaps cost is holding us back? The UN Department of Economic and Social Affairs found that to 'overcome poverty, increase food production to eradicate hunger without degrading land and water resources, and avert the climate change catastrophe' will cost $1.9 trillion a year for the next forty years.[42] At least half of this amount needs to be invested in developing countries. This figure isn't much more than the annual global defence budget, currently at about $1.7 trillion.[43] (For decades, the US military budget has accounted for close to half of this rising total.) When politicians are asked to justify this enormous amount of money, the well-worn phrase 'national security' quickly makes an appearance. It's an odd phrase, even ironic, when you consider that the same politicians are slashing social security, forcing families into unrepayable debt and accelerating climate catastrophe. What security do people have if they cannot keep their homes, feed their children, afford university, receive healthcare, or anticipate a future free of famine, drought, hurricanes, fire and flooding? Climate change is the greatest security threat humanity has ever faced. If we can collectively sacrifice for war, why not for survival? If high levels of international cooperation are possible when creating complex trade deals, why not for a global ban on carbon?

A commitment from every government to divert 30 per cent of their military budget to climate solutions could raise over half a trillion dollars each year. A global financial transaction tax could raise $650 billion a year.[44] According to well-established projections, a tax on carbon in developed nations could raise between $250 billion and $450 billion a year.[45] An extremely conservative estimate from 2012 suggested that if fossil fuel subsidies were cut by all nations, $1 trillion would be saved every year.[46] This already takes us beyond the $1.9 trillion threshold. However, more recent research by the IMF shows that government subsidies to the fossil fuel industry are far higher than originally thought, totalling $5.3 trillion a year – more than twice the money needed to address climate change. The IMF also found that ending these subsidies would reduce global carbon emissions by 20 per cent.[47] These figures show that there is no shortage of money to address climate change. How could there be? Can we seriously place a price tag on our own survival?

It is madness on the grandest scale to draw up a list of the costs and benefits of protecting the conditions for life on Earth. According to leading climate scientists, a 4 °C rise in global temperatures would be catastrophic for our species. What's more, it is unlikely that temperatures would stabilise at that level. Feedback loops could take us to 5 °C or 6 °C. It's also important to bear in mind that talk of a 4 °C rise on pre-industrial levels refers to a global average. On land it would be closer to 5 °C and in some places it would be up to 15 °C.[48] Predictions vary, but it seems likely that warming of such magnitude would result in the deaths of not hundreds of millions but billions of people. A 2012 report by the Potsdam Institute for the World Bank concluded that 'there is . . . no certainty that adaptation to a 4 °C world is possible'.[49] Professor Neil Adger of the Tyndall Centre, an expert on adaptation to a warmer world, told *The Guardian* newspaper in 2008 that 'Thinking through the implications of 4 degrees of warming shows that the impacts are so significant that the only real adaptation strategy is to avoid that at all cost because of the pain and suffering that is going to cost. There is no science on how we are going to adapt to 4 degrees warming. It is actually pretty alarming.'[50] Kevin Anderson echoes this: 'There's no evidence to suggest that humanity can actually survive at this sort of temperature. Small pockets of human beings might continue to exist but I don't consider that to be a success.'[51] He estimates that 'If you have got a population of nine billion by 2050 and you hit 4C, 5C or 6C, you might have half a billion people surviving.'[52] Professor Hans Joachim Schellnhuber, one of the world's leading climate scientists, Director of the Potsdam Institute for Climate Impact Research and adviser to the German government and the Pope, stated that a four-degree rise would lead to a planet able to support 'below 1 billion people'.[53]

Even if these predictions are way off – even if two, three, four or five billion people could survive a 4 °C temperature rise – it would still mean billions are wiped out. This would be suffering on a scale without precedent in human history. The resource wars that would almost certainly accompany such a temperature rise could themselves take the lives of many millions more. If nations armed with nuclear weapons start to fight over increasingly limited energy sources, arable land and fresh water, mutual obliteration becomes a real possibility. Bertrand Russell paints a sobering picture of the outcome: 'Our ruined lifeless planet [would] continue for countless ages to circle aimlessly round the sun unredeemed by the joys and loves, the occasional wisdom and the power to create beauty which have given value to human life.'[54]

Thinking about these scenarios is uncomfortable but serves a useful purpose: it shows what may be at stake, it frames the problem as a unique and urgent moral challenge, and exposes the profound inadequacy of the global response so far. Our species faces an existential threat. We have the technology to overcome it and we know how to raise the money to foot the bill. So why has the global response been such a failure?

Capitalism versus the climate

When James Hansen delivered his findings about the dangers of climate change to a packed US congressional hearing in 1988, it seemed like a turning point. Suddenly law-makers, journalists and the popular media were talking about the 'greenhouse effect' and the dangers of a warming climate. International conferences were organised, and that same year, the United Nations Intergovernmental Panel on Climate Change held its first meeting. Strong commitments to sustainability were made and it looked as if the world's nations were serious about action over climate change.

The mass movements of the 1960s had ushered in something of a golden era for environmentalism. On both sides of the Atlantic, laws had been introduced to regulate corporate activity in the interest of public health. Toxic substances were banned and corporations were forced to clean up the pollution they produced. For a time, there was a cross-party consensus about the need to restrain capitalism in order to protect our forests, oceans, wildlife, air and soil. All this came to an end in 1981 with the election of President Ronald Reagan.

By the end of the 1980s, the ideology of neoliberalism – with its familiar policy package of privatisation, deregulation and lower taxes – had reversed the trend. A year after Hansen's speech, the Berlin Wall fell and the world entered an era of free-market triumphalism. Corporate power increased, inequality soared, and far-reaching free trade deals were struck. Just as the climate threat started making headlines in 1988, the ideology of unfettered markets was taking root in the world's most powerful institutions. The mantra for the age became 'leave it to the market'.

Profit was seen as the solution, not the problem: greed was good for everyone. Growth was emphasised over sustainability, competition over cooperation, corporate freedom over democracy, tax cuts over public spending, globalisation over localism, and private ownership over public ownership. People and planet came to be regarded as resources for exploitation rather than protection, and governments were to be judged not by the health of the planet but by the 'health' of the economy.

Environmentalists faced some serious dilemmas. The tools needed to tackle climate change were ruled out by the neoliberal mindset. How do you get polluters to pay when political parties are funded and lobbied by the most polluting corporations? How do you support community-owned renewable energy, or share cleaner technologies with developing nations if you're locked into trade agreements that make it illegal? How do you invest billions in green technology when taxes have been cut, public utilities privatised, and austerity has become official policy? How do you create sustainability while trying to expand the economy? What environmentalists did have on their side were the facts – and facts were the first casualties in the battles over climate change.

Individually and collectively, our capacity to create a future that protects our health and well-being depends on the accuracy of the maps of reality we employ. If our beliefs are false, our actions may destroy what we value. The sense data that flood our nervous system every waking moment continually update our internal maps. Yet our senses are blunt instruments with limited reach. For an informed picture of the world, we depend on the scientific community to collect and interpret vast amounts of information. However, as the Berlin Wall came down in 1989, the demands of science were set on a collision course with free-market economics.

In their book, *Merchants of Doubt,* Naomi Oreskes and Erik Conway describe in detail how the findings of climate science have been systematically distorted.[55] For decades, a small group of well-connected scientists have been casting doubt over established scientific findings – from the dangers of smoking and acid rain to the threats of a depleted ozone layer and climate change – in order to create the illusion of disagreement within the scientific community. Initially, this core group consisted of Fred Seitz and Bill Nierenberg (physicists who started their careers in the atomic weapons programme), Fred Singer (a government scientist) and Robert Jastrow (a long-time employee of NASA). They were 'fiercely anti-communist' and regarded science as a crucial weapon for containing the spread of communist ideology. After the fall of the Soviet Union, they came to believe that environmentalism posed the greatest threat to 'free market capitalism'. They saw environmentalists as 'watermelons': green on the outside, red on the inside.[56] They denied and obfuscated the link between tobacco and cancer. They dismissed as fraudulent the evidence demonstrating the dangers of second-hand smoke. They blamed the hole in the ozone layer on volcanoes. And, over a period of twenty years, they systematically attacked the findings of climate science. According to Oreskes and Conway:

> First they claimed there was none, then they claimed it was just natural variation, and then they claimed that even if it was happening and it was our fault, it didn't matter because we could just adapt to it. In case after case, they steadfastly denied the existence of scientific agreement, even though they, themselves, were pretty much the only ones who disagreed.[57]

The fear was that environmentalists would be able to justify heavy regulation of industry and, ultimately, undermine the ideology of free markets. If they showed that the free market could not be trusted to preserve and protect the conditions of our survival, people might ask whether it could be trusted at all. Initially, these scientists were funded largely by the tobacco industry, but, as the political terrain shifted, new money from the fossil fuel industry started to flow in their direction. ExxonMobil, which has made more profit in recent years than any company in history, has consistently used its wealth to obscure the public's understanding of climate science and to obstruct a meaningful international response. In the 1980s, Exxon was a leading researcher into climate change, but by 1990, having grasped that carbon emissions were raising global temperatures and that this could have profound implications for its business model, it shifted its focus from research to denial.[58] In an internal memo from 1988 it was decided that the company should 'Emphasise the uncertainty' of the science.[59] This marked the beginning of a multimillion-dollar operation.

With other leading oil companies, ExxonMobil was part of the Washington-based Global Climate Coalition, which staunchly opposed a reduction in greenhouse gas emissions late into the 1990s. The coalition spent $13 million on one anti-Kyoto campaign.[60] The Heartland Institute, funded by Exxon and the billionaire Koch brothers (owners of Koch Industries), have been persistent and vocal climate deniers, holding regular conferences and providing a public platform for hand-picked scientists to lie about the science. Its tactics include placing newspaper ads attacking government research into climate change, emphasising the need for 'further climate research' before political action is taken, as well as paying for billboards which suggested that those who believed in climate change were mass murderers.[61]

In 2009, as Barack Obama was developing his energy policies, there were 2,340 registered Washington lobbyists working on climate change – roughly four lobbyists for every Congressman – almost all of whom were dedicated to slowing down any government response.[62] From 2002 to 2010, anonymous tycoons donated $120 million to more than 100 groups working to discredit climate change science. *The Guardian* newspaper in the UK reported that the funds were used to help 'build a vast network of think tanks and activist groups working to a single purpose: to redefine climate change from neutral scientific fact to a highly polarising "wedge issue" for hardcore conservatives'.[63]

Whitney Ball, chief executive of one of the donor trusts that channels these millions to climate denial groups, said of her organisation, 'We exist to help donors promote liberty which we understand to be limited government, personal responsibility, and free enterprise.'[64] Fossil fuel interests have spent a total of almost half a billion dollars a year on campaign donations, PR, think tanks and lobbying.[65] This money has had an impact. Although 97 per cent of climate scientists believe in human-caused climate change, polls show that for many years the percentage of the public who agree has been falling. In 2007, a Harris poll showed that 71 per cent of Americans believed fossil fuels change the climate. Four years on, the figure had dropped to just 44 per cent.[66] Similar trends have been observed in the UK and Australia. Thankfully, more recent polls indicate a swing in the other direction.[67]

Money opens doors – even, it would seem, when that money comes from fossil fuel companies and the doors lead to the biggest green groups on the planet. The World Wide Fund for Nature (WWF), the Nature Conservancy, the Conservation Fund, Conservation International and the World Resources Institute have all either taken money from, invested money in, or developed 'strategic ties' with fossil fuel companies. Incredibly, the Nature Conservancy – perhaps the largest environmental organisation on the planet, commanding assets of over $6 billion – has for years been drilling for oil and gas on one of its own nature reserves, while also investing tens of millions of dollars in the fossil fuel industry.[68]

Predictably, such ties have compromised these groups. Instead of calling for the kinds of measures demanded by the science – a global cap on carbon, an end to fossil fuel subsidy, a rejection of economic growth, a green energy revolution – they have pushed for 'market solutions' such as carbon trading, while advocating natural gas and nuclear power as greener alternatives to oil and coal. The outcome of this strategy has been predictable: their assets have soared hand-in-hand with global emissions.

It hasn't always been about the money. Some environmentalists genuinely believed that fossil fuel companies could be reformed. If their wealth and political power could be used to kick-start a renewable energy revolution then things could change fast. Some wondered if it was just a matter of helping dirty energy companies to understand that it was in their own long-term interests to change. Jonathan Porritt, one of the UK's leading environmentalists, once believed the idea might actually work. He had been a key figure in the Ecology Party (later rebranded the Green Party), a former Director of Friends of the Earth and, in the mid 1990s, co-founder of Forum for the Future, a group dedicated to 'working globally with business and government to create a sustainable future'. Part of the strategy of Forum for the Future was to work with giant fossil fuel companies like BP to facilitate a green transition. In 2015, after years of effort and optimism, Porritt concluded that 'it was impossible for today's oil and gas majors to adapt in a timely and intelligent way to the imperative of radical decarbonisation'.[69] Ignorance is not the problem. As Porritt points out, 'these are companies whose senior managers know, as an irrefutable fact, that their current business model threatens both the stability of the global economy and the longer-term prospects of humankind as a whole'. This knowledge has not resulted in action. Porritt witnessed 'first hand the intricate patterns of denial and self-deception that they were forced to adopt'. His story is a cautionary tale to all those concerned with the changing climate: 'This has been quite a painful journey for me personally. I so badly wanted to believe that the combination of reason, rigorous science and good people would enable elegant transition strategies to emerge in those companies.'

It's not all about fossil fuel, however. Although they have presented themselves as a key part of the solution, multinational agribusiness corporations are also a significant part of the problem.[70] Successes in slowing down deforestation mean that agriculture is now the main source of land-based greenhouse gas emissions.[71] Large sums of money have been spent to promote the idea that industrial agriculture is compatible with fighting climate change. The evidence contradicts this. According to a 2012 study, food systems, particularly meat and dairy production, currently contribute over 20 per cent of greenhouse gases.[72] Another study in 2014 found that, in the words of one of its authors, 'without dietary change at the global level, the two-degrees goal is pretty much off the table'.[73] The alternative is agroecology − a sustainable approach to food production that aims to optimise use of limited resources while minimising negative impacts. Olivier De Schutter, who from 2008 to 2014 was the UN's Special Rapporteur on the Right to Food, argues that 'A large segment of the scientific community now acknowledges the positive impacts of agroecology on food production, poverty allevi-ation and climate change mitigation − and this is what is needed in a world of limited resources.'[74] Numerous studies show the advantages of agroecology. The evidence suggests that crop yields can be doubled or even tripled. According to De Schutter, 'agroecological projects have shown an average crop yield increase of 80 per cent in 57 developing countries'.[75] When combined with food sovereignty (placing control of food systems in the hands of local communities), the whole process is democratised and food security is increased for entire communities, who are able to share what is produced and ensure that no one goes hungry.

By organising society for short-term profit, capitalism condemns much of our species to short-term survival. As author and social activist Naomi Klein puts it, 'our economic model is at war with life on Earth'.[76] At the heart of this war has been a battle of narratives. Scientific find-ings have to traverse the political battleground of the corporate-owned mass media before they can permeate the public consciousness. They have to struggle against the tide of corporate lobbyists, think tanks and party donors to reach and sway politicians. In the space between peer-reviewed results and public and political action, the most impor-tant scientific warnings of our time have been corrupted by concerted campaigns of disinformation, funded and organised by one of the most profitable industries the world has ever seen. Our civilisation has a complex nervous system, but not a brain capable of responding to the information it collects. The result is a society stumbling into the future, blinded by the imperatives of power and profit.

This sabotage is a crime against humanity. The motive may be profit rather than human devastation but the outcomes they are predicted to produce will be equivalent to the gravest of war crimes. To the people who die of starvation, drought, drowning and resource wars, it is little consolation to hear that their deaths were not the primary goal of the fossil fuel industry but collateral damage in the pursuit of profit. Choosing to accelerate climate change is, as American writer Rebecca Solnit points out, an act of violence, the scale of which may eclipse anything that occurred in the twentieth century. This violence has distinct racial and class dimensions. Lacking the resources to protect themselves, the Global South, the world's poorest, will be affected first and most severely, though historically they bear the least responsibility for the crisis. The growing refugee crisis – already the worst in recorded history – is a sign of what's to come.

The growth problem

A few decades ago, system analysts at MIT predicted many of the ecological problems we now face. European industrialists and members of a think tank called the Club of Rome commissioned them to investigate the relationship between Earth's natural systems and humanity's economic systems. The outcome was a book published in 1972, *The Limits to Growth*. It was translated into thirty languages and sold 30 million copies. Bringing together reams of data and entering them into complex computer models, the authors arrived at a sobering prediction: over the coming decades human systems would overwhelm the natural resources on which we depend, leading to widespread collapse. They reported that, if present growth trends continue, 'the limits to growth on this planet will be reached sometime within the next one hundred years'.[77] They maintained it was still 'possible to alter these growth trends and to establish a condition of ecological and economic stability that is sustainable far into the future'.

The book had a big impact, inspiring a sense of urgency and leading to political action and a shift in popular opinion. A few years on, a poll showed that more Americans were against growth than in favour of it.[78] However, the report was also heavily criticised as being unnecessarily apocalyptic. Critics claimed that technology would overcome the problems it had identified and that new energy sources would be found. Decades on, the warnings have been largely vindicated. In 2008, Australian academic Graham Turner evaluated every system examined in the book – population, agriculture, industry, pollution, and resource consumption – and found that 'for the first thirty years of the model, the world has been tracking along the unsustainable trajectory of the book's business as usual scenario' with economic collapse predicted sometime before 2050.[79]

For over half a century, GDP has functioned as the barometer of progress – a shortcut for measuring how things are going in the economy. Bigger is assumed to be better. The ideology of growth has united interests across the political spectrum and the social hierarchy. In the words of environmentalist Bill McKibben, growth has become 'the organizing ideology for corporations and individuals, for American capitalists and Chinese communists, for Democrats and Republicans'.[80] Even in the face of near economic and environmental collapse, growth is vaunted as the solution to our problems. The current system is structured to make us dependent on growth. When it stalls, recession ensues, businesses struggle, unemployment rises and people suffer.

Placing GDP at the top of policy priorities is a recent phenomenon. The concept was developed by economist Simon Kuznets, who warned against it being used as a measure of social welfare. His warnings have been largely ignored, but his measure has not. It took a few years, but by the end of the 1950s growth had become the overriding policy objective in the US and elsewhere. According to economist historian H. W. Arndt, it came to be regarded as a 'remedy for all the major current ailments of Western economies'.[81] Since then, the dominant narrative has led us to believe that society is improving as long as GDP increases at a healthy rate each year.

Growth hasn't always been a bad idea. When Adam Smith wrote *The Wealth of Nations*, the world was a very different place. Fewer than 800 million people roamed the Earth, most of the world's resources were untapped, and the continents were relatively uninhabited.[82] Today, the world's population is 7.4 billion. The economic system that Smith described emerged in a world in which ecological limits were out of sight and out of mind, and meeting basic human needs was still a technological challenge. Economic growth held out the promise of increased material prosperity for many in desperate need (as it does today for developing nations).

Prior to the invention of the steam engine by Thomas Newcomen in 1712, the standard of living for humanity had remained, on average, relatively stable for more than four millennia, with only slow and incremental progress. Newcomen's invention marked a major turning point. This world-changing event and the Industrial Revolution that followed were only possible because of humanity's new-found capacity to exploit the coal, gas and oil hidden beneath the Earth's surface. All the major technological changes that followed depended on bountiful reserves of fossil fuel. The modern world was built with this miraculous supply of concentrated energy.

To think clearly about the limits of economic growth we need to understand the concept of 'throughput'. Throughput is defined as the physical matter (including energy) that enters the economy as useful inputs and exits as waste. Earth has finite physical resources and a finite capacity to absorb waste. Today, the world uses eight times more physical resources (by weight) than it did a century ago.[83] On a finite planet, this rate of expansion cannot continue. We have already hit crucial environmental limits, the most pressing of which come not from resource depletion, as was once feared, but from the planet's capacity to absorb safely the waste we produce through economic activity.

Throughput is not the same as GDP. When economists speak of economic growth they mean GDP – the value of all the goods produced and services delivered in a year, expressed in dollars, pounds or yen. However, GDP and throughput are closely linked because economic activity almost always involves physical resources and energy. The hope that we can continue to increase GDP each year without also extracting more resources and producing more waste seems little more than a dangerous fantasy. If the global economy grows at 3 per cent a year, its GDP will increase a hundredfold after 156 years. To maintain the same level of throughput as today would mean shrinking throughput per dollar of GDP to 1 per cent of its current level. That's already a staggering amount of decoupling. It would take just 312 years at the same rate of growth for the global economy to reach 10,000 times its current size. To avoid an increase in the flow of resources through the economy would then require a drop in throughput per dollar to just 0.01 per cent of its current level. Evidently, unless we create an immaterial economy, perpetual growth of GDP is impossible. Yet most economists are firmly attached to the growth paradigm. According to Larry Summers, Treasury Secretary under President Clinton and one of President Obama's chief economic advisers, 'The idea that we should put limits on growth because of some natural limit is a profound error.'[84] Harvard professor N. Gregory Mankiw dedicates just a few paragraphs in his economics textbook of over 800 pages to the idea that nature places restrictions on economic growth. Dismissing the possibility of such constraints, he writes, 'Market prices give no reason to believe that natural resources are a limit to economic growth.'[85]

When confronted with questions of ecological limits, the typical response is to speak of technological salvation as a way of decoupling growth in dollars from growth in throughput. The hope is that technology will allow economies to continue to grow without breaching ecological limits. In theory, groundbreaking technological advances could enable enough decoupling to take place for economic growth to continue for a while without adverse environmental impacts. In reality, although new technologies will play a part in creating a sustainable economy, they are unlikely to come close to solving our ecological problems.[86] As we have seen, given current rates of growth, the amount of decoupling necessary to stay within ecological limits boggles the mind. And when we pin our hopes on technological miracles, we tend to neglect the solutions that are already available.[87]

Another reason we cannot leave it at all to techno-fixes is that it takes time to transition to new technologies, and time is not on our side. Canadian scholar Vaclav Smil points out that, although large industry began burning coal in the mid-1700s, it took about 140 years for the US to burn more coal than wood, and 200 years for Asia to pass this threshold. It took fifty years for the commercial production of oil to capture just one-tenth of the global energy market. Looking at the historical record, Smil concluded that 'because of the requisite technical and infrastructural imperatives and because of numerous (and often entirely unforeseen) socio-economic adjustments, energy transitions in large economies and on a global scale are inherently protracted affairs'.[88] Although it is under way, the transition to renewable technology will also take time, which is why halting fossil fuel-dependent growth is part of the solution. Of course, this needs to happen as green investments grow to a scale unparalleled since the levels of investment that transformed the US into a wartime economy in 1939. These investments need to respond to today's urgent threats – the advance not of fascism but climate change. Executive Secretary of the UN Framework Convention on Climate Change (UNFCC), Christiana Figueres, summed it up in 2015: 'Where capital goes over the next fifteen years is going to decide whether we're actually able to address climate change and what kind of a century we are going to have.'[89]

It is foolish to pin all our hopes on techno-fixes that currently do not exist, to ignore the problems surrounding the dogged pursuit of economic growth while equating social progress with GDP. The folly of this conflation was highlighted by some of the world's leading economists in a report in 2010 commissioned by then President of France, Nicolas Sarkozy. Led by Nobel prize-winning economists Joseph Stiglitz and Amartya Sen, their objective 'was to align better the metrics of well-being with what actually contributes to quality of life . . . Our economy is supposed to increase our well-being. It too is not an end in itself.'[90] The report challenged the way we think about traditional trade-offs between economic growth and other social goals, such as environmental sustainability: 'Current metrics suggest that . . . one can improve the environment only by sacrificing a growth measure. But if we had a comprehensive measure of well-being, perhaps we would see this as a false choice: it could indicate an increase in well-being if we improve the environment, even if conventionally measured output went down.'[91]

The cost of growth is increasing all the time. China's 'economic miracle', for instance, has resulted in air pollution that kills over 4,000 of its people a day.[92] So bad has the problem become that a Canadian company has started selling bottles of clean air from the Rocky Mountains to Chinese citizens – a good example of economic growth thriving on the destruction it creates.[93] This is fast becoming a global problem. According to one estimate from the World Health Organization, disease and premature death caused by poisoned air in Europe amount to financial costs of more than $1.6 trillion a year – close to 10 per cent of the EU's GDP in 2013.[94] And already more people die from pollution than malaria and HIV combined.[95]

There is a problem with basing all of our decisions on a single indicator. Not all values can be reduced to a single number: the more we simplify, the more we conceal. Many ecological economists argue that we should use a range of indicators and at the very least separate environmental factors from social ones. Better metrics for social progress exist, such as the Human Development Index, the Genuine Progress Indicator, and the Happy Planet Index. Although each has its shortcomings, they represent a significant improvement on GDP.

Quality, not quantity

Earth has a limited capacity to supply us with land and materials and absorb the waste we produce. The economy is a subsystem of the biosphere. If it grows too big, we risk damaging the biosphere on which it depends. A society that recognised this fact would design a system that, on reaching an optimum scale, would consume a steady and sustainable level of resources. Such an economy has a name. It is called a 'steady state economy'.[96]

In a steady state economy, a limit is set to the use of resources, and the right to exploit them is controlled so that the physical scale of the overall system does not change. The optimal scale of the economy is one that enables the health of the ecosystem to be preserved, renewable resources to be extracted at a rate no faster than they can be regenerated, non-renewable resources to be consumed at a rate no faster than they can be replaced by renewable substitutes, and waste to be deposited into the environment at a rate no faster than it can be safely absorbed.

If these four conditions could be met while GDP grew, perpetual economic growth would pose no problems (at least not in environmental terms). Aiming for zero growth is not an end in itself – investing in green jobs, for instance, would constitute a temporary boost to GDP – the point is to prevent our fixation on GDP obstructing the pursuit and protection of the conditions on which our survival and prosperity depend. Our first priority as a civilisation should be to meet these conditions. They should be regarded as inviolable parameters within which we pursue our economic goals.

Once an optimum scale has been reached in a steady state economy, some things are maintained at a constant level, others are not. What remains steady is the population, the stock of built capital – buildings, roads, tunnels – and the quantity of material resources flowing through the economy (throughput).[97] Everything else – knowledge, community, compassion, wisdom, innovation and freedom – can grow indefinitely.

To speak of the end of growth in throughput is to speak of the end of just one form of growth – a form that depletes Earth's resources and overwhelms its capacity to absorb safely the waste we create. Change in a steady state is continuous. To make sense of the idea of change within a system of fixed resources, ecological economists use the analogy of a forest that does not grow in size but is home to a complex set of relationships between species that cooperate and compete. Animals evolve and new relationships emerge – change and dynamism exist at all levels, even though the scale of the whole system remains invariant.

The pioneer of 'steady state economics' is Herman Daly, who was once a senior economist at the World Bank. He argues that an economy should only grow if the benefits (such as more income and products) outweigh the costs (such as environmental degradation). As soon as the costs of growth in GDP exceed the benefits it is no longer economic growth at all but 'uneconomic growth', because each dollar of additional growth impoverishes rather than enriches us.

The principle of a steady state economy is not new. Some notable early economists foresaw the need to achieve an economy of a stable size. Over a century ago, John Stuart Mill envisioned a time when economies would cease to increase in scale, and saw in such economies 'as much scope as ever for all kinds of mental culture, and moral and social progress'.[98] Seeing no necessary connection between economic growth and human improvement, he argued that the 'Art of Living' would flourish 'when minds cease to be engrossed by the art of getting on'.

Bigger doesn't necessarily mean better. A range of needs must be met for communities to flourish, but, beyond a certain level, increased consumption does not appear to improve people's lives. In spite of fifty years of economic growth, most people in wealthy nations seem to be no better off. In the UK, per capita GDP grew by 66 per cent between 1973 and 2003, but there was no discernible difference in life satisfaction.[99] From 1958 to 1986, Japan experienced a fivefold increase in per capita income, again with no reported increase in satisfaction.[100] These findings have been corroborated in numerous studies covering many countries. We may fly more miles, own more cars, buy more clothes, watch bigger TVs and use more gadgets, but, as Bill McKibben puts it, 'All that material progress – and all the billions of barrels of oil and millions of acres of trees that it took to create it – seems not to have moved the satisfaction meter an inch.'[101]

The ideology of growth has provided a long-standing justification for inequality, but, if the economic pie cannot perpetually increase in size, calls to redistribute wealth gain extra weight. Henry Wallich, former governor of the US Federal Reserve, argued that 'growth is a substitute for equality of income. So long as there is growth there is hope, and that makes large income differentials tolerable.'[102] The reality is that growth has not been a substitute for equality. Over the last century, the global economy grew twenty-five times larger, yet at the turn of the millennium over a billion people still lived on less than $1 per day and 2.7 billion people lived on less than $2 per day.[103] The view expressed by Anne Krueger of the IMF, that 'Poverty reduction is best achieved through making the cake bigger, not by trying to cut it up in a different way', is refuted by the facts.[104] For every $100 of global economic growth that occurred between 1990 and 2001, only 60 cents went to those living below the $1 per day threshold.[105]

Although growth in wealthy nations has not been making us happier, the stability of the present system requires it to continue. The transition to a steady state economy therefore requires structural changes to address the interconnected features of the current system that combine to create a powerful growth imperative. Our dependency on growth begins with the drive at the heart of the market economy to increase profits, which exerts a powerful pressure on the whole system to expand. Last year's profits must find somewhere to go – if investment opportunities cannot be found there is great pressure to create them. This dynamic sees competition drive the expansion of wants, markets, production and debt, while nature is reduced to a commodity for exploitation in ever more ways.

Over the twentieth century, the productive capacity of corporations has accelerated rapidly, bringing with it the challenge of how to increase demand along with supply. One part of the solution was planned obsolescence – intentionally limiting the lifespan of a product to force the faster replacement of goods – which has depleted scarce natural resources more rapidly. Investment in advertising also ensured that the demand to consume kept pace with the capacity to produce. In an unequal society, social comparisons fan the flames of an aspirational culture in which people strive to attain the symbols of material success. People acquire goods simply to keep up with others: overall consumption increases, the economy expands, but no one gets any happier. As wages are pushed down to boost profits, money for increased consumption must be found elsewhere: the result is high levels of indebtedness. In effect, debt is a promise of future productivity. People borrow today with the expectation of greater productivity tomorrow: debt exacerbates the growth imperative.

Standard economic measures – which may overestimate slightly – reveal that between 1950 and 2000, productivity in the American economy increased fivefold.[106] In spite of these gains, the average American worked more hours a week in 2000 than in 1950.[107] A fivefold increase in productivity could have radically reduced the length of the working week. Part of the explanation for why this did not happen is that gains in productivity were captured almost completely by those at the top of the economic hierarchy. From 1966 to 2001, 90 per cent of American workers saw their incomes rise more slowly than overall productivity in the economy.[108] And from 1997 to 2001, the top 1 per cent of earners captured more of the growth than the bottom 50 per cent of the population combined.[109] Ordinary people have been working harder for fewer rewards.

Trade unions typically fear that a slow down of economic growth will create unemployment for those they represent, but recent research looking at the relationship between growth and unemployment suggests the two are not necessarily linked.[110] However, even if under the current system unemployment increases when the economy slows, the solution would be to change the system, not defend growth. In any case, the path to a greener economy will be a powerful creator of jobs. Getting to where we need to be will take a lot of work – decades of high-level employment. There will of course be costs associated with the transition to a new system, and these should be borne fairly. People who have been engaged in unsustainable forms of employment should be supported and retrained to enter the green economy. Spreading these costs equitably is not only fair, it's essential if we are to generate enough support to guide society down this path.

Green jobs are an important part of the picture, but a sustainable economy requires us to do more than change the kind of work we do. It demands that we change the way we think about work itself. Many jobs in our society are unnecessary. As David Graeber points out, labour is only virtuous if it helps others.[111] Stated this way it becomes clear that a lot of the most useful work in society goes unpaid anyway: the work of mothers, fathers, carers and friends. The aim of society should not be to produce more jobs but to enable better lives. If we share out the necessary work (by all working less) and convert productivity gains into more time rather than more profit, full employment can be achieved without incomes being reduced.

We need an economy of sustainable scale, one that generates a fairer distribution of the world's resources. In the short term we urgently need to impose resource caps to protect natural resources from over-exploitation. In the longer term we need to address the growth imperative at the heart of the economy, change the way we measure progress, move away from consumer culture, take power back from corporations, rejuvenate democracy, share work, cancel debts and significantly reduce inequality. There are many internal arrangements possible within a steady state economy; by taking the initiative now, a progressive movement can frame and lead the transition to a sustainable system of the most democratic and egalitarian form possible.

Building a movement

Bill McKibben has long been one of the world's leading environmentalists. He is credited as the first author to write about climate change for a general audience. After decades of writing, lecturing and organising, he has arrived at a sobering judgement: '[T]his fight, as it took me too long to figure out, was never going to be settled on the grounds of justice or reason. We won the argument, but that didn't matter: like most fights it was, and is, about power.'[112]

Power determines the future. Books, articles, films, speeches and campaigns are some of the tools we can use to shift the balance of power, but movements provide the force to sweep away the obstacles to change. Movements coordinate actions on a scale large enough to turn shared values into shared reality. They bring about deep shifts in ideas, attitudes and behaviour, making the impossible suddenly inevitable. Yet movements do not build themselves – they erupt and swell through the dedicated actions of countless people, driven by rage, love, fear and hope.

Achieving meaningful change is hard. The best strategies of the disempowered often fail, while the worst strategies of the powerful usually succeed. That is the nature of power. Looking the climate problem squarely in the face is not easy. The impulse to turn away, focus on something else and push it to the back of our minds is a persistent obstacle to action. Jason Box argues that even most scientists are 'burying overt recognition of the awful truths of climate change in a protective layer of denial'.[113] He is 'amazed how few climatologists have taken an advocacy message to the streets, demonstrating for some policy action'.

Choosing to ignore climate change, even when we understand its seriousness, has less to do with not caring than not knowing how to respond. Some even fear that it is too late to respond. The issue is huge and terrifying, and can seem beyond our control. What's more, there are other pressing issues of importance that require our attention: war, inequality, racism, corporate power – on top of the daily personal challenges of existence. From this angle, our prospects look bleak, but we should nevertheless bear two things in mind: first, even if a serious climate catastrophe is by now unavoidable, our actions can either slow down or accelerate the process and the way we respond can either exacerbate or reduce suffering along the way; second, the scale of the climate threat presents us with a valuable opportunity.

Climate change exposes all the flaws in our social, economic and political systems: the corrupting influence of corporate power, the shortcomings of mainstream media, the hollowness of our democracies, the failings of markets, the pervasiveness of racial injustice, the breakdown of local communities, the dangers of consumerism, problems with industrial agriculture, the unsustainability of perpetual growth, and deep inequalities within and between nations. As Naomi Klein puts it, 'It is a civilisational wake-up call. A powerful message – spoken in the language of fires, floods, droughts and extinctions – telling us that we need an entirely new economic model and a new way of sharing this planet.'[114] To understand what climate science requires of us, she points out, is to understand that it's 'the most powerful weapon progressives have ever had in the fight for equality and social justice'.

Climate change provides an opportunity to build the kind of movement that can win the depth of change we so urgently need. It is not an additional issue to tack onto our list of problems: it is a unifying force that can help us join the dots between the crises erupting around us, all symptoms of the failings of a single system. It is an opportunity to see that our most serious problems share common causes and common solutions. It is a vindication of the arguments that have been made by progressives for centuries, grounding an old critique in hard science.

The fights for racial justice, refugee welfare, gender equity, disability rights, public services, economic equality, meaningful democracy and lasting peace are not unrelated. The challenge is to transform the causal links between these issues into networks of solidarity, to weave their solutions into a coherent, inspiring and urgent vision that can take us beyond the deadly certainties of the present system and win a society that not only cuts emissions, bans fracking, protects forests and heals sick oceans, but reduces inequalities, addresses injustices, eradicates unemployment, rescues public services and deepens democracy.

To get there, we need a spectrum of tactics and people from all walks of life. As well as powerful and symbolic acts of resistance and defiance, we need high levels of organisation and participation. The role of unions in this regard could be decisive. For too long, a mutual suspicion has divided environmentalists and social justice campaigners, each believing the other has the wrong priorities – but things are starting to change. One British union leading the way has been the Public and Commercial Services Union (PCS). Its General Secretary, Mark Serwotka, argues that the environmental and union movements go 'together like hand in glove'. The PCS represents people in the aviation industry, the Ministry of Defence and until recently the nuclear industry. Yet, Serwotka explains, 'as a union, we have a position of total opposition to nuclear power, we have a position against the expansion at Heathrow, and we have a position of opposition to all nuclear weapons, and indeed we are affiliated to the Campaign for Nuclear Disarmament'. How did this happen? '[W]e went to the members who worked in these industries . . . we wrote to every single person that we represented and we argued that if we did not renew Trident, if we did not have nuclear weapons, if we freed up the billions and billions of pounds to do something productive, they could be re-employed, re-skilled to do things that would benefit all of us. And you know what, the members actually accepted it.'[115]

In 2009, a coalition of trade unions and green groups in Britain released a pioneering report detailing how a million climate jobs could be created and paid for by the government in just one year.[116] Now in its third edition, it is an attractive plan, even for workers in highly polluting industries, because anyone who loses a job in an old high-carbon sector is guaranteed a permanent job in the green economy. The jobs that a green transition would create include producing and installing vast numbers of wind turbines and solar panels; building energy-efficient housing; retrofitting old buildings; transitioning to small-scale sustainable agriculture; building more railways, tramlines and bicycle routes; and strengthening flood defences. The struggle to democratise capital, to channel it where it is most needed, is at the forefront of the climate fight.

More and more people are realising that the same logic that treats human beings as economic inputs to be exploited and discarded also treats nature as a garbage can for corporate waste; the same trade deals that attack workers' rights are also at war with Earth's life-support systems, undermining the transition to renewable energy; and that the same racism that systematically disempowers non-white communities is blithely sentencing whole nations to carbon-induced droughts and flooding. Fighting the many corrosive symptoms of a profit-driven system in isolation means we will always be on the back foot, overwhelmed by battles on many fronts. But if we join together and fight for a vision that unites us, we give ourselves a chance of winning deep and lasting change.

There is already much to inspire hope. In June 2015, campaigners in Holland, on behalf of 900 Dutch citizens, won a case against their own government, which was ordered to reduce greenhouse gas emissions by at least 25 per cent by 2020.[117] Similar cases are being fought in Belgium and the Philippines, suggesting that this could be the beginning of a wave of climate-driven legal challenges. That same month, Pope Francis dedicated a chapter of his encyclical to the urgent need to engage in the protection of nature. Speaking of an 'ecological conversion', he argued that, 'Living our vocations to be protectors of God's handiwork is essential to a life of virtue; it is not an optional or a secondary aspect of our Christian experience.'[118] On a blustery day in July 2015, 140 per cent of Denmark's electricity needs were met by wind farms.[119] In Toronto, over 10,000 people took to the streets united by the call for 'Jobs, Climate and Justice'. Led by First Nations activists, the march comprised not just environmentalists but labour unions, faith groups, anti-poverty campaigns, health workers and immigration rights activists.[120] In August 2015, it was revealed that hundreds of people had succeeded in shutting down Europe's largest open-cast coal mine – the source of much of the continent's carbon emissions – with little more than courage, discipline and unity.[121] In the same month, it was reported that renewable energy had become the second largest source of electricity across the globe, overtaking natural gas.[122] In September, in response to years of bold campaigning and direct action, Shell declared it would withdraw from oil and gas drilling in the Arctic. About the same time, Brazil, the world's seventh biggest polluter, committed to emission cuts of 37 per cent by 2025 (from 2005 levels) and 43 per cent by 2030, and the global divestment movement secured a remarkable $2.6 trillion in pledges to divest from fossil fuels.[123] In November, President Barack Obama agreed to cancel the Keystone pipeline, which would have lit the fuse of the 'carbon bomb' that is the Alberta tar sands. This incomplete list, covering a single year, demonstrates that when people come together to protect and create what they value, it is possible to win, even in the face of powerful resistance. Activism works. Indeed, it may be our only hope.

Those on the frontlines of this fight need support. According to research from Global Witness, every week at least two people are killed defending their land from environmental destruction. To pick just one of many examples: 'on 18th September 2015, Rigoberto Lima Choc was shot dead in broad daylight opposite the courthouse in Sayaxché, Guatemala. On the same day, three other activists – Hermelindo Asij, Lorenzo Pérez and Manuel Mendoza – were kidnapped'. It was reported that they had been threatened with being burned alive.[124] They were targeted because 'Lima Choc and his colleagues were the first to document the catastrophic environmental destruction caused by palm oil company REPSA in the Río de la Pasión'. The Ministry of the Environment and Natural Resources described the damage as 'ecocide . . . the most serious environmental problem of its kind in national territory in living memory'.

Since 2002, close to a thousand environmental activists have been murdered for their campaigning, the majority of attacks taking place in Latin America and Asia. Many more have been injured, threatened or arrested. These people are sacrificing their lives because their communities are already struggling for survival. Men, women and children are dying and being displaced as a result of climate-driven disasters, but the people who suffer the most have been largely omitted from debates on climate change, which are invariably dominated by Western governments and NGOs. This has had an impact on how the problem is framed. In fact, the coalitions responsible for the largest climate marches on both sides of the Atlantic conceal deep rifts on these questions among their member organisations. Behind closed doors many of the largest campaigning groups – and often those with the deepest pockets – have been pushing to sanitise the imagery and language, downplay the implications of the science and exaggerate the progress being made.

A global climate deal needs to reflect the fact that neither the benefits nor the costs of burning fossil fuel have been spread equally. The rich nations, comprising about 20 per cent of the global population, are responsible for releasing about 70 per cent of the greenhouse gases currently in the atmosphere. The injustice is striking. According to one estimate, the development model of the richer nations has externalised $5 trillion of costs onto poorer nations in the form of ecological damage.[125] If we take into account – as we ought to – the vast debts incurred from centuries of colonialism, imperialism and slavery, the figure is far higher. Given this context, the extraction of billions of dollars a year from poorer nations in the form of debt repayments to institutions such as the World Bank and IMF only adds insult to injury.

The fact that we are hitting ecological limits to growth means that richer nations need to free up the ecological space into which poorer nations can grow, if they are to develop sustainably. If richer countries want poorer ones to tread a sustainable path, they will have to do their bit to make it happen. This means providing the necessary resources to build renewable infrastructure and compensating poorer nations for not exploiting the billions of dollars' worth of oil, gas and coal that lie within their borders. The money for this should come from the richest, most polluting corporations. This may be a hard sell in the Global North but, if poorer nations attempt to emulate the development path of richer nations, in climate terms, nothing the rich nations do will matter.

To enable poorer regions, such as sub-Saharan Africa, to benefit from a spurt of economic growth before reaching an optimal size, the wealthy nations of Western Europe and North America need to pursue a course of de-growth on the way to sustainable steady state economies. The world's nations need to converge on an economic scale that can fit comfortably within ecological limits.[126] Guided by historical responsibility for emissions, and taking into account the 'capacity to contribute', researchers have fleshed out in great detail, country by country, what a fair approach to greenhouse-gas reduction would look like.[127]

Those with their hands on the levers of power have shown themselves incapable of doing what is necessary to protect life on Earth, not because they seek to wreak destruction but because they are in thrall to the expansionist logic of the current system, driven by profit and blinkered by the dishonest framing of 'national interest'. To achieve a meaningful transformation, the logic of the system itself needs to be overhauled. The nature and scale of the climate challenge require that we defy the professional and cultural expectations that too often tame and dehumanise us. It requires that we recognise the fundamental obligations we owe to each other, to future generations, and the natural world. To achieve this transformation, it will take a great many people, a great deal of cooperation and creativity, and the triumph of hope over cynicism and courage over fear.

★

'[T]he American way of life is not negotiable,' declared President George H. W. Bush at the 1992 Earth summit.[128] It was a statement brimming with the delusional arrogance that has characterised the response of states and corporations to the climate threat. It is the laws of nature and the needs of our own biology with which we cannot negotiate. Whether we like it or not, our survival requires that civilisation make some profound changes. A war against nature cannot be won.

The scale of the climate threat challenges us to break out of old ways of thinking. Storms, floods and droughts do not respect the arbitrary borders of nations. Pollution in China is everyone's problem. A nuclear meltdown in Japan is everyone's problem. Excessive consumption in the

US is everyone's problem. When it comes to the climate, there is no easily identifiable 'national interest'. Climate change compels us to recognise our interdependence. We will not compete our way to a solution. Now, more than ever, we need to revive the art of cooperation and transcend the illusory divisions of borders and beliefs.

Moving away from the endless pursuit of consumption and profit not only benefits the natural world but helps us to discard a damaging value-system – one that drives us to chase things that don't matter and disconnect from things that do. We are not separate from the world around us. Its health is our health. We emerged from it, depend on it and will soon disappear into it. Our physiology reminds us of this intimate relationship: our lungs are an anticipation of the atmosphere that clings to this spinning rock; our eyes an anticipation of the light waves that illuminate the world; our bodies an anticipation of a narrow band of temperatures, beyond which we cannot survive. The evolution of human society is inextricable from the history of our natural environment. The more this dependency is acknowledged, the more we empower ourselves. The more we understand our limitations, the better placed we are to adapt to them.

The idea that we are products of forces over which we have no control exposes the fact that we are not as free as we'd like to believe, but it also reveals how we are literally the walking embodiment of the relationships we have with our natural and social environment. The level of social and ecological violence in the world is an ugly testament to just how blind we have become to this interdependence. To see beyond the illusion of ultimate responsibility requires a broader form of identification, one in which the individual is not seen as separate from the rest of the universe, but as temporary and changing manifestations of it, intimately connected to all its facets. As we let go of the illusion, we gain something else of immeasurable value: a deep sense of interconnectedness. For creative freedom to survive, we must hold sacred the conditions that make it possible.

Beyond the thin layer of gases that comprise Earth's atmosphere is a cold, desolate, unforgiving universe. Remove this protective layer and we perish. We know of nowhere else in this vast universe capable of supporting life. Earth is the only home we have. For all the suffering that exists in the world, for all the injustice, greed, ignorance and violence, our planet remains a fount of great beauty and potential, the source of the endlessly creative permutations of life. If ever there was something to treasure, worship, protect and fight for, it is the soil and forests, the oceans and the air that generously sustain us all – the source of all our freedom.

12

Empathy

We differ from each other in countless ways – height, weight, health, wealth and intelligence, aggression, kindness, courage and confidence – but in one important respect we are all the same. Without exception, none of us is ultimately responsible for who we are or what we do. This perspective creates the possibility for a deep solidarity between human beings, one built on the understanding that, had I truly been in your situation, I would have done as you did. A profound equality emerges from this realisation that provides a firm basis for compassion and empathy, two ideals that have infused the pages of this book. All systems of oppression and exploitation depend on the denial of this equality. Contrary to the fears some may have, learning to view ourselves more objectively does not undermine ethical standards or the capacity for love. It places them on firmer ground.

For centuries, Western philosophers, politicians and economists have asserted that humans are essentially greedy, concerned primarily with their own preservation, pleasure and comfort. Neoclassical economists postulate that humans are rational and selfish, focused on the maximisation of their own well-being, which is often defined in narrow, materialistic terms. This caricature does not fit the facts. Research across a range of disciplines has converged on a different conclusion: empathy, the capacity to 'step into another's shoes' and get a sense of how things look and feel from their perspective, is an integral part of what makes us human and is central to the practice of compassion.[1]

Child psychologists have observed that three-year-olds have the capacity to view things from another's perspective.[2] At twelve months, infants seem able to empathise with the distress of others, offering them toys, stroking them when they look upset and helping strangers who appear to be struggling, even if they have to clamber over obstacles to do so.[3] Quite automatically, our brains 'mirror' the brain states of others: the neurons that begin to fire when we encounter the emotions and actions of someone else are called 'mirror neurons'. Recent research suggests that they are part of a more complex 'circuit of empathy' comprising at least ten regions of the brain.[4] This empathy circuit facilitates our understanding of the experiences of other people. Damage to these neurons seriously impairs empathetic potential.

Primatologists have no doubt that our cousins on the evolutionary tree of life, the great apes, regularly display empathetic behaviour. Chimpanzees frequently console and reassure one another. When a chimpanzee loses a fight or crosses paths with a predator, others embrace and groom it to calm it down. Numerous experiments with primates also point to a powerful instinct for fairness. In a classic experiment conducted by American psychiatrist Jules Masserman, rhesus monkeys refused to pull a cord that gave them food while simultaneously administering an electric shock to another monkey. Monkeys would sometimes go for days without pulling the cord, starving themselves rather than hurt a companion. In another case, a bonobo chimp was observed looking after a wounded bird in captivity and trying to free it from its enclosure by climbing to the top of a tree, helping it to spread its wings and releasing it into the air. The first attempt failed, but, after protecting it for a while longer and allowing it to heal, he tried again and the bird successfully flew to freedom.[5]

Frans de Waal, one of the world's leading primatologists, sees important implications arising from our enriched understanding of human nature. Speaking of politicians who justify policies by claiming that nature is a selfish struggle for life, he states: 'They read into nature what they want to, and I feel it is my task to point out that they got it all wrong. There are many animals that survive through cooperation, and our own species in particular comes from a long line of ancestors dependent on each other. Empathy and solidarity are bred into us, so that our society's design ought to reflect this side of the human species, too.'[6] The central role played by cooperation in the survival of our species is now widely accepted among biologists.

Empathy is the ability to identify what someone else is feeling and thinking, and respond to them appropriately. The capacity for profound empathy and the compassion it engenders exist in almost everyone, but the degree to which we empathise is not fixed. Culture influences and channels our potential for empathy. It can be stunted or constrained by many factors, from ideology and early experiences, to genes, hormones and neurology.[7] A serious lack of empathy makes it easy to treat people as less than human, to ignore their subjective inner world and see them as objects to be used for our own purposes. The interesting question is not whether we have the capacity to be empathetic, but why we extend our empathy to some groups and not others.

Dehumanisation

Renowned criminologist Nils Christie began his career studying German and Norwegian concentration camp guards in the wake of the Second World War. The guards fell into two broad groups: those who maltreated prisoners, killing or torturing them, and those who treated prisoners relatively well. Christie wanted to understand why the second group behaved more humanely. After interviewing numerous guards at length about their experiences, he arrived at a telling conclusion: there was indeed a difference between them, one that left an indelible mark on his life, and it lay in their ability to 'see the prisoners as human beings', the ability to be close enough to the prisoners to understand that these people who were 'miserable, starving, dirty' and willing to betray a friend to get their hands on a crust of bread were only doing what they themselves would likely do in those same circumstances.[8] Christie found that the guards who had behaved more humanely had spent more time with the prisoners and developed closer relationships. They had spoken with their captives and seen photos of them from before their incarceration. Christie argued this contact had humanised the prisoners in the eyes of the guards. Later research supports this conclusion. One of the major findings from studies of extermination camps, as well as from controlled psychological experiments, is that, in Christie's words, 'Distance makes killing and torture possible . . . Distance makes it possible to lose sight of the victim as an ordinary human being.' This distance is not necessarily 'measured in yards or metres' – it may be 'of a social sort', and quite consciously inculcated.

The way we relate to other groups and individuals is heavily influenced by how we categorise them. Our language abounds with labels that define and distinguish between people: believer/non-believer; illegal immigrant/citizen; criminal/victim; terrorist/civilian; patriot/traitor; black/white; man/woman. The categories go on and on and, depending on the prejudices that accompany them, our attitudes towards their members change dramatically. The neuroscience of dehumanisation has demonstrated just how powerful the act of categorisation can be. When exposed to stigmatised groups – such as homeless people and drug addicts – the region of the brain normally associated with considerate and social behaviour is not activated.[9]

The categories in which we place people reflect a hierarchy of human value. The philosopher Peter Singer uses the term 'moral circle' to describe how we place some beings in a privileged category – worthy of our full moral concern – and others outside it.[10] Those within the circle of altruism become part of our moral community and, with respect to them, preferential principles of fairness, conduct, respect, resource allocation and justice apply. The smaller our moral circle, the more people are excluded from it.[11] Those who don't make the cut are judged unworthy of the same level of concern, in which case a different ethical code applies.[12]

It is useful to think not of a single moral circle but a series of concentric circles, bounding zones of moral concern. The further someone is from the epicentre of these circles, the less deserving of humane treatment they are judged to be. In extreme cases, certain categories of people are judged to be sub-human. Research into moral exclusion suggests that humanising privileged 'in-groups' while dehumanising 'out-groups' is a ubiquitous phenomenon.[13]

Immigrants, foreigners, the poor, the working class, women, the unemployed, the disabled, the obese, the young, the old and prisoners are routinely described in derogatory terms that chip away at their status as human beings worthy of our full moral concern. Racism, sexism and classism are all ways of defining the boundaries of our moral circles in order to keep some people firmly out. Moral exclusion can run in both directions, however: the oppressed can dehumanise their oppressors as much as their oppressors can dehumanise them – the crucial difference being the power each group has to turn prejudice into persecution.

One of the important implications of research into dehumanisation is that thinking of people in terms of good and bad, ethical and unethical, is too simplistic. Moral behaviour isn't just a reflection of character; it's also an indication of the categories we impose on each other, and the prejudices that accompany them. You may be loving, caring and loyal to those within your moral circle, yet callous and brutal to those outside it. The suffering of those within our moral circle tugs at our heartstrings; that of outsiders does not. We are adept at compartmentalising our morality.

Language reinforces psychological distance. From Nazi Germany to apartheid South Africa, labels that reduce people to the status of animals have been a standard way of justifying persecution. People are called 'beasts', 'dogs', 'pigs' or 'parasites'. Employing the clinical language of hygiene takes this process further so that people become objects of revulsion: 'filth', 'scum' or 'trash' that must be 'cleansed' and 'eradicated'. Jews in Nazi Germany were routinely described as 'rats' and 'vermin'. In the Rwandan genocide, the terms 'lice' and 'cockroaches' were used. Bosnians in the Balkan wars suffered similar comparisons.

The philosopher Jonathan Glover has identified degradation as a common feature of dehumanisation.[14] It is far easier to think of people as objects of revulsion if they are forced to live in conditions that provoke disgust. Confining people in dirty and humiliating conditions, be it a prison cell, concentration camp or just extreme poverty, makes it easier to treat them as sub-human. A scruffy, unwashed appearance adds to the impression that they are different and inferior. It's a small jump to assume they belong in the same category as diseases or dirty animals, and that they lack the higher faculties of civilised people. You don't reason with an animal. You don't enter into a dialogue with a disease.

"The Good Old Days": *The Holocaust as Seen by Its Perpetrators and Bystanders* is a remarkable, if disconcerting book that includes letters from concentration camp guards to their families and the diary entries of people involved in carrying out the Holocaust.[15] The accounts challenge our impulse to label their authors as monsters, instead revealing people who were capable of caring behaviour when relating to those within their moral circles. These were men who loved their children, missed their wives and felt loyalty to their friends and colleagues. They were also engaged in the mass slaughter of those who had been placed beyond their moral circle by a culture in which categories of moral worth were carefully controlled.

As Nils Christie points out, 'It's easier to think in terms of bad people: make monsters of the concentration-camp guards.'[16] Yet, having spent time with many concentration-camp guards from the Nazi extermination camps, he is of the opinion that some were 'nice and kind people'.[17] In his account of his twelve years as a slave, Solomon Northup wrote of one of his 'masters' that 'there never was a more kind, noble, candid, Christian man', but that his influences 'blinded him to the inherent wrong at the bottom of the system of Slavery'.[18] This is a jarring idea. It feels wrong to describe the perpetrators of terrible crimes as, in any sense, 'kind', yet it makes more sense when we understand that they did not regard the people they were killing or enslaving as fully human. An ordinary person could not participate in such crimes against fellow human beings, but perhaps they could do so when their victims shared the status of animals – 'rats' or 'vermin'. It may be sickening to attempt to see things this way, but understanding the roots of such behaviour is essential if we are to avoid repeating it.

From December 1937 to January 1938, thousands of Chinese civilians – men, women and children – were killed, mutilated and raped by Japanese soldiers. Philosopher David Livingstone Smith, who has written extensively on dehumanisation, presses home the point that 'the soldiers who committed these atrocities were neither madmen nor monsters. They were, for the most part, ordinary people. People like you.'[19] When one veteran, Yoshio Tshuchiya, was later interviewed about his crimes, he was explicit about what made such acts possible: 'We called the Chinese "chancorro", that meant below human, like bugs or animals. The Chinese didn't belong to the human race. That was the way we looked at it. . . . If I'd thought of them as human beings I couldn't have done it . . . But I thought of them as animals or below human beings.'[20] In general, dehumanisation of the enemy is encouraged by all sides of a conflict. The Second World War saw Russian political art depict Germans and Italians as rats, pigs, dogs and apes. One prominent Russian poet wrote that 'there is nothing more amusing for us than a heap of German corpses'. The Japanese depicted American and British leaders as monsters and devils with fangs, claws and tails. In the US and Britain, the Japanese were often presented as monkeys, apes, cockroaches and rodents.[21]

There is a strong temptation to dehumanise those who dehumanise others, but the uncomfortable truth, as history teaches us, is that treating others inhumanely is very much within the scope of our nature. Indeed, by dehumanising those who have dehumanised others we clearly demonstrate our own capacity for moral exclusion. The evidence suggests that what separates us from those whose actions we deplore is not innate moral superiority but circumstances – and not just circumstances that shape our character but the circumstances that determine our options. As Thomas Nagel puts it, 'Someone who was an officer in a concentration camp might have led a quiet and harmless life if the Nazis had never come to power in Germany. And someone who led a quiet and harmless life in Argentina might have become an officer in a concentration camp if he had not left Germany for business reasons in 1930.'[22]

The same psychological mechanisms of dehumanisation are at work whenever we encounter systematic killing, oppression or torture. In the Rwandan genocide of 1994, hundreds of thousands of Tutsis were slaughtered by the Hutu majority. The underlying prejudices were consciously fostered by European colonialists, particularly the Belgians, as part of a 'divide and rule' strategy. Insidious theories of racial superiority were established and reinforced institutionally by political, economic and educational means. The Tutsi minority were granted privileges and invited to help rule the Hutu majority, fomenting the anger and resentment that eventually exploded into the violence of the 1990s. Examples abound. Dutch colonialism created the conditions for South African apartheid by systematically denying black South Africans fundamental rights and condemning them to humiliating and degrading conditions.

Paul Connolly, an academic from Northern Ireland, found that the process of moral exclusion can be observed in children as young as three.[23] The combination of cultural and familial influences meant that, by that age, children raised as Catholics were twice as likely to express negative and aggressive behaviour towards presumably pro-British police officers as children raised in Protestant homes. At six years old, a third of children, on both sides of the religious divide, already identified strongly with their community.

Daniel Bar-Tal from Tel-Aviv University has conducted research into the formation of attitudes and stereotypes among Jewish children in Israel, focusing specifically on the concept of 'Arab' because it is 'probably the most significant outgroup for Israeli Jews'. He found that Israeli children begin to use the word 'Arab' between the ages of twenty-four and thirty months, making it one of the first social categories they learn. When asked what they knew about Arabs, the majority of children described them as violent and aggressive. Children aged between five and six held more negative attitudes towards Arabs than younger children, and were more reluctant to entertain the possibility of social contact. These attitudes contrasted with their positive emotions towards 'Jews'. Bar-Tal's research led him to the broad conclusion that 'when Israeli children characterise Arabs, many of them use delegitimising categories, mostly those of "killers" and "murderers"'.[24] Parents were thought to be the main source of their attitudes. According to Patricia G. Devine, a professor of psychology at the University of Wisconsin, stereotypes 'are well established in children's memories before children develop the cognitive ability and flexibility to question or critically evaluate the stereotype's validity or acceptability'.[25] In 2015, it was reported that Israel had banned a novel that told the story of a romance between an Arab man and a Jewish woman.[26] Reasons given for the ban included the fear that 'young people of adolescent age don't have the systemic view that includes considerations involving maintaining the national-ethnic identity of the people and the significance of miscegenation [the interbreeding of people believed to be of different races]'. The need to maintain 'the identity and heritage of students' was asserted because 'intimate relations between Jews and non-Jews threatens the separate identity' cultivated by the Israeli state.

The selective channelling of compassion begins early and continues in a multitude of ways. Indirect forms of dehumanisation can be among the most powerful; for example in media coverage. In his 2002 book, *Brown Tide Rising*, Otto Santa Ana explored the representation of Mexican immigrants in US culture. He found that many newspaper articles made tacit comparisons to insects, parasites, diseases, weeds, burdens, outsiders and invaders.[27] He argued that the power of the metaphor allows implicit, derogatory associations to be made – overtly racist terms are implied, hinted at and evoked but not directly stated. This use of language is fairly standard. In 2015, David Cameron described refugees living in appalling conditions in Calais as 'a swarm' trying to reach Britain.[28]

For millennia, legal categories have been used to codify hierarchies of moral concern, bestowing some groups – whether united by gender, race, religion, sexual orientation, political beliefs, class, wealth or ability – with more rights than others. The attributes used to isolate groups can be almost anything. Once a category has been imposed, people are segregated into the worthy and unworthy. The hierarchies are accompanied by evocative myths about the superiority of the in-group and the dangers of an out-group. Standing up to the outsiders is framed as an act of courage. Indeed, the dehumanisation and persecution of the 'other' is often presented as a virtuous act – a demonstration of patriotism, solidarity and loyalty.

Many slave owners believed their slaves did not possess a soul. Using the rule of law to advance the process of dehumanisation, Chief Justice of the US Supreme Court Roger Brooke Taney declared in 1856 that the black man 'had no rights which the White man was bound to respect . . . the Negro might justly and lawfully be . . . treated as an ordinary article of merchandise and traffic'.[29] Dehumanisation has always been fostered to concentrate power and justify violence. How can a country grow rich on slave labour if its population regards slaves as fully human? How can military leaders destroy native populations and establish new territories if those natives have equal rights? How can rich nations justify their hugely disproportionate consumption of the world's resources without implicitly believing in their own superiority?

Dehumanisation has long been wired into the systems that dominate the world.[30] Capitalism has to foster moral exclusion to justify the extreme inequality it creates. States are fictional entities that methodically constrain empathy through the cultivation of patriotism. If we are to reduce dehumanisation in the world, we need to overcome the physical and psychological distance maintained by borders and bank balances.

The human exchange rate

As of 24 November 2014, attempts to kill forty-one targeted individuals under the US drone programme sacrificed an estimated 1,147 innocent people.[31] On average, according to human rights group Reprieve, each attempt to assassinate one person has resulted in the deaths of twenty-eight innocent civilians, many of them children. In fact, the victims of these strikes are far more numerous. A major study by two US universities found that the psychological impact of killer drones was profound, inducing deep trauma in those living in and around targeted areas. Symptoms include 'emotional breakdowns, running indoors or hiding when drones appear above, fainting, nightmares and other intrusive thoughts, hyper startled reactions to loud noises, outbursts of anger or irritability, [insomnia] and loss of appetite and other physical symptoms'.[32] In a number of instances, the targets themselves walked away unharmed as innocent civilians lay dead and communities felt terrorised. President Obama calls this 'targeted killing'.

In 2012, it was revealed by the UK-based Bureau of Investigative Journalism that civilian rescuers of drone victims, as well as those who attend their funerals, are themselves intentionally targeted.[33] According to Christof Heyns, the UN Special Rapporteur on extrajudicial, summary and arbitrary executions, such killings are 'a war crime'. Former drone operators have started to speak out against the programme, at great personal risk. Michael Haas, a twenty-nine-year-old sensor operator, described how operators speak of children as 'fun-size terrorists'.[34] Killing them is compared to 'cutting the grass before it grows too long'. As a flight instructor, Haas was reprimanded by superiors for refusing to pass a student who seemed overly eager to kill.

Along with Haas, three other whistleblowers penned an open letter to Obama in which they declared, 'This administration and its predecessors have built a drone program that is one of the most devastating driving forces for terrorism and destabilization around the world . . . We cannot sit silently by and witness tragedies like the attacks in Paris, knowing the devastating effects the drone program has overseas and at home.'[35] Haas asks, 'Ever step on ants and never give it another thought? That's what you are made to think of the targets – as just black blobs on a screen . . . You had to kill part of your conscience to keep doing your job every day – and ignore those voices telling you this wasn't right.'[36]

A hierarchy of moral concern guides the foreign policy of nation states. Almost without exception, it is framed as the protection of the 'national interest'. This justification routinely passes without comment, but should it be accepted? Apart from the fact that there are many competing interests within any nation, is it right that a government should always and automatically prioritise what they claim advances 'national interest' or 'national security'? What if that means killing innocent people elsewhere, as it often does? What if it means undermining democracies elsewhere, as it often has? Such questions rarely enter into policy debates.

From the Roman Empire to European colonialists, those with the most powerful militaries have used violence to increase their wealth and consolidate their control of resources. Policies of colonialism, imperialism, exploitation and genocide are pursued precisely because they are believed by those in power to be in their interest.[37] National borders are the physical manifestation of legally mandated boundaries of moral exclusion. They demarcate a specific community to whom preferential principles apply. The careful and persistent cultivation of patriotism is, in effect, a form of state-sanctioned dehumanisation aimed not at eradicating empathy but channelling it to where it is politically useful.

British Foreign Secretary Lord Palmerston declared in 1848, 'We have no eternal allies and we have no perpetual enemies. Our interests are perpetual and eternal and those interests it is our duty to follow.'[38] It is generally taken for granted that, as Hans Morgenthau, a major figure in the study of international relations, puts it, 'International politics, like all politics, is a struggle for power.'[39] Carne Ross, a former UK Foreign Office employee, writes: 'In our ministry's culture, it was often deemed "emotional" or "immature" to burden arguments with moral sentiment. Real diplomats were cold-eyed and hard-headed, immune to the arguments of liberal protesters, journalists and other soft-heads who did not understand how the "real world" worked.'[40]

A brief look at the foreign policy records of the US and UK shows that this 'hard-headed' approach – even when practised by some of the most advanced democracies on the planet – is all that is needed to allow the most extreme forms of dehumanisation to pass as policy. Britain has not been at peace with the world for over a hundred years. As *The Guardian* reported in 2014, 'Since Britain's declaration of war against Germany in August 1914, not a year has passed without its forces being involved in conflict.'[41] Prior to the Second World War, the British Empire oversaw the deaths of, according to some estimates, over twenty million innocent people by pursuing brutal policies that turned droughts and crop failure into devastating famines.[42] Since the Second World War, it has been complicit in the deaths of over 10 million people globally.[43] Between 1945 and 2005, the United States has attempted to overthrow fifty governments around the world, many of them democracies; it has dropped bombs on close to thirty countries; attempted to assassinate more than fifty foreign leaders; installed and supported some of the most oppressive regimes on the planet; and is responsible – directly and indirectly – for the deaths of many millions of innocent people.[44] Throughout the 1990s, the US and Britain pursued a policy of debilitating sanctions in Iraq – debilitating for the people of Iraq not Saddam Hussein, whose ability to maintain power was unaffected. By the middle of that decade, the best available evidence indicated that up to a million people had died as a result of the sanctions. According to two authoritative studies – one by the UN Food and Agriculture Organization, the other by UNICEF with support from the World Health Organization – half of those who died were children under five.[45] One US establishment journal, *Foreign Affairs*, estimated in 1999 that Iraqi deaths from sanctions exceeded the number 'slain by all so-called weapons of mass destruction throughout history'.[46] In 2000, seventy members of the US Congress signed a letter to President Clinton to end the embargo and cease what they called 'infanticide masquerading as policy'.[47] Senior UN officials in charge of implementing the oil-for-food programme in Iraq were so outraged by the impact of sanctions that a number of them resigned in protest.[48] One of them – Denis Halliday – called it 'a programme that satisfies the definition of genocide' and 'a deliberate policy that has effectively killed well over a million individuals'.[49] Perhaps nowhere was the admission of dehumanisation as policy more clear than in the words of Clinton's Secretary of State, Madeleine Albright, in an exchange about the Iraqi death toll from sanctions on the TV show *60 Minutes*, in May 1996:

INTERVIEWER: We have heard that a half million children have died. I mean, that's more children than died in Hiroshima. And, you know, is the price worth it?

ALBRIGHT: I think this is a very hard choice, but the price – we think the price is worth it.

States are violent institutions – empires even more so. Throughout history, elites within nation states – whether Russia, Japan, France, Spain, Israel, Indonesia, Germany, Britain, or the US, to name a few – have repeatedly shown a willingness to sacrifice the lives of vast numbers of people in the quest for profit and power. Since 1945, the US has possessed by far the most powerful military in the world, enabling it to dominate other nations and take control of a disproportionate share of Earth's resources.

In 1948, Director of the US State Department's Policy Planning Staff, George Kennan, summed up the position of his country:

> [W]e have about 50% of the world's wealth but only 6.3% of its population . . . In this situation, we cannot fail to be the object of envy and resentment. Our real task in the coming period is to devise a pattern of relationships which will permit us to maintain this position of disparity without positive detriment to our national security. To do so, we will have to dispense with all sentimentality and day-dreaming; and our attention will have to be concentrated everywhere on our immediate national objectives. We need not deceive ourselves that we can afford today the luxury of altruism and world-benefaction.[50]

Valuable natural resources have always attracted the attention of powerful states. In 1947, US planners sought 'the removal or modification of existent barriers to the expansion of American foreign oil operations' and to 'promote . . . the entry of additional American firms into all phases of foreign oil operations'.[51] The Middle East was described by British officials as 'a vital prize for any power interested in world influence or domination'.[52] British Foreign Secretary Selwyn Lloyd noted in 1956 that, 'We must at all costs maintain control of this oil.'[53] Decades later, Henry Kissinger made it clear that 'oil is much too important a commodity to be left in the hands of the Arabs'. And at the turn of the millennium, General Anthony Zinni, Commander in Chief of the US Central Command in the Middle East, testified in Congress that the Gulf region was a 'vital interest' of 'long-standing importance' and that the US 'must have free access to the region's resources'.[54] Between 1900 and 1989, the US population tripled, but its consumption of raw materials increased seventeen-fold. In 2000, 'with less than 5 per cent of world population', the US consumed 'one-third of the world's paper, a quarter of the world's oil, 23 per cent of the coal, 27 per cent of the aluminum, and 19 per cent of the copper' and by 2010 it was estimated to possess 39 per cent of the world's wealth.[55]

Powerful corporations often stand to benefit from the wars waged by their governments. The invasion of Iraq in 2003 transferred $138 billion from the public purse to private security firms and reconstruction contractors.[56] Between them, the top ten contractors secured contracts worth more than $72 billion. As the *Financial Times* reported, 'The controversial former subsidiary of Halliburton, which was once run by Dick Cheney, vice-president to George W. Bush, was awarded at least $39.5bn in federal contracts related to the Iraq war over the past decade.'[57] A 2011 commission on Wartime Contracting found that as much as $12 million a day for the preceding decade had been lost to the corruption or dysfunction of defence contractors.[58]

As conflict escalated in the Middle East in 2015, major defence contractors assured their investors at a conference in West Palm Beach that they stood to gain from the violence. A year earlier, Bank of America analyst Ronald Epstein summed up the attitude: 'Let's paint a picture of the world right now . . . You've got the Europeans worried about what the Russians are doing in their backyard; we've got our hands full right now in Iraq; you've got the Israelis with their hands full in their region; and then you have the Chinese and Japanese in the South China Sea. As an investor, with this much regional conflict in the world, at least from a sentiment point of view, that can't be bad.'[59]

Governments and corporations are not shy about profiting from the human rights abuses of oppressive regimes. The leading exporters of arms and surveillance equipment are the US, Russia, France, Britain and Germany. In 2015, the world's largest importer of these arms was Saudi Arabia.[60] Ruled by an absolute monarchy, Saudi Arabia makes extensive use of the death penalty; it denies fundamental rights to women, who must seek permission from men to work, travel or leave the house; and it has banned all public gatherings. Dissidents face imprisonment, torture and death. In 2014, three lawyers were sentenced to up to eight years in prison for tweets that were deemed too critical of the Ministry of Justice. Two years earlier, teenager Ali Mohammed al-Nimr was arrested for taking part in protests during the Arab Spring and sentenced to death by beheading and crucifixion. In 2015, the Saudis intervened in a civil war in Yemen. The United Nations later reported that it was disproportionately killing civilians in its military operations, calling the outcome a 'humanitarian catastrophe'.[61] Thousands of civilians died and numerous hospitals and schools were bombed by Saudi forces. As this was happening, Britain sold over £1 billion worth of bombs and missiles to the Saudi regime. In response to criticism, British Foreign Secretary Philip Hammond declared he wanted to sell even more weapons to the country. 'We'd always like to do more business, more British exports, more British jobs and in this case very high end engineering jobs protected and created by our diplomacy abroad.'[62] When the Saudi King Abdullah died in early 2015, US Secretary of State John Kerry called him a 'man of wisdom and vision'. Obama praised his 'enduring contribution to the search for peace'.[63]

It's almost as if foreign policy operates according to a state-sanctioned human exchange rate. How many Syrians count for one French citizen? How many Iraqi lives count for one American? How many Afghani children count for one Briton? Just as the value of currencies in different nations increases and decreases in relation to each other, so does the value of human life according to geopolitical priorities. Monetising and comparing lives is standard practice in policy circles. Drafting the second report for the IPCC (Intergovernmental Panel on Climate Change), a group of economists pushed hard for the report to evaluate human lives in monetary terms: the fine print showed that it valued a life in rich countries at $1.5 million, a life in middle-income countries at $300,000, and a life in the lowest-income countries at $100,000. The final draft of the report took a more cautious approach, despite the lack of consensus.[64] In 2005, siding with the economists, a House of Lords committee in the UK published an influential report urging the IPCC to monetise all its costs and benefits.

In a now notorious memo – intended to be private but subsequently leaked – Larry Summers, Chief Economist at the World Bank, applied standard economic reasoning to the problem of toxic waste:

> Just between you and me, shouldn't the World Bank be encouraging *more* migration of the dirty industries to the LDCs [Least Developed Countries]? . . . The measurements of the costs of health-impairing pollution depends on the foregone earnings from increased

morbidity and mortality. From this point of view a given amount of health-impairing pollution should be done in the country with the lowest wages. I think the economic logic behind dumping a load of toxic waste in the lowest-wage country is impeccable and we should face up to that.[65]

Raj Patel, a former employee of the World Bank, writes that it 'costs corporations in Europe $1,000 to dispose of every ton of hazardous toxic waste – in Somalia the same waste can disappear for $2.50'.[66] After the tsunami of 2005, barrels of toxic waste that had been dumped offshore washed up on the Somali coastline, causing a range of chronic illnesses amongst local inhabitants. That Somalis are exposed to these risks rather than higher paid Europeans is perfectly logical according to prevalent cost–benefit assumptions. While there is nothing ethically problematic with comparing benefits and costs, viewing them in exclusively financial terms, and in ways that give preferential treatment to the wealthy, is misleading and unjust. As Patel argues, a Somali woman 'values her children no less than a German or American, and wants them to grow up healthy just as much as her richer counterparts', but when the value of life is viewed through the lens of the market, or measured according to the geopolitical priorities of rich nations, that's not how things appear.[67]

Actively taking lives is not easy. For soldiers, a first kill can be followed by bouts of vomiting, weeping, incontinence and trembling.[68] Troops are not taught to cut themselves off from their empathy but to channel it towards their fellow soldiers. It is drummed into marines that their actions affect not only themselves but the whole unit, so that a reluctance to kill might result in the death of 'one of their own'. Compassion, love and empathy are thus directed at the in-group, and the 'other' is pushed beyond the scope of moral concern. Resistance amongst the general population to killing in wartime is overcome in an analogous way. Domestic populations often have the power to constrain the dehumanising policies of their governments – and resistance to war has been growing in recent decades. In the lead-up to the 2003 invasion of Iraq, a million people took to the streets in Britain, and many more did so around the world. Protest on this scale preceding the start of war is a new development and not welcomed by state power. As 'hard-headed' as the decisions of governments may be, in order to secure public support and galvanise the soldiers who must carry out the killing, foreign policy aims – and a nation's military history – are generally cloaked in the highest ideals. There are always politicians on hand to explain why killing is noble and necessary.

Centuries ago, David Hume wrote that 'When our own nation is at war with any other, we detest them under the character of cruel, perfidious, unjust and violent: but always esteem ourselves and allies equitable, moderate and merciful.'[69] Every government, in every era, justifies its own violence in noble terms while condemning in harsh tones the violence of enemies. While gearing up for the 'war on terror', after the terrorist attacks of September 2001, George W. Bush declared that 'Our enemies send other people's children on missions of suicide and murder . . . We stand for a different choice . . . We choose freedom and the dignity of every life.'[70] The following year, he described the illegal and unprovoked invasion of Iraq as a fight for 'the cause of liberty and for the peace of the world'.[71] In November 2015, Barack Obama condemned the appalling murders in Paris, for which ISIS took responsibility, as 'an attack on all of humanity and the universal values we share'.[72] Weeks later, after the UK parliament voted to bomb ISIS in Syria, Chancellor George Osborne declared to an American think tank that Britain had 'got its mojo back' and was ready to join the US in the struggle to 'reassert Western values'.[73] At the heart of these values were, according to Obama, 'life, liberty, the pursuit of happiness'.[74]

In pursuit of power and profit, Western states have supported slavery, colonialism, torture, apartheid, illegal invasions, tyrannical dictators, the overturning of foreign democracies and the destruction of the environment. For many in the world, they have shown themselves to be a remarkably stubborn obstacle to 'life, liberty, and the pursuit of happiness'. The 'hard-headed' approach to foreign policy has caused unimaginable suffering on a scale that no terrorist group has come close to replicating, often without even achieving its stated aims. Former director of the US Defense Intelligence Agency Michael Flynn conceded in 2015 that the drone programme has created more terrorists than it has killed and argued that the Iraq war was a 'huge error', without which the Islamic State would not exist.[75] The human cost of this 'error', according to an authoritative study in 2013, is close to half a million Iraqi lives.[76]

Meanwhile the myth of 'Western benevolence' is closely guarded and cultivated in order to retain enough public support for the next round of violence. Decades of evidence, from official sources and declassified files, have exposed the hypocrisy of this myth, yet it is held in place with remarkable discipline by the organs of the state and much of the media. If people internalise the idea of a nation's 'moral mission' deeply enough, they will come to support state violence as a matter of principle. Drone strikes, for instance, remain popular with the majority of Americans.[77] And a US poll in 2015 found that 30 per cent of Republicans and 19 per cent of Democrats would support the bombing of 'Agrabah', the fictional city in Disney's version of *Aladdin*.[78] By contrast, soon after this poll was released, grandmother Mary Anne Grady Flores was sentenced to six months in prison for participating in a peaceful anti-drone protest in New York.[79]

Though Western leaders are heavily criticised for the strategies they endorse, their motivation is rarely questioned. As William Blum puts it, 'A terrorist is someone who has a bomb but doesn't have an air force.'[80] Even when the evidence is overwhelming, the idea that a Western leader could be a war criminal, a mass murderer or a terrorist remains taboo. History is written by the victors, and the victors determine whose dehumanisation is condemned and whose is quietly suppressed. Winston Churchill – celebrated for his role in defeating the racist ideology of Nazi Germany – himself endorsed a profoundly racist philosophy. He once advocated the use of chemical weapons against the 'uncooperative Arabs' fighting British rule: 'I am strongly in favour of using poison gas against uncivilised tribes . . . [it] would spread a lively terror.'[81] As millions were dying during the Bengal famine of 1943–4, he ignored pleas from his Secretary of State for India to divert scarce shipping to Calcutta, declaring that 'the starvation of anyway underfed Bengalis' was 'less serious [than that of] sturdy

Greeks', particularly as Indians would, in any case, go on breeding 'like rabbits'. In 1945, his private secretary heard him assert that Hindus were a foul race 'protected by their mere pullulation from the doom that is their due' and heard him wish that he could 'send some of his surplus bombers to destroy them'.[82] The secretary commented that 'On the subject of India, Winston is not quite sane . . . I didn't see much difference between his outlook and Hitler's.'[83] Indeed, his dehumanising worldview provided ample justification for genocide:

> I do not agree that the dog in a manger has the final right to the manger even though he may have lain there for a very long time. I do not admit that right. I do not admit for instance, that a great wrong has been done to the Red Indians of America or the black people of Australia. I do not admit that a wrong has been done to these people by the fact that a stronger race, a higher-grade race, or, at any rate, a more worldly-wise race, to put it that way, has come in and taken their place.[84]

It could be claimed that leaders such as Clinton, Bush, Blair, Cameron and Obama do not set out to kill innocent people, whereas the likes of ISIS and al-Qaeda do. This may be true but it is hardly much better. To know that, on average, you will kill twenty-eight innocent people and terrorise many more for every drone strike, or that hundreds of thousands of children are dying because of your sanctions, or that obstructing climate negotiations may have dire consequences for billions of people, while deciding again and again that 'the price is worth it', demonstrates an extreme form of moral exclusion. It is unclear which action is more dehumanising: one that results from an intention to kill or one that results from the knowledge that an action will kill and yet the decision is taken to do it anyway. Noam Chomsky compares the second action to someone 'killing ants while walking down the street': the intention may not be to kill the ants, but they know they're doing it and the lives they are destroying are not important enough for them to stop.[85]

Vast inequalities of wealth always require brutal violence to maintain them. As empathy transcends the dehumanising distinctions of nation states, it becomes increasingly difficult to justify the sacrifice of innocent people. The idea that the lives of all people – whatever their nationality, religion, gender, abilities or legal status – are of equal value is incompatible with extreme inequality and a foreign policy that maintains it. We have to reject the human exchange rate calibrated according to the latest geopolitical aims of elite interests, and extend our empathy far beyond the artificial borders of nation states that divide and dehumanise. Indiscriminate empathy is a revolutionary force.

The wealth gap

In May 2007, three-year-old Madeleine McCann went missing from a holiday resort in Portugal. Her parents had popped out for dinner with friends, leaving her in bed in their hotel room. When they returned she was gone. Soon after the disappearance, Madeleine's mother was seen on televised appeals for information and the safe return of her child. Within two weeks, the British press had published well over a thousand articles about the disappearance. A sum of £2.6 million was offered for her return, with high-profile donors including Richard Branson, Simon Cowell and J. K. Rowling.[86] A sense of national solidarity took hold, with parliamentarians wearing yellow ribbons to show their support. Coverage continued for many months.

Does such an outpouring of solidarity signify our potential for human empathy, our capacity to imagine the torture of losing one's child? It does – but it also demonstrates the opposite. According to the World Health Organization, roughly 18,000 children under the age of five die every day, mainly from preventable causes.[87] Five in every 1,000 children born in the UK die before their fifth birthday – the highest child death rate in Western Europe, excluding Malta.[88] The deaths are not random: experts have identified increased poverty and deprivation, exacerbated by cuts in welfare, as the prime causes. Globally, there are six million child deaths every year, the majority of which are attributable to preventable causes such as neonatal infection, pre-term delivery, lack of oxygen at birth, diarrhoea, pneumonia and malaria. How many thousands of children could £2.6 million save? The geographical and cultural distance of these dying children, concealed behind plain statistics, allows the media largely to ignore them while disproportionately fixating on a single tragic event.

Numerous experiments have demonstrated the inconsistent ways in which our empathy manifests itself. For instance, psychologists Tehila Kogut and Ilana Ritov asked a group of people how much money they would donate to help develop a drug that would save one child's life.[89] They then asked another group how much they would donate to save the lives of eight children. The answers given were, on average, almost exactly the same. With a third group, the researchers provided specific details about the single child. Participants were told her name, age and were shown a photograph of her. Donations to save her life soon dwarfed the amount raised for the anonymous group of eight. This is known as the 'identifiable victim effect': a vivid, flesh-and-blood description humanises a victim, engaging our empathy in a way that statistics never do. We often feel more visceral emotion for the suffering of fictional characters than the real pain of millions of people. Our innate biases direct our compassion in morally unjustifiable ways. Peter Singer posed the following thought experiment:

> The path from the library at my university to the humanities lecture theatre passes a shallow ornamental pond. Suppose that on my way to give a lecture I notice that a small child has fallen in and is in danger of drowning. Would anyone deny that I ought to wade in and pull the child out? This will mean getting my clothes muddy and either cancelling my lecture or delaying it until I can find something dry to change into; but compared with the avoidable death of a child this is insignificant.[90]

Who would disagree with this judgement? Would the obligation to save the drowning child disappear if others in a position to help failed to do so? Or if you couldn't be sure that your efforts would make any difference to the outcome? Or if you'd saved another child's life last week? Or if you knew that saving this child's life wouldn't solve the more general problem of water safety? Elementary moral principles suggest the answer in each case should be 'no'. None of these considerations remove the obligation to save the child.

Singer offers a simple principle to guide behaviour: 'if it is in our power to prevent something very bad from happening, without thereby sacrificing anything of comparable moral significance, we ought to do it'.[91] The apparent simplicity of this principle is deceptive. If it were taken seriously, our lives and world would be transformed. The principle applies 'not just to rare situations in which one can save a child from a pond, but to the everyday situation in which we can assist those living in absolute poverty'.[92] Every non-essential pound that we spend could plausibly be used to save those living in desperate need of food, water and medicine. At all times, there are many people (including children) around the world suffering and dying from the effects of poverty. At the same time, charities have been set up to raise money for these people. When someone chooses to buy a non-essential item – a fifth pair of shoes, a sports car or a yacht – they are also choosing not to give this money to others in dire need. Try as we might, it is difficult to find any morally significant difference between choosing to keep walking as a girl drowns in a nearby pond and choosing, over the course of a lifetime, to buy non-essential goods with money that might have saved the lives of children dying from a lack of clean water or medicine. The difference between the two examples is distance, both physical and social. We have to widen the context of our choice far beyond what is required by the drowning girl to think of the child dying from a lack of medicine, and this takes more effort. Distance may not be morally significant but it is psychologically important. One example immediately tugs at our heartstrings; the other does not. Consequently, writes Singer, 'Few could stand by and watch a child drown; many can ignore a famine in Africa.'[93]

The moral calculations of consumerism don't occur to most of us, but, when the scope of concern is widened, the choices of consumers take on moral significance, particularly for those with large disposable incomes. Many people are mired in debt, struggling to pay bills and rent while hoping to save something to see them through an uncertain future. Singer's experiment has little relevance to those already striving to make ends meet – it is not intended to provoke guilt for every treat and pleasure – but it does challenge the values of consumer culture and expose the immorality of excessive consumption. We can debate what counts as a 'non-essential good', and whether giving money to a charity is the best way to help people, but when discussing the consumption choices of the rich – or the choice to lock up wealth in bank accounts and capital investments – the moral force of the thought experiment is hard to deny. Society and nature are damaged by excessive consumption of the inane, the trivial and the luxurious, but our economic system demands such consumption so it is celebrated.

Evidence suggests that wealth itself can impact on our capacity for empathy and compassion. Research seems to show that the wealthier we are the less ethically we behave, and the less empathetic and compassionate we become. In 2011, a UK report found that the poor are more generous than the rich when it comes to giving to good causes, regularly giving a higher proportion of their earnings to charity irrespective of age, class or beliefs.[94] In the same year, the top 20 per cent of US earners – gave on average 1.3 per cent of their incomes to charity while Americans in the bottom 20 per cent income bracket donated more than double that at 3.2 per cent.[95]

The wealthy tend to prefer giving to (often elite) universities, arts organisations and museums, while the poor tend to give to religious organisations and social-service charities. Yet the link between wealth and greed is not set. When groups of both rich and poor people were shown a video about child poverty that was intended to elicit sympathy, the compassion of the wealthier group – though initially less than that of the poor group – began to increase until both displayed an almost identical willingness to help. Studies like this have led researchers to conclude that the empathy deficit among the rich is, at least in part, down to isolation from poverty.

The tendency for the affluent to be more selfish has been confirmed in the laboratory. Berkeley psychologists Paul Piff and Dacher Keltner have conducted a number of studies which explore how social class impacts on empathy. They concluded that as people gained wealth and status, their capacity for compassionate feelings declined.[96] Piff found that 'the rich are way more likely to prioritize their own self-interests above the interests of other people'. Over seven studies it was found that wealthier individuals were more likely than poorer ones to break the law while driving, take valuable goods from others, lie in negotiations, cheat to increase their chances of winning a prize, and endorse unethical behaviour at work.

Part of the explanation for these findings, according to the data collected from participants, is that upper-class participants had a more favourable attitude towards greed, and that such attitudes were a good predictor of the degree of empathetic and compassionate behaviour they were likely to exhibit. Wealthier people were more likely to agree with the statement that 'greed is justified, beneficial, and morally defensible'. When asked to explain economic inequalities, wealthy people believed environmental causes were less significant than personal qualities, in effect taking credit for their privilege and placing the blame for poverty on personal failings.

Another set of studies by Keltner and his colleagues found that, even after controlling for factors such as gender, ethnicity and spiritual beliefs, poorer participants were more likely than affluent ones to agree with statements such as, 'It's important to take care of people who are vulnerable.'[97] This research builds on previous studies which found that upper-class people tend to be worse at identifying the emotions of others and less likely to pay full attention to those with whom they are interacting.

To establish whether selfishness leads to wealth or wealth leads to selfishness, researchers carried out another experiment that asked participants to spend a few minutes comparing themselves either to those more affluent than themselves or to those who were poorer. Afterwards, both groups were shown a jar and told they could take as many sweets as they wanted from it. They were told that whatever candy was left would go to children in a nearby laboratory. The participants that compared themselves to richer people took significantly less candy out of the jar than those who compared themselves to poorer people. Feeling richer than others, it seems, can erode our sense of solidarity and generosity. People at all levels of society tend to become less attentive when interacting with people below them in the hierarchy.

Reason and imagination

Broadly speaking, our cognitive biases channel our empathy towards specific, vivid, observable examples of human suffering, and away from stigmatised groups, while our social conditioning channels our empathy in directions that serve the interests of those with the power to do the conditioning, determining which groups are stigmatised and to what degree. Citizens are encouraged to empathise with their compatriots, soldiers with their unit, religious followers with members of their faith, and so on. The general pattern is that the political class, aided by a compliant media, exploit these biases to channel the public's empathy where it is politically expedient. Reason and imagination can compensate for these biases. They can correct for our insensitivity to scale and distance and enable us to question the hierarchies of moral concern that we internalise from our culture.

Reason is amoral. Our ethical instincts are the raw material from which any moral system is built. They are what galvanise us to act in the face of injustice. Yet selective empathy can be as much a cause of cruelty as a solution to it. That is why acting in accordance with principles is so important. Without principles, our empathetic instincts are as likely to facilitate the process of dehumanisation as to restrain it. There is no formula for balancing instincts against the logic of moral reasoning – a tension between the two exists, as numerous thinkers have identified – but engaging with this tension rather than denying its existence, and employing all our faculties rather than limiting ourselves to potent emotions or cold logic, is perhaps the only path available to take us beyond the dehumanisation that blights our world.

Imagination has an important part to play. It transports us across time, class, gender and race. A story, painting or poem enables us to step into the shoes of someone we would otherwise find difficult to understand. A skilfully constructed narrative can lead us down a different life path, providing glimpses into the experiences of others – vagrant, criminal, oppressed, oppressor – and enable us to see how we might have turned out given a different set of influences and opportunities. It helps us to see the world through the eyes of others, to understand the rationale for different value systems, cultural norms and behaviour. By thinking about how things could look from another perspective, the 'self' doing the imagining is changed. As author Ian McEwan puts it, 'Imagining what it is like to be someone other than yourself is at the core of our humanity. It is the essence of compassion, and it is the beginning of morality.'[98]

The empathy-enhancing value of using our imagination has stood up to experimental tests. In one study, people were shown a photograph of a young black man and asked to write a short account of a day in his life. Those who were instructed to put themselves in his shoes and look at the world through his eyes showed the most positive attitudes towards him, compared with a group who were asked to suppress their prejudices and a control group who received no additional instructions.[99]

Empathy is malleable. Programmes to increase compassion and empathy, in both adults and children, have been shown to produce positive results. For instance, the charity Roots of Empathy periodically brings a baby from the local community into classrooms over the course of a year, and follows the child's development while trying to understand what it is experiencing. Studies have shown that these empathy programmes significantly improve social and emotional skills, resulting in more caring behaviour, while reducing levels of stress, depression and aggression. Where it has been introduced, bullying and classroom disruption have been reduced.

Many steps could be taken to create a more compassionate world. The development of empathy owes much to our early experiences. On fostering empathy, Simon Baron-Cohen warns that 'when we fail to nurture young children with parental affection, we deprive them of the most valuable birthright we can give them and damage them almost irreversibly'.[100] But a nurturing upbringing is not enough. If we are to expand the categories of people to whom we extend our empathy, we have to engage our reason and imagination, individually and collectively. We have to question the loyalties, assumptions and values at the heart of our identity and the system that shapes it. As the activist and writer Daniel Voskoboynik puts it:

> [T]he colours of morality sharpen over time. Arguments reasoned in the past appear unthinkable today. The ethical confusion that reigned around issues such as slavery, suffrage or the acceptance of Jewish refugees, seems absurd in a modern light. Dissident and 'radical' voices, marginalized at the time, become uncontroversial as years pass . . . We look back, often with certainty, confident that we have learnt the lessons and corrected our myopias. Yet the lessons are evasive. The ethical clarity afforded to the past rarely translates to the present. Our moral instincts persistently fail us.[101]

They are meant to fail us. The political and economic edifice of which we are a part requires it. Unbounded empathy cannot coexist with the system that has so far prevailed. For one to flourish, the other must fade. Yet reason and imagination can tip the balance, closing the gap that separates us. We need to ask ourselves how it would it feel to be a refugee fleeing war – risking our life and the lives of people we love – in the hope of finding sanctuary and security abroad. Or how it would feel to have innocent friends and family murdered by a distant drone or have our country occupied by a foreign power that dictates our every move. Solutions to problems are not always clear, but justice demands that we never stop trying to see the world through the eyes of others, especially those who are vulnerable, oppressed and disadvantaged.

Politics is applied morality. It is easy to commit to abstract ethical ideals, far harder to apply them. Real life is messy and complicated. It is all too easy to find reasons to relinquish our fundamental moral principles. There is never any shortage of people telling us that in this instance, for this or that reason, it would be inappropriate, impractical or foolish to apply them. 'Don't be naïve', we are admonished, 'these are dangerous times. Ideals are luxuries that we simply cannot afford. In crisis, difference rules apply. We must be strong, vigilant, realistic. We must look after our own, secure our borders, defend our values.' Narratives of fear accompany every war and crisis. Fear stifles empathy and elevates hate – fear for our safety, for our jobs, for our children; fear of what will happen if we don't drop more bombs, lock more people up, keep more people out. Fear drives the cycle of inhumanity that makes good people support terrible things. There are always pressures to distance ourselves from certain groups by placing them in categories of a different status, but as soon as we allow ourselves to do this we have opened the door to insidious forms of dehumanisation.

Hope

In 1984, Patrick Magee booked himself into Brighton's Grand Hotel under a false name, and planted a bomb. Magee was a member of the Irish Republican Army. Four weeks later, on the 12th of October, when the hotel was hosting the annual Conservative Party conference, the bomb exploded, killing five people and injuring dozens more. The British Prime Minister, Margaret Thatcher, and her husband narrowly escaped harm.

Magee was captured and sentenced to thirty-five years in prison. Under the terms of the Good Friday Agreement, he was granted early release in 1999. Around this time, he received an unexpected request. Jo Berry, the daughter of Sir Anthony Berry, a Cabinet minister who was killed in the blast, wanted to meet him. She hoped that meeting him might help her deal with her anger and psychological pain. 'I wanted to meet Patrick to put a face to the enemy, and see him as a real human being. At our first meeting I was terrified, but I wanted to acknowledge the courage it had taken him to meet me. We talked with an extraordinary intensity. I shared a lot about my father, while Patrick told me some of his story . . .'.[102]

Since that first meeting, Patrick and Jo have met many times. They have developed a remarkable friendship and have spoken together on many platforms and as part of many workshops. Jo has since founded a charity, Building Bridges for Peace, which focuses on non-violent resolution to conflict. Getting to know Pat, she writes, 'I feel I've been recovering some of the humanity I lost when that bomb went off.' Jo's perspective courageously embodies the philosophy of moving beyond the framework of blame and trying to step into the shoes of someone else to understand their behaviour.

> I don't talk about 'forgiveness'. To say 'I forgive you' is almost condescending – it locks you into an 'us and them' scenario keeping me right and you wrong. That attitude won't change anything. But I can experience empathy . . . Sometimes when I've met with Patrick, I've had such a clear understanding of his life that there's nothing to forgive . . . I've realised that no matter which side of the conflict you're on, had we all lived each other's lives, we could all have done what the other did.[103]

The effect of Jo's enlightened approach on Patrick Magee is equally remarkable. Describing his first meeting with her, he speaks of how it changed his outlook:

> Jo's openness, calmness; her apparent lack of hostility – in fact her willingness to listen and to try to understand, disarmed me. Had Jo instead shown anger, however justifiable, it would for me have been easier to cope with. The political hat would have remained firmly attached. But in the presence of such composure and decency, as I said, I felt disarmed . . . As an individual I carried the heavy weight of knowing I had caused profound hurt to this woman . . . A political obligation henceforth became a personal obligation. I now realised more fully that I was guilty of something I had attributed to the other: that our enemies demonised, dehumanised, marginalised, reduced us. I began from that moment to see Jo's father in a fuller light and to begin the process of understanding his view. I was also guilty of adhering to a reduced view and of not perceiving the other's full humanity; instead apprehending our enemies in terms of their uniform or solely from their political colours. All that I came to admire and respect in Jo was surely due in part to his gift of values so apparent in her. And that was a measure of the loss. Jo's loss of her father; her daughters' loss of a grandfather. But loss also in terms of my own humanity. For war

does rob combatants of something of what it is to be human, of an essential capacity to empathise and to see the world through the eyes of others.[104]

Life brings suffering and pain, making it difficult to stay connected to the hope and compassion within us. We may find temporary protection by cutting off the empathy that connects us to others, steeling ourselves for future disappointment and hurt. But we lose something of value in the process, something that can only be saved by reconnecting. The Forgiveness Project, set up by Marina Cantacuzino in 2004, has collected an extensive selection of remarkable stories revolving around the themes of empathy and forgiveness – each, in its own way, as inspiring, moving and provocative as that of Patrick and Jo. A recurring idea in these personal accounts is that the refusal to succumb to fear and hate is extremely liberating and empowering, and is often the only way to move beyond the trauma caused by the actions of another. Empathy is not always within our immediate reach, but responding to hate with compassion and breathing meaning into pain may be the only way to preserve or recover aspects of ourselves that we value deeply. In a world of division, injustice and cruelty, an empathetic response is a creative act signalling the change we want to see.

Decades of sociological research into disasters have shed important light on this potential. The standard picture of people panicking, of order breaking down and desperation leading to violent anarchy is false. On the contrary, experiencing the worst tends to bring out the best. People affected by large-scale disasters – floods, earthquakes, hurricanes and bombings – tend to undergo a dramatic transformation. Spontaneous communities emerge, altruism becomes the norm; people focus their energies on looking after themselves, their families, neighbours and strangers with equal vigour. Resources are shared, public spaces become makeshift centres of organisation and community, and novel networks of support spring into existence amidst extreme physical hardship. In her book *A Paradise Built in Hell*, Rebecca Solnit writes:

377

In the wake of an earthquake, a bombing, or a major storm, most people are altruistic, urgently engaged in caring for themselves and those around them, strangers and neighbours as well as friends and loved ones. The image of the selfish, panicky, or regressively savage human being in times of disaster has little truth to it . . . The prevalent human nature in disaster is resilient, resourceful, generous, empathetic, and brave.[105]

What is most surprising is that, in the midst of disaster, as homes lie in rubble or under water, as food stocks run low and people endure arduous conditions, the survivors speak not of their fear and sadness but of having experienced a deep joy and happiness as they worked with others in the aftermath. Accounts of smiling faces are common, and many survivors remember the time with fondness. Initially this is perplexing. What is there to be joyful about in a disaster? People die. Families lose their homes. According to the accounts of survivors, the source of their joy is to be found in the connectedness and sense of common purpose that emerges. Without an established hierarchy in place, people take charge of their situations, work together, and help others and themselves. They experience deep satisfaction from doing meaningful work, rejuvenated by the generosity and courage of those around them who otherwise would be no more than nameless strangers, part of the background scenery of their life.

As Solnit describes, research into disasters really got going after the Second World War. One of its pioneers was Charles E. Fritz, a graduate in sociology and an American soldier stationed in England. Five years into the war, in a period marked by severe shortages of food, clothing and housing, Fritz was surprised to find 'a nation of gloriously happy people, enjoying life to the fullest, exhibiting a sense of gaiety and love of life that was truly remarkable'.[106] At the end of the war, Fritz was assigned a role on the US Strategic Bombing Survey, which was conducting an in-depth study into the effectiveness of bombing on the German population. Fritz found that those 'living in heavily bombed cities had significantly higher morale than people living in the lightly bombed cities'.[107] Similar observations were later made in Japan. This surprising phenomenon has been observed and documented over many years and in many places. No one welcomes a disaster, or the suffering it brings, but many welcome the humanity that springs from themselves and others as a response to it. Many experience joy as they engage in new forms of social relations, unencumbered by the trappings of status that normally define social interactions, undermining simple compassion.

Not only does this research inspire confidence in our capacity for solidarity, mutual aid and compassion, and affirm our need for purposeful cooperation with others, it demonstrates what is possible when we decommission the framework of entitlement. Part of what distinguishes disasters from everyday life is that they reduce our readiness to impute responsibility. When a flood strikes, the earth quakes, or a bomb falls, it is clear that those who suffer are not responsible for their predicament. The role of luck is obvious to all – there is no place for blame. The existence of hunger becomes reason enough to be fed, that of illness reason enough to be treated. Questions of entitlement and desert do not arise. Each according to their need becomes the default operating principle. Equality becomes the social norm. As floods sweep away buildings, they can take with them the carefully maintained markers of social status that sustain the psychological chasms between us. For the duration of a disaster, those affected are in a very real sense 'all in it together'. Class, race, religion, gender and nationality are temporarily transcended by shared experience. This commonality creates the space for greater empathy.

Of course, there are notable exceptions – prejudices never completely vanish – but the general trend is that categorical divisions become far less important. Our challenge is to break down these divisions the rest of the time. Floods, hurricanes, droughts and fires are increasing in number and severity as the climate warms. If our apathy continues, essential resources – food, water and energy – will become increasingly scarce. Wars will result and the numbers of refugees will continue to rise rapidly. In the face of divisive propaganda and difficult circumstances, our capacity to respond with compassion and empathy may be the difference between survival and destruction, between solidarity and barbarism. Will we let borders bound the limits of our empathy? Will we allow carefully cultivated prejudices to overwhelm our humanity? After centuries of highly profitable exploitation, will the Global North continue to ignore the incalculable debt it owes to those in the Global South? The further our empathy reaches, and the more deeply it is felt, the more obvious it becomes that Earth's resources should be shared and that people should have a say over the decisions that impact their lives. Life is not fair, but society can do a lot to compensate for this. Politics should be about fighting the inherent unfairness of existence.

Transforming society is a daunting task. The problems we face are enormous and each of us has limited time, energy and resources. Yet the small actions of many people add up. Each day, the bonds of friendship, family and community are renewed through simple acts of love. As we widen our moral circle, these bonds multiply and strengthen. It is essential to join the dots between the problems we face, to see that war, poverty, mental health problems, climate change, racism and sexism share common causes and common solutions. A systemic critique emerges from a deep understanding of any of these issues. Our future depends on the recognition of our interdependence.

At each stage of social improvement we need to be receptive to the needs of the moment – to modify strategies and priorities accordingly. However, some things are already clear. Serious social change involves large numbers of people working together around common goals and beyond the confines of thought and behaviour that have brought us to our present situation. Every day, the structures of society are recreated through the collective choices of millions of people. These structures exist in our collective imagination. If enough of us change the way we think about politics, democracy, freedom and each other, our actions will cease to reproduce the world as we know it. A revolution in belief and imagination creates a revolution in possibility. Whatever class, race or gender we belong to, we all have the potential to contribute to the creation of something better. There is so much valuable work to be done – much of it challenging, yet rewarding. Abilities, resources, time and interests vary, but whoever we are, there will be others with whom we can work. In a million different ways, large and small, individually and collectively, we must interrupt the patterns of obedience and conformity that run through society to create the change that we need.

Social change is not something that we get done 'out there' simply by changing laws and procedures. Whatever rights are granted, whatever procedures are in place, social systems are brought to life by the people who participate in them. The attempt to increase control over our lives and produce outcomes we value is inextricable from the attempt to deepen our understanding and develop our character. Ultimately, this is a moral challenge. We are the timber from which the future will be constructed – the stronger the timber, the more solid the construction.

The first obstacles to overcome on the path to creating freedom will always be internal, for what we do is a reflection of who we are. If we want a more compassionate society, we must try to be more compassionate. If we want a more informed society, we must try to become more informed. If we want a freer society, we must try to live as if we are already free. Compassion, truth and freedom are not distant goals to be won once we destroy a system or vanquish an ideology. They are tools for creating the world we desire. Outbreaks of collective empathy have overwhelmed corrupt regimes, ended wars and abolished slavery, expanding the liberty of millions of men, women and children in the process. We need to rediscover that potential. A commitment to empathy, truth and freedom needs to be the starting point for economics, politics, culture and education – the foundation for our civilisation.

Decades of conditioning have told us that greed is good, that society is an illusion, and that people tend to get what they deserve. We have been sold an impoverished vision of humanity, one that binds our imagination and erodes our hope. We are told this is freedom. Deep down we know this is a myth – one that is promoted to justify a world of destruction, exploitation and injustice. Behind the technical debates of economists, the ideological rows of politicians, the pursuit of corporate profit and the passionate protests of the public is the most important question we can ask: what is life for? To compete, accumulate and dominate? Or is it to love and be loved – to create, share and experience beauty?

Every human being inevitably suffers hardship, loses loved ones and, some day, passes away. Life is rare, delicate and short. Given all this, why would we not join together to do what we can, for the brief time we have air in our lungs and strength in our bodies, to transform this world into a place of joy and wonder for all those passing through – a place where all can flourish, contribute and create? After all, it is only through the creation of what we deeply value that we find the fullest expression of our freedom. And what could be more valuable than that?

Notes

All websites listed were accessed between November 2015 and February 2016.

1 Luck

1.   Either the immaterial soul that survives death has always existed or it has not. If not, it has a beginning, so we have merely pushed the problem of self-creation back to this point. If it has always existed, then, by definition, it could not have created itself (that would imply a beginning!). In each case, the idea of self-creation is incoherent.

2.   David Eagleman, *Incognito: The Secret Lives of the Brain* (Edinburgh: Canongate Books, 2011), pp. 154–5.

3.   For extensive information about the ACE study, see http://acestudy.org/

4.   Robert Anda, 'The Health and Social Impact of Growing Up With Alcohol Abuse and Related Adverse Childhood Experiences: The Human and Economic Costs of the Status Quo'. This document, summarising the findings of the ACE study, was presented to the National Association for Children of Alcoholics and resides on their website. See http://www.nacoa.org/pdfs/Anda%20NACoA%20Review_web.pdf

5.   Dr Gabor Maté, 'Embraced by the Needle', posted on the author's website, July 2013. See http://drgabormate.com/article/embraced-by-the-needle/

6.   David Eagleman, *Incognito*, pp. 174–5.

7.   David Eagleman, *Incognito*, p. 173

8.   David Eagleman, *Incognito*, p. 173.

9. In Einstein's 1931 essay *The World As I See It*, he writes: 'In human freedom in the philosophical sense I am definitely a disbeliever. Everybody acts not only under external compulsion but also in accordance with inner necessity. Schopenhauer's saying, that "a man can do as he will, but not will as he will," has been an inspiration to me since my youth up, and a continual consolation and unfailing well-spring of patience in the face of the hardships of life, my own and others. This feeling mercifully mitigates the sense of responsibility which so easily becomes paralysing, and it prevents us from taking ourselves and other people too seriously; it conduces to a view of life in which humour, above all, has its due place.' (Albert Einstein, *The World As I See It* [1935, repr. San Diego: The Book Tree, 2007] p. 2).

10. Kim Wombles, 'An Interview with Simon Baron-Cohen on Zero-Empathy, Autism, and Accountability', Science 2.0, June 2011. See http://www.science20. com/countering_tackling_woo/interview_simon_baroncohen_zeroempathy_ autism_and_accountability-79669

11. Kim Wombles, 'An Interview with Simon Baron-Cohen on Zero-Empathy, Autism, and Accountability'.

12. Galen Strawson, *Freedom and Belief* (1986; New York: Oxford University Press, 2010), p. 25.

13. David Eagleman, *Incognito*, p. 4.

14. Ludwig Wittgenstein, *Philosophical Investigations* (1953; 3rd edn, Oxford: Blackwell Publishing, 2001), p. 40c.

15. It's also unproblematic to speak of someone being 'responsible for someone or something', as in: 'He has a responsibility to safeguard the welfare of his children.' This is just another way of expressing that someone has a duty or obligation. Whether they are ultimately responsible for meeting that obligation is a separate issue.

16. Traditionally, the free will debate has focused on the notion of determinism. Consider two kinds of universe: the first deterministic, the second indeterministic. A deterministic universe is one in which there exists only one possible future. In his 1812 essay on the deterministic universe, the French mathematician Pierre-Simon, Marquis de Laplace summed up the concept as follows: 'An intellect which at a given moment knew all the forces that animate Nature, and the mutual positions of the beings that comprise it, if this intellect were vast enough to submit its data to analysis, could condense into a single formula the movement of the greatest bodies of the universe and that of the lightest atom: for such an intellect nothing would be uncertain; and the future just like

the past would be present before its eyes.' If Laplace is right, then were the above conditions satisfied, your reading of this sentence could have been predicted thirteen and a half billion years ago at the birth of the universe. Of course, in practice, there is no way that Laplace's conditions could be met. But *if* the universe works as Laplace assumes it does, what implications might it have for human freedom?

Broadly speaking, there are three main positions in the debate on free will. (These can be subdivided in various ways, but a full taxonomy would not serve our purposes here.) There are 'compatibilists', who believe that a deterministic universe is compatible with free will. They do not consider a deterministic universe restrains our freedom; instead, many argue that it is a necessary condition for it. Opposing this view are the 'incompatibilists', who believe that freedom is incompatible with a deterministic universe. One category of incompatibilism – libertarianism (nothing to do with political libertarianism) – holds that if the universe is indeterministic *in the right kind of way*, free will is still possible. If we can break the causal chain that links a choice to its cause, and that cause to another cause, all the way back to the birth of the universe, and if this break occurs in the brain as part of our decision-making process (a causal break elsewhere does nothing to preserve free will), they argue that our belief in free will might yet be vindicated. This line of reasoning faces a devastating objection. An event not determined by an antecedent cause is a random event (what else could it be?) and a random event in our decision-making process does not vindicate free will. This objection deals a fatal blow to the libertarian project. To make choices for our own reasons, our decision-making process cannot be random. Some incompatibilists – 'sceptics' – accept this and conclude that we therefore lack free will, for neither a deterministic universe nor an indeterministic universe provides the conditions necessary for its realisation.

Compatibilists as we have seen disagree. In their view, the thesis of determinism does not pose a threat to free will. To many, this is a counter-intuitive conclusion. A universe with only one possible future appears, at least initially, to leave no room for freedom. Of course, it all depends on the definitions we use. Suppose we have to make a prediction about how Jim would behave in situation Y. It is reasonable to assume that, all else being equal, as our understanding of Jim and Y increases, the accuracy of our prediction, would also increase. Now, suppose it were possible for us to know everything there is to know about Jim and situation Y: in a deterministic universe, assuming we possessed the requisite intelligence, we would now be able to predict Jim's behaviour with complete accuracy. Our ability to make this prediction, however, would not depend on Jim being compelled by some *external* force to behave as predicted, but on a perfect understanding of Jim and situation Y. Our ability to make an accurate prediction is perfectly compatible with Jim acting in accordance with the beliefs and values he holds. If we want to define 'free will' as 'the capacity, given the options available to us, to act in accordance with the beliefs and values we happen to hold' then free will is possessed by almost everyone, almost all of the time. Yet, however we define free will, the facts about responsibility remain unchanged.

Consider the use of language. As linguist Noam Chomsky often says, a typical verbal response will be appropriate to, but not determined by, a situation. Our mental capacities enable us to be creative in that sense. We might say that the response, a particular choice of words, 'emerges' from the interaction between a stimulus and our internal structure. So, while a choice may be a reaction to stimuli, the stimuli do not, on their own, cause or determine the choice.

It is clear that across time and space the range of options available to people differs enormously. A deterministic universe does not prevent us from acting in accordance with the beliefs and values we hold, or from learning, changing and growing over time. Daniel Dennett claims that such a universe offers us all the varieties of free will worth wanting. This is a judgement some would challenge. Undoubtedly, some people feel that 'ultimate responsibility', incoherent as it may be, is a variety of freedom worth wanting.

Not enough is known about the nature of the universe to define it as deterministic or indeterministic. The debate is highly technical and its results are generally thought to be inconclusive. In any case, the capacity to make choices according to the beliefs and values we hold does not require a deterministic universe because an indeterministic universe can still be highly ordered. Randomness may play a part in our existence but there are compelling reasons to believe we inhabit a highly ordered universe. The Cosmos appears to follow predictable laws. Things usually work as we expect them to and, when they do not, most of the time we can isolate the reason why. Personalities and character traits are ordinarily stable over time. As I type these words my fingers are hitting the keys I want them to hit and the letters appearing on my screen match the keys I am hitting. The regularities in nature are remarkable and imply a highly non-random universe. Experience justifies the belief that the integrity of our decision-making process is not compromised by randomness.

17.   For instance, Robert Sapolsky, Joshua Greene, Paul Bloom, Sam Harris, Wolf Singer,

Chris Frith, V. S. Ramachandran, Patrick Haggard, Daniel Wegner, Stephen Hawking, Lawrence Krauss, and of course Albert Einstein. For a more comprehensive list, take a look at the website of Sam Snyder. See http://samsnyder.com/free-will/

18. Friedrich Nietzsche, *Beyond Good and Evil* (1886; New York: Vintage Books, 1966), p. 21.

19. Francis Wheen, *How Mumbo-Jumbo Conquered the World* (London: Harper Perennial, 2004), p. 47.

20. Rhonda Byrne, *The Secret* (London: Simon and Schuster, 2006), p. 28.

21. Abigail Saguy and Rene Almeling, 'Fat Devils and Moral Panics: News Reporting on Obesity Science', SOMAH workshop, UCLA Department of Sociology, June, Vol. 1, 2005.

22. Raj Patel, *Stuffed and Starved* (London: Portobello Books, 2007), p. 254.

23. J. Michael McGinnis, Jennifer Appleton Gootman, Vivica I. Kraak (eds), Institute of Medicine, *Food Marketing to Children and Youth: Threat or Opportunity?* (Washington DC: The National Academies Press, 2006), p. 4.

24. Erica Goode, 'Study Finds TV Alters Fiji Girls' View of Body', *New York Times*, 20 May 1999. See http://www.nytimes.com/1999/05/20/world/study-finds-tv-alters-fiji-girls-view-of-body.html

25. Rhonda Byrne, *The Secret*, p. 60.

26. These figures are taken from the project website for *The Secret*. See http://www.thesecret.tv/about/rhonda-byrnes-biography/

27. John Milton Berdan and John Richie Schultz, Hewette Elwell Joyce (eds), *Modern Essays* (New York: Macmillan, 1916), p. 347. See https://archive.org/details/modernessays01joycgoog

28. Charles Murray, 'Charles Murray and the Underclass: The Developing Debate', ed. Ruth Lister, The IEA Health and Welfare Unit, Choice in Welfare, No. 33, 1996, p. 86. See http://www.civitas.org.uk/content/files/cw33.pdf

29. Charles Murray, 'Charles Murray and the Underclass', p. 86.

30. Charles Murray, 'Charles Murray and the Underclass', p. 86.

31. Charles Murray, 'Charles Murray and the Underclass', p. 85.

32. Barbara H. Fried, 'Beyond Blame', *Boston Review*, 28 June 2013. See http://www.bostonreview.net/forum/barbara-fried-beyond-blame-moral-responsibility-philosophy-law

33. Barbara H. Fried, 'Beyond Blame'.

34. Steve Pearlstein, 'Hermanomics: Let them eat pizza', *The Washington Post*, 15 October 2011. See http://www.washingtonpost.com/business/economy/hermanomics-let-them-eat-pizza/2011/10/11/gIQAgT0mmL_story.html

35. Howard G. Buffet with a foreword by Warren G. Buffet, *Forty Chances: Finding Hope in a Hungry World* (New York: Simon and Schuster, 2013) p. xiii.

36. Daniel C. Dennett, *Freedom Evolves* (2003; London: Penguin Books, 2004), p. 273.

37. 'The State of the World's Children 2015 (Executive Summary): Reimagine the Future – Innovation for Every Child', United Nations Children's Fund (UNICEF), 2015, pp. 36–41. See http://www.data.unicef.org/corecode/uploads/document6/uploaded_pdfs/corecode/SOWC_2015_Summary_and_Tables_210.pdf

38. This figure is taken from the US Centers for Disease Control and Prevention website. See http://www.cdc.gov/reproductivehealth/maternalinfanthealth/infantmortality.htm

39. This figure is taken from the UNICEF website. See http://www.data.unicef.org/child-mortality/under-five.html

40. Anne Fernald, Virginia A. Marchman, Adriana Weisleder, 'SES differences in language processing skill and vocabulary are evident at 18 months', *Developmental Science* 16:2, 2013, pp. 234–48.

41. Betty Hart and Todd R. Risley, 'The Early Catastrophe: The 30 Million Word Gap by Age 3', *American Educator*, Spring 2003. See http://www.aft.org/pdfs/americaneducator/spring2003/theearlycatastrophe.pdf

42. For the latest findings from this ongoing study, visit the 'Growing Up in Scotland' website. See: http://growingupinscotland.org.uk/about-gus/key-findings/#2

43. This point has been denied by some compatibilists. Although they accept that everything about us may be down to forces that we do not control, they claim that we are still blameworthy. It is a strange position to hold, though it should be said that at times the disagreement is really about how to define 'blame'. If all that is meant by blaming someone is that our attitudes towards them change (for instance we become less trusting and wish to end our association with them), there is no conflict with the position outlined here. We may distrust and dislike a person without blaming them for being the way they are. The sort of blame denied in this chapter is the sort that depends on holding a person responsible for the way they are, the sort that implies a person *deserves* to suffer in some way for failing to meet certain standards of behaviour.

44. It would be perfectly consistent for a society to accept that we are not absolutely responsible, and all that follows from this conclusion, but to agree to implement certain laws and impose certain penalties for pragmatic reasons. Everything in our environment has the potential to shape our behaviour. If we find that because of the way our human nature is constituted, more behaviour of the sort we value is produced when we introduce a given law, punishment or

incentive into the environment, then we might decide to adopt it even if we consider it to be unfair on some. What's important is that the ethical implications of people not being ultimately responsible are factored into our societal decisions about punishment, reward and other social institutions.

45. Email from Daniel C. Dennett, 24 February 2012.

46. Daniel C. Dennett, *Darwin's Dangerous Idea* (1995; London: Penguin Books, 1996), p. 17.

47. Daniel C. Dennett, *Darwin's Dangerous Idea*, pp. 22–3.

48. Paul H. Barrett et al. (eds), *Charles Darwin's Notebooks, 1836–1844* (New York: Cornell University Press, 1987), p. 608.

49. To learn more about this research, a good place to start is: Gregg D. Caruso (ed.), *Exploring the Illusion of Free Will and Moral Responsibility* (Lanham MD: Lexington Books, 2013).

50. To challenge this claim, some have cited an influential paper appearing to suggest that exposing the myth of responsibility will tend to have a negative impact on moral behaviour. The paper in question (K. D. Vohs, J. W. Schooler, 'The Value of Believing in Free Will: Encouraging a Belief in Determinism Increases Cheating', *Psychological Science*, January 2008, pp. 49–54) found that exposure to arguments in favour of determinism increased the likelihood of cheating on a subsequent task. The deeper point, however, is that the impact of a new idea will always depend on the web of beliefs into which it is introduced. The meaning of facts and ideas change as we consider them from different perspectives. It is unsurprising that in a culture that propagates the responsibility myth, kneejerk responses to it being exposed will sometimes be based on a misunderstanding of the implications. It takes time to assimilate facts that challenge our foundational beliefs.

That said, it is significant that other researchers have failed to replicate the results of Vohs and Schooler. (Rolf Zwaan, 'The Value of Believing in Free Will: A Replication Attempt', 18 March 2013. See http://rolfzwaan.blogspot. co.uk/2013/03/the-value-of-believing-in-free-will.html.) It has emerged that most of the participants in the original study were Mormons and held views on morality that were not representative of the broader population. A number of commentators have criticised the text used to prime the participants in the study precisely because it lends itself to misinterpretation. Also, after its publication it was discovered that some of the original results had not been analysed correctly and, when this was taken into account, the effect that had been detected turned out to be smaller than initially stated. (For more information on this, see the blog by psychologist Rolf Zwaan posted on the London School of Economics website. See http://blogs.lse.ac.uk/impactofsocialsciences/2013/04/19/pre-publication-posting-and-post-publication-review/) To explore these issues further, see James B. Miles, '"Irresponsible and a Disservice": The integrity of social psychology turns on the free will dilemma', *British Journal of Social Psychology*, Vol. 52, No. 2, June 2013, pp. 205–18. In the paper, Miles writes: 'Almost all of the work on free will published to date by social psychologists appears methodologically flawed, misrepresents the state of academic knowledge, and risks linking social psychology with the irrational.'

51.   A. F. Shariff, J. D. Greene, J. C. Karremans, J. B. Luguri, C. J. Clark, J. W. Schooler, R. F. Baumeister, K. D. Vohs, 'Free will and punishment: A mechanistic view of human nature reduces retribution', *Psychological Science*, published online 10 June 2014. pp. 1–8.

52.   I'm paraphrasing Sam Harris, who writes: 'In fact, it seems immoral not to recognize just how much luck is involved in morality itself.' Sam Harris, *Free Will* (New York: Free Press, 2012), p. 54.

53.   Charles J. Westbrook, Don E. Davis, Brandon J. Griffin, Joshua N. Hook, Cirleen DeBlaere, Man Yee Ho, Chris Bell, Daryl R. Van Tongeren, Everett L. Worthington Jr., 'Forgiving the Self and Physical and Mental Health Correlates: A Meta-Analytic Review, *Journal of Counseling Psychology*, Vol. 62, No. 2, April 2015, pp. 329–35; P. A. Mauger, J. E. Perry, T. Freeman, D. C. Grove, A. G. McBride, K. E. McKinney, 'The measurement of forgiveness', *Journal of Psychology and Christianity*, 11, 1992, pp. 170–80.

54.   That said, the impact of a new idea will always depend on the web of beliefs into which it is introduced. To clarify, then, self-forgiveness should not be confused with trivialising or disregarding the hurt caused to others. To truly forgive ourselves requires that we recognise the full extent of the suffering caused by our actions. It requires the cultivation of empathy, a crucial step to more compassionate behaviour.

55.   Daniel Kahneman, *Thinking, Fast and Slow* (London: Allen Lane, 2011), p. 27.

56.   Bertrand Russell, *Logic and Knowledge* (1956; London: Routledge, 1997), p. 149.

57.   Thomas Nagel, *A View From Nowhere* (Oxford: Oxford University Press, 1986), p. 4.

2 Punishment

1.   The eighteenth-century German philosopher Immanuel Kant, for instance, argued in *The Science of Right* (1790) that 'Judicial punishment can never be

used merely as a means to promote some other good for the criminal himself or for civil society, but instead it must in all cases be imposed on him only on the ground that he has committed a crime.'

2. YouGov poll, 'Death Penalty', 13 August 2014; YouGov poll, 'Prospect Social, Moral and Political Issues', 18 November 2010.

3. Gallup poll, 'Americans' views of the Death Penalty', 7–11 October 2015.

4. Daniel Kahneman, *Thinking, Fast and Slow* (London: Allen Lane, 2011), p. 308.

5. Nathalia Gjersoe, 'The moral life of babies', *The Guardian*, 12 October 2013. See http://www.theguardian.com/science/2013/oct/12/babies-moral-life

6. Robert Wright, *The Moral Animal* (1994; London: Abacus, 2006), p. 205.

7. *United States* v. *Grayson*, 438 U.S. 41, 52 (1978).

8. *Smith* v. *Armontrout*, 865 F.2d 1502, 1506 (8th Cir. 1988) ('The whole presupposition of the criminal law is that most people, most of the time, have free will within broad limits.'); *Steward Machine Co.* v. *Davis*, 301 U.S. 548, 590 (1937) ('the law has been guided by a robust common sense which assumes the freedom of the will as a working hypothesis in the solution to its problems'.); *Bethea* v. *United States*, 365 A.2d 64, 83 n.39 (D.C. 1976) (Although the deterministic theory of behaviour may have 'some adherents, the notion that a person's conduct is a simple function of extrinsic forces and circumstances over which he has no control is an unacceptable contradiction of the concept of free will, which is the sine qua non of our criminal justice system'.); Rachel J. Littman, 'Adequate Provocation, Individual Responsibility, and the Deconstruction of Free Will', *Albany Law Review*, Vol. 60, No. 4, 1997 (Individuals are 'rational, free thinkers with strong inner selves and the capacity to exercise free will'.); Sanford H. Kadish, *Blame and Punishment: Essays in the Criminal Law* (New York: Macmillan, 1987), p. 77 ('Much of our commitment to democratic values, to human dignity and self-determination, to the value of the individual, turns on the pivot of a view of man as a responsible agent entitled to be praised or blamed depending upon his free choice of conduct.')

9. Stephen J. Morse, 'New Neuroscience, Old Problems: Legal Implications of Brain Science', in *Neuroscience and the Law: Brain, Mind, and the Scales of Justice*, ed. B Garland (New York: Dana Press, 2004), pp. 157–98. See http://www.dana.org/Cerebrum/Default.aspx?id=39169

10. Stephen J. Morse, 'New Neuroscience, Old Problems: Legal Implications of Brain Science'.

11. Stephen J. Morse, 'New Neuroscience, Old Problems: Legal Implications of Brain Science'. ('Nor is the truth of a fully physically caused universe [sometimes

referred to as "determinism"] part of the criteria for any legal doctrine that holds some people non-responsible. Thinking that causation itself excuses, including causation by abnormal variables, is an analytic error that I have termed the fundamental psycho-legal ... All behavior may be caused in a physical universe, but not all behavior is excused, because causation per se has nothing to do with responsibility.')

12. A. F. Shariff, J. D. Greene, J. C. Karremans, J. B. Luguri, C. J. Clark, J. W. Schooler, R. F. Baumeister, K. D. Vohs, 'Free will and punishment: A mechanistic view of human nature reduces retribution', *Psychological Science*, published online 10 June 2014, p. 7.

13. Richard Wilkinson, Kate Pickett, *The Spirit Level: Why Equality is Better for Everyone* (2009; revd edn, London: Penguin, 2010), pp. 154–5.

14. Paul Gendreau, Claire Goggin, 'The Effects of Prison Sentences on Recidivism', Centre for Criminal Justice Studies, University of New Brunswick, and Francis T. Cullen, Department of Criminal Justice, University of Cincinnati, 1999. See http://www.prisonpolicy.org/scans/gendreau.pdf

15. A number of studies have demonstrated this pattern. See Patrick A. Langan, David J. Levin, 'Recidivism of Prisoners Released in 1994', US Department of Justice, Office of Justice Programs, 2002. See also Matthew R. Durose, Alexia D. Cooper, Howard N. Snyder, 'Recidivism of Prisoners Released in 30 States in 2005: Patterns from 2005 to 2010', Bureau of Justice Statistics Special Report, April 2014.

16. Ministry of Justice, Green Paper, Evidence Report – *Breaking the cycle: effective punishment, rehabilitation and sentencing of offenders*, 7 December 2010.

17. James Gilligan, *Preventing Violence* (New York: Thames & Hudson, 2001), p. 117.

18. See, for instance, Steven Pinker, *The Blank Slate* (2002; London: Penguin Books, 2003), p. 183.

19. Daniel Dennett, *Freedom Evolves* (2003; London: Penguin Books, 2004), p. 272.

20. Richard A. Posner (ed.), *The Essential Holmes* (Chicago: The University of Chicago Press, 1996), p. 216.

21. Rita J. Simon, Dagny A. Blaskovich, *A Comparative Analysis of Capital Punishment: Statutes, Policies, Frequencies and Public Attitudes the World Over* (New York: Lexington Books, 2002), p. 40.

22. Rita J. Simon, Dagny A. Blaskovich, *A Comparative Analysis of Capital Punishment: Statutes, Policies, Frequencies and Public Attitudes the World Over*, p. 40.

23. Amnesty International Public Statement, Index: ACT 50/004/2014, 23 December, 2014, p. 3. (The most comprehensive study carried out by the UN in 1988 and

updated in 2008 concluded: '[R]esearch has failed to provide scientific proof that executions have a greater deterrent effect than life imprisonment. Such proof is unlikely to be forthcoming. The evidence as a whole still gives no positive support to the deterrent hypothesis.')

24. A useful summary of this evidence can be found at the Death Penalty Information Centre. See http://www.deathpenaltyinfo.org/law-enforcement-views-deterrence

25. The United Nations Convention Against Torture and Other Cruel, Inhuman or Degrading Treatment or Punishment, Part I, Article 1. See http://www.hrweb.org/legal/cat.html

26. New York State Bar Association Committee on Civil Rights, Report to the House of Delegates, 'Solitary Confinement in New York State', 25 January 2013, pp. 4–5. See https://www.nysba.org/solitaryreport/

27. New York City Bar, 'Supermax Confinement in U.S. Prisons', Committee on International Human Rights, September 2011. See http://www2.nycbar.org/pdf/report/uploads/20072165-TheBrutalityofSupermaxConfinement.pdf

28. Richard Wilkinson, Kate Pickett, *The Spirit Level*, p. 152.

29. Richard Wilkinson, Kate Pickett, *The Spirit Level*, p. 152.

30. Paul Gendreau, Claire Goggin, 'The Effects of Prison Sentences on Recidivism', p. 4.

31. Valerie Wright, *Deterrence in Criminal Justice, Evaluating Certainty vs. Severity of Punishment*, The Sentencing Project, November 2010. See http://www.sentencingproject.org/doc/Deterrence%20Briefing%20.pdf

32. Erwin James, 'Bastøy: the Norwegian prison that works', *The Guardian*, 4 September 2013. See http://www.theguardian.com/society/2013/sep/04/bastoy-norwegian-prison-works

33. Erwin James, 'Bastøy: the Norwegian prison that works'.

34. Lois M. Davis, Robert Bozick, Jennifer L. Steele, Jessica Saunders, Jeremy N. V. Miles, 'Evaluating the Effectiveness of Correctional Education'(Santa Monica, CA: RAND Corporation, 2013), p. xvi. See http://www.rand.org/content/dam/rand/pubs/research_reports/RR200/RR266/RAND_RR266.pdf

35. 'US prison courses collapse', *The Times Higher Education*, 29 September 1995. See https://www.timeshighereducation.com/news/us-prison-courses-collapse/95448.article

36. Audrey Bazos, Jessica Hausman, 'Correctional Education as a Crime Control Program', UCLA School of Public Policy and Social Research, March 2004, p. 2. See http://www.ceanational.org/PDFs/ed-as-crime-control.pdf

37. Joanna Shapland, Gwen Robinson, Angela Sorsby, *Restorative Justice in Practice*

(London: Routledge, 2011). For a summary of these results, see: https://www.restorativejustice.org.uk/resources/ministry-justice-evaluation-implementing-restorative-justice-schemes-crime-reduction-3

38.   Lawrence W. Sherman, Heather Strang, *Restorative Justice: The Evidence* (London: The Smith Institute, 2007). See http://www.iirp.edu/pdf/RJ_full_report.pdf

39.   James Gilligan, Bandy Lee, 'The Resolve to Stop the Violence Project: Reducing Violence Through a Jail-Based Initiative', *Journal of Public Health*, Vol. 27, No. 2, April 2005, pp. 143–8.

40.   Katherine Reynolds Lewis, 'What if Everything You Knew About Disciplining Kids Was Wrong?', *Mother Jones*, July/August 2015. See http://www.motherjones.com/politics/2015/05/schools-behavior-discipline-collaborative-proactive-solutions-ross-greene

41.   Katherine Reynolds Lewis, 'What if Everything You Knew About Disciplining Kids Was Wrong?'

42.   Katherine Reynolds Lewis, 'What if Everything You Knew About Disciplining Kids Was Wrong?'

43.   Katherine Reynolds Lewis, 'What if Everything You Knew About Disciplining Kids Was Wrong?'

44.   Katherine Reynolds Lewis, 'What if Everything You Knew About Disciplining Kids Was Wrong?'

45.   Kwame Anthony Appiah, *Experiments in Ethics* (Cambridge, MA: Harvard University Press, 2008), p. 41.

46.   Kwame Anthony Appiah, *Experiments in Ethics*, p. 41.

47.   Daniel Kahneman, *Thinking, Fast and Slow*, pp. 43–4.

48.   Richard Wilkinson, 'Why is Violence More Common Where Inequality is Greater?', *Annals of the New York Academy of Science*, Vol. 1036, December 2004, pp. 1–12.

49.   The outliers in this data set are Finland and Singapore. Finland is a very equal society but has a high homicide rate. Singapore is extremely unequal but has a relatively low homicide rate. The explanation for this appears to be the level of gun ownership in each nation. Finland has one of the highest rates of gun ownership in the world, while Singapore has one of the lowest.

50.   James Gilligan, *Violence: Our Deadly Epidemic and its Causes* (New York: G. P. Putnam, 1996), p. 110.

51.   Tom Moroney, 'America's Mentally Ill Prisoners Outnumber Hospital Patients, Tenfold', Bloomberg Business, 8 April 2014. See http://www.bloomberg.com/news/articles/2014-04-08/americas-mentally-ill-prisoners-outnumber-hospital-patients-tenfold

52.   Helena Kennedy, *Just Law* (London: Random House, 2004), p. 284.

53.   Helena Kennedy, *Just Law*, p. 292.

54.   Christopher Ingraham, 'You Really Can Get Pulled Over For Driving While Black, Federal Statistics Show', *The Washington Post*, 9 September 2014. See http://www.washingtonpost.com/blogs/wonkblog/wp/2014/09/09/you-really-can-get-pulled-over-for-driving-while-black-federal-statistics-show/. Oliver Laughland, Jon Swaine, Jamiles Lartey, 'US police killings headed for 1,110 this year, with black Americans twice as likely to die', *The Guardian*, 1 July 2015. See http://www.theguardian.com/us-news/2015/jul/01/us-police-killings-this-year-black-americans

55.   Devah Pager, 'The Mark of a Criminal Record,' *American Journal of Sociology*, Vol. 108, No. 5, March 2003, p. 958.

56.   'King's Dream Remains an Elusive Goal; Many Americans See Racial Disparities', Pew Research Center, 22 August 2013. See http://www.pewsocialtrends.org/2013/08/22/kings-dream-remains-an-elusive-goal-many-americans-see-racial-disparities/

57.   'How Fair is Britain? Equality, Human Rights and Good Relations in 2010: The First Triennial Review', Equality and Human Rights Commission, 23 May 2011, p. 162. See https://www.gov.uk/government/publications/how-fair-is-britain-equality-human-rights-and-good-relations-in-2010-the-first-triennial-review

58.   James Chapman, 'Clegg: Young black men are more likely to end up in prison than at a top university', *Daily Mail*, 24 November 2011. See http://www.dailymail.co.uk/news/article-2065427/Clegg-Young-black-men-likely-end-PRISON-university.html

59.   For a detailed breakdown of this figure, see the Inquest website: http://www.inquest.org.uk/statistics/bame-deaths-in-prison

60.   Anita Mukherjee, 'Do Private Prisons Distort Justice? Evidence on Time Served and Recidivism', Social Sciences Research Network, 15 March 2015. See http://papers.ssrn.com/sol3/papers.cfm?abstract_id=2523238

61.   Glenn Greenwald, *With Liberty and Justice for Some* (New York: Picador, 2011), pp. 257–8.

62.   Vicky Pelaez, 'The Prison Industry in the United States: Big Business or a New Form of Slavery?', Global Research, 31 March 2014. See http://www.globalresearch.ca/the-prison-industry-in-the-united-states-big-business-or-a-new-form-of-slavery/8289

63.   Helena Kennedy, *Just Law*, p. 283.

64. 'The Cost of a Nation of Incarceration', CBS News, 23 April 2012. See http://www.cbsnews.com/news/the-cost-of-a-nation-of-incarceration/

65. Lisa Bloom, 'When will the US stop mass incarceration?', CNN, 3 July 2012. See http://edition.cnn.com/2012/07/03/opinion/bloom-prison-spending/

66. Lisa Bloom, 'When will the US stop mass incarceration?'

67. Douglas Husak, *Overcriminalization* (Oxford: Oxford University Press, 2008), p. 12.

68. Penny Green, Andrew Rutherford (eds), *Criminal Policy in Transition* (Oxford: Hart Publishing, 2000), p. 20.

69. Donald Macintyre, 'Major On Crime: "Condemn More, Understand Less"', *The Independent*, 21 February 1993. See http://www.independent.co.uk/news/major-on-crime-condemn-more-understand-less-1474470.html

70. Richard Wilkinson, Kate Pickett, *The Spirit Level*, pp. 148–9.

71. Richard Wilkinson, Kate Pickett, *The Spirit Level*, p. 149.

72. Richard Wilkinson, Kate Pickett, *The Spirit Level*, pp. 148–9.

73. Richard Wilkinson, Kate Pickett, *The Spirit Level*, p. 147.

74. 'Netherlands Close Eight Prisons Due to Lack of Criminals', Huffington Post UK, 26 June 2013. See http://www.huffingtonpost.co.uk/2013/06/26/netherlands-prisons-close--lack-of-criminals-_n_3503721.html

75. Helena Kennedy, *Just Law*, p. 282.

76. Helena Kennedy, *Just Law*, p. 281.

77. James Slack, 'Labour is dreaming up 33 new crimes a month . . . including barring you from swimming into the *Titanic*', *Daily Mail*, 22 January 2010.

78. Richard Wilkinson, Kate Pickett, *The Spirit Level*, p. 145.

79. Matt Taibbi, 'Cruel and Unusual Punishment: The Shame of Three Strikes Laws', *Rolling Stone*, 27 March 2013.

80. Arundhati Roy, *Ordinary Person's Guide to Empire* (London: Penguin Books, 2006), p. 146.

81. Glenn Greenwald, *With Liberty and Justice for Some*, p. 227.

82. Glenn Greenwald, *With Liberty and Justice for Some*, pp. 19–20.

83. Calvin Woodward, Jeff Wilson, 'Cheney Hails Ford's Pardon of Nixon', *The Washington Post*, 30 December 2006. See http://washingtonpost.com/wp-dyn/content/article/2006/12/30/AR006123000977_pf.html

84. Shadee Ashtari, 'Former Counterterrorism Czar Richard Clarke: Bush, Cheney Committed War Crimes', Huffington Post, 29 May 2014.

85. David Johnston, Charlie Savage, 'Obama Reluctant to Look into Bush Programs', *New York Times*, 11 January 2009. See http://www.nytimes.com/2009/01/12/us/politics/12inquire.html?pagewanted=all&_r=0

86. Glenn Greenwald, *With Liberty and Justice for Some*, p. 133.

87. Joseph E. Stiglitz, *The Price of Inequality* (London: Allen Lane, 2012), p. 200.

88. Joseph E. Stiglitz, *The Price of Inequality*, p. 198.

89. Alan Beattie, 'Summers 'outrage' at AIG bonuses', *Financial Times*, 15 March 2009. See http://www.ft.com/cms/s/0/31bafc52-1192-11de-87b1-0000779fd2ac.html

90. Edward Luce, 'Obama Says Bonuses Are Part of Free Market', *Financial Times*, 10 February 2010. See http://www.ft.com/cms/s/0/50e597e0-1678-11df-bf44-00144feab49a.html

91. Sean Martin, 'Judge Takes Pity on "Embarrassed" RBS Bankers Who Committed £3m Fraud', *International Business Times*, 26 November 2014. See http://www.ibtimes. co.uk/two-rbs-bankers-walk-free-after-committing-3m-property-fraud-1476786

92. Matt Taibbi, 'The US justice divide: why crime and punishment in Wall Street and Ferguson are so different', *The Guardian*, 17 October 2014. See http://www. theguardian.com/us-news/2014/oct/17/us-justice-divide-crime-punishment-wall-street-ferguson

93. Yanis Varoufakis, *The Global Minotaur* (2011; 2nd edn, London: Zed Books, 2015), p. 125.

94. Richard Luscombe, '90-year-old among Florida activists arrested for feeding the homeless', *The Guardian*, 5 November 2014. See http://www.theguardian.com/ us-news/2014/nov/05/fort-lauderdale-pastors-arnold-abbott-arrested-feeding-homeless

95. Though this quote is widely attributed to Jefferson, I was not able to confirm its source. A similar quote has been attributed to Justice Felix Frankfurter: 'It is a wise man who said that there is no greater inequality than the equal treatment of unequals', *Dennis v. United States*, 339 U.S. 162, (1950).

96. Katie Engelhart, 'The UK is Going To Send Billions In Arms Exports To Countries on the Human Rights Blacklist', Vice News, 20 March 2015. See https://news. vice.com/article/the-uk-is-going-to-send-billions-in-arms-exports-to-countries-on-the-human-rights-blacklist

97. Adam Smith, *The Wealth of Nations*, Book 5, Chapter 1. https://www.marxists. org/reference/archive/smith-adam/works/wealth-of-nations/book05/ch01b.htm

98. *"Take back the streets": Repression and criminalization of protest around the world*, International Network of Civil Liberties Organizations, October 2013, p. 3. See https://www.aclu.org/files/assets/global_protest_suppression_report_inclo.pdf

99. *"Take back the streets": Repression and criminalization of protest around the world*, p. 11.

100. *"Take back the streets": Repression and criminalization of protest around the world.* p. 4.

101. Richard A. Posner (ed.), *The Essential Holmes*, p. 216.

3 Reward

1. Les Leopold, 'America's New Math: 1 Wall Street Hour = 21 Years of Hard Work For the Rest of Us', Huffington Post, 22 April 2013. Available at http://www.huffingtonpost.com/les-leopold/americas-new-math-1-wall-_b_3134022.html.

2. Graeme Wearden, 'Oxfam: 85 richest people as wealthy as poorest half of the world', *The Guardian*, 20 January 2014. See: http://www.theguardian.com/business/2014/jan/20/oxfam-85-richest-people-half-of-the-world

3. Amartya Sen, *On Ethics and Economics* (1987; Cambridge, MA: Blackwell Publishing, 2011), p. 2.

4. Among economists, there is much debate about how capital should be defined. For present purposes I have followed Thomas Piketty's definition and conflated wealth with capital.

5. Thomas Piketty, *Capital in the Twenty-First Century* (Cambridge, MA: Harvard University Press, 2014), p. 440.

6. Thomas Piketty, *Capital in the Twenty-First Century*, p. 431.

7. According to Piketty, this is because the rate of return on capital has, on average, been higher than the growth rate of the economy as a whole. The period from the end of the Second World War to the 1980s was anomalous, an exception to the rule of wealth concentration that was prompted by two world wars, the Great Depression, higher taxes, rising populations and more comprehensive social services.

8. Thomas Piketty, *Capital in the Twenty-First Century*, p. 428.

9. James Nye, 'America's wealthiest families revealed: from the Rockefellers to the Waltons, the 185 clans all worth more than $1 billion . . . and yes, most of them are Republicans', *Daily Mail*, 9 July 2014. See http://www.dailymail.co.uk/news/article-2686395/Americas-wealthiest-families-revealed-From-Rockefellers-Kennedys-185-clans-worth-1billion-yes-Republicans.html

10. Thomas Piketty, *Capital in the Twenty-First Century*, p. 244.

11. Thomas Piketty, *Capital in the Twenty-First Century*, p. 257. By comparison, historically the wealthiest 10 per cent of wage earners have received between 25 to 30 per cent of total income, and the bottom 50 per cent have received between a quarter and a third: Thomas Piketty, *Capital in the Twenty-First Century*, p. 244.

12. Jamie Doward, 'Inheritance: how Britain's wealthy still keep it in the family', *The Guardian*, 31 January 2015. See http://www.theguardian.com/society/2015/jan/31/inheritance-britain-wealthy-study-surnames-social-mobility

13. John J. Havens, Paul G. Schervish, 'A Golden Age of Philanthropy Still Beckons: National Wealth Transfer and Potential for Philanthropy Technical Report',

Center on Wealth and Philanthropy, Boston College, 28 May 2014. For a summary of the results, see http://www.bc.edu/content/dam/files/research_sites/cwp/pdf/Wealth%20Press%20Release%205.28-9.pdf

14. Robin Hahnel, *Economic Justice and Democracy* (New York: Routledge, 2005), p. 22.

15. Robin Blackburn, 'Enslavement and Industrialisation', BBC website, 17 February 2011. See http://www.bbc.co.uk/history/british/abolition/industrialisation_article_01.shtml

16. Robert Beckford, *Documentary as Exorcism* (London: Bloomsbury Academic, 2014), p. 165.

17. Sanchez Manning, 'Britain's colonial shame: Slave-owners given huge payouts after abolition', *The Independent*, 24 February 2013. See http://www.independent.co.uk/news/uk/home-news/britains-colonial-shame-slave-owners-given-huge-payouts-after-abolition-8508358.html

18. Alexandra Sims, 'Vast scale of British slave ownership revealed', *The Independent*, 13 July 2015. See http://www.independent.co.uk/news/uk/vast-scale-of-british-slave-ownership-revealed-10383768.html

19. Thomas Piketty, *Capital in the Twenty-First Century*, p. 443.

20. Ashley Gray, 'David Beckham toppled by Lionel Messi as Barcelona star leads football earner charts on £570,000 a week!', *Daily Mail*, 24 March 2010.

21. Royal College of Nursing, NHS Agenda for Change pay scales – 2010/2011, Agenda for Change pay bands effective from 1 April 2010. See http://www.rcn.org.uk/__data/assets/pdf_file/0018/233901/003303.pdf

22. Ha-Joon Chang, *23 Things They Don't Tell You About Capitalism* (London: Allen Lane, 2010), p. 30.

23. Joseph E. Stiglitz, *The Price of Inequality* (London: Allen Lane, 2012), p. 19.

24. Press Association, 'Well-off families create "glass floor" to ensure children's success, says study', *The Guardian*, 26 July 2015. See http://www.theguardian.com/society/2015/jul/26/well-off-families-create-glass-floor-to-ensure-childrens-success-says-study?CMP=share_btn_fb

25. Milton Friedman, *Capitalism and Freedom* (1962; Chicago: University of Chicago Press, 2002), p. 164.

26. All work requires effort. Imagine two teenagers: one about to leave school to seek employment, and one about to enter university to study medicine. Over the next decade, who will work harder? Does going to school require more effort or personal sacrifice than working? It's certainly not obvious that this is the case. In many instances the reverse is true. Appealing to 'effortful training'

does nothing to justify the rewards people receive for innate ability. The very fact that we feel the need to highlight the fact that talent takes effort to develop betrays an awareness that talent alone does not warrant great rewards.

27. Suppose we grade the usefulness of our contribution from zero to one – 'zero' indicating our efforts have no social value, 'one' indicating our efforts are as socially useful as it is possible for them to be. Rewarding people according to their socially useful effort would mean that anyone who scores above zero, even by the tiniest of amounts, ought to be remunerated as much as someone who scores 'one', *if the efforts made are equivalent*. The problem is that someone who scores literally zero, through no fault of their own, no matter how much effort they expend, will fail to be remunerated at all. This seems an arbitrary distinction. It is worth noting that all of us at any time can become ill or disabled through no fault of our own, and youth and old age are, of course, universal phases of human existence. These are not side issues; they are central to the question of fairness.

28. Closely linked to the concept of effort is the idea of sacrifice. As a basis for a fair reward, it is far more promising. A sacrifice implies the loss of something – the loss of well-being for instance. But, a well-being deficit is a deficit irrespective of its origin, whether it is the result of socially useful work, effortful training, bereavement, poor judgement, or a genetic predisposition. Ultimately, we are not responsible for the way we are, or what follows from that, and so the source of our deficit makes us no more or less deserving of compensation.

29. Some principles of reward, it should be said, are preferable to others, not because they are intrinsically fairer but because they happen to produce more egalitarian outcomes. For instance, rewarding people for the value of their personal contribution is preferable to rewarding people according to the value of their capital. This is because capital is far less evenly distributed throughout the population than talent, the capacity to make efforts, or educational opportunities, all of which help to determine the value of our personal contribution.

30. No policy proposals follow *necessarily* from this conclusion. A gap exists between a principle of fairness and the creation of actual policy.

31. If fairness implies equality, we need to ask 'equality of what'? Amartya Sen has argued that competing political and economic philosophies do not dispute the case for equality, but rather what it is that should be equalised. Various answers have been proposed: equality of income, happiness, opportunity, resources, primary goods, freedom, treatment before the law. In other words, even those philosophies that have rejected traditional notions of wealth equality are still

founded on a conception of equality of some kind. So where does this leave us? Well, certain things are clear: human beings share some fundamental needs that must be met in order to flourish and live decent, dignified lives. In our world, access to material resources, and the income that provides that access, is fundamental to meeting many of these needs and securing many of the rights that diverse groups agree are fundamental to human flourishing. Material inequality, therefore, is only fair when it is used to compensate for a form of inequality that is generally considered to be more fundamental.

32.   The rate of profit is determined by an analogous process involving the 'marginal product of capital' and the revenue a business would lose as capital is incrementally removed.

33.   Orley Ashenfelter, Stepan Jurajda, 'Cross-Country Comparisons of Wage Rates: The Big Mac Index', paper given at conference, Unemployment in Transition Economies: Developments, Challenges and Lessons from the EU and the US, 26–28 October 2001.

34.   Ha-Joon Chang, *23 Things They Don't Tell You About Capitalism*, p. 30.

35.   'Women in the workplace', Chartered Management Institute, December 2012, p. 3. See http://www.managers.org.uk/~/media/Angela%20Media%20Library/ pdfs/Policies/Women%20in%20the%20Workplace.pdf

36.   Joseph Stiglitz, *The Price of Inequality*, p. 41.

37.   Daniel Kahneman, *Thinking, Fast and Slow* (London: Allen Lane, 2011), p. 219.

38.   Daniel Kahneman, *Thinking, Fast and Slow*, p. 261.

39.   Moshe Adler, *Economics for the Rest of Us* (New York: The New Press, 2009), pp. 143–5.

40.   Jill Treanor, 'Barclays condemned over £2.4bn bonuses', *The Guardian*, 11 February 2014. See http://www.theguardian.com/business/2014/feb/11/barclays-hikes-bonuses-profits-slide

41.   Lawrence Mishel, Alyssa Davis, 'Top CEOs Make 300 Times More Than Typical Workers', Economic Policy Institute, 21 June 2015. See http://www.epi.org/ publication/top-ceos-make-300-times-more-than-workers-pay-growth-surpasses-market-gains-and-the-rest-of-the-0-1-percent/

42.   Robert Reich, 'How to Fix Sky-High CEO Pay in Companies that Pay Workers Like Serfs', Alternet, 22 April 2014. See http://www.alternet.org/economy/ robert-reich-how-fix-sky-high-ceo-pay-companies-pay-workers-serfs

43.   Mainstream economists acknowledge the great disparity between the theory of wages and the reality, but they blame these disparities on distortions of the market, not failings in the theory. They believe that the theory is close enough to reality

to justify using as an approximation but concede that the real world does not always produce the results they would predict. They place the blame for this discrepancy on factors such as union, state and corporate power distorting the market. And so, in response to criticisms of the theory, they argue that we need to slash regulation, end monopolies, disempower unions and remove other obstacles to the free functioning of the market. In other words, we should change the world to fit the theory rather than the other way around. Apart from the fact that it does nothing to address the problem of measuring a worker's individual contribution, and that the system of rewards described by the theory would be unfair even if it were true, this response is problematic. Our world is so far from conforming to the perfectly competitive, highly abstracted markets of economic modelling that it makes little sense to design policy based on them. The prescriptions of economists to remove distortions from the market are often flawed in another way. If you have both monopolies and unions, getting rid of just one – and invariably the focus is on unions – will take you a step closer to the abstract models of economists, but even according to mainstream analysis it will result in workers getting far less than their contribution. The point being that if we have one form of market distortion it is better to have a countervailing distortion than to apply the crude rule of thumb that 'all market intervention is bad'.

44.   Thomas Piketty, *Capital in the Twenty-First Century*, p. 331.

45.   Adam Smith, *The Wealth of Nations*, Book 1, Chapter 8. See http://www.marxists. org/reference/archive/smith-adam/works/wealth-of-nations/book01/ch08.htm

46.   Robert L. Heilbroner, William Milberg, *The Making of Economic Society* (1962; Boston, MA: Pearson, 2012), p. 62.

47.   Thomas Piketty, *Capital in the Twenty-First Century*, p. 40.

48.   Thomas Piketty, *Capital in the Twenty-First Century*, p. 438.

49.   Adam Smith, *The Wealth of Nations*, Book 4, Chapter 8. See https://www. marxists.org/reference/archive/smith-adam/works/wealth-of-nations/book04/ ch02.htm. A close reading of the text shows that Smith used the term 'invisible hand' in a much narrower sense than it is generally used today.

50.   Jack Shenker, 'After the massacre: life in South Africa's platinum mining belt', *The Guardian*, 15 August 2014. See http://www.theguardian.com/world/2014/ aug/15/-sp-south-africa-platinum-mining-massacre-strike

51.   Mark Ames, 'Revealed: Apple and Google's wage-fixing cartel involved dozens more companies, over one million employees', Pando, 22 March 2014. See https://pando.com/2014/03/22/revealed-apple-and-googles-wage-fixing-cartel-involved-dozens-more-companies-over-one-million-employees/

52. Joseph E. Stiglitz, *The Price of Inequality*, p. 61.

53. Thomas Piketty, *Capital in the Twenty-First Century*, p. 265.

54. Robert Reich, 'Work and Worth', 2 August 2014. See http://robertreich.org/post/93632709170

55. Eugene V. Debs, Ohio Anti-War Speech, delivered 16 June 1918. Available at http://www.marxists.org/archive/debs/works/1918/canton.htm

56. David Ricardo believed that the theory of marginal productivity could only be applied in very specific circumstances, namely, to what he called 'doses' (a combination of a labourer and her tools) and only in agriculture, not industry. For an extended discussion of this topic, see: Moshe Adler, *Economics for the Rest of Us*, pp. 113–42.

57. John Bates Clark, *The Distribution of Wealth: A Theory of Wages, Interest, and Profits* (New York: Macmillan, 1908), Chapter One. Available at http://www.econlib.org/library/Clark/clkDW1.html

58. Amartya Sen, *On Ethics and Economics*, p. 1.

59. Michael Tomasello, Felix Warneken, 'Extrinsic Rewards Undermine Altruistic Tendencies In 20-Month-Olds', *Developmental Psychology*, Vol. 44, No. 6, 2008, pp. 1785–8.

60. Edward L. Deci, 'Effects of Externally Mediated Rewards on Intrinsic Motivation', *Journal of Personality and Social Psychology*, Vol. 18, No. 1, 1971, pp. 105–14.

61. Edward L. Deci, 'Intrinsic Motivation, Extrinsic Reinforcement, and Inequity', *Journal of Personality and Social Psychology*, Vol. 22, No.1, April 1972, pp. 113–20.

62. Daniel H. Pink, *Drive: The Surprising Truth About What Motivates Us* (Edinburgh: Canongate, 2010), p. 10.

63. Daniel H. Pink, *Drive*, pp. 42–3.

64. Dan Ariely, Uri Gneezy, George Lowenstein, Nina Mazar, 'Large Stakes and Big Mistakes', Federal Reserve Bank of Boston Working Paper, No. 05-11, 23 July 2005.

65. Samuel Bowles, Sandra Polania Reyes, 'Economic Incentives and Social Preferences: A Preference-Based Lucas Critique of Public Policy', Economics Department Working Paper Series, Paper 5, University of Massachusetts, Amherst, 2009.

66. Stefan Stern, 'Are chief executives so very valuable?', *Financial Times*, 15 October 2015.

67. Joseph E. Stiglitz, *The Price of Inequality*, p. 104.

68. Thomas Piketty, *Capital in the Twenty-First Century*, p. 511.

69. YouGov poll, 'Meaningless Labour of British Working Adults', August 2015. See https://yougov.co.uk/news/2015/08/12/british-jobs-meaningless/

70. Elizabeth W. Dunn, Lara B. Aknin, Michael I. Norton, 'Spending Money on

Others Promotes Happiness', *Science*, 319, March 2008, p. 1687; Lara B. Aknin, Christopher P. Barrington-Leigh, Elizabeth W. Dunn, John F. Helliwell, Robert Biswas-Diener, Imelda Kemeza, Paul Nyende, Claire E. Ashton-James, 'Prosocial spending and well-being: Cross-cultural evidence for a psychological universal', *Journal of Psychology and Social Psychology*, Vol. 104, No. 4, 2013, pp. 635–52.

71. Elizabeth W. Dunn, Lara B. Aknin, Kiley Hamlin, 'Giving Leads to Happiness in Young Children', PLOS, 14 June 2012, ONE 7(6): e39211. doi:10.1371/journal. pone.0039211.

72. There is plenty of room for difference within a society that places a high value on the flourishing of all its members. Diversity is something to celebrate, but all the more so within a context in which it is accepted that the needs of every human being matter, in which no one is judged to be more or less deserving of what life has to offer, and in which no group is systematically privileged or exploited.

73. Peter Kropotkin, *Anarchism* (1927; New York: Dover Publications, 2002), p. 71.

74. Peter Kropotkin, *Anarchism*, p. 71.

75. Bertrand Russell, *Roads to Freedom: Socialism, Anarchism and Syndicalism* (1918; Oxford: Routledge, 1996), p. 87.

76. Howard Zinn, 'On Rewarding People for Talent and Hard Work', *The Zinn Reader* (1997; New York: Seven Stories Press, 2009), p. 235.

77. Ha-Joon Chang, *Economics: The User's Guide* (London: Pelican Books, 2014), p. 91.

78. The evidence against 'trickle down' theory is overwhelming. An IMF paper of 2015 says: 'we find an inverse relationship between the income share accruing to the rich (top 20 per cent) and economic growth. If the income share of the top 20 per cent increases by 1 percentage point, GDP growth is actually 0.08 percentage point lower in the following five years, suggesting that the benefits do not trickle down. Instead, a similar increase in the income share of the bottom 20 per cent (the poor) is associated with 0.38 percentage point higher growth. This positive relationship between disposable income shares and higher growth continues to hold for the second and third quintiles (the middle class). This result survives a variety of robustness checks, and is in line with recent findings for a smaller sample of advanced economies (OECD 2014).' In Era Dabla-Norris, Kalpana Kochhar, Nujin Suphaphiphat, Frantisek Ricka, Evridiki Tsounta, 'Causes and Consequences of Income Inequality: A Global Perspective', International Monetary Fund, Strategy, Policy, and Review Department, June 2015. See https://www.imf.org/external/pubs/ft/sdn/2015/sdn1513.pdf. A report by the OECD arrived at similar conclusions, summarised in the following article:

Lee Williams, 'It's official – benefits and high taxes make us all richer, while inequality takes a hammer to a country's growth', *The Independent*, 10 December 2014. See http://www.independent.co.uk/voices/comment/its-official-benefits-and-high-taxes-make-us-all-richer-while-inequality-takes-a-hammer-to-a-9914941.html

79. John Kenneth Galbraith, *A History of Economics* (1987; London: Penguin Books, 1991), p. 7.

80. Daniel Kahneman, *Thinking, Fast and Slow*, p. 397.

81. David Ransom, Vanessa Baird (eds), *People First Economics* (2009; 2nd edn, Oxford: World Changing, 2010), pp. 157–8.

4 Control

1. This example comes from Daniel C. Dennett, *Breaking the Spell: Religion as a Natural Phenomenon* (2006; London: Penguin Books, 2007), pp. 3–4.

2. Samuel Bowles, Arjun Jayadev, 'One Nation Under Guard', *New York Times*, 15 February 2014. See http://opinionator.blogs.nytimes.com/2014/02/15/one-nation-under-guard/?_php=true&_type=blogs&_r=1

3. Samuel Bowles, Arjun Jayadev, 'One Nation Under Guard'.

4. Samuel Bowles, Arjun Jayadev, 'One Nation Under Guard'.

5. Niall Ferguson, *The Cash Nexus* (London: Allen Lane, 2001), p. 28.

6. Niall Ferguson, *The Cash Nexus*, p. 43.

7. Thomas Pakenham, *The Scramble for Africa* (1991; London: Abacus, 2011), p. xxiii.

8. Joseph Conrad, 'Geography and Some Explorers', *National Geographic*, March 1924. See http://www.ric.edu/faculty/rpotter/temp/geog_and_some.html

9. Adam Hochschild, *King Leopold's Ghost* (1998; London: Pan Books, 2006), p. 38.

10. Adam Hochschild, *King Leopold's Ghost*, p. 233.

11. Thomas Piketty, *Capital in the Twenty-First Century* (Cambridge: Harvard University Press, 2014), p. 69.

12. Adam Hochschild, *Bury the Chains* (London: Pan Books, 2005), p. 2.

13. Adam Hochschild, *Bury the Chains*, p. 2.

14. Astra Taylor, 'You are not a loan: it's time to bring student debt down to zero', *The Guardian*, 18 November 2014. See http://www.theguardian.com/comment-isfree/2014/nov/18/loan-student-debt-zero-free-tuition

15. Blake Ellis, 'Grieving Parents Hit With $200,000 In Student Loans', CNN Money, 28 July 2014. See http://money.cnn.com/2014/07/28/pf/parents-student-loans/

16. Tim Ross, 'Six in 10 students will have their debts written off', *The Telegraph*, 5 April 2014.

17. But when does shaping an identity qualify as control? When do attempts to influence ideas, beliefs and desires qualify as manipulation? What distinguishes indoctrination from education? We will take up these questions in Part Three, but for now we will assume the following: the cause of freedom is served by deepening our understanding of how and why we come to possess the beliefs and desires that we do.

18. Evolutionary psychology offers a simple explanation for the vulnerability of young minds. The trust children place in their elders tends to enhance survival prospects. Parental figures familiar with the dangers and pitfalls of their environment have essential information to pass on to their progeny. Children who don't take these warnings seriously will be exposed to greater risks. Natural selection, so the argument goes, would favour genes that predisposed children to trust the community elders on whom their safety depends. If this theory is correct, it would mean that children would not only accept the useful advice given to them by their carers such as 'That root is poisonous; do not eat it', they would accept any serious warning given to them by a recognised authority.

19. For instance, Elizabeth L. Eisenstein, *The Printing Press as an Agent of Change* (Cambridge: Cambridge University Press, 1980).

20. Zaid Jilani, 'Top GOP Strategist Admits He's "Scared" of Occupy Wall Street Because It's Having an Impact', ThinkProgress, 1 December 2011. See http://thinkprogress.org/special/2011/12/01/379365/frank-luntz-occupy-wall-street/

21. Following the Bolshevik revolution of 1917, education and cultural engineering were seen as central to building a new communist society. A vision of the ideal male citizen was articulated: the 'New Soviet Man'. He was to be educated, selfless, fit, disciplined, committed to the socialist revolution and prepared to sacrifice his life for the collective. Schools were viewed as an essential part of the socialisation process, a microcosm of society. The cultivation of socialist values lay at the heart of the curriculum. The initial educational achievements of the revolution were substantial and innovative. Large investments were ploughed into the education system, making it free for every child between the ages of three and sixteen. Serious attempts were made to combat sexism and to provide schools for students with disabilities. In an attempt to bring democracy into the classroom, student governments were established who worked with teachers to manage the schools. Many new libraries were built, and nationwide literacy campaigns were launched. Early on in the Russian

revolution, families were encouraged to live in communal apartments in which the private sphere would be significantly reduced and communal living would foster collective values. For a short period, while collectivist ideals were at their height, architects took these ideas to the extreme and designed 'commune houses' in which all property would be held collectively, everybody would sleep in large dormitories along gender lines (with private rooms for sex), and childcare, along with other domestic tasks, would be assigned to teams on a rotating schedule.

Mao's China offers another example. After emerging victorious from a ten-year civil war in 1949, the Communist Party took power in China. One of its first acts was to take control of all forms of public media. Criticism of the regime was not tolerated. In 1951, the Chairman of the Party, Mao Zedong, launched a programme of thought reform that aimed explicitly to expunge attitudes of individualism and promote his personal ideology. The programme took place in educational institutions, prisons, government offices and peasant organisations. Mao was particularly concerned about those who he termed 'intellectuals'. This was a broad and vague category that included anyone with significant education, and ranged from teachers and doctors to students and engineers. Active participants in the revolution were expected to attend weekly meetings for 'thought examination', in which they had to criticise themselves and be subjected to the criticism of others. The personal was regarded as polit-ical and so privacy was heavily discouraged. Many witch-hunts were launched by Mao, while detailed files were kept on millions of Chinese. And people were often persecuted for connections to supporters of the old regime. The victims of these purges were pressured into incriminating others, generating an atmos-phere of paranoia and distrust. Mutual surveillance, forced confessions, the threat of heavy penalties and intense propaganda exerted a tight grip over the thoughts and behaviour of millions.

22. Philip Pilkington, 'What is Debt? – An Interview with Economic Anthropologist David Graeber', Naked Capitalism, 26 August 2011. See http://www.nakedcapitalism. com/2011/08/what-is-debt-%E2%80%93-an-interview-with-economic-anthropo-logist-david-graeber.html

23. David Graeber, Debt: The First 5,000 Years (New York: Melville House Publishing, 2011), p. 5.

24. For instance, when France invaded Madagascar in 1895, declaring it a French colony henceforth, heavy taxes were imposed on the Malagasy population to cover the cost of the invasion and the subsequent large-scale infrastructure

projects that were carried out (imposed, not requested). Subsequent decades saw hundreds of thousands of dissenting Malagasy killed by the French, yet to this day Madagascar still owes money to France.

25. Jubilee Debt Campaign, Philippines: Country Case Study. See http://jubileedebt.org.uk/countries/philippines

26. Mechele Dickerson, *Homeownership and America's Financial Underclass: Flawed Premises, Broken Promises, New Prescriptions* (New York: Cambridge University Press, 2014), p. 96.

27. Torture is an extreme form of control, combining a regime of mental and physical violence, along with a sophisticated blend of psychological techniques. In the 1980s a CIA handbook for interrogation found its way into the public domain. A number of techniques for breaking down the resistance of individuals were described, including use of mind-altering drugs, physical abuse and sensory deprivation. Central to these techniques was a focus on regression, the wiping clean of a person's sense of identity. As the handbook explains: 'All of the techniques employed to break through an interrogation roadblock, the entire spectrum from simple isolation to hypnosis and narcosis, are essentially ways of speeding up the process of regression. As the interrogatee slips back from maturity toward a more infantile state, his learned or structured personality traits fall away. . . . [On reaching this point, a prisoner finds himself in a state of psychological shock and paralysis and is] far more open to suggestion, far likelier to comply.' Modern interrogation techniques aim to raise the costs of non-compliance while eroding the psychological resources that make resistance possible. It is a two-step process: first deprive the prisoner of sensory inputs, then overwhelm them with stimulation, whether in the form of beatings, pounding music or electric shocks. This induces a state of profound confusion and fear, in which resisting the commands of the interrogator becomes excruciatingly difficult, if not impossible.

28. Only from 8000 BC onwards does the archaeological record show any evidence of institutionalised warfare. From then on, as anthropologists Jonathan Haas and Matthew Piscitelli write, we begin to observe 'a steady – if episodic – trickle of such indicators'. During this period, growing populations, food storage, limited farmland, the threat of famine arising from crop failure and animal disease, social and political hierarchy, created the preconditions for conflict between neighbouring settlements. And by the time we reach the Copper age, evidence of warfare is unambiguous. Once institutionalised warfare did arise, competition between states set a powerful evolutionary logic in motion that would shape

the development of human civilisation from then on. See Douglas P. Fry (ed.), *War, Peace, and Human Nature* (New York: Oxford University Press, 2013).

29. Any picture of the development of early Neolithic communities is necessarily speculative due to the limited evidence available, but general trends seem clear.

30. John Maynard Keynes, 'Economic Possibilities for our Grandchildren', 1930.

31. Yanis Varoufakis, Joseph Halevi, Nicholas J. Theocarakis, *Modern Political Economics* (Abingdon, Oxon: Routledge, 2011), pp. 23–5.

32. Yanis Varoufakis, *The Global Minotaur* (London: Zed Books, 2011), p. 30.

33. Owen Jones, *The Establishment: And how they get away with it* (London: Allen Lane, 2014), p. 5.

34. James Madison, *The Papers of James Madison*, Appendix to the debates, Volume 1, 1841. See https://archive.org/details/papersjamesmadi09madigoog

35. David Graeber, *The Democracy Project* (London: Allen Lane, 2013), p. 165.

36. Francis Dupuis-Déri, 'The Political Power of Words: The Birth of Pro-Democratic Discourse in the Nineteenth Century in the United States and France', *Political Studies*, Vol. 52, No. 1, March 2004, pp. 118–34.

37. Stuart Ewen, *PR! A Social History of Spin* (New York: Basic Books, 1996), p. 66.

38. Joseph A. Schumpeter, *Capitalism, Socialism and Democracy* (1943; Abingdon, Oxon: Routledge, 2010), p. 253.

39. Joseph A. Schumpeter, *Capitalism, Socialism and Democracy*, p. 264.

40. Theodore M. Porter, Dorothy Ross (eds), *The Cambridge History of Science*: Volume 7: *The Modern Social Sciences* (New York: Cambridge University Press, 2003), p. 316.

41. David Hume, *Essays and Treatises on Several Subjects*, Volume 1 (London, 1777), p. 33. See http://www.davidhume.org/texts/etv1.html

42. Yanis Varoufakis, *The Global Minotaur*, pp. 29–30.

5 Elections

1. Stuart Ewen, *PR! A Social History of Spin* (New York: Basic Books, 1996), p. 67.

2. Quoted in Stuart Ewen, *PR! A Social History of Spin*, p. 73.

3. Quoted in Stuart Ewen, *PR! A Social History of Spin*, p. 61.

4. He articulated his ideas in two seminal essays: *Public Opinion* (1922) and *The Phantom Public* (1925).

5. Stuart Ewen, *PR! A Social History of Spin*, p. 106.

6. Quoted in Stuart Ewen, *PR! A Social History of Spin*, p. 112.

7. Stuart Ewen, *PR! A Social History of Spin*, pp. 103–11.

8. Edward Bernays, *Propaganda* (1928; New York: Ig Publishing, 2005), p. 37.

9. Walter Lippmann, *Public Opinion* (1922; South Dakota: NuVision Publishing, 2007), p. 142.

10. Quoted in Alex Carey, *Taking the Risk Out Of Democracy* (Chicago: University of Illinois Press, 1997), p. 13. The emergence of democracy in the UK brought with it its own pioneers of public relations. One of its earliest practitioners of corporate propaganda was Charles Higham, an advertising executive recruited by the British government during the First World War. He was perturbed by what he saw as the 'amazing ignorance' of the newly enfranchised masses, and firmly believed in the importance and potential of shaping public opinion: 'there is no good habit or lofty idea that could not be inculcated in a people in a few short years if the right methods were used . . . we can move human energy in any direction by organised and public persuasion.' David Miller, William Dinan, *A Century of Spin* (London: Pluto Press, 2008), p. 39.

11. Walter Lippmann, *Public Opinion*, p. 29.

12. Edward Bernays, *Propaganda*, p. 97.

13. Stuart Ewen, *PR! A Social History of Spin,* p. 169.

14. Walter Lippmann, *Public Opinion*, pp. 119–20.

15. Walter Lippmann, *Public Opinion*, p. 136.

16. Walter Lippmann, *Public Opinion*, p. 21.

17. Unfortunately, this wording unnecessarily excludes many other significant political developments of the twentieth century, such as the great achievements of feminism and the civil rights movement. Alex Carey, *Taking the Risk Out of Democracy*, p. 18.

18. Joel Bakan, *The Corporation* (London: Constable & Robinson, 2004), p. 14.

19. Joel Bakan, *The Corporation*, p. 38.

20. Joel Bakan, *The Corporation*, p. 149.

21. Joel Bakan, *The Corporation*, p. 35.

22. Quoted in Raj Patel, *The Value of Nothing* (London: Portobello Books, 2011), p. 48.

23. Alex Carey, *Taking the Risk Out of Democracy*, p. 21.

24. Stuart Ewen, *PR! A Social History of Spin*, pp. 42–3.

25. In response to this threat, a powerful British organisation called National Propaganda was founded in 1919. Throughout its existence, it had close ties with government and the secret services, both of which provided it with funding and intelligence. One of its early anti-communist campaigns was run by former undercover agent Sidney Walton, who claimed to be able to plant 'authoritative

signed articles' in over 1,200 newspapers through 'bribery on a substantial scale'. By 1921, Walton, with the help of government funding, was able to 'budget for up to £100,000 a week if needed'. In 1925, National Propaganda was rechristened the Economic League. Writing to its members, it described its mission in the following terms: 'What is required is some years of propaganda for capitalism as the finest system that human ingenuity can devise, to counteract forty years of propaganda for socialism.' It would take a while, but eventually the aims of National Propaganda would be achieved. David Miller, William Dinan, *A Century of Spin*, p. 41.

26. Edward Bernays, *Propaganda*, p. 75.
27. Yanis Varoufakis, *The Global Minotaur* (London: Zed Books, 2011), p. 41.
28. David Stuckler, Sanjay Basu, *The Body Economic* (London: Allen Lane, 2013), p. 7.
29. Stuart Ewen, *PR! A Social History of Spin*, p. 234.
30. Quoted in Stuart Ewen, *PR! A Social History of Spin*, p. 235.
31. Quoted in Arthur M. Schlesinger, *The Coming of the New Deal, 1933–1935*, Vol. 2: *The Age of Roosevelt* (Boston and New York: Houghton Mifflin, 2003), p. 22.
32. Quoted in Alex Carey, *Taking the Risk Out of Democracy*, p. 21.
33. Quoted in Alex Carey, *Taking the Risk Out of Democracy*, p. 24.
34. According to the labour press, the formula consisted of the following steps:

'When a strike is threatened, label the union leaders as 'agitators' to discredit them with the public and their own followers. Conduct balloting under the foremen to ascertain the strength of the union and to make possible misrepresentation of the strikers as a small minority. Exert economic pressure through threats to move the plant, align bankers, real estate owners and businessmen into a 'Citizens' Committee'.

Raise high the banner of 'law and order', thereby causing the community to mass legal and police weapons against imagined violence and to forget that employees have equal rights with others in the community.

Call a 'mass meeting' to coordinate public sentiment against the strike and strengthen the Citizens' Committee.

Form a large police force to intimidate the strikers and exert a psychological effect. Utilise local police, state police, vigilantes and special deputies chosen, if possible, from other neighbourhoods.

Convince the strikers their cause is hopeless with a 'back-to-work' movement by a puppet association of so-called 'loyal employees' secretly organised by the employer.

When enough applications are on hand, set a date for opening the plant by having such opening requested by the puppet 'back-to-work' association.

Stage the 'opening' theatrically by throwing open the gates and having the employees march in a mass protected by squads of armed police so as to dramatize and exaggerate the opening and heighten the demoralising effect.

Demoralise the strikers with a continuing show of force. If necessary turn the locality into a warlike camp and barricade it from the outside world.

Close the publicity barrage on the theme that the plant is in full operation and the strikers are merely a minority attempting to interfere with the right to work. With this, the campaign is over – the employer has broken the strike.' (Quoted in David Miller, William Dinan, *A Century of Spin*, p. 53.)

35. Quoted in Alex Carey, *Taking the Risk Out of Democracy*, p. 26.

36. Quoted in Alex Carey, *Taking the Risk Out of Democracy*, p. 24.

37. Quoted in Alex Carey, *Taking the Risk Out of Democracy*, p. 138.

38. Quoted in David Miller, William Dinan, *A Century of Spin*, p. 57.

39. John Kenneth Galbraith, *A History of Economics* (1987; London: Penguin Books, 1991), pp. 252–3.

40. Alex Carey, *Taking the Risk Out of Democracy*, p. 30.

41. Alex Carey, *Taking the Risk Out of Democracy*, p. 28.

42. Quoted in Alex Carey, *Taking the Risk Out of Democracy*, p. 31.

43. Alex Carey, *Taking the Risk Out of Democracy*, p. 31.

44. Elizabeth Fones-Wolf, *Selling Free Enterprise* (Champaign, IL: University of Illinois Press, 1994), p. 189.

45. Quoted in Elizabeth Fones-Wolf, *Selling Free Enterprise*, p. 195.

46. Elizabeth Fones-Wolf, *Selling Free Enterprise*, p. 198.

47. Elizabeth Fones-Wolf, *Selling Free Enterprise*, p. 10.

48. Friedrich Hayek, *The Road to Serfdom* (1944; New York: Routledge, 2009), p. 5.

49. *The Collected Works of F. A. Hayek*, Vol. X, *Socialism and War: Essays, Documents, Reviews*, ed. Bruce Caldwell (1997; Chicago: University of Chicago Press, 2012), p. 225.

50. Friedrich Hayek, *The Road to Serfdom*, p. 168.

51. A steady source of funding came from right-wing foundations such as the Earhart Foundation, the William Volker Fund, and the Reim Foundation, and wealthy individuals such as Charles Koch, Richard Mellon Scaife, and Joseph Coors.

52. Quoted in David Miller, William Dinan, *A Century of Spin*, p. 77.

53. Quoted in Richard Cockett, *Thinking the Unthinkable: Think-Tanks and the Economic Counter-Revolution 1931–1983* (New York: Harper Collins, 1994), p. 173.

54. Quoted in David Miller, William Dinan, *A Century of Spin*, p. 74.

55. Daniel Stedman-Jones, *Masters of the Universe: Hayek, Friedman and the Birth of Neoliberal Politics* (Woodstock, Oxon: Princeton University Press, 2012), p. 50.

56. This information comes from their own website. See http://businessroundtable. org/about

57. Michel J. Crozier, Samuel P. Huntington, Joji Watanuki, *The Crisis of Democracy: Report on the Governability of Democracies to the Trilateral Commission* (New York: New York University Press, 1975), p. 61. See https://archive.org/stream/TheCrisisOf Democracy-TrilateralCommission-1975/crisis_of_democracy_djvu.txt

58. Michel J. Crozier, Samuel P. Huntington, Joji Watanuki, *The Crisis of Democracy*, p. 113.

59. Michel J. Crozier, Samuel P. Huntington, Joji Watanuki, *The Crisis of Democracy*, p. 185.

60. Quoted in Daniel Stedman Jones, *Masters of the Universe*, p. 163.

61. David Harvey, *A Brief History of Neoliberalism* (New York: Oxford University Press, 2005), p. 115.

62. Ha-Joon Chang, *Economics: The User's Guide* (London: Pelican Books, 2014), p. 89.

63. Ha-Joon Chang, *23 Things They Don't Tell You About Capitalism* (London: Allen Lane, 2010), p. 60.

64. 'Inflation's back', *The Economist*, 22 May 2008. See http://www.economist.com/ node/11409414

65. Ha-Joon Chang, *23 Things They Don't Tell You About Capitalism*, p. 55. The experience of a number of countries supports this claim. During the 1960s and 1970s, Brazil had an average inflation rate of 42 per cent but was also one of the world's fastest growing economies. Over the same period, South Korea's economy grew at 7 per cent a year in spite of an inflation rate of almost 20 per cent.

66. Quoted in David Harvey, *A Companion to Marx's Capital* (London: Verso, 2010), p. 284.

67. John Kenneth Galbraith, *A History of Economics* (1987; London: Penguin Books, 1991), p. 275.

68. Milton Friedman, *Capitalism and Freedom* (1962; Chicago: University of Chicago Press, 2002), p. xiv.

69. Ben H. Bagdikian, *The New Media Monopoly* (Boston, MA: Beacon Press, 2004), p. 158.

70. David Harvey, *A Brief History of Neoliberalism*, p. 52.

71. Robin Hahnel, *The ABCs of Political Economy* (London: Pluto Press, 2002), p. 153.

72. In the lead-up to the strike, a man named Ian MacGregor was appointed to head

the National Coal Board. MacGregor was known for his 'uncompromising union-busting' tactics in the US. One of MacGregor's advisers, echoing the strategists of US strike breakers from the 1930s, argued that 'the way to break the strike was to launch an offensive on three fronts: first a massive propaganda campaign to encourage miners to return to work; second, organise and finance working miners to catalyse this process; and third, wear down the NUM by legal action, using the government's new employment laws'. Such strategies were ultimately successful. (David Miller, William Dinon, *A Century of Spin*, pp. 133–5.)

73. Ronald Butt, 'Mrs Thatcher: The First Two Years', Interview for the *Sunday Times*, 3 May 1981. See http://www.margaretthatcher.org/document/104475

74. Douglas Keay, 'Aids, education and the year 2000!', *Woman's Own*, 31 October 1987. https://www.margaretthatcher.org/document/106689

75. R. Ormston, J. Curtice (eds), *British Social Attitudes Survey 32* (London: NatCen Social Research, 2015). See http://www.bsa.natcen.ac.uk/latest-report/british-social-attitudes-32/welfare.aspx

76. Alison Park, John Curtice, Elizabeth Clery, Caroline Bryson (eds), *British Social Attitudes 27th Report* (London: Sage Publications, 2010), p. 37.

77. Niall Ferguson, *The Cash Nexus* (2001; London: Penguin Books, 2002), p. 255.

78. Joel Bakan, *The Corporation*, p. 103.

79. Ben Bagdikian, *The New Media Monopoly*, p. 19.

80. For up-to-date information on this, take a look at the work of the Center for Responsive Politics. See http://www.opensecrets.org

81. Simon Johnson, James Kwak, *13 Bankers* (New York: Random House, 2010), p. 90.

82. Andrew Katz, 'Congress Is Now Mostly A Millionaires' Club,' *Time Online*, 9 January 2014. See http://swampland.time.com/2014/01/09/congress-is-now-mostly-a-millionaires-club/

83. Thomas J. Hayes, 'Responsiveness in an Era of Inequality', *Political Research Quarterly*, Vol. 66, No. 3, September 2013, pp. 585–99. See http://prq.sagepub.com/content/66/3/585.abstract

84. Sahil Kapur, 'Scholar Behind Viral "Oligarchy" Study Tells You What It Means', *Talking Points Memo*, 22 April 2014, an interview with Martin Gilens about his study (with Benjamin I. Page), 'Testing Theories of American Politics: Elites, Interest Groups, and Average Citizens'. See http://talkingpointsmemo.com/dc/princeton-scholar-demise-of-democracy-america-tpm-interview

85. Martin Gilens, Benjamin I. Page, 'Testing Theories of American Politics: Elites, Interest Groups, and Average Citizens', *Perspectives on Politics*, Vol. 12, No. 3, September 2014, pp. 564–81. See https://scholar.princeton.edu/sites/default/

files/mgilens/files/gilens_and_page_2014_-testing_theories_of_american_politics.doc.pdf

86. Antonia Juhasz, *The Tyranny of Oil* (New York: William Morrow, 2008), p. 210.

87. These appointees included Gale Norton, a Secretary of the Interior, a former lawyer for Delta Petroleum; Don Evans, Secretary of Commerce, an ex-CEO and Chair of Tom Brown Inc., a billion-dollar oil and gas company; Condoleezza Rice, National Security Advisor, who for ten years had been a member of Chevron's board of directors; Dick Cheney, Vice President, a former CEO of Halliburton, one of the largest oil services company in the world; and, of course, George Bush, himself a 'failed oil man'. See Antonia Juhasz, *The Tyranny of Oil*, p. 210.

88. Antonia Juhasz, *The Tyranny of Oil*, p. 225.

89. Simon Johnson, James Kwak, *13 Bankers*, p. 91.

90. Quoted in Simon Johnson, James Kwak, *13 Bankers*, p. 92.

91. Simon Johnson, James Kwak, *13 Bankers*, p. 192.

92. Wall Street's influence extends to universities too. In 2013, *The New York Times* published an article entitled 'Academics Who Defend Wall St. Reap Reward'. Their investigation revealed that 'major players on Wall Street and elsewhere have been aggressive in underwriting and promoting academic work' as part of 'a sweeping campaign to beat back regulation and shape policies that affect the prices that people around the world pay for essentials like food, fuel and cotton'. See David Kocieniewski, 'Academics Who Defend Wall St. Reap Reward', *New York Times*, 27 December 2013. See http://www.nytimes.com/2013/12/28/business/academics-who-defend-wall-st-reap-reward.html

93. David Beetham, *Unelected Oligarchy: Corporate and Financial Dominance in Britain's Democracy*, paper published by Democratic Audit UK, London School of Economics, 26 July 2011, p. 11. See http://democraticaudituk.files.wordpress.com/2013/06/oligarchy-1.pdf

94. David Beetham, *Unelected Oligarchy*, p. 12.

95. 'Not More Lords!', Electoral Reform Society, 8 August 2014. See http://www.electoral-reform.org.uk/blog/more-lords

96. Quoted in David Beetham, *Unelected Oligarchy*, p. 7.

97. Aditya Chakrabortty, 'Direct aid, subsidies, tax breaks – the hidden welfare budget we don't debate', *The Guardian*, 7 July 2015. See http://www.theguardian.com/politics/2015/jul/07/direct-aid-subsidies-tax-breaks-the-hidden-welfare-budget-we-dont-debate

98. Simon Bowers, 'UK tax policy dictated by companies not ministers says leading treasury expert', *The Guardian*, 28 June 2015. See http://www.theguardian.com/

global/2015/jun/28/uk-tax-policy-dictated-by-big-companies-not-ministers-treasury-adviser

99. David Beetham, *Unelected Oligarchy*, p. 16.

100. David Beetham, *Unelected Oligarchy*, p. 16.

101. 'Addicted to tax havens: The secret life of the FTSE 100', Action Aid report, 11 October 2011. See https://www.actionaid.org.uk/sites/default/files/doc_lib/addicted_to_tax_havens.pdf

102. David Beetham, *Unelected Oligarchy*, p. 18.

103. Sociologists David Miller and William Dinan describe the case of Alan Donnelly, a former Labour MEP, who set up the lobbying firm Sovereign Strategy in 2000. Donnelly explains, 'I'd been on the receiving end of lobbying for 11 years, I'd seen the good approaches and the bad ones, and over time I'd developed my own ideas about how I'd do it.' Donnelly brought in a team of former MPs, MEPs and ministers, including, in 2005, Lewis Moonie and Alan Milburn, who had recently stood down as Parliamentary Under-Secretary for Defence and Health Secretary respectively. Milburn's job, in his own words, would be 'to teach clients how to lobby government'. See: David Miller, William Dinan, *A Century of Spin*, pp. 158–60.

104. Katie Allen, 'Osborne claims businesses must defend free market from unions and charities', *The Guardian*, 30 October 2014. See http://www.theguardian.com/politics/2014/oct/03/george-osborne-businesses-case-free-market

105. David Beetham, *Unelected Oligarchy*, p. 21.

106. Thomas Ferguson, *Golden Rule* (London and Chicago: University of Chicago Press, 1995), p. 22.

107. Quoted in Joel Bakan, *The Corporation*, pp. 104–5.

108. Joel Bakan, *The Corporation*, p. 105.

109. 'The Affluent Ante Up for the Presidency', *New York Times*, 14 August 2015. See http://www.nytimes.com/2015/08/15/opinion/the-affluent-ante-up-for-the-presidency.html?_r=2

110. Thomas Ferguson, *Golden Rule*, p. 28.

111. Matt Dathan, Jon Stone, 'The 9 charts that show the "left-wing" policies of Jeremy Corbyn the public actually agrees with', *The Independent*, 23 July 2015. See http://www.independent.co.uk/news-14-5/the-jeremy-corbyn-policies-that-most-people-actually-agree-with-10407148.html

112. Lee William, 'What is TTIP? And six reasons why the answer should scare you', *The Independent*, 12 October 2015. See http://www.independent.co.uk/voices/comment/what-is-ttip-and-six-reasons-why-the-answer-should-scare-you-9779688.html

113. Take, for instance, the trade investment agreement struck between Australia and Hong Kong. It has since allowed the Hong Kong-based tobacco company Philip Morris to sue the Australian government for millions of dollars after the Australian government, backed by the Australian Supreme Court, decided to force cigarette companies to print large health warnings alongside graphic images of the consequences of smoking. In another case, the Argentinian government was sued by international utility companies for freezing energy and water bills in response to rapid price increases. The companies won and received over a billion dollars in compensation from the Argentine state. El Salvador is currently being sued by a Canadian company that was refused access to a vast gold mine (on the back of mass public protests).

114. Dan O'Neill, Rob Dietz, *Enough is Enough* (Abingdon, Oxon: Routledge, 2013) pp. 144–5.

6 Markets

1. I take this example from Ha-Joon Chang, *23 Things They Don't Tell You About Capitalism* (London: Allen Lane, 2010), p. 2.

2. The Global South is a different story, where today the same arguments against the outlawing of child workers are made as were put forward in nineteenth-century England.

3. Raj Patel, *The Value of Nothing* (2009; London: Portobello Books, 2011), p. 17.

4. Ha-Joon Chang, *23 Things They Don't Tell You About Capitalism,* p. 1.

5. Ha-Joon Chang, *23 Things They Don't Tell You About Capitalism,* p. 10.

6. Milton Friedman, *Capitalism and Freedom* (1962; Chicago: University of Chicago Press, 2002), p. 14.

7. Milton Friedman, Rosa D. Friedman, *Two Lucky People: Memoirs* (Chicago: University of Chicago Press, 1998), p. 605.

8. Adam Smith, *The Wealth of Nations*, Book IV, Chapter II. Available at https://www.marxists.org/reference/archive/smith-dam/works/wealth-of-nations/book04/ch02.htm. A close reading of the text shows that Smith used the term 'invisible hand' in a much narrower sense than it is generally used today.

9. Oscar Wilde has one of his characters in *Lady Windermere's Fan* comment on a man who 'knows the price of everything and the value of nothing'. It's a profound insight. In neoclassical economics, which dominate the world's most powerful institutions, the prices arrived at by the workings of a market are meant to provide the information necessary for the whole system to function

efficiently. In a perfectly competitive market, prices are meant to represent the social cost of every product and every service. As Adam Smith pointed out, the market, as if by magic, should lead us to produce the socially optimal quantity of every single good – no more and no less than we really want. What Smith didn't take into account was that it is extremely difficult for prices to accurately fulfil this function. If prices are to reflect the true social cost of a product: (1) customers must make their decisions based on price alone, and not be swayed by the billions of dollars spent on branding and advertising; and (2) no buyer or seller can have the power to impact prices. This pretty much ignores the existence of monopolies and unions, both of which use their power to impact prices. (3) All buyers and sellers must have *complete* information about all known products and their prices. For this to be the case, all consumers must be credited with a form of omniscience. (4) All firms must have equal access to technology and resources, meaning that land, labour and capital would need to be perfectly mobile. This assumes the end of all border controls. (5) Market transactions must not affect anyone other than those participating in the transaction. For this to be the case, there can be no externalities.

Not a single one of the above five conditions has been met in our economy (it is hard to imagine how they could be met in any economy). As economist Peter Victor writes: 'The price of something might be inflated simply because a few companies control supply and force the price up to increase their profits. Advertisers may persuade us that two products that are essentially identical are different and that we should choose one brand over another for no good reason. The information that we have about products and their prices is less than complete and so we make ill-informed decisions about what to produce, what to buy and what to sell. Technologies are not equally available to all; there is an entire set of legal protections in the form of patent and copyright law to keep it that way. Most egregious of all is the pervasiveness of externalities and, in particular, the widespread damage to the environment caused by economic activity.' See Peter A. Victor, *Managing Without Growth* (Cheltenham: Edward Elgar Publishing, 2008), p. 42.

10. Milton Friedman, *Capitalism and Freedom*, p. 15.

11. Greenspan was a disciple of Ayn Rand, a purveyor of an extreme form of market fundamentalism, whose objectivist moral philosophy holds that the moral purpose of each individual is to advance their own self-interest, a sentiment summed up by the title of her book: *The Virtue of Selfishness* (1964). She advocates a form of capitalism that reduced the role of government to providing 'the police, to protect men from criminals – the armed services, to protect men from foreign

invaders – the law courts, to settle disputes among men according to objectively defined laws'. See: Ayn Rand, *Capitalism: The Unknown Ideal* (1967 repr. New York: Signet, 2008) p. 43.

12. Quoted in Raj Patel, *The Value of Nothing*, p. 5.

13. Quoted in Raj Patel, *The Value of Nothing*, p. 6.

14. John D. McKinnon, 'Bush Aims to Lift Confidence', *The Wall Street Journal*, 20 September 2008. See http://www.wsj.com/news/articles/SB122186559923558649

15. For a useful discussion of this topic, see: Robin Hahnel, *The ABCs of Political Economy* (New York: Pluto Press, 2002), Chapter 10.

16. Owen Jones, *The Establishment: And how they get away with it* (London: Allen Lane, 2014), p. 11.

17. Kirkpatrick Sale, *Rebels Against the Future* (New York: Basic Books, 1995), p. 34.

18. David Harvey, *A Companion to Marx's Capital* (London: Verso, 2010), p. 284.

19. Karl Polanyi, *The Great Transformation* (1944; 2nd edn, Boston, MA: Beacon Press, 2001), p. 37.

20. Quoted in Noam Chomsky, *On Power and Ideology – The Managua Lectures* (New York: South End Press, 1987), p. 14.

21. Joseph Stiglitz, *Globalization and Its Discontents* (London: Allen Lane, 2002), p. 62.

22. A famous argument by the economist David Ricardo was instrumental in selling the benefits of free trade to poorer nations, and justifying it more generally. In Ricardo's time, two hundred years ago, it was believed that international trade only made sense when one country could make something more cheaply than its trading partner. But Ricardo showed that international trade increased efficiency even when one of the trading partners could not make *anything* more cheaply. This is because of what he called 'comparative advantage'. Ricardo's insight was profound and has since had a big influence. But apart from the fact that Ricardo's reasoning has nothing to say about who will primarily benefit from the efficiency gains of international trade – rich nations can use their superior bargaining power to take the lion's share – his arguments only work if we focus our attention on immediate short-term gains, taking for granted the level of development in a country. How can a poorer country develop a more technologically advanced economy if it ploughs all its resources into low-tech industries?

23. Quoted in Andre Gunder Frank, *Capitalism and Underdevelopment in Latin America: Historical Studies of Chile and Brazil* (revd edn, New York: Monthly Review Press, 1967), p. 164.

24. Ha-Joon Chang, *Bad Samaritans* (London: Random House, 2007), p. 54.

25. The industries in which the US has had a technological lead over international

competition – whether we consider computers, semiconductors, aircraft, pharmaceuticals or biotechnology – have all received significant financial support from government.

26. The case of Japan's automobile industry is instructive. In 1958, after more than twenty years of state support in the form of large subsidies and high tariffs on foreign imports, Japan's leading automobile manufacturer, Toyota, exported its first batch of cars to the US. Even after this extended period of support, the products proved to be extremely unpopular and were soon withdrawn from the US market. Japanese officials then faced a conundrum. Should Japan cut its losses and open its markets to foreign cars again or invest more in Toyota and try again? Many within Japan thought that it should cut its losses and focus on traditional industries such as textiles. But these voices did not win out and Toyota models went on to compete remarkably successfully on the global market. Had Japan followed the neoliberal rulebook, this would never have happened. Japan is not an exceptional case.

27. Not only does mainstream theory predict that markets will systematically over-produce goods and services whose production or consumption produce negative externalities (though it has long underestimated the prevalence of such external effects), it predicts that markets will systematically under-produce goods and services that have *positive* externalities. Health and education are good examples of services whose benefits to society go beyond the direct benefit to those who consume them. That is to say, the benefit to society is larger than the private benefit to the individual. To the extent that it is a positive externality, this benefit will not be reflected in the price people pay for the service, with the result that it becomes more expensive than it should be and so is under-consumed.

28. Joan Robinson, *Collected Economic Papers of Joan Robinson*, Vol. 4 (New York: Humanities Press, 1973), p. 102.

29. Rod Hill, Tony Myatt, *The Economics Anti-Textbook* (London: Zed Books, 2010), p. 154.

30. Quoted in Robin Hahnel, *The ABCs of Political Economy*, p. 92.

31. Raj Patel, *The Value of Nothing*, pp. 43–6.

32. Nancy Dunne, 'Why a hamburger should cost 200 dollars – the call for prices to reflect ecological factors', *Financial Times*, 12 January 1994.

33. Karl Marx, *Wage-Labour and Capital* (1849: Rockville, MD: Wildside Press, 2008), p. 33.

34. Paul Krugman, 'Building a Green Economy', *New York Times*, 7 April 2010. See http://www.nytimes.com/2010/04/11/magazine/11Economy-t.html

35. Damian Carrington, 'Fossil fuels subsidised by $10m a minute, says IMF', *The Guardian*, 18 May 2015. See http://www.theguardian.com/environment/2015/may/18/fossil-fuel-companies-getting-10m-a-minute-in-subsidies-says-imf

36. 'Natural Capital At Risk: The Top 100 Externalities Of Business', Report by Trucost for TEEB for Business Coalition, 15 April 2013. See http://www.trucost.com/published-research/99/natural-capital-at-risk-the-top-100-externalities-of-business

37. Raj Patel, *The Value of Nothing*, p. 50.

38. Joseph E. Stiglitz, *The Price of Inequality* (London: Allen Lane, 2012), p. 213.

39. Milton Friedman, *Capitalism and Freedom*, p. 14. ('The consumer is protected from coercion by the seller because of the presence of other sellers with whom he can deal. The seller is protected from coercion by the consumer because of other consumers to whom he can sell. The employee is protected from coercion by the employer because of other employers for whom he can work, and so on.' Milton Friedman, *Capitalism and Freedom*, p. 13.)

40. Quoted in Karl Marx, *Theories of Surplus Value*, Chapter 7. See https://www.marxists.org/archive/marx/works/1863/theories-surplus-value/ch07.htm

41. Aditya Chakrabortty, 'The woman who nearly died making your iPad', *The Guardian*, 5 August 2013. See http://www.theguardian.com/commentisfree/2013/aug/05/woman-nearly-died-making-ipad

42. Friedrich Hayek, *The Road to Serfdom* (1944; New York: Routledge, 2009), p. 26.

43. I happen to agree that there is an important distinction to be made between freedom and power (to be discussed in later chapters), but it is not the one made by neoliberals.

44. John Rawls, *A Theory of Justice* (Cambridge: Harvard University Press, 1971), p. 204.

45. To see this, imagine a society with no money, in which the state controls what people can do by apportioning tickets to them, detailing bundles of activities that they may perform: eating at a restaurant, flying to Scotland, driving a sports car, and so on. Any deviation from these licensed bundles of activities will be met with armed force. In this society, the degree of state interference in one's life is proportionate to the amount and quality of permissible activities on one's ticket. These tickets dictate the freedoms people possess. In such a society, those with fewer and less appealing options on their ticket would be subject to greater state interference. This thought experiment was constructed by Gerald Cohen to demonstrate that in our own society a given sum of money functions in much the same way as these tickets – as a highly abstract permission slip from the state which allows certain bundles of activities but not others. See: Gerald

Cohen, *Self-Ownership, Freedom and Equality* (New York: Cambridge University Press, 1995), p. 58.

46. Neoliberal theory, particularly in its early incarnations, is more nuanced than the free-market fundamentalism that has since colonised the halls of power. Hayek, for instance, conceded the need for 'some minimum of food, shelter, and clothing, sufficient to preserve health and the capacity to work', and accepted the case of some degree of social security. He recognised that market competition was not always effective, and accepted the need for state intervention to correct for market failures. And Friedman advocated a negative income tax, a progressive measure that would mean people earning below a certain amount would receive money rather than pay tax. But to those with the resources to really champion it, the freedom-praising ideology of neoliberalism was a convenient means to an end: eroding democratic control of corporate power.

47. Robert Nozick, *Anarchy, State, and Utopia* (Oxford: Blackwell Publishing, 1974), p. 262.

48. Gerald Cohen, *Self-Ownership, Freedom and Equality* (New York: Cambridge University Press, 1995), p. 36.

49. Robert Nozick, *Anarchy, State, and Utopia*, p. 30.

50. Quoted in Stuart Ewen, *Captains of Consciousness* (1976; New York: Basic Books, 2001), p. 38.

51. Quoted in Stuart Ewen, *Captains of Consciousness*, pp. 178-9.

52. Quoted in Stuart Ewen, *Captains of Consciousness*, pp. 179-80.

53. Milton Friedman, *Price Theory* (1986; New Jersey: Transaction Publishers, 2009), p. 13.

54. Rod Hill, Tony Myatt, *The Economics Anti-Textbook*, p. 79.

55. Douglas Dowd, *Capitalism and Its Economics: A Critical History* (2000; new edn, London: Pluto Press, 2004), p. 84.

56. David Miller, William Dinan, *A Century of Spin* (London: Pluto Press, 2008), p. 36.

57. Quoted in Stuart Ewen, *Captains of Consciousness*, p. 39.

58. Hayley Leaver, 'Companies growing fat as you slim: The growth of the weight loss market', *Metro*, 30 January 2014. See http://metro.co.uk/2014/01/30/companies-growing-fat-as-you-slim-the-growth-of-the-weight-loss-market-4282903/; 'Global Cosmetic Surgery and Service Market Report 2015-2019', PR Newswire, 11 March 2015. See http://www.prnewswire.com/news-releases/global-cosmetic-surgery-and-service-market-report-2015-2019-295910691.html

59. Naomi Wolf, *The Beauty Myth* (London: Chatto & Windus, 1990), p. 185.

60. Eileen L. Zurbriggen, Rebecca L. Collins, Sharon Lamb, Tomi-Ann Roberts, Deborah L. Tolman, L. Monique Ward, Jeanne Blake, 'Report of the APA Task

Force on the Sexualization of Girls' (Washington DC: American Psychological Association, 2007). See http://www.apa.org/pi/women/programs/girls/report-summary.pdf

61. 'The Good Childhood Report 2014: Executive Summary' (London: The Children's Society, 2014), p. 6. See http://www.york.ac.uk/inst/spru/research/pdf/GCR14sum.pdf

62. Kate Devlin, 'One in five young women "has an eating disorder"', *The Telegraph*, 30 January 2009. See http://www.telegraph.co.uk/news/health/news/4389444/One-in-five-young-women-has-an-eating-disorder.html

63. Monisha Rajesh, 'India's unfair obsession with lighter skin', *The Guardian*, 14 August 2013. See http://www.theguardian.com/world/shortcuts/2013/aug/14/indias-dark-obsession-fair-skin

64. Tim Kasser, *The High Price of Materialism* (Cambridge, MA: MIT Press, 2002), p. 22.

65. David G. Myers, Ed Diener, 'The Pursuit of Happiness', *Scientific American*, 16 April 1996, pp. 54–6.

66. Richard Wilkinson, Kate Pickett, *The Spirit Level: Why Equality is Better for Everyone* (2009; revd edn, London: Penguin, 2010), p. 65.

67. 'The Good Childhood Report 2014: Executive Summary', The Children's Society and the University of York, 2014. See http://www.childrenssociety.org.uk/sites/default/files/The%20Good%20Childhood%20Report%202014%20summary%20FINAL.pdf; 'A million children now suffer from mental health problems', *Daily Mail*, 20 June 2007. See http://www.dailymail.co.uk/news/article-463194/A-million-children-suffer-mental-health-problems.html

68. Richard Wilkinson, Kate Pickett, *The Spirit Level*, pp. 63–5.

69. Oliver James, *The Selfish Capitalist* (London: Vermilion, 2008), p. 26.

70. Oliver James, *The Selfish Capitalist*, p. 1.

71. Richard Wilkinson, Kate Pickett, *The Spirit Level*, p. 75.

72. Quoted in Oliver James, *The Selfish Capitalist*, p. 49.

73. Kathleen Taylor, *Brainwashing: The Science of Thought Control* (Oxford: Oxford University Press, 2004), p. 51.

74. Susan Linn, interviewed in the documentary film, *The Corporation* (2004), Mark Achbar, Jennifer Abbot, Joel Bakan. See http://www.thecorporation.com/

75. Lucy Hughes, interviewed in the documentary film, *The Corporation* (2004), Mark Achbar, Jennifer Abbot, Joel Bakan.

76. Susan Linn, interviewed in the documentary film, *The Corporation* (2004), Mark Achbar, Jennifer Abbot, Joel Bakan.

77. Joel Bakan, *Childhood Under Siege* (London: The Bodley head, 2011), p. 16.

78. Rod Hill, Tony Myatt, *The Economics Anti-Textbook*, p. 82.

79. Richard Wilkinson, Kate Pickett, *The Spirit Level*, p. 52.

80. Richard Wilkinson, Kate Pickett, *The Spirit Level*, p. 61.

81. Raj Patel, *The Value of Nothing*, pp. 30–31.

82. Daniel Kahneman, *Thinking, Fast and Slow*, pp. 55–6.

83. Quoted in Robin Hahnel, *The ABCs of Political Economy*, p. 100.

84. Karl Polanyi, *The Great Transformation*, p. 265.

85. Joseph E. Stiglitz, *The Price of Inequality*, p. xiii.

86. Quoted in Robert Leeson (ed.), *Hayek: A Collaborative Biography: Part IV, England, the Ordinal Revolution and the Road to Serfdom, 1931–1950* (New York: Palgrave Macmillan, 2015), p. 16.

87. Quoted in Robert Leeson (ed.), *Hayek: A Collaborative Biography: Part IV, England, the Ordinal Revolution and the Road to Serfdom, 1931–1950*, p. 17.

88. Ben Chu, 'Bill Gates: Why do we care more about baldness than malaria?', *The Independent*, 16 March 2013. See http://www.independent.co.uk/news/world/americas/bill-gates-why-do-we-care-more-about-baldness-than-malaria-8536988.html

7 Media

1. Robert W. McChesney, *Digital Disconnect* (New York: The New Press, 2013), p. 1; Joe Mayes, 'We now spend more time in front of a screen than in bed, Ofcom study shows', *The Independent*, 7 August 2014. See http://www.independent.co.uk/life-style/gadgets-and-tech/news/we-now-spend-more-time-in-front-of-a-screen-than-in-bed-ofcom-study-shows-9652631.html

2. James Curran, Jean Seaton, *Power Without Responsibility*, (1981; 2nd edn, London: Methuen, 1985), p. 7.

3. James Curran, Jean Seaton, *Power Without Responsibility*, 2nd edn, p. 9.

4. Quoted in James Curran, Jean Seaton, *Power Without Responsibility* (7th edn, London: Routledge, 2010), p. 14.

5. In 1834, the Lord Chancellor wondered how the people 'shall read in the best manner; how they shall be instructed politically, and have political habits formed the most safe for the constitution of the country'. Quoted in James Curran, Jean Seaton, *Power Without Responsibility*, 7th edn, p. 17.

6. Quoted in James Curran, Jean Seaton, *Power Without Responsibility*, 2nd edn, p. 13.

7. Quoted in James Curran, Jean Seaton, *Power Without Responsibility*, 7th edn, p. 20.

8.   Noam Chomsky, Edward S. Herman, *Manufacturing Consent* (1988; New York: Pantheon Books, 2002), p. 4.

9.   James Curran, Jean Seaton, *Power Without Responsibility*, 7th edn, p. 92.

10.   Many consider the state-owned BBC an important exception. But at the BBC the most senior positions are selected by the British government. This gives the government huge power to influence its political direction. Unsurprisingly, the government appoints figures likely to be supportive rather than antagonistic. At times, the threat of overt state control is made explicit. In late 2013, leading Conservative Cabinet minister Grant Shapps threatened the BBC with cuts to its licence fee if its reporting did not become more 'balanced' in the lead-up to the next general election. Many of the forces that mould privately owned media output also operate on the BBC, producing output that broadly supports state and corporate interests. Its owners are drawn from the elite establishment, its sources tend to be corporate and state representatives, and it is as vulnerable to state and corporate discipline as any other media institution.

11.   Quoted in James Curran, Jean Seaton, *Power Without Responsibility*, 7th edn, p. 81.

12.   Quoted in Owen Jones, *The Establishment: And how they get away with it* (London: Allen Lane, 2014), pp. 97–98.

13.   Quoted in James Curran, Jean Seaton, *Power Without Responsibility*, 7th edn, p. 70.

14.   James Curran, Jean Seaton, *Power Without Responsibility*, 7th edn, p. 329.

15.   Quoted in Owen Jones, *The Establishment: And How They Get Away with It*, p. 92.

16.   Gary Younge, 'A web of privilege supports this so-called meritocracy', *The Guardian*, 7 May 2012. See http://www.theguardian.com/commentisfree/2012/may/06/leveson-murdoch-cameron-brooks-privilege

17.   Media Reform Coalition, 'The elephant in the room: a survey of media ownership and plurality in the United Kingdom', 2014, p. 1. See http://www.mediareform.org.uk/wp-content/uploads/2014/04/ElephantintheroomFinalfinal.pdf

18.   Quoted in James Curran, Jean Seaton, *Power Without Responsibility*, 7th edn, p. 329.

19.   Norman Solomon, 'The Military-Industrial-Media Complex', Fairness & Accuracy in Reporting (FAIR), 1 August 2005. See http://fair.org/extra-online-articles/the-military-industrial-media-complex/

20.   George Arnett, 'Elitism in Britain – breakdown by profession', *The Guardian*, 28 August 2014. See http://www.theguardian.com/news/datablog/2014/aug/28/elitism-in-britain-breakdown-by-profession

21.   George Arnett, 'Elitism in Britain – breakdown by profession'.

22. James Curran, Jean Seaton, *Power Without Responsibility*, 2nd edn, p. 41.

23. James Curran, Jean Seaton, *Power Without Responsibility*, 7th edn, p. 29.

24. James Curran, Jean Seaton, *Power Without Responsibility*, 2nd. edn, p. 41.

25. Quoted in James Curran, Jean Seaton, *Power Without Responsibility*, 7th edn, p. 30.

26. Noam Chomsky, Edward S. Herman, *Manufacturing Consent*, p. 15.

27. Quoted in James Curran, Jean Seaton, *Power Without Responsibility*, 7th edn, p. 64.

28. Quoted in James Curran, Jean Seaton, *Power Without Responsibility*, 7th edn, p. 83.

29. Ben Bagdikian, *The New Media Monopoly* (Boston, MA: Beacon Press, 2004), p. 222.

30. James Curran, Jean Seaton, *Power Without Responsibility*, 7th edn, p. 171.

31. Quoted in Ben Bagdikian, *The New Media Monopoly*, p. 243.

32. Quoted in Ben Bagdikian, *The New Media Monopoly*, p. 239.

33. Quoted in Ben Bagdikian, *The New Media Monopoly*, p. 240.

34. Media Lens, 'The Fictitious Firewall', 10 October 2006. See http://www.medialens.org/index.php/alerts/alert-archive/2006/477-the-fictitious-firewall.html

35. Without the need to attract advertising, the radical press of the nineteenth and twentieth century – which commanded the largest audiences of its day by a significant margin – would have remained politically radical and materially successful, impacting the views of its millions of readers and, by implication, the political direction of the country. This is all speculation, of course, but speculation of this sort is necessary to begin to assess the impact of advertising on today's world.

36. Media Buying, 'Total Media Ad Spending Growth Slows Worldwide', eMarketer, 15 September 2015. See http://www.emarketer.com/Article/Total-Media-Ad-Spending-Growth-Slows-Worldwide/1012981

37. David Edwards, David Cromwell, *Guardians of Power* (London: Pluto Press, 2006), p. 7. This figure has come down in recent years but remains over 50 per cent.

38. Andrew Marr, *My Trade* (London: Macmillan, 2004), p. 112.

39. Noam Chomsky, Edward S. Herman, *Manufacturing Consent*, p. 22.

40. Nick Davies, *Flat Earth News* (London: Chatto & Windus, 2008), p. 52.

41. Quoted in Nick Davies, *Flat Earth News*, p. 97.

42. These agencies, although benefiting from a virtual monopoly of the international news market, have themselves suffered a severe culling of jobs and resources. Thousands of jobs have been cut over the last two decades. In fact, 130 countries have no TV crew from either agency. And research suggests that the entire US media – every paper and TV network – depend on only 141 foreign correspondents to cover the entire world. See Nick Davies, *Flat Earth News*, p. 99.

43. Quoted in Nick Davies, *Flat Earth News*, p. 83.

44. Nick Robinson, '"Remember the last time you shouted like that?" I asked the spin doctor', *The Times*, 16 July 2004.

45. Quoted in David Edwards, David Cromwell, '*Newspeak in the 21st Century* (London: Pluto Press, 2009)

46. Nick Davies, *Flat Earth News*, p. 96.

47. Noam Chomsky, Edward S. Herman, *Manufacturing Consent*, p. 26.

48. Nick Davies, *Flat Earth News*, p. 122.

49. In recent years, one of the most active and influential lobby groups has been the Israeli lobby. John Pilger – twice winner of Britain's Journalist of the Year Award, having dedicated much of his long career to exposing human rights abuses around the world – made a film entitled *Palestine Is Still the Issue* which aired in September 2002 on ITV, one of the largest TV networks in Britain. It highlighted, in Pilger's words, the 'daily humiliation and cultural denigration of the Palestinians', while dedicating a 'significant part of the film' to the official Israeli position. Before it aired, 'virtually every word and frame was subjected to a forensic legal examination both for accuracy and to ensure compliance with the balance and fairness regulations in the UK Broadcasting Act'.

    The response was impressive, if unnerving. 'Several thousand emails arrived at the film's production company Carlton Televison', describing Pilger, among other things, as a 'demonic psychopath', 'a purveyor of hate and evil', 'an anti-Semite of the most dangerous kind'. One person suggested that the murder of his family was 'not a bad idea'. Pilger received a number of death threats at home. This was a coordinated attack. Many of the emails originated from an organisation in New York called Honest Reporting, with subscribers from around the world. According to Pilger, it 'drafted complaints, provided generic material and coached people on how to attack allegedly "anti-Jewish" work they had not seen'. After a protracted period of criticism that included many threatening emails and phone calls, and Carlton's own chairman condemning the film, the Independent Television Commission announced that it rejected all complaints, instead praising the 'journalistic integrity', the 'care and thoroughness with which [the film] was researched' and the 'comprehensiveness and authority' of its historical sources. As welcome as this vindication was, the effectiveness of flak does not depend on exposing errors. The point of such persistent and threatening criticism is to cordon off certain topics and perspectives as 'highly risky' so that media organisations self-censor the next time around. For a full account of this story, see John Pilger, *Freedom Next Time* (London: Bantam Press, 2006), pp. 187–98.

Honest Reporting claims that since 2000, it has 'prompted hundreds of apologies, retractions and revisions from news outlets. These efforts are changing the face of the media and reporting of Israel throughout the world.' See http://honestreporting.com/a/digitaldiplomats/html/introOld.html. Investigative journalist Nick Davies, in his book *Flat Earth News*, cites the testimony of a senior journalist at the BBC: 'The [Israeli] lobby insinuates a sense of fear. If the editor of the *Today* programme knows that an item will make the phone ring off the hook, he may think twice about running it. Sure the lobby works. I can think of numerous examples where I have felt the brunt of it.' The effect has been that 'the BBC routinely gives more airtime to Israeli voices than to Palestinian and that it focuses more frequently on Israeli victims than on Palestinians.' Glasgow University's media group conducted a study (see *Bad News from Israel* (London: Pluto Press, 2004) which concluded that British television reflected 'an overwhelming bias towards the policies of the State of Israel'. Greg Philo and co-author of the study Mike Berry found that Israelis are quoted and speak in interviews more than twice as much as Palestinians, and there are major differences in the language used to describe the two sides – terms such as 'murder', 'atrocity' and 'savage, cold-blooded killing' were reserved for the killing of Israelis.

50. Maxwell T. Boykoff, Jules M. Boykoff, 'Balance as bias: global warming and the US prestige press', *Global Environmental Change*, Vol. 14 (2004), pp. 125–36. See http://sciencepolicy.colorado.edu/admin/publication_files/2004.33.pdf

51. Aaron Huertas, Dena Adler, 'Is News Corp. Failing Science?', Union of Concerned Scientists, September 2012. See http://www.ucsusa.org/global_warming/solutions/fight-misinformation/news-corporation-climate-science-coverage.html

52. Andrew Marr, *News at Ten*, BBC1, 9 April 2003. While interviewing Tony Blair on the *Andrew Marr Show*, on 25 September 2005, Marr said: '25,000 civilians have died in Iraq over the last two years . . . About a third of those people were killed, no doubt in absolutely legitimate operations, by British and American soldiers.' And on 20 March 2006, BBC diplomatic correspondent Bridget Kendall declared on the *Six O'clock News*, 'There's still bitter disagreement over invading Iraq. Was it justified or a disastrous miscalculation?' Other questions, such as whether the war had been illegal or immoral, were simply not raised.

53. Matt Wells, 'Study deals a blow to claims of anti-war bias in BBC news', *The Guardian*, 4 July 2003. See http://www.theguardian.com/media/2003/jul/04/Iraqandthemedia.politicsandthemedia

54. Quoted in David Edwards, David Cromwell, *Newspeak in the 21st Century*, p. 28.

55. Glenn Greenwald, 'CNN/MSNBC Reporter: Corporate executives forced pro-Bush, pro-war narrative', *Salon*, 29 May 2008. See http://www.salon.com/2008/05/29/yellin/

56. Glenn Greenwald, 'CNN/MSNBC Reporter: Corporate executives forced pro-Bush, pro-war narrative'.

57. Chris Hedges' speech is available on YouTube. See http://www.youtube.com/watch?v=SAWMgYyAtHU

58. Chris Hedges, *Death of the Liberal Class* (New York: Nation Books, 2010), p. 130.

59. Interview with Amy Goodman, New York, July 2009.

60. Amy Goodman with David Goodman, *The Exception to the Rulers* (London: Arrow Books, 2004), pp. 241–6.

61. No prior rules had been established. Goodman writes that the 'administration threatened to ban me from the White House and suggested to a Newsday reporter that they might punish me for my attitude by denying me access – not that I had any to lose.' (Amy Goodman, *The Exception to the Rulers*, pp. 246–7.)

62. Quoted in Amy Goodman, *The Exception to the Rulers*, p. 192.

63. *The Situation Room*, CNN, 28 May 2008. The transcript is available online. See http://transcripts.cnn.com/TRANSCRIPTS/0805/28/sitroom.01.html

64. Glenn Greenwald, 'CNN/MSNBC Reporter: corporate executives forced pro-Bush, pro-war narrative'.

65. Nick Davies, *Flat Earth News*, p. 330.

66. Quoted in Nick Davies, *Flat Earth News*, p. 350.

67. Alan Rusbridger, 'David Miranda, schedule 7 and the danger that all reporters now face', *The Guardian*, 19 August 2013. See http://www.theguardian.com/commentisfree/2013/aug/19/david-miranda-schedule7-danger-reporters

68. Nicholas Watt, 'David Cameron makes veiled threat to media over NSA and GCHQ leaks', *The Guardian*, 28 October 2013. See http://www.theguardian.com/world/2013/oct/28/david-cameron-nsa-threat-newspapers-guardian-snowden

69. Alan Rusbridger, 'MPs' questions to Alan Rusbridger: do you love this country', *The Guardian*, 3 December 2013. See http://www.theguardian.com/media/2013/dec/03/keith-vaz-alan-rusbridger-love-country-nsa

70. Dr Glen O'Hara, Oxford Brookes University, 'History lessons on the public debt', letter to *The Guardian*, 3 March 2010. See http://www.theguardian.com/business/2010/mar/03/history-lessons-on-public-debt

71. Barry Kushner, Saville Kushner, *Who Needs the Cuts?* (London: Hesperus Press, 2010), p. 39.

72. For a rigorous account of the historical failure of austerity, see Mark Blyth, *Austerity* (New York: Oxford University Press, 2013).

73. For instance, Alberto Alesina, Silvia Ardagna, 'Large Changes in Fiscal Policy: Taxes Versus Spending', National Bureau of Economic Research, Working Paper No. 15438, October 2009. See also: Carmen Reinhart, Kenneth Rogoff, 'Growth in a Time of Debt', National Bureau of Economic Research, Working Paper No. 15639, January 2010.

74. Paul Krugman, 'The case for cuts was a lie. Why does Britain still believe it? The austerity delusion', *The Guardian*, 29 April 2015. See http://www.theguardian.com/business/ng-interactive/2015/apr/29/the-austerity-delusion

75. George Eaton, 'Exclusive: Osborne's supporters turn on him', *New Statesman*, 15 August 2012. See http://www.newstatesman.com/blogs/politics/2012/08/exclusive-osbornes-supporters-turn-him

76. Paul Krugman, 'The case for cuts was a lie. Why does Britain still believe it? The austerity delusion'.

77. Paul Krugman, 'The case for cuts was a lie. Why does Britain still believe it? The austerity delusion'.

78. Simon Wren-Lewis, 'The Austerity Con', *London Review of Books*, Vol. 37, No. 4, 19 February 2015, pp. 9–11. See http://www.lrb.co.uk/v37/n04/simon-wren-lewis/the-austerity-con

79. Ben Chu, 'Two thirds of economists say Coalition austerity harmed the economy', *The Independent*, 1 April 2015. See http://www.independent.co.uk/news/business/news/two-thirds-of-economists-say-coalition-austerity-harmed-the-economy-10149410.html

80. Simon Wren-Lewis, 'The economic consequences of George Osborne: covering up the austerity mistake', *New Statesman*, 22 April 2015. See http://www.newstatesman.com/politics/2015/04/economic-consequences-george-osborne-covering-austerity-mistake

81. Ha-Joon Chang, 'Why did Britain's political class buy into the Tories' economic fairytale?', *The Guardian*, 19 October 2014. See http://www.theguardian.com/commentisfree/2014/oct/19/britain-political-class-tories-economic-fairytale

82. Ha-Joon Chang, 'Why did Britain's political class buy into the Tories' economic fairytale?'

83. 'Budget 2010: Full text of George Osborne's statement', *The Telegraph*, 22 June 2010. See http://www.telegraph.co.uk/finance/budget/7846849/Budget-2010-Full-text-of-George-Osbornes-statement.html

84. Liam Halligan, 'It's time to come clean about our national debt', *The Telegraph*,

25 October 2014. See http://www.telegraph.co.uk/finance/economics/11187727/Its-time-to-come-clean-about-our-national-debt.html

85. B. Barr, D. Taylor-Robinson, D. Stuckler, R. Loopstra, A. Reeves, M. Whitehead, '"First, do no harm": are disability assessments associated with adverse trends in mental health? A longitudinal ecological study', *Journal of Epidemiology and Community Health*, 16 November 2015. See http://jech.bmj.com/content/early/2015/10/26/jech-2015-206209

86. Phillip Inman, 'Bank of England governor blames spending cuts on bank bailouts', *The Guardian*, 1 March 2011. See http://www.theguardian.com/business/2011/mar/01/mervyn-king-blames-banks-cuts

87. Joseph E. Stiglitz, *The Price of Inequality* (London: Allen Lane, 2012), p. 215.

88. Tom Clark, 'Tories retake poll lead but appear at odds with public on 50p tax', *The Guardian*, 19 March 2012. See http://www.theguardian.com/politics/2012/mar/19/tories-poll-lead-50p-tax-rate

89. Lord Mayor's Banquet 2013: Prime Minister's Speech, 11 November 2013. See https://www.gov.uk/government/speeches/lord-mayors-banquet-2013-prime-ministers-speech

90. Paul Krugman, 'The case for cuts was a lie. Why does Britain still believe it? The austerity delusion'.

91. 'The complaints come marching in', *Financial Times*, 25 March 2011. See http://www.ft.com/cms/s/0/30f5fc14-5721-11e0-9035-00144feab49a.html

92. 'A brave budget that pulls Britain back from the brink', *The Telegraph*, 22 June 2010. See http://www.telegraph.co.uk/finance/budget/7847905/A-brave-Budget-that-pulls-Britain-back-from-the-brink.html

93. Quoted in Barry Kushner, Saville Kushner, *Who Needs the Cuts?*, p. 17.

94. Quoted in Barry Kushner, Saville Kushner, *Who Needs the Cuts?*, p. 17.

95. Simon Wren-Lewis, 'The Austerity Con'.

96. 'Osborne wins the battle on austerity', *Financial Times*, 10 September 2013. See http://www.ft.com/cms/s/0/03137634-1a13-11e3-93e8-00144feab7de.html

97. Julien Mercille, 'The British Media, Cheerleaders for Austerity', Truthout, 26 June 2013. See http://www.truth-out.org/opinion/item/17209-the-british-media-cheerleaders-for-austerity

98. Mike Berry, 'Hard Evidence: How biased is the BBC?', *The Conversation*, 23 August 2013. See http://www.newstatesman.com/broadcast/2013/08/hard-evidence-how-biased-bbc

99. Mike Berry, 'Hard Evidence: How biased is the BBC?'

100. 'Gordon Brown to keep spending high despite recession, Ed Balls indicates',

The Telegraph, 28 June 2009. See http://www.telegraph.co.uk/news/politics/5677741/Gordon-Brown-to-keep-spending-high-despite-recession-Ed-Balls-indicates.html

101. Peter Moore, 'Austerity: the new normal', YouGov UK website, 24 April 2013. See https://yougov.co.uk/news/2013/04/24/austerity-new-normal/

102. Tom Clark, 'Voters trust Cameron-Osborne most with the economy, poll finds', *The Guardian*, 6 October 2014. See http://www.theguardian.com/politics/2014/oct/06/voters-trust-cameron-osborne-most-with-the-economy-poll-finds

103. Jonathan Paige, 'British public wrong about nearly everything, survey Shows', *The Independent*, 9 July 2013. See http://www.independent.co.uk/news/uk/home-news/british-public-wrong-about-nearly-everything-survey-shows-8697821.html

104. Louise Ridley, 'Jeremy Corbyn "Systematically" Attacked by British Press the Moment He Became Leader, Research Claims', *The Huffington Post*, 26 November 2015. See http://www.huffingtonpost.co.uk/2015/11/26/jeremy-corbyn-media-coverage_n_8653886.html?1448557116

105. Steerpike, 'Nick Robinson tackles anti-Corbyn bias at the BBC', *The Spectator*, 16 November 2015. See http://blogs.new.spectator.co.uk/2015/11/nick-robinson-tackles-anti-corbyn-bias-at-the-bbc/

106. 'Cracks in the crust', *The Economist*, 11 December 2008. See http://www.economist.com/node/12762027

107. Karin Hammar, 'Iceland Makes Strong Recovery From 2008 Financial Crisis', *IMF Survey Magazine*, 13 March 2015. See http://www.imf.org/external/pubs/ft/survey/so/2015/car031315a.htm

108. Tracey Greenstein, 'Iceland's Stabilized Economy Is A Surprising Success Story', *Forbes*, 20 February 2013. See http://www.forbes.com/sites/traceygreenstein/2013/02/20/icelands-stabilized-economy-is-a-surprising-success-story/

109. *The Big Idea*, BBC2, 14 February 1996. The programme is available on YouTube. See https://www.youtube.com/watch?v=GjENnyQupow

110. In one study, members of the public were presented with different causes of death and asked to guess which was more frequent by indicating what they thought the ratio of the two frequencies would be. The results showed that although strokes cause double the number of deaths as all accidents combined, 80 per cent of responders guessed that accidental death would be more likely. See Daniel Kahneman, *Thinking, Fast and Slow* (London: Allen Lane, 2011), p. 62.

111. The effect is not limited to humans.

112. Daniel Kahneman, *Thinking, Fast and Slow*, pp. 66–7. Experiments have identified

similar behaviour in a number of animals; in fact Robert Zajonc claims it extends to all species.

113. John Nichols, 'The Discourse Suffers When Trump Gets 23 Times As Much Coverage As Sanders', *The Nation*, 14 December 2015. See http://www.thenation.com/article/the-discourse-suffers-when-trump-gets-23-times-as-much-coverage-as-sanders/

114. Janet Elder, 'Packaging 9/11, Terror and the War in Iraq', *The New York Times*, 17 October 2007. See http://www.nytimes.com/2007/10/17/us/politics/17web-elder.html

115. Steven Kull, 'Misperceptions, the Media and the Iraq war', Program on International Policy Attitudes (PIPA), 2 October 2003. See http://www.pipa.org/onlineReports/Iraq/IraqMedia_Oct03/IraqMedia_Oct03_rpt.pdf

116. Simon Jeffery, 'WikiLeaks: Julian Assange returns to court and the latest developments', *The Guardian*, 11 January 2011. See http://www.theguardian.com/news/blog/2011/jan/11/wikileaks-latest-developments

117. Quoted in Robert W. McChesney, *Digital Disconnect*, p. 173.

118. The figures, however, varied significantly: ABC Television: 91 per cent, MSNBC: 81 per cent, *The Guardian*: 62 per cent, CNN: 59 per cent, and so on. The content reproduced by internet companies such as Yahoo! and AOL was far higher, averaging 85 per cent.

119. James Curran, Jean Seaton, *Power Without Responsibility*, 7th edn, p. 276.

8 Creativity

1. Stanley Milgram, *Obedience to Authority* (1974; London: Pinter and Martin, 2005).

2. Stanley Milgram, *Obedience to Authority*, p. 32.

3. Thomas Blass, 'The Obedience Experiments At 50', *Observations*, Association for Psychological Science, 31 August 2011. ('I believe that one of the most important aspects of Milgram's legacy is that, in demonstrating our extreme readiness to obey authorities, he has identified one of the universals, or constants, of human behavior, straddling time and place.') See http://www.psychologicalscience.org/index.php/publications/observer/obsonline/the-obedience-experiments-at-50.html. For further investigation, see Thomas Blass, *The Man Who Shocked the World: The Life and Legacy of Stanley Milgram* (New York: Basic Books, 2004) and also Jerry M. Burger, 'Replicating Milgram', *American Psychologist*, Vol. 64, No. 1, January 2009, pp. 1–11.

4. Thomas Blass, 'The Obedience Experiments At 50'.

5. Stanley Milgram, *Obedience to Authority*, pp. 179–80.

6. Stanley Milgram, *Obedience to Authority*, pp. 183–6.

7. Stanley Milgram, *Obedience to Authority*, p. xviii.

8. Hannah Arendt, *The Life of the Mind* (1971; Boston: Houghton Mifflin Harcourt, 1981), p. 180.

9. Stanley Milgram, *Obedience to Authority*, p. 9.

10. It is conceivable that a man locked in a cell – though he lacks power to act on the outside world – could possess more creative freedom than his low-paid, stressed-out jailer.

11. The accuracy of our personal maps is essential for our freedom, but only when it bears on the realisation of our deepest values. Some truths may simply cause pain without any enhancement of creative freedom.

12. George Orwell, 'In Front of Your Nose' *Tribune*, 22 March 1946. See http://www.orwell.ru/library/articles/nose/english/e_nose

13. John Maynard Keynes, 'Economic Possibilities for our Grandchildren', 1930. See https://www.marxists.org/reference/subject/economics/keynes/1930/our-grandchildren.htm

14. The comment was made by Friedrich Hayek in an interview with Bernard Levin on a show called 'The Levin Interviews', which was broadcast on the BBC on 31 May 1980. See https://www.youtube.com/watch?v=gVjT98208M4

15. Kathleen Taylor, *Brainwashing* (Oxford: Oxford University Press, 2004), p. 122.

16. Viktor Frankl, *Man's Search for Meaning* (1946; London: Ebury Publishing, 2004), p. 53.

17. Nicholas Kristof, 'Is Delhi So Different From Steubenville?', *New York Times*, 12 January, 2013. See: http://www.nytimes.com/2013/01/13/opinion/sunday/is-delhi-so-different-from-steubenville.html?_r=0. In the US, close to three women are murdered each day by a spouse or ex-spouse, a beating takes place every nine seconds, and a rape is reported every 6.2 minutes. (Most rapes go unreported – estimates indicate that a rape may take place almost every minute.)

18. Edward Skidelsky, 'Are people frightened of leisure time?', *The Guardian*, 10 September 2013. See http://www.theguardian.com/sustainable-business/are-people-frightened-leisure-time.

19. Adam Smith, *The Wealth of Nations*, Book 1, Chapter 2, See https://www.marxists.org/reference/archive/smith-adam/works/welath-of-nations/book01/ch02.htm

20. It is debatable whether or not Keynes ever really said this. The first attribution

was in 1951. See George Schuster, *Christianity and Human Relations in Industry* (London: Epworth, 1951), p. 109.

21.   John Maynard Keynes, 'Economic Possibilities for our Grandchildren', 1930. See https://www.marxists.org/reference/subject/economics/keynes/1930/our-grandchildren.htm

22.   The comment was made in an interview with Bernard Levin on a show called 'The Levin Interviews', which was broadcast on the BBC on 31 May 1980. See https://www.youtube.com/watch?v=gVjT98208M4

23.   E. F. Schumacher, *Small Is Beautiful* (London: Vintage, 1993), p. 12.

24.   David Graeber, *Toward an Anthropological Theory of Value* (New York: Palgrave, 2001), p. xi.

25.   Taken from the transcript of a speech, 'The Pricing of Everything', by George Monbiot, at the Sheffield Political Economy Research Institute Annual Lecture, 2014. See http://www.monbiot.com/2014/07/24/the-pricing-of-everything/

26.   Kimberly Vosburgh, 'Ocean Assets Valued At $24 Trillion, But Dwindling Fast', WWF website, 22 April 2015. The World Wildlife Fund recently put a monetary value on the world's oceans: $24 trillion.

27.   Shamim Adam, 'Global Financial Assets Lost $50 Trillion Last Year, ADB Says', Bloomberg, 9 March 2009. See http://www.bloomberg.com/apps/news?pid=newsarchive&sid=aZ1kcJ7y3LDM

28.   Friedrich Hayek, *The Road to Serfdom*, (1944; Abingdon, Oxon, and New York: Routledge Classics, 2001), p. 60.

29.   Friedrich Hayek, *The Road to Serfdom*, p. 154.

30.   Joel Bakan, *Childhood Under Siege* (London: The Bodley Head, 2011), p. 11.

31.   Friedrich Hayek, *The Road to Serfdom*, p. 157.

32.   Friedrich Hayek, *The Road to Serfdom*, p. 164.

33.   Friedrich Hayek, *The Road to Serfdom*, p. 166.

34.   Friedrich Hayek, *The Road to Serfdom*, p. 151.

35.   Friedrich Hayek, *The Road to Serfdom*, p. 153.

36.   A number of thinkers have argued that the state of society – its level of development – should be measured according to the freedoms it affords its people. Amartya Sen has pioneered this approach in texts such as *Development as Freedom* (Oxford: Oxford University Press, 1999). (Sen's conception of freedom in terms of capabilities is a radical departure from the formulations that justify the economic and political systems that prevail today. He acknowledges the difficulty not just of attaining what is valuable but identifying it: 'seeing freedom in terms of the power to bring about the outcome one wants with reasoned assessment,

there is, of course, the underlying question whether the person has had an adequate opportunity to reason about what she really wants'; Amartya Sen, *The Idea of Justice* [London: Penguin Books, 2010], p. 301.)

37. Philip Pullella, Sarah Marsh, 'Pope calls for new economic order, criticizes capitalism', Reuters, 9 July 2015. See http://www.reuters.com/article/us-pope-latam-bolivia-idUSKCN0PJ29B20150710#7RT6dFUqSdi4P5mA.97

38. Bertrand Russell, *The Prospects of Industrial Civilization* (1923; London: Routledge, 1996), p. 229.

39. Solomon Northup, *Twelve Years a Slave* (1853; London: Penguin Classics, 2012), pp. 135–6.

40. There is also a paradox worth highlighting. The only way to authentically endorse values which conflict with creative freedom is to achieve some degree of autonomy. In other words, embracing freedom is necessary if we're to discover good grounds for its rejection.

41. This formulation comes from William F. Buckley. He made the comment in a televised debate with Gore Vidal in 1968. The debate is the subject of the 2015 documentary *Best of Enemies*, directed by Robert Gordon and Morgan Neville.

42. A division exists among those seeking radical social change. It is based not so much on where we want to go but how we get there. Broadly speaking, some people favour reform, others favour revolution. Revolutionaries argue that real and lasting change can only come through a forcible overthrow of the existing social order. If a head-on confrontation with existing power structures results in victory, the idea is that existing institutions can then be dismantled and new ones rapidly built in their place. Destruction precedes creativity. Famous examples include the Bolshevik October Revolution of 1917 in Russia and the Cuban revolution of 1959.

Reformists favour an evolutionary approach, trying to achieve change within the present system. This involves rewriting laws and experimenting with new forms of organisation, often non-hierarchical in character, within the spaces permitted by the dominant system: starting up cooperatives, democratising workplaces, establishing eco-villages or alternative communities. Changing laws can make life better for people right away, while also expanding the possibility for future democratic gains. Building alternatives within the system, as well as empowering people, shows that different ways of working and living are possible.

It is not hard to identify problems with both approaches. To the extent it depends on violent overthrow, the revolutionary approach seems hopeless most of the time in the face of state power. Any head-on confrontation with modern armies, police forces and intelligence services will almost certainly result in a state victory. Genuine opportunities for system overthrow are extremely rare, and in today's technologically advanced, militarised states they seem remote. However, even if conditions changed enough to weaken state power considerably and strengthen the political opposition, history would suggest that the revolutionary approach is more likely to result in an enhancement of authoritarian state power than a deeply egalitarian and democratic society. There is little guarantee that after old structures of power have been demolished, something better will emerge in its place. Power vacuums are dangerous things.

The reformist approach also has its problems. Building alternatives within the system can create pockets of valuable democratic structures, but there are systemic obstacles that stand in their way, making it hard for them to overcome the concentrations of power that already exist. Getting laws changed through campaigning, lobbying and civil disobedience has been remarkably successful at certain points in history, leading to real improvements in people's lives. The welfare state in the UK and the New Deal in the US are good examples. Yet incremental progressive change did not alter the fundamental institutions of power enough to prevent many gains being eroded by corporate power under the guise of neoliberalism. Reformist strategies can underestimate the systemic nature of the problems we struggle against, focusing disproportionately on symptoms over causes.

Whether through reform or revolution, overcoming the mechanisms which concentrate wealth and power is a precondition for significantly expanding freedom. To state the obvious, achieving social change is hard. Nevertheless, history teaches us that profound changes do take place. All kinds of victories have been won over the centuries. What is most damaging is to allow disagreement over strategy to weaken those groups who are trying to win liberating change. Power can be corrupting but so can its absence.

The distinction between reform and revolution is less clear than it initially appears. Whatever we believe the long-term goals should be, the short-term strategies largely remain the same. We need to educate ourselves and each other; develop networks of mutual support and solidarity around shared concerns in the community, workplace, and around issues of national significance. When networks are strengthened, and more people participate, larger scale actions become possible: strikes, marches, protests, and acts of mass civil disobedience – electoral victory for radical candidates and parties also becomes a possibility. We also need bold experiments in social institutions such as worker-owned enterprises, independent media, democratic schools and collectives of various kinds. These experiments address the hard challenge of actually living, associating and cooperating as free people here in the present. They act as a model of the future we wish to create.

Hopefully there is no limit to what constructive reform can achieve. Hopefully by continually pressing the existing structures to succumb to popular control, it will be possible to grow new structures from within the present society which, over time, will create a qualitatively different system. Cumulative institutional reforms may be able to achieve fundamental change, but to reach this point we need a revolution in common sense about what politics is, what democracy is, what freedom is, and what we are.

43. Adam Hochschild, *Bury the Chains: The British Struggle to Abolish Slavery* (Basingstoke: Macmillan, 2005), p. 5.

44. Adam Hochschild, *Bury the Chains*, p. 5.

45. For an enlightening account of the abolitionists' struggle, see Adam Hochschild, *Bury the Chains*.

46. Viktor Frankl, *Man's Search for Meaning*, p. 91.

47. Viktor Frankl, *Man's Search for Meaning*, p. 85.

48. Howard Zinn, *You Can't Be Neutral on a Moving Train*, 2nd edn (Boston, MA: Beacon Press, 2002), p. 208.

9 Knowledge

1. Adam Smith, *The Theory of Moral Sentiments* (1759; New York: Cosimo Classics, 2007), p. 111.

2. Hannah Arendt, *Lectures on Kant's Political Philosophy* (Chicago: University of Chicago Press, 1982), p. 43. Of course, our capacity to 'go visiting', and the penalties for openly attempting it, depend on our particular circumstances.

3. They have this characteristic in common with the 'hard sciences', yet they attempt to achieve something far more difficult. We ascend the ladder of complexity as we move from physics to chemistry to biology to psychology to questions of economics, politics and sociology. With each rung, things become less amenable to the precision, measurement and elegance exemplified by fundamental science.

4. To deepen our understanding of what is valuable, we need to pay special attention to the factual assumptions upon which our values are based. Most things we pursue, we do so because we believe they are a means to something more fundamental. Interrogating the causal connections between means and ends is vital. It is one thing to want the best for our children, to wish for greater personal happiness and fulfilment, and dream of a safer, fairer world – it is quite

another to know how to pursue these things most effectively. Improving our understanding of the consequences of our actions – on ourselves, our intimates and the wider world – is a lifelong journey.

5. An exception might be certainty of your own existence: 'I think, therefore I am' as Descartes famously put it.

6. There are exceptions. Important discoveries that challenge beliefs are sometimes made by accident, but even then a degree of humility is necessary to recognise and accept the implications of what has been discovered.

7. A striking bit of evidence about the value of uncertainty comes from a study focused on problem-solving. When things are going well, when we perceive no need to increase our effort, we feel what psychologists call 'cognitive ease'. But when conscious, effortful thinking is mobilised, we feel a sense of 'cognitive strain'. Studies have shown that our performance at solving problems that trigger an intuitive yet incorrect answer improves dramatically when the problem is written in a less legible font. One study involved forty Princeton students, half of whom saw two puzzles in normal font, while the other half saw them in a faded, small, washed-out print. Ninety per cent of students who saw the problems in normal font made at least one mistake on the test, accepting the intuitive answer that popped into their head. For those students given a less legible font, the figure dropped to 35 per cent. Cognitive strain brought on by the faded font raised the likelihood that students double-checked their intuitive response with a dose of effortful thinking. Daniel Kahneman, *Thinking, Fast and Slow* (London, Allen Lane, 2011), p. 65.

8. Richard Feynman, *The Pleasure of Finding Things Out* (1999; London: Penguin, 2007), pp. 146–9.

9. Alice Calaprice, *The New Quotable Einstein* (New Jersey: Princeton University Press, 2005), p. 291.

10. The neural pathways created, reinforced and secured throughout the process of learning make previously complicated actions – speaking, typing, walking – so easy that the conscious mind doesn't have to think about them. Once these actions become automatic, additional thought tends to inhibit the fluency of their execution. A lot of activities benefit from habitual responses. Uncertainty can sometimes hinder rather than help our performance. In general, habitual responses are preferred when a level of continuity is desired, for these allow us to maintain and make use of the patterns we've learnt. But when progress is desired and discoveries sought, as in our pursuit of truth, knowledge and personal and social improvement, the value of uncertainty to keep us open-minded, alert and sceptical is indispensable. Incidentally, attempts by philosophers of science

to formalise the scientific method have so far failed to encompass the behaviour of scientists in making their discoveries. See Alan Chalmers, *What is This Thing called Science?* (1978; 3rd edn, Maidenhead, Berks: Open University Press, 1999).

11. The following discussion of cognitive biases draws on Daniel Kahneman, *Thinking, Fast and Slow* (London, Allen Lane, 2011).

12. Robert B. Cialdini, *Influence: Science and Practice*, 5th edn (Boston, MA.: Pearson, 2009) p. 3.

13. Robert B. Cialdini, *Influence: Science and Practice*, p. 3.

14. Steven Pinker, *The Blank Slate: The Modern Denial of Human Nature* (London: Allen Lane, 2002), p. 203.

15. Donaldo Macedo (ed.), *Chomsky on MisEducation* (Lanham, MD: Rowman and Littlefield, 2000), p. 3.

16. Paul Jay, 'TRNN Veteran's Day Replay: Training That Makes Killing Civilians Acceptable', The Real News Network, 12 May 2010. See http://therealnews.com/t2/index.php?option=com_content&task=view&id=31&Itemid=74&jumival=11913

17. Paul Jay, 'TRNN Veteran's Day Replay: Training That Makes Killing Civilians Acceptable'.

18. Paul Jay, 'TRNN Veteran's Day Replay: Training That Makes Killing Civilians Acceptable'.

19. Kathryn Schultz, 'My Country Right or Wrong: Conscientious Objector Josh Stieber on Being Wrong About the Military', *Slate* online magazine, 16 December 2010. See http://www.slate.com/blogs/thewrongstuff/2010/12/16/my_country_right_or_wrong_conscientious_objector_josh_stieber_on_being_wrong_about_the_military.html

20. Kathryn Schultz, 'My Country Right or Wrong: Conscientious Objector Josh Stieber on Being Wrong About the Military'.

21. Dan Kahan, Donald Braman, Paul Slovic, John Gastil, Geoffrey Cohen, *The Second National Risk and Culture Study: Making Sense of – and Making Progress in – the American Culture War of Fact*, Cultural Cognition Project, Yale Law School, 2007.

22. Dan M. Kahan, Paul Slovic, 'Cultural Evaluations of Risk: "Values" or "Blunders"?', *Public Law & Legal Theory* Research paper series, Yale Law School, No. 111, p. 8.

23. 'Two Nature Features Provide Insights on Need for Better Communications', Yale Climate Connections, 11 February 2010. See http://www.yaleclimateconnections.org/2010/02/two-nature-features-2/

24. Tim McDonnell, 'Schools Are Doing a Terrible Job Teaching Your Kids About Global Warming', *Mother Jones*, 11 February 2016.

25. Upton Sinclair, *I, Candidate for Governor: And How I got Licked* (1935; Berkeley: University of California Press, 1994), p. 109.

26. Rebecca Solnit, 'The Longest War', TomDispatch, 24 January, 2013. See: http://www.tomdispatch.com/blog/175641/tomgram%3A_rebecca_solnit%2C_the_longest_war

27. Dan Bilsker, Jennifer White, 'The silent epidemic of male suicide', *BCMJ*, Vol. 53, No. 10, December 2011; Jamie Doward, 'Let's reach out to men to halt shocking suicide rate', *The Guardian,* 31 October, 2015. See: http://www.theguardian.com/society/2015/oct/31/social-media-campaign-male-suicide

28. Indre Viskontas, Chris Mooney, 'The Science of Your Racist Brain', Mother Jones, 9 May 2014. See http://www.motherjones.com/environment/2014/05/inquiring-minds-david-amodio-your-brain-on-racism

29. Alexander Green, Dana Carney, Daniel Pallin, Long Ngo, Kristal Raymond, Lisa Lezzoni, Mahzarin Banaji, 'Implicit Bias Among Physicians and Its Prediction of Thrombolysis Decisions for Black and White Patients', *Journal of General Internal Medicine,* Volume 22, No. 9, September 2007, pp. 1231–8.

30. Privilege is a relative concept. It is possessed only in relation to what other people have.

31. Paulo Freire, *Pedagogy of the Oppressed* (1970; London: Penguin, 1996), pp. 26–7.

32. W. E. B. Du Bois, *The Souls of Black Folks* (1903; New York: Penguin, 1989), p. 3.

33. Bertrand Russell, *Principles of Social Reconstruction* (1916; New York: Routledge, 1997), p. 115.

34. Scott Barry Kaufman, Carolyn Gregoire, *Wired to Create* (New York: Penguin Random House, 2015). Some of the findings are summarised in: Scott Barry Kaufman, Carolyn Gregoire, 'The Surprising Benefit of Going Through Hard Times', *Huffington Post,* 2 January 2016. See http://www.huffingtonpost.com/entry/post-traumatic-growth-creativity_568426c0e4b014efe0d9d8e8

35. Scott Barry Kaufman, Carolyn Gregoire, *Wired to Create*, p. 149.

36. Quoted in Scott Barry Kaufman, Carolyn Gregoire, *Wired to Create*, p.151.

37. George F. DeMartino, Deirdre N. McCloskey (eds), *The Oxford Handbook of Professional Economic Ethics* (Oxford and New York: Oxford University Press, 2016), p. 273.

38. After the crash, the Dutch economist Dirk Bezemer scoured the academic literature to find which economists, if any, made predictions that satisfied the following criteria: they forecast a real estate crisis and a severe recession caused by the financial sector; they described the mechanisms by which this would happen; they gave a time period; and they made their prediction public. Bezemer

found twelve economists who fitted these criteria: Dean Baker, Wynne Godley, Fred Harrison, Michael Hudson, Eric Janszen, Steve Keen, Jakob Brochner Madsen, Jens Kjaer Sorensen, Kurt Richebacher, Nouriel Roubini, Peter Schiff and Robert Shiller. None is identified with the neoclassical school of economics. (See George F. DeMartino, Deirdre N. McCloskey [eds], *The Oxford Handbook of Professional Economic Ethics*, p. 272.)

39. Robert E. Prasch, *How Markets Work: Supply, Demand and the 'Real World'* (Cheltenham: Edward Elgar, 2008), p. 4.

40. For a rigorous critique of textbook economics, see Rod Hill, Tony Myatt, *The Economics Anti-Textbook*, (London: Zed Books, 2010).

41. Thomas Piketty, *Capital in the Twenty-First Century* (Cambridge, MA: Harvard University Press, 2014), p. 32.

42. See the International Student Initiative for Pluralism in Economics website: http://www.isipe.net/open-letter/

43. Long Wang, Deepak Malhotra, Keith Murnighan, 'Economics Education and Greed', *Academy of Management Learning and Education*, Vol. 10, No. 4, 1 December 2011, pp. 643–60.

44. Neil Gandal, Sonia Roccas, Lilach Sagiv, Amy Wrzesniewski, 'Personal Value Priorities of Economists', *Human Relations*, Vol. 58, No. 10, October 2005, pp. 1227–52.

45. David Colander, *The Making of an Economist* (New Jersey: Princeton University Press, 2007), p. 21.

46. Robert Frank, Thomas Gilovich, Dennis Regan, 'Does Studying Economics Inhibit Cooperation?', *The Journal of Economic Perspectives*, Vol. 7, No. 2, 1993, pp. 159–71.

47. Ha-Joon Chang gives the example of neoclassical economists who reject criticism of low-wage factories in developing nations on the basis that the alternative would be no job at all. As he writes, 'This is true, if we take the underlying socio-economic structure as given. However, once we are willing to change the structure itself, there are a lot of alternatives to those low-wage jobs. With new labour laws that strengthen worker rights, land reform that reduces the supply of cheap labour to factories (as more people stay in the countryside) or industrial policies that create high-skilled jobs, the choice for workers can be between low-wage jobs and higher-wage ones, rather than between low-wage jobs and no jobs.' (Ha-Joon Chang, *Economics: The User's Guide* [London: Pelican, 2014], pp. 126–7.)

48. 'Rhodes must not fall', YouGov, 18 January 2016. See https://yougov.co.uk/news/2016/01/18/rhodes-must-not-fall/

49. For instance, in 2005 Gordon Brown declared that 'the days of Britain having to apologise for its colonial history are over', adding that 'we should celebrate much of our past rather than apologise for it'. See Benedict Brogan, 'It's time to celebrate the Empire, says Brown', *Daily Mail*, 15 January 2005. See http://www.dailymail.co.uk/news/article-334208/Its-time-celebrate-Empire-says-Brown.html In 2009, David Cameron said, 'We must never forget that Britain is a great country with a history we can be truly proud of.' (David Cameron MP: Proud to be British, *Conservative Home*, 10 July 2009. See http://www.conservativehome.com/platform/2009/07/david-cameron-proud-to-be-british.html). For examples of contemporary historians who celebrate and defend the empire, see the work of Niall Ferguson, Lawrence James and Andrew Roberts.

50. Ian Cobain, Owen Bowcott, Richard Norton-Taylor, 'Britain destroyed records of colonial crimes', *The Guardian*, 18 April 2012. See http://www.theguardian.com/uk/2012/apr/18/britain-destroyed-records-colonial-crimes?newsfeed=true

51. Ian Cobain, Owen Bowcott, Richard Norton-Taylor, 'Britain destroyed records of colonial crimes'.

52. George Monbiot, 'Deny the British empire's crimes? No, we ignore them', *The Guardian*, 23 April 2012. See http://www.theguardian.com/commentisfree/2012/apr/23/british-empire-crimes-ignore-atrocities

53. Mark Curtis, *Web of Deceit: Britain's Real Role in the World* (London: Vintage, 2003) p. 21.

54. Mark Curtis, *Web of Deceit*, pp. 21–2.

55. Mark Curtis, *Web of Deceit*, p. 24.

56. Mark Curtis, *Unpeople* (London: Vintage, 2004), p. 105.

57. Mark Curtis, *Unpeople*, p. 105.

58. Mark Curtis, *Unpeople*, p. 108.

59. Mark Curtis, *Unpeople*, p. 48.

60. Mark Curtis, *Unpeople*, p. 49.

61. 'Deception on Capitol Hill', *New York Times*, 15 January 1992. See http://www.nytimes.com/1992/01/15/opinion/deception-on-capitol-hill.html

62. R. W. Apple Jr, '25 Years Later; Lessons From the Pentagon Papers', *New York Times*, 23 June 1996.

63. Arthur Neslen, 'TTIP talks: EU alleged to have given ExxonMobil access to confidential strategies', *The Guardian*, 26 November 2015. See http://www.theguardian.com/environment/2015/nov/26/ttip-talks-eu-alleged-to-have-given-exxonmobil-access-to-confidential-papers

64. Jon Stone, 'George Osborne defends blocking analysis that shows how much

money he takes from the poor and gives to the rich', *The Independent*, 24 March 2016. See: http://www.independent.co.uk/news/uk/politics/george-osborne-defends-scrapping-analysis-that-shows-how-much-money-he-takes-from-the-poor-and-gives-a6949981.html

65. Randeep Ramesh, Alex Hern, 'Conservative party deletes archive of speeches from internet', *The Guardian*, 13 November 2013. See http://www.theguardian.com/politics/2013/nov/13/conservative-party-archive-speeches-internet

66. Randeep Ramesh, Alex Hern, 'Conservative party deletes archive of speeches from internet'.

67. Alan Travis, 'Snooper's charter: wider police powers to hack phones and access web history', *The Guardian*, 1 March 2016. See http://www.theguardian.com/uk-news/2016/mar/01/snoopers-charter-to-extend-police-access-to-phone-and-internet-data?CMP

68. Ben Goldacre, 'It's a scandal drug trial results are still being withheld', *The Guardian*, 5 January 2014. See http://www.theguardian.com/commentisfree/2014/jan/05/scandal-drugs-trials-withheld-doctors-tamiflu

69. David Pilling, 'Lunch with the FT: Ha-Joon Chang', *Financial Times*, 29 November 2013. See http://www.ft.com/cms/s/2/27a2027e-5698-11e3-8cca-00144feabdc0.html

70. There are as many perspectives as there are people, but groups that have certain traits in common, because of systematic prejudice in society, come to share similar experiences.

10 Power

1. Mike Davis, *Late Victorian Holocausts* (London: Verso, 2002), p. 7.

2. Mike Davis, *Late Victorian Holocausts*, p. 46.

3. Mike Davis, *Late Victorian Holocausts*, p. 31.

4. Mike Davis, *Late Victorian Holocausts*, p. 33.

5. Amartya Sen, 'Democracy as a Universal Value', *Journal of Democracy*, Vol. 10, No. 4, October 1999, p. 7.

6. Amartya Sen, *Development as Freedom* (1999; Oxford: Oxford University Press, 2001), p. 152.

7. Mike Davis, *Late Victorian Holocausts*, p. 7.

8. Stephen Devereux, 'Famine in the Twentieth Century', Institute of Development Studies, Working Paper 105, January 2000. See http://www.ids.ac.uk/publication/famine-in-the-twentieth-century

9. Samuel P. Huntington, *The Third Wave* (Norman, OK: University of Oklahoma Press, 1991), p. 9.

10. Quoted in E. Wayne Ross (ed.), *The Social Studies Curriculum* (New York: State University of New York Press, 2006), p. 328.

11. The aims of government can appear uncontroversial when stated in the most general terms. Such generality allows diverse groups to interpret a vision of the future in their own way, but this only staves off conflict until the details are elaborated. Furthermore, people may agree about goals but disagree about the proper means for achieving those goals. And their disagreement may be on moral, rather than strategic, grounds.

12. Robert A. Dahl, *Democracy and Its Critics* (London: Yale University Press, 1989), p. 77.

13. Mary Wollstonecraft, *A Vindication of the Rights of Woman* (1792; London: Penguin, 1982), p. 127.

14. For more information on Finland's education system, see Pasi Sahlberg, *Finnish Lessons: What Can the World Learn from Educational Change in Finland?*(New York: Teachers College Press, 2011).

15. Richard Garner, 'Finland schools: Subjects scrapped and replaced with "topics" as country reforms its education system', *The Independent*, 20 March 2015. See http://www.independent.co.uk/news/world/europe/finland-schools-subjects-are-out-and-topics-are-in-as-country-reforms-its-education-system-10123911.html

16. Peter Wilby, 'Finland's education ambassador spreads the word', *The Guardian*, 1 July 2013. See http://www.theguardian.com/education/2013/jul/01/education-michael-gove-finland-gcse

17. David L. Kirp, 'Make School A Democracy', *New York Times*, 28 February 2015. See http://www.nytimes.com/2015/03/01/opinion/sunday/make-school-a-democracy.html

18. For more information, see the Center for Education Innovations (CEI) website: http://www.educationinnovations.org/program/escuela-nueva

19. Paulo Freire, *Pedagogy of the Oppressed* (1970; London: Penguin, 1996), p. 16.

20. Howard Zinn, *The Politics of History* (Champaign, IL.: University of Illinois Press, 1970; 2nd edn, 1990), pp. 1 and 3.

21. 'Dr. John Dewey Dead at 92; Philosopher a Noted Liberal', *New York Times*, 2 June 1952. See http://www.nytimes.com/learning/general/onthisday/bday/1020.html

22. Giles Tremlett, 'Mondragon: Spain's giant co-operative where times are hard but few go bust', *The Guardian*, 7 March 2013. See http://www.theguardian.com/world/2013/mar/07/mondragon-spains-giant-cooperative

23. Giles Tremlett, 'Mondragon: Spain's giant co-operative where times are hard but few go bust'.

24. See his book on the topic, which has informed much of my analysis: Richard Wolff, *Democracy at Work* (Chicago: Haymarket Books, 2012).

25. Adam Smith, *The Wealth of Nations*, Book 5, Chapter 1, Part 3, Article 2. See https://www.marxists.org/reference/archive/smith-adam/works/wealth-of-nations/book05/ch01c-2.htm

26. Gore's website has information about its work practices and history. See http://www.gore.com/en_xx/aboutus/culture/index.html

27. Gar Alperovitz, *America Beyond Capitalism* (Hoboken, NJ: John Wiley and Sons, Inc., 2005), p. 87.

28. Dan O'Neill, Rob Dietz, *Enough is Enough* (Abingdon, Oxon: Routledge, 2013) p. 131.

29. Dan O'Neill, Rob Dietz, *Enough is Enough*, pp. 132–3.

30. Ben Craig, John Pencavel, 'Participation and Productivity: A Comparison of Worker Cooperatives and Conventional Firms in the Plywood Industry', Brookings Papers on Economic Activity: Microeconomics 1995, 1 July 1995. See also Richard B. Freeman, Joel Rogers, *What Workers Want* (New York: ILR Press, 2006); and Justin Schwartz, 'Where Did Mill Go Wrong?: Why the Capital-Managed Firm Rather than the Labor-Managed Enterprise is the Predominant Organizational Form in Market Economies', *Ohio State Law Journal*, Vol. 73, No. 2, 2012, pp. 219–85.

31. M. G. Marmot, G. Rose, M. Shipley, P. J. Hamilton, 'Employment Grade and Coronary Heart Disease in British Civil Servants', *Journal of Epidemiology and Community Health*, Vol. 32, 1978, pp. 244–9. A follow-up study conducted in 1997 found similar results.

32. Bruce Ackerman, *Voting With Dollars: A New Paradigm for Campaign Finance* (New Haven: Yale University Press, 2004).

33. Erik Olin Wright, *Envisioning Real Utopias* (London: Verso, 2010), pp. 169–70.

34. Robert W. McChesney, *Digital Disconnect* (New York: The New Press, 2013), p. 212.

35. Thomas Piketty, *Capital in the Twenty-First Century* (Cambridge, MA: Harvard University Press, 2014), p. 493.

36. Thomas Piketty, *Capital in the Twenty-First Century*, p. 513.

37. Richard Murphy, 'New Report: The Tax Gap Is £119.4 Billion And Rising', Tax Research UK, 22 September 2014. See http://www.taxresearch.org.uk/Blog/2014/09/22/new-report-the-tax-gap-is-119-4-billion-and-rising/

38. Graham Black, 'End the cuts to staff dealing with tax avoiders', *The Guardian*,

17 April 2012. See http://www.theguardian.com/society/2012/apr/17/end-cuts-staff-tax-avoiders

39. Jesse Drucker, Renee Dudley, 'Wal-Mart Has $76 Billion in Undisclosed Overseas Tax Havens', Bloomberg, 17 June 2015. See http://www.bloomberg.com/news/articles/2015-06-17/wal-mart-has-76-billion-in-overseas-tax-havens-report-says

40. Nicholas Shaxson, 'Follow the money: inside the world's tax havens', *The Guardian*, 19 June 2015. See http://www.theguardian.com/business/2015/jun/19/tax-havens-money-cayman-islands-jersey-offshore-accounts

41. Nicholas Shaxson, 'Follow the money: inside the world's tax havens'.

42. John Christensen, Richard Murphy, 'Tax Us If You Can', 2nd edn, Tax Justice Network, 2012, p. 3. See http://www.taxjustice.net/cms/upload/pdf/TUIYC_2012_FINAL.pdf

43. Julia Werdigier, 'Tax Evasion Costs Governments $3.1 Trillion Annually, Report Says', *New York Times*, 28 November 2011. See http://www.nytimes.com/2011/11/28/business/global/26iht-tax26.html?_r=0

44. Thomas Piketty, *Capital in the Twenty-First Century*, p. 528.

45. John Weeks, 'Inequality Trends in Some Developed OECD Countries', Working Paper No. 6, *Economic and Social Affairs*, October 2005. See http://www.un.org/esa/desa/papers/2005/wp6_2005.pdf

46. For a detailed breakdown of figures across Europe, and a list of sources, see the worker-participation.eu website: http://www.worker-participation.eu/National-Industrial-Relations/Across-Europe/Collective-Bargaining2

47. Gar Alperovitz, *America Beyond Capitalism*, p. 15.

48. Joseph E. Stiglitz, *The Price of Inequality* (London: Allen Lane, 2012), pp. 72–3.

49. 'Americans' Views on Income Inequality and Workers' Rights', *New York Times*, 3 June 2015. See http://www.nytimes.com/interactive/2015/06/03/business/income-inequality-workers-rights-international-trade-poll.html?_r=0. Will Dahlgreen, 'Voters choose greater equality over greater wealth', YouGov, 30

50. Amartya Sen, *Resources, Values and Development* (Cambridge, MA.: Harvard University Press, 1984), p. 103.

51. Bill Gates interviewed by James Bennet, 'We Need An Energy Miracle', *The Atlantic*, November 2015. See http://www.theatlantic.com/magazine/archive/2015/11/we-need-an-energy-miracle/407881/

52. David Stuckler, Sanjay Basu, *The Body Economic* (London: Allen Lane, 2013), p. 102.

53. David Stuckler, Sanjay Basu, *The Body Economic*, p. 101.

54. David Stuckler, Sanjay Basu, *The Body Economic*, p.101.

55. David Stuckler, Sanjay Basu, *The Body Economic*, p.101.

56.	Karen Davis, Cathy Schoen, Kristof Stremikis, 'Mirror, Mirror on the Wall: How the Performance of the U.S. Health Care System Compares Internationally, 2010 Update', The Commonwealth Fund, June 2010. See http://www.common-wealthfund.org/Publications/Fund-Reports/2010/Jun/Mirror-Mirror-Update.aspx?page=all

57.	'Health expenditure per capita (current US$)', The World Bank. See http://data.worldbank.org/indicator/SH.XPD.PCAP; see the World Health Organization's profiles for each country. US: http://www.who.int/countries/usa/en/ and Cuba: http://www.who.int/countries/cub/en/

58.	Ian Taylor, Lynn Sloman, 'Rebuilding Rail', Transport for Quality of Life, June 2012. See http://www.aslef.org.uk/files/133517/FileName/Rebuilding_Rail_1_Report.pdf

59.	Ian Taylor, Lynn Sloman, 'Rebuilding Rail'.

60.	Emily Gosden, 'Big Six energy companies' profits increased tenfold since 2007', Daily Mail, 16 March 2015. See http://www.telegraph.co.uk/news/earth/energy/11475989/Big-Six-energy-companies-profits-increased-tenfold-since-2007.html

61.	Simon Read, '24,000 die in winter as fuel poverty climbs', The Independent, 30 November 2012. See http://www.independent.co.uk/money/spend-save/24000-die-in-winter-as-fuel-poverty-climbs-8372461.html

62.	Simon Read, 'Big Six energy companies overcharging loyal customers by up to £234 a year says watchdog', The Independent, 18 February 2015. See http://www.independent.co.uk/news/business/news/big-six-energy-companies-overcharg-ing-loyal-customers-by-up-to-234-a-year-says-watchdog-10053050.html

63.	Tom Bawden, 'Should the Big Six be Nationalised?', The Independent, 3 December 2013. See http://www.independent.co.uk/environment/should-the-big-six-be-nationalised-8981112.html

64.	Andrew Cumbers, 'Policy paper: Renewing Public Ownership', Centre for Labour and Social Studies (Class), July 2014, p. 7. See http://classonline.org.uk/docs/Renewing_Public_Ownership_-_Andrew_Cumbers_FINAL.pdf

65.	Andrew Cumbers, 'Policy paper: Renewing Public Ownership', p. 25.

66.	David Cameron, 'Scotland's Community Land Ownership Story', Open Democracy UK, 28 August 2014. See https://www.opendemocracy.net/ourkingdom/david-cameron/scotlands-community-land-ownership-story

67.	Derek Wall, 'Defend, extend and deepen the commons', Red Pepper, 10 December 2015. See http://www.redpepper.org.uk/defend-extend-and-deepen-the-commons/

68.	Derek Wall, 'Defend, extend and deepen the commons'.

69. Michael Kumhof, Speech at the 31st Annual Monetary and Trade Conference, 17 April 2013. See https://vimeo.com/64807284

70. Lord Adair Turner, Speech to Stockholm School of Economics, 12 September 2013. See http://ineteconomics.org/sites/inet.civicactions.net/files/Adair%20 Turner%20Stockholm%20School%20of%20Economics%20September%2012.pdf

71. Paul Tucker, Speech to the Monetary Policy and the Markets Conference, 13 December 2007. See http://www.bankofengland.co.uk/archive/Documents/ historicpubs/speeches/2007/speech331.pdf

72. Sir Mervyn King, Speech to the South Wales Chamber of Commerce at the Millennium Centre, Cardiff, 23 October 2012. See http://www.bankofengland. co.uk/publications/Documents/speeches/2012/speech613.pdf

73. Michael Kumhof, Speech at the 31st Annual Monetary and Trade Conference, 17 April 2013. See https://vimeo.com/64807284

74. For an in-depth discussion, see Josh Ryan-Collins, Tony Greenham, Richard Werner, Andrew Jackson, *Where Does Money Come From,* 2nd edn (London: New Economics Foundation, 2012).

75. Andrew Jackson, Ben Dyson, 'Banking vs Democracy', Positive Money, February 2012. See http://positivemoney.org/wp-content/uploads/2012/06/Banking_Vs_ Democracy_Web.pdf

76. Josh Ryan-Collins, Tony Greenham, Richard Werner, Andrew Jackson, *Where Does Money Come From?*, p. 68.

77. Herman Daly, 'Nationalise Money, Not Banks', Center for the Advancement of the Steady State Economy, 4 February 2013. See http://steadystate.org/nation- alize-money-not-banks/

78. Andrew Jackson, Ben Dyson, *Modernising Money* (London: Positive Money, 2012), pp. 167-8.

79. This is a big part of the reason why the property boom was possible. Flooded with loans, the housing market saw prices increase far more quickly than wages, as more money chased the same number of houses. The think tank Positive Money calculated that while 'in 1996 the amount of take-home salary that a person on an average salary buying an average house would spend on their mortgage was 17.5 per cent, by 2008 this had risen to 49.3 per cent. In London the figures are even more shocking, rising from 22.2 per cent of take-home pay spent on their mortgage in 1997 to 66.6 per cent in 2008.'

80. Some of this comes back to us via the interest we get from savings accounts and the taxes that banks pay, but it's still a vast sum that serves to increase inequality. In effect, banks are able to rent out the money they create from

nothing. Positive Money has found that: 'The bottom 90% of the UK pays more interest to banks than they ever receive from them, which results in a redistribution of income from the bottom 90% of the population to the top 10%. Collectively we pay £165m every day in interest on personal loans alone (not including mortgages), and a total of £213bn a year in interest on all our debts.' See http://www.positivemoney.org/issues/inequality/

81. Lord Adair Turner, Speech at the South African Reserve Bank, 2 November 2012. See http://www.fsa.gov.uk/static/pubs/speeches/1102-at.pdf

82. Jaromir Benes, Michael Kumhof, 'The Chicago Plan Revisited', IMF Working Paper, August 2012, See https://www.imf.org/external/pubs/ft/wp/2012/wp12202.pdf

83. These include: '(1) Much better control of a major source of business cycle fluctuations, sudden increases and contractions of bank credit and of the supply of bank-created money. (2) Complete elimination of bank runs. (3) Dramatic reduction of the (net) public debt. (4) Dramatic reduction of private debt, as money creation no longer requires simultaneous debt creation.' (Jaromir Benes, Michael Kumhof, 'The Chicago Plan Revisited'.)

84. Andrew Jackson, a lead author of the proposal, writes: 'Lending occurs in this system when people move their money from their transaction account (held at the central bank) to an "investment account". This will be broadly similar to a time deposit today – there will be minimum notice periods, however, unlike today they will also carry some risk (i.e. if the underlying assets go bad they may lose some of their money). The money transferred to the banks will then be transferred to a borrower. So in this system lending by banks merely transfers money around the system, no new money or purchasing power is created when loans are made. Because in this system all money is held on the central bank's balance sheet any bank can be allowed to fail, without any effect on the money supply.' See Andrew Jackson, 'The Chicago Plan & Positive Money's proposals – What is the difference?', Positive Money blog, 23 January 2013. See https://www.positivemoney.org/2013/01/the-chicago-plan-versus-positive-money/

85. Some people worry that this newer system would provide less credit, with serious implications for the stability of the economy. For a discussion of this concern, see Andrew Jackson, 'Why there will be no "shortage of money"', Positive Money blog, 29 April 2014. See http://positivemoney.org/2014/04/ann-pettifor-there-will-be-no-shortage-of-money/

86. Nigel Morris, 'New Economic Crash Fears As British Families Run £40bn Deficit', The Independent, 21 December 2015. See http://www.independent.

co.uk/news/uk/home-news/fears-of-new-economic-crash-as-british-families-run-40bn-deficit-a6782221.html

87. Taken from their site. See http://www.federalreserve.gov/faqs/about_14986.htm

88. Following the example of the Federal Reserve since the 1980s, the primary focus of central banks has been to keep inflation low. The argument is that keeping inflation very low (below 2 per cent) is essential for a market system to prosper, as it maintains economic stability. The fact that the single-minded pursuit of this policy led to the massive and costly economic recession of 2008 has not dampened the enthusiasm of its supporters, even though the slight loss of efficiency due to a small rise in inflation is nothing compared to the gargantuan loss incurred by the collapse of the whole financial system.

89. Ha-Joon Chang, *Bad Samaritans* (London: Random House, 2007), p. 154.

90. Ha-Joon Chang, *Bad Samaritans*, p. 154.

91. Christopher Adolph, *Bankers, Bureaucrats, and Central Bank Politics: The Myth of Neutrality* (New York: Cambridge University Press, 2013).

92. Joseph Stiglitz, *The Price of Inequality*, p. 48.

93. For instance, participatory economics (Parecon), devised by Michael Albert and Robin Hahnel, attempts to transcend the failings of state-planning and free markets by introducing a mechinism that combines the best of both systems. It involves a nested structure of democratic worker councils and consumer councils. Each year, these councils formulate comprehensive plans for production and consumption which are then revised in an iterative process overseen by a facilitation board in order to converge on a single coherent plan for the year. It takes a while to grasp, but the idea has been worked out quite formally, having been fleshed out and debated over a few decades. It's an original solution to the problem of economic coordination and is worthy of serious consideration and experimentation.

94. David Schweickart, *After Capitalism* (2nd edn, Lanham, MD.: Rowman and Littlefield, 2011).

95. David Schweickart, *After Capitalism*, p. 46.

96. In fact, at times, Schweickart suggests, this per-capita criteria could be dropped in order to channel extra investment to those regions that are underdeveloped and underprivileged, but this would have to be settled democratically and transparently.

97. David Schweickart, *After Capitalism*, p. 54.

98. However, these grants do not constitute a completely free giveaway because the investment increases the assets of the enterprise thereby increasing its tax burden

and raising the level of its contribution to the national investment fund. The larger an enterprise's assets, the more tax it ends up paying. This tax can be thought of as the payment of interest on the grant, but not the repayment of the grant itself.

99. Schweickart sums up his model as follows: 'A flat-rate tax on the capital assets of all productive enterprises is collected by the central government, then plowed back into the economy, assisting those firms needing funds for purposes of productive investment. These funds are dispersed throughout society, first to regions and communities on a per capita basis, then to public banks in accordance with past performance, then to those firms with profitable project proposals. Profitable projects that promise increased employment are favoured over those that do not. At each level, national, regional, and local, legislatures decide what portion of the investment fund coming to them is to be set aside for public capital expenditures, then send down the remainder, no strings attached, to the next lower level. Associated with most banks are entrepreneurial divisions, which promote firm expansion and new firm creation.' (David Schweickart, *After Capitalism*, p. 56.)

11 Survival

1. This line comes from the 'Overview of the Millennium Ecosystem Assessment' on the project's website. See http://www.millenniumassessment.org/en/About.html

2. Will Steffen, Katherine Richardson, Johan Rockström, Sarah E. Cornell, Ingo Fetzer, Elena Bennett, Reinette Biggs, Stephen R. Carpenter, Wim de Vries, Cynthia A. de Wit, Carl Folke, Dieter Gerten, Jens Heinke, Georgina M. Mace, Linn M. Persson, Veerabhadran Ramanathan, Belinda Reyers, Sverker Sörlin, 'Planetary Boundaries: Guiding human development on a changing planet', *Science*, Vol. 347, No. 6223, 13 February 2015. For a summary of findings, see http://www.stockholmresilience.org/21/research/research-news/1-15-2015-planetary-boundaries-2.0---new-and-improved.html

3. Core writing team, R. K. Pachauri and L. A. Meyer (eds), 'IPCC, 2014: Climate Change 2014: Synthesis Report. Contribution of Working Groups I, II and III to the Fifth Assessment Report of the Intergovernmental Panel on Climate Change', Synthesis Report, Summary for Policymakers, p. 2. See https://www.ipcc.ch/pdf/assessment-report/ar5/syr/AR5_SYR_FINAL_SPM.pdf

4. Core writing team, R. K. Pachauri and L. A. Meyer (eds.), 'IPCC, 2014: Climate Change 2014: Synthesis Report', p. 8.

5. Edward A. G. Schuur, A. D. McGuire, C. Schädel, G. Grosse, J. W. Harden, D. J. Hayes, G. Hugelius, C. D. Koven, P. Kuhry, D. M. Lawrence, S. M. Natali, D. Olefeldt, V. E. Romanovsky, K. Schaefer, M. R. Turetsky, C. C. Treat, J. E. Vonk, 'Climate change and the permafrost carbon feedback', *Nature*, Vol. 520, No. 7576, 9 April 2015. See http://www.nature.com/nature/journal/v520/n7546/full/nature14338.html; Edward A. G. Schuur, James Bockheim, Josep G. Canadell, Eugenie Euskirchen, Christopher B. Field, Sergey V. Goryachkin, Stefan Hagemann, Peter Kuhry, Peter M. Lafleur, Hanna Lee, Galina Mazhitova, Frederick E. Nelson, Annette Rinke, Vladimir E. Romanovsky, Nikolay Shiklomanov, Charles Tarnocai, Sergey Venevsky, Jason G. Vogel, Sergei A. Zimov, 'Vulnerability of Permafrost Carbon to Climate Change: Implications for the Global Carbon Cycle', *BioScience*, Vol. 58, No. 8, 2008, pp. 701–14. See http://bioscience.oxfordjournals.org/content/58/8/701

6. John H. Richardson, 'When the End of Human Civilization is Your Day Job', *Esquire*, 7 July 2015. See http://www.esquire.com/news-politics/a36228/ballad-of-the-sad-climatologists-0815/

7. Dirk Bryant, Daniel Nielsen, Laura Tangley, *The Last Frontier Forests: Ecosystems and Economies on the Edge* (Washington DC: WorldWide Resource Institute, 1997), p. 1. For online e-book, see pdf.wri.org/lastfrontierforests.pdf

8. Key Findings, 'Global Forest Resource Assessment, Food and Agriculture Organization of the United Nations', 2010, p. 2. See http://foris.fao.org/static/data/fra2010/KeyFindings-en.pdf

9. Roddy Scheer, Doug Moss, 'Deforestation and Its Extreme Effect on Global Warming', *Scientific American*, 13 November 2012. See http://www.scientificamerican.com/article/deforestation-and-global-warming/

10. Juliette Jowit, 'Humans driving extinction faster than species can evolve, say experts', *The Guardian*, 7 March, 2010. See http://www.theguardian.com/environment/2010/mar/07/extinction-species-evolve

11. Nafeez Ahmed, 'Scientific model supported by UK Government Taskforce flags risk of civilisation's collapse by 2040', *Insurge Intelligence*, 19 June 2015. See https://medium.com/insurge-intelligence/uk-government-backed-scientific-model-flags-risk-of-civilisation-s-collapse-by-2040-4d121e455997#.6pvn5b6rx

12. James Hansen, Makiko Sato, Pushker Kharecha, David Beerling, Valerie Masson-Delmotte, Mark Pagani, Maureen Raymo, Dana L. Royer, James C. Zachos, 'Target Atmospheric CO_2: Where Should Humanity Aim?', *The Open Atmospheric Science Journal*, Vol. 2, 7 April 2008, pp. 217–31. See http://droyer.web.wesleyan.edu/Target_CO2_%28Hansen_et_al%29.pdf

13. Andrew Simms, Victoria Johnson, Peter Chowla, 'Growth Isn't Possible', New Economics Foundation, January 2010. See http://s.bsd.net/nefoundation/ default/page/file/f19c45312a905d73c3_rbm6iecku.pdf

14. Matt McGrath, 'Warming to Breach 1°C Threshold', BBC News website, 9 November 2015. See http://www.bbc.co.uk/news/science-environment-34763036

15. Steve Connor, 'Father of Climate Change: 2°C Limit is Not Enough', *The Independent*, 8 December 2011. See http://www.independent.co.uk/environment/ climate-change/father-of-climate-change-2c-limit-is-not-enough-6273721.html. Another useful article is Suzanne Goldenberg, 'UN's 2°C target will fail to avoid a climate disaster, scientists warn', *The Guardian*, 3 December 2013. See http:// www.theguardian.com/environment/2013/dec/03/un-2c-global-warming-climate- change

16. Adam Vaughan, 'Paris climate talks: what difference will temperature rises really make?', *The Guardian*, 4 December 2015. See http://www.theguardian.com/ environment/2015/dec/04/paris-climate-talks-what-difference-will-temperature -rises-really-make

17. Duncan Clark, 'How much of the world's fossil fuel can we burn?', *The Guardian*, 25 March 2015. See http://www.theguardian.com/environment/keep-it-in-the-ground- blog/2015/mar/25/what-numbers-tell-about-how-much-fossil-fuel-reserves- cant-burn

18. Kevin Anderson, 'Duality in Climate Science', *Nature Geoscience*, Vol. 8, 12 October 2015. See http://kevinanderson.info/blog/category/papers-reports/

19. Kevin Anderson, 'Duality in Climate Science'.

20. 'Six years worth of current emissions would blow the carbon budget for 1.5 degrees', Carbon Brief, 13 November 2014. See http://www.carbonbrief.org/ six-years-worth-of-current-emissions-would-blow-the-carbon-budget-for-1-5- degrees. For a 50 per cent chance of staying below 1.5 °C, assuming the same emission levels, we have a carbon budget that lasts until 2025.

21. Mike Berners-Lee, Duncan Clark, *The Burning Question* (London: Profile Books, 2013), p. 27.

22. Mike Berners-Lee, Duncan Clark, *The Burning Question*, p. 27.

23. Kevin Anderson, Alice Bows, 'A 2°C Target? Get Real, Because 4°C is on its Way', *Parliamentary Brief*, Vol. 13, No. 3, December 2010, p. 19. See http:// kevinanderson.info/blog/wp-content/uploads/2012/11/Parliamentary-Brief- p19-Dec-20101.pdf

24. Sarah Morrison, 'Leaked climate change report: Scientific body warns of "devas- tating rise of 4–5°C if we carry on as we are"', *The Independent*, 12 April 2014. See http://www.independent.co.uk/environment/climate-change/leaked-

climate-change-report-scientific-body-warns-of-devastating-rise-of-4-5c-if-we-carry-on-as-we-9256708.html

A 5°C increase is predicted by Michael E. Mann, 'The Power of Paris: Climate Challenge Remains, But Now We're on the Right Path', *Huffington Post*, 12 December 2015. See http://www.huffingtonpost.com/michael-e-mann/paris-climate-change_b_8799764.html

25.   For a summary of the effects of climate change that we are already experiencing, see Bill McKibben, *Eaarth: Making a Life on a Tough New Planet* (New York: Henry Holt & Co., 2010).

26.   Kiley Kroh, 'UN Chief Scientist Urges Action On Climate Change: "We Have Five Minutes Before Midnight"', *Think Progress*, 3 September 2013. See http://thinkprogress.org/climate/2013/09/03/2561751/climate-scientist-midnight/

27.   Damian Carrington, 'Carbon reserves held by top fossil fuel companies soar', *The Guardian*, 19 April 2015. See http://www.theguardian.com/environment/2015/apr/19/carbon-reserves-held-by-top-fossil-fuel-companies-soar

28.   Bill McKibben, 'Global Warming's Terrifying New Maths', *Rolling Stone*, 19 July 2012. See http://www.rollingstone.com/politics/news/global-warmings-terrifying-new-math-20120719

29.   Increases in energy efficiency appear to have increased our overall emissions. This is known as the 'rebound effect'. It occurs because increased efficiency reduces costs and this frees up money that can then be spent on additional consumption. The effect was first identified in the nineteenth century by William Stanley Jevons in his study of the efficiency gains of using coal as a fuel source. The rebound effect does not mean innovation and new technologies will not play a central role in creating a sustainable world. It just means it won't be enough without a global cap on emissions to prevent the rebound effect taking place.

30.   Consider the mechanism known as 'fee and dividend', which is an alternative to the watered down, inadequate cap-and-trade proposals that have garnered the most support from politicians and fossil fuel companies. Numerous economists support this proposal as well as leading climatologist turned activist James Hansen. Fee and dividend works surprisingly simply. A fee is charged at the source of fossil fuel production, or at the port of entry for each fuel (coal, gas and oil). This fee is uniform and amounts to a given number of dollars for every ton of carbon dioxide that the fuel will release when burned. The increased price in fuel would lead to an increased price in goods in proportion to the amount fossil fuels are used in their production. The fee for carbon would rise gradually over time, allowing people and businesses to

adjust their behaviour accordingly in response to the rising prices of fossil-fuel intensive products. So what happens to the money generated by the fees collected? The money would be distributed equally across society to every adult (with half shares for children). A uniform disbursement of the fees would function as a progressive tax, as the wealthy would end up paying much more on the fossil-fuel intensive goods they consume than the portion of the fee they receive. This measure would provide a financial incentive for everyone to reduce their carbon footprint, the power of which would grow as the carbon fee was steadily raised. Alternatively, Oliver Tickle sets out an effective and sophisticated cap-and-trade mechanism in his important book *Kyoto2* (London: Zed Books, 2008). His system would raise about $1 trillion a year through the auction of carbon permits which would be used to 'tackle the causes and consequences of climate change'. Contraction and convergence is another model. It would involve permits being handed to nations, initially to reflect their current emissions, but with each year the amount allocated would drop and become more equitable so that, by a given date in the future, permits would be handed out in proportion to population (and of course the total number of permits would not exceed the global cap).

31. Naomi Klein, 'This Changes Everything: Capitalism vs. The Climate', *Huffington Post*, 6 March 2015. See http://www.huffingtonpost.ca/naomi-klein/naomi-klein-book_b_6812200.html

32. John Vidal, 'Carbon targets pledged at Copenhagen "fail to keep temperature rise to 2°C"', *The Guardian*, 12 February 2010. See http://www.theguardian.com/environment/2010/feb/12/copenhagen-carbon-emission-pledges

33. Fiona Harvey, 'World Bank president celebrates "game changer" Paris talks', *The Guardian*, 13 December 2015. See http://www.theguardian.com/business/2015/dec/13/world-bank-president-celebrates-game-changer-paris-talks

34. Kelly Levin, Taryn Fransen, 'INSIDER: Why Are INDC Studies Reaching Different Temperature Estimates?', World Resources Institute, 9 November 2015. See http://www.wri.org/blog/2015/11/insider-why-are-indc-studies-reaching-different-temperature-estimates

35. Kevin Anderson, 'The Paris Agreement: 10/10 for presentation; 4/10 for content. Shows promise . . .', 13 December 2015. See http://kevinanderson.info/blog/the-paris-agreement-1010-for-presentation-410-for-content-shows-promise/

36. Pete Smith, Steven J. Davis, Felix Creutzig, Sabine Fuss, Jan Minx, Benoit Gabrielle, Etsushi Kato, Robert B. Jackson, Annette Cowie, Elmar Kriegler, Detlef P. van Vuuren, Joeri Rogelj, Philippe Ciais, Jennifer Milne, Josep G.

Canadell, David McCollum, Glen Peters, Robbie Andrew, Volker Krey, Gyami Shrestha, Pierre Friedlingstein, Thomas Gasser, Arnulf Grübler, Wolfgang K. Heidug, Matthias Jonas, et al., 'Biophysical and economic limits to negative CO2 emissions', *Nature Climate Change*, Vol. 6, 7 December 2015. See http://www.nature.com/nclimate/journal/v6/n1/full/nclimate2870.html

37. Mark Z. Jacobson, Mark A. Delucchi, 'A Plan to Power 100 Percent of the Planet with Renewables', *Scientific American*, 1 November 2009. See http://www.scientificamerican.com/article/a-path-to-sustainable-energy-by-2030/; Mark Z. Jacobson, Mark A. Delucchi, 'Providing all global energy with wind, water, and solar power, Part I: Technologies, energy resources, quantities and areas of infrastructure and materials', *Energy Policy*, Vol. 39, No. 3, pp. 1154–69.

38. Louis Bergeron, 'The World Can Be Powered By Alternative Energy, Using Today's Technology, In 20–40 Years, Says Stanford Researcher Mark Z. Jacobson', *Stanford News*, 26 January 2011. See http://news.stanford.edu/news/2011/january/jacobson-world-energy-012611.html

39. Mark Fischetti, '139 Countries Could Get All of Their Power from Renewable Sources', *Scientific American*, 19 November 2015. See http://www.scientificamerican.com/article/139-countries-could-get-all-of-their-power-from-renewable-sources1/

40. 'Latin America and the Caribbean could cover all their electricity needs using renewable resources: IDB report', Inter-American Development Bank, News, 13 June 2013. See http://www.iadb.org/en/news/webstories/2013-06-18/renewable-energy-in-latin-america-and-the-caribbean,10486.html

41. Jonathan Watts, 'Uruguay makes dramatic shift to nearly 95% electricity from clean energy', *The Guardian*, 3 December 2015. See http://www.theguardian.com/environment/2015/dec/03/uruguay-makes-dramatic-shift-to-nearly-95-clean-energy

42. 'World Economic and Social Survey 2011: The Great Green Technological Transformation', United Nations Department of Economic and Social Affairs, 2011, pp. xxii, p. 174. See http://www.un.org/en/development/desa/policy/wess/wess_current/2011wess.pdf

43. Simon Rogers, 'Military Spending: How much does the military cost each country, listed', *The Guardian*, 17 April 2012. See http://www.theguardian.com/news/datablog/2012/apr/17/military-spending-countries-list

44. 'Innovative financing at a global and European level', European Parliament Resolution, 8 March 2011, p. 5. See http://www.europarl.europa.eu/sides/getDoc.do?pubRef=-//EP//NONSGML+TA+P7-TA-2011-0080+0+DOC+PDF+V0//EN

45. 'Mobilizing Climate Finance: A paper prepared at the request of G20 Finance Ministers', World Bank group, 6 October 2011, p. 15. See https://www.imf.org/external/np/g20/pdf/110411c.pdf

46. Duncan Clark, 'Campaigners demand an end to $1tn fossil fuel subsidies', *The Guardian*, 18 June 2012. See http://www.theguardian.com/environment/blog/2012/jun/18/campaigners-end-fossil-fuel-subsidies

47. Damian Carrington, 'G20 countries pay over $1,000 per citizen in fossil fuel subsidies, says IMF', *The Guardian*, 4 August 2015. See http://www.theguardian.com/environment/2015/aug/04/g20-countries-pay-over-1000-per-citizen-in-fossil-fuel-subsidies-say-imf

48. 'Climate change: Too hot to handle', *The Scotsman*, 28 November 2009. See http://www.scotsman.com/news/climate-change-too-hot-to-handle-1-1363112

49. 'Turn Down the Heat', A Report for the World Bank by the Potsdam Institute for Climate Impact Research and Climate Analytics, November 2012, p. xviii. See http://climateanalytics.org/files/turn_down_the_heat_11-16-12.pdf

50. James Randerson, 'Climate change: Prepare for global temperature rise of 4°C, warns top scientist', *The Guardian*, 7 August 2008. See http://www.theguardian.com/environment/2008/aug/06/climatechange.scienceofclimatechange

51. 'Climate change: Too hot to handle', *The Scotsman*.

52. Jenny Fyall, 'Warming will "wipe out billions"', *The Scotsman*, 29 November 2009. The original article no longer seems to be online.

53. James Kanter, 'Scientist: Warming could cut population to 1 billion', *New York Times*, 13 March 2009. See http://dotearth.blogs.nytimes.com/2009/03/13/scientist-warming-could-cut-population-to-1-billion/?_r=0

54. Bertrand Russell, *Autobiography* (1975; New York: Routledge, 2010), p. 620.

55. Naomi Oreskes, Erik M. Conway, *Merchants of Doubt* (New York: Bloomsbury Press, 2010).

56. A group of ideological fellow travellers would soon join these scientists in their attempts to discredit inconvenient truths. These included Dixy Lee Ray (a zoologist and former chair of the Atomic Energy Commission) and Patrick Michaels (a climatologist).

57. Naomi Oreskes, Erik M. Conway, *Merchants of Doubt*, p. 7.

58. Suzanne Goldenberg, 'Exxon knew of climate change in 1981, email says – but it funded deniers for 27 more years', *The Guardian*, 8 July 2015. See http://www.theguardian.com/environment/2015/jul/08/exxon-climate-change-1981-climate-denier-funding

59. Katie Jennings, Dino Grandoni, Susanne Rust, 'How Exxon went from leader

to skeptic on climate change research', *Los Angeles Times*, 23 October 2015. See http://graphics.latimes.com/exxon-research/

60. Teena Gabrielson, Cheryl Hall, John M. Meyer, David Schlosberg (eds), *The Oxford Handbook of Environmental Political Theory* (Oxford: Oxford University Press, 2016), p. 452.

61. Katie Jennings, Dino Grandoni, Susanne Rust, 'How Exxon went from leader to skeptic on climate change research'.

62. Jay Yarow, '2,340 lobbyists have an opinion on how best to enact climate policy', *Business Insider*, 25 February 2009. See http://www.businessinsider.com/2340-lobbyists-have-an-opinion-on-how-best-to-enact-climate-policy-2009-2

63. Suzanne Goldenberg, 'Secret funding helped build vast network of climate denial thinktanks', *The Guardian*, 14 February 2013. See http://www.theguardian.com/environment/2013/feb/14/funding-climate-change-denial-thinktanks-network

64. Suzanne Goldenberg, 'Secret funding helped build vast network of climate denial thinktanks'.

65. Mike Berners-Lee, Duncan Clark, *The Burning Question*, p. 173.

66. 'Big drop in those who believe that global warming is coming', Harris Interactive, Press Release, 2 December 2009. See http://media.theharrispoll.com/documents/Harris-Interactive-Poll-Research-Global-Warming-2009-12.pdf? 'Most Americans think devastating natural disasters are increasing', Harris Interactive, Press Release, 7 July 2011. See http://www.theharrispoll.com/politics/Most_Americans_Think_Devastating_Natural_Disasters_Are_Increasing.html

67. Emma Howard, 'Rising numbers of Americans believe climate science, poll shows', *The Guardian*, 13 October 2015. See http://www.theguardian.com/environment/2015/oct/13/rising-numbers-of-american-believe-climate-science-poll-shows; Bruce Stokes, Richard Wike, Jill Carle, 'Global concern about climate change, broad support for limiting emissions', Pew Research Centre, 5 November 2015. See http://www.pewglobal.org/2015/11/05/global-concern-about-climate-change-broad-support-for-limiting-emissions/

68. Naomi Klein, *This Changes Everything* (London: Allen Lane, 2014), pp. 195–6.

69. Jonathan Porritt, 'It is "impossible" for today's big oil companies to adapt to climate change', *The Guardian*, 15 January 2015. See http://www.theguardian.com/environment/2015/jan/15/it-is-impossible-todays-big-oil-companies-adapt-climate-change-jonathon-porritt

70. 'Silent But Deadly', Global Justice Now, Policy Briefing, December 2015. See http://www.globaljustice.org.uk/sites/default/files/files/resources/cop-paris-briefing-online.pdf

71. Robert McSweeney, 'Farming overtakes deforestation and land use as a driver of climate change', Carbon Brief, 12 January 2015. See http://www.carbonbrief.org/farming-overtakes-deforestation-and-land-use-as-a-driver-of-climate-change

72. Sonia J. Vermeulen, Bruce M. Campbell, 'Climate Change and Food Systems', Annual Review of Environment and Resources, Vol. 37, 30 July 2012, pp. 195–222. See https://sustainabledevelopment.un.org/content/documents/881annurev.pdf

73. Robert McSweeney, 'Meat and dairy consumption could mean a two-degree target is "off the table"', Carbon Brief, 2 December 2014. See http://www.carbonbrief.org/meat-and-dairy-consumption-could-mean-a-two-degree-target-is-off-the-table

74. 'Eco-farming can double food production in 10 years, says new UN report', United Nations Human Rights website, 8 March 2011. See http://www.ohchr.org/en/NewsEvents/Pages/DisplayNews.aspx?NewsID=10819&LangID=E

75. 'Eco-farming can double food production in 10 years, says new UN report'.

76. Naomi Klein, 'How will everything change under climate change?', The Guardian, 8 March 2015. See http://www.theguardian.com/environment/2015/mar/08/how-will-everything-change-under-climate-change

77. Donella H. Meadows, Dennis L. Meadows, Jorgen Randers, William W. Behrens III, 'The Limits to Growth: A Report to The Club of Rome' (Short Version), 1972. See http://web.ics.purdue.edu/~wggray/Teaching/His300/Illustrations/Limits-to-Growth.pdf

78. Bill McKibben, Eaarth, p. 93.

79. Jeff Hecht, 'Prophesy of Economic Collapse "Coming True"', New Scientist, 17 November 2008. See https://www.newscientist.com/article/dn16058-prophesy-of-economic-collapse-coming-true/. The full study is Graham Turner, 'A Comparison of the Limits of Growth with Thirty Years of Reality', Socio-Economics and the Environment in Discussion, CSIRO Working Paper Series 2008–09, June 2008. See http://www.manicore.com/fichiers/Turner_Meadows_vs_historical_data.pdf

   For a summary, read Graham Turner, Cathy Alexander, 'Limits to growth was right. New research shows we're nearing collapse', The Guardian, 2 September 2014. See http://www.theguardian.com/commentisfree/2014/sep/02/limits-to-growth-was-right-new-research-shows-were-nearing-collapse

80. Bill McKibben, Deep Economy (New York: Henry Holt, 2007), p. 10.

81. H. W. Arndt, The Rise and Fall of Economic Growth (Sydney: Longman Cheshire, 1978), p. 30.

82. Robin Hahnel, Green Economics (New York: Routledge, 2010), p. 4.

83. Fridolin Krausmann, Simone Gingrich, Nina Eisenmenger, Karl-Heinz Erb, Helmut Haberl, Marina Fischer-Kowalski, 'Growth in global materials use, GDP and population during the 20th century', *Ecological Economics*, Vol. 68, No. 10, August 2009, pp. 2696–705.

84. Donella H. Meadows, Jorgen Randers, Dennis L. Meadows, *The Limits To Growth: The 30-Year Update* (White River Junction, VT: Chelsea Green, 2004), p. 204.

85. N. Gregory Mankiw, *Principles of Economics*, 7th edn (Mason, OH: South-Western Cengage Learning, 2015), p. 532.

86. Tim Jackson, *Prosperity Without Growth* (Abingdon, Oxon and New York: Earthscan, 2009).

87. Tim Jackson, *Prosperity Without Growth*, p. 14.

88. Vaclav Smil, 'Moore's Curse and the Great Energy Delusion', *The American*, 19 November 2008. See http://www.vaclavsmil.com/wp-content/uploads/docs/ smil-article-20081119-the_American.pdf

89. Elizabeth Kolbert, 'The Weight of the World', *New Yorker*, 24 August 2015. See http://www.newyorker.com/magazine/2015/08/24/the-weight-of-the-world

90. Joseph E. Stiglitz, Amartya Sen, Jean-Paul Fitoussi, *Mis-Measuring Our Lives: Why GDP Doesn't Add Up*, The Report by the Commission on the Measurement of Economic Performance and Social Progress (New York: The New Press, 2010), p. xvii.

91. Joseph E. Stiglitz, Amartya Sen, Jean-Paul Fitoussi, *Mis-Measuring Our Lives*, p. xx.

92. Associated Press, 'Air pollution in China is killing 4,000 people every day, a new study finds', *The Guardian*, 14 August 2015. See http://www.theguardian. com/world/2015/aug/14/air-pollution-in-china-is-killing-4000-people-every- day-a-new-study-finds

93. Jennifer Pak, 'Chinese buy up bottles of fresh air from Canada', *The Telegraph*, 15 December 2015. See http://www.telegraph.co.uk/news/worldnews/asia/ china/12051354/Chinese-buy-up-bottles-of-fresh-air-from-Canada.html

94. John Vidal, 'Air pollution: a dark cloud of filth poisons the world's cities', *The Guardian*, 16 January 2016. See http://www.theguardian.com/global- development/2016/jan/16/winter-smog-hits-worlds-cities-air-pollution-soars? CMP=share_btn_fb

95. John Vidal, 'Air pollution: a dark cloud of filth poisons the world's cities'.

96. For a useful and accessible introduction to steady state economics, see Dan O'Neill, Rob Dietz, *Enough Is Enough* (Abingdon, Oxon: Routledge, 2013).

97. Population growth also drives economic growth. All else being equal, we

approach ecological limits at a faster pace when there are more of us. In order to stabilise our emissions and the scale of our economy we must also stabilise our numbers. As conditions worsen globally, which they will whatever we do, certain areas of the world will become less habitable. If this happens, as populations increase, more and more people will be forced to live in locations that have a high risk of severe flooding and other extreme natural disasters. There are a number of progressive measures that can serve the goal of population stabilisation. Making effective forms of contraception available to those who have previously had little access is essential. Working to increase the rights and opportunities of women globally, apart from being an extremely important social goal in itself, has proven to be an effective check on population growth. We should be encouraged by the strong correlation between diminishing birth rates, increased economic well-being, and expanding women's rights.

98. John Stuart Mill, *Principles of Political Economy*, Book IV, Chapter VI. See http://www.econlib.org/library/Mill/mlP61.html

99. Ann Pettifor (ed.), *Real World Economic Outlook* (Basingstoke: Palgrave Macmillan, 2003), p. 135.

100. Robert Frank, *Luxury Fever* (New York: The Free Press, 2000), p. 73.

101. Bill McKibben, *Deep Economy*, pp. 34–5.

102. George Monbiot, 'In this age of diamond saucepans, only a recession makes sense', *The Guardian*, 9 October 2007. See http://www.theguardian.com/commentisfree/2007/oct/09/comment.economy

103. David Woodward, Andrew Simms, 'Growth is failing the poor: the unbalanced distribution of the benefits and costs of global economic growth', DESA Working Paper No. 20, *Economic and Social Affairs*, March 2006. See http://www.un.org/esa/desa/papers/2006/wp20_2006.pdf

104. Anne Krueger, 'Letting the future in: India's continuing reform agenda', Speech at the Stanford India conference, Stanford University, 4 June 2004. See https://www.imf.org/external/np/speeches/2004/060404.htm

105. David Woodward, Andrew Simms, 'Growth is failing the poor: the unbalanced distribution of the benefits and costs of global economic growth'.

106. Robin Hahnel, *Green Economics*, p. 81.

107. Robin Hahnel, *Green Economics*, p. 81

108. Ian Dew-Becker, Robert J. Gordon, 'Where Did the Productivity Growth Go? Inflation Dynamics and the Distribution of Income', Brookings Papers on Economic Activity, Fall Issue, 2005, pp. 67–150. See http://www.brookings.edu/~/media/Projects/BPEA/Fall2005/2005b_bpea_dewbecker.PDF

109. Ian Dew-Becker, Robert J. Gordon, 'Where Did the Productivity Growth Go? Inflation Dynamics and the Distribution of Income'.

110. Daniel O'Neill, 'The economics of enough', *The Guardian*, 1 May 2013. See http://www.theguardian.com/business/economics-blog/2013/may/01/economics-of-enough

111. David Graeber, 'A Practical Utopian's Guide to the Coming Collapse', *The Baffler*, No. 22, 2013. See http://thebaffler.com/salvos/a-practical-utopians-guide-to-the-coming-collapse

112. Bill McKibben, 'Climate fight won't wait for Paris: vive la resistance', *The Guardian*, 9 March 2015. See http://www.theguardian.com/environment/2015/mar/09/climate-fight-wont-wait-for-paris-vive-la-resistance

113. John H. Richardson, 'When the End of Human Civilization is Your Day Job'.

114. Naomi Klein, 'Why Unions Need to Join the Climate Fight', speech at the founding convention of UNIFOR, 1 September 2013. See http://www.naomiklein.org/articles/2013/09/why-unions-need-join-climate-fight

115. 'Mark Serwotka: Trade Unions And The Environmental Movement Are Natural Allies', Desmog UK, 9 April 2015. See http://www.desmog.uk/2015/04/09/mark-serwotka-trade-unions-and-environmental-movement-are-natural-allies

116. 'One Million Climate Jobs', Campaign Against Climate Change, 2014. See http://www.campaigncc.org/sites/data/files/Docs/one_million_climate_jobs_2014.pdf

117. 'Netherlands ordered to cut greenhouse gas emissions', BBC News, 24 June 2015. See http://www.bbc.co.uk/news/world-europe-33253772

118. Pope Francis, 'Encyclical Letter *Laudato Si.*' Of The Holy Father Francis, On Came For Our Common Home', 17 June 2015, para. 217. See http://w2.vatican.va/content/francesco/en/encyclicals/documents/papa-francesco_20150524_enciclica_laudato-si.html

119. Doug Bolton, 'Denmark produces 140 per cent of its electricity needs through wind power', *The Independent*, 10 July 2015. See http://www.independent.co.uk/environment/denmark-produces-140-per-cent-of-its-electricity-needs-through-wind-power-10381648.html

120. Martin Lukacs, '"Historic" Toronto climate march calls for new economic vision', *The Guardian*, 6 July 2015. See http://www.theguardian.com/environment/true-north/2015/jul/06/historic-toronto-climate-march-calls-for-new-economic-vision?CMP=share_btn_fb

121. John Jordan, 'The day we stopped Europe's biggest polluter in its tracks', *The*

Guardian, 27 August 2015. See http://www.theguardian.com/commentis-free/2015/aug/27/europes-biggest-polluter-protesters-lignite-mine-germany-direct-action

122. 'Renewable Electricity Generation Climbs To Second Place After Coal', International Energy Agency, 6 August 2015. See http://www.iea.org/newsroomandevents/news/2015/august/renewable-electricity-generation-climbs-to-second-place-after-coal.html

123. Karl Ritter, 'Brazil pledges to cut greenhouse gas emissions', Associated Press, 27 September 2015. See http://bigstory.ap.org/article/546bf2c0c20d4a99-adf59cf5321b3dd2/brazil-pledges-cut-greenhouse-gas-emissions; Nick Visser, 'The World Has Pledged to Divest $2.6 Trillion from Fossil Fuels', *Huffington Post*, 22 September 2015. See http://www.huffingtonpost.com/entry/fossil-fuel-divestment_56016c87e4b0fde8b0cfc539

124. 'Countdown to the Climate Summit', Global Witness, 20 November 2015. See https://www.globalwitness.org/campaigns/environmental-activists/7-days-until-climate-summit/

125. U. Thara Srinivasan, Susan P. Carey, Eric Hallstein, Paul A. T. Higgins, Amber C. Kerr, Laura E. Koteen, Adam B. Smith, Reg Watson, John Harte, Richard B. Norgaardd, 'The Debt of Nations and the Distribution of Ecological Impacts from Human Activities', *Proceedings of the National Academy of Sciences*, Vol. 105, No. 5, 5 February 2008, pp. 1768–73.

126. Daniel W. O'Neill, 'The Proximity of Nations to a Socially Sustainable Steady-State Economy', *Journal of Cleaner Production*, Vol. 108, Part A, December 2015, pp. 1213–31. See http://www.sciencedirect.com/science/article/pii/S0959652615010471

127. See the Climate Fairshares website: http://www.climatefairshares.org/. Also, the Greenhouse Development Rights website: http://gdrights.org/

128. John Vidal, 'Rio+20: Earth summit dawns with stormier clouds than in 1992', *The Guardian*, 19 June 2012. See http://www.theguardian.com/environment/2012/jun/19/rio-20-earth-summit-1992-2012

12 Empathy

1. Two varieties of empathy have been distinguished: affective and cognitive. Affective empathy refers to the capacity to share in another person's emotional state, the capacity to feel anguish when we see someone else in anguish, for instance. Cognitive empathy refers to the capacity to take another's perspective, to understand their mental state. Researchers have suggested that psychopaths

possess cognitive empathy, but not affective, and people with autism possess affective empathy, but not cognitive. Empathy, as discussed in this chapter, refers to both of these capacities.

2. Morten Kringelbach, Helen Phillips, *Emotion: Pleasure and Pain in the Brain* (Oxford: Oxford University Press), pp. 104–5.

3. Nathalia Gjersoe, 'The moral life of babies', *The Guardian*, 12 October 2013. See http://www.theguardian.com/science/2013/oct/12/babies-moral-life

4. Simon Baron-Cohen, *Zero Degrees of Empathy* (London: Penguin, 2011), p. 20.

5. Roman Krznaric, *Empathy: Why It Matters, and How To Get It* (London: Ebury Publishing, 2014), pp. 17–20.

6. Roman Krznaric, 'In Search of Our Inner Ape: An Interview with Frans de Waal', Outrospection, 14 November 2009. See http://www.romankrznaric.com/outrospection/2009/11/14/152

7. Simon Baron-Cohen, *Zero Degrees of Empathy*, p. 103.

8. Nils Christie, 'Too Much of Nothing. The Senseless Prisons'. See https://www.youtube.com/watch?v=Jah_txmOf-k

9. Susan Fiske, 'From Dehumanization and Objectification to Rehumanization: Neuroimaging Studies on the Building Blocks of Empathy', *Annals of the New York Academy of Sciences*, Vol. 1167, 24 June 2009, pp. 32–4.

10. Peter Singer, *The Expanding Circle* (1981; repr. Oxford: Princeton University Press, 2011).

11. Peter Singer's own views on who should be included in the circle of altruism are problematic. His stance on who should count as a 'person', on infanticide, particularly his beliefs about infants born with a severe disability, are overly simplistic and offensive to many.

12. I will use the idea of moral exclusion interchangeably with the idea of dehumanisation. Both occur on a spectrum.

13. Susan Opotow, 'Moral Exclusion and Injustice: An Introduction', *Journal of Social Issues*, Vol. 46, No. 1, Spring 1990, pp. 1–20.

14. Jonathan Glover, *Humanity: A Moral History of the Twentieth Century* (London: Jonathan Cape, 1999).

15. Ernst Klee, Willi Dressen, Volker Riess (eds), *"The Good Old Days": The Holocaust as Seen by Its Perpetrators and Bystanders* (Saybrook: Konecky & Konecky, 1988).

16. 'Crime and Civilization: An Interview with Nils Christie', *New Internationalist*, Issue 282, August 1996. See http://newint.org/features/1996/08/05/crime/

17. 'Crime and Civilization: An Interview with Nils Christie', *New Internationalist*.

18. Solomon Northup, *Twelve Years a Slave* (1853; London: Penguin Classics, 2012), pp. 56–7.

19. 'David Livingstone Smith: Psychology of Violence', *Forbes India*, 4 June 2010. See http://www.forbes.com/2010/06/15/forbes-india-david-livingstone-smith-psychology-of-violence-opinions-ideas-10-smith.html

20. David Livingstone Smith, *Less Than Human* (New York: St Martin's Press, 2011), p. 18.

21. David Livingstone Smith, *Less Than Human*, pp. 17–19.

22. Thomas Nagel, *Mortal Questions* (1979; Cambridge: Cambridge University Press, 1991), p. 26.

23. Paul Connolly, Alan Smith, Bernie Kelly, 'Too Young To Notice?', Community Relations Council, 2002. See http://www.unescocentre.ulster.ac.uk/pdfs/pdfs_alan/2002_Too_Young_to_Notice.pdf

24. Daniel Bar-Tal, 'Development of social categories and stereotypes in early childhood: the case of "the Arab" concept formation, stereotype and attitudes by Jewish children in Israel', *International Journal of Intercultural Relations*, Vol. 20, Issues 3–4, Summer–Autumn, 1996, pp. 341–70.

25. Patricia G. Devine, 'Stereotypes and prejudice: Their automatic and controlled components', *Journal of Personality and Social Psychology*, Vol. 56, January 1989, pp. 5–18.

26. Or Kashti, 'Israel Bans Novel on Arab-Jewish Romance From Schools for "Threatening Jewish Identity"', Haaretz, 31 December 2015. See http://www.haaretz.com/israel-news/.premium-1.694620

27. Otto Santa Ana, *Brown Tide Rising* (Austin: University of Texas, 2002).

28. Jessica Elgot, Matthew Taylor, 'Calais crisis: Cameron condemned for "dehumanising" description of migrants', *The Guardian*, 30 July 2015. See http://www.theguardian.com/uk-news/2015/jul/30/david-cameron-migrant-swarm-language-condemned

29. Phillip Atiba Goff, Jennifer L. Eberhardt, Melissa J. Williams, Matthew Christian Jackson, 'Not Yet Human: Implicit Knowledge, Historical Dehumanization, and Contemporary Consequences', *Journal of Personality and Social Psychology*, Vol. 94, No. 2, 2008, pp. 292–306.

30. In 2015, in a desperate bid to reach safety, thousands of refugees – men, women and many children – drowned in the Mediterranean. Most of them were fleeing war yet the UN did little to help them. Outrage was minimal. In the same year, a terrorist attack in Beirut killed over forty people, injuring hundreds more. A father, Adel Termos, courageously wrestled one of the bombers to the ground, saving many lives in the process, while sacrificing his own. It was barely reported.

The very next day another terrorist attack killed over 100 people, this time in Paris. Newspapers and television networks across the world covered it. In an act of solidarity, many countries projected the French flag onto some of their significant monuments and buildings. Facebook even provided its users with the option of placing a transparent French flag over their profile picture. Outrage was palpable.

31. Spencer Ackerman, '41 men targeted but 1,147 people killed: US drone strikes – the facts on the ground', *The Guardian*, 24 November 2014. See http://www.theguardian.com/us-news/2014/nov/24/-sp-us-drone-strikes-kill-1147

32. Chris Woods, '"Drones causing mass trauma among civilians," major study finds', *The Bureau of Investigative Journalism*, 25 September 2012. See https://www.thebureauinvestigates.com/2012/09/25/drones-causing-mass-trauma-among-civilians-major-study-finds/

33. Jack Serle, 'UN expert labels CIA tactic exposed by bureau "a war crime"', *The Bureau of Investigative Journalism*, 21 June 2012. See https://www.thebureauinvestigates.com/2012/06/21/un-expert-labels-cia-tactic-exposed-by-bureau-a-war-crime/

34. Ed Pilkington, 'Life as a drone operator: "ever step on ants and never give it another thought"?', *The Guardian*, 19 November 2015. See http://www.theguardian.com/world/2015/nov/18/life-as-a-drone-pilot-creech-air-force-base-nevada

35. See full letter here: https://www.documentcloud.org/documents/2515596-final-drone-letter.html

36. Ed Pilkington, 'Life as a drone operator: "ever step on ants and never give it another thought?"'

37. One might argue that as long as governments do not break international laws (as they often do), they are justified in fighting for their self-perceived interest. But the international legal framework is itself a product of powerful nations attempting to secure advantages over other nations, and so it can be terribly unjust.

38. Dominic Raab, 'Time for a foreign policy that puts Britain first', *The Telegraph*, 14 September 2011. See http://www.telegraph.co.uk/news/uknews/defence/8762714/Time-for-a-foreign-policy-that-puts-Britain-first.html

39. Hans J. Morgenthau, *Politics Among Nations: The Struggle for Power and Peace* (New York: Alfred A. Knopf, 1948).

40. Carne Ross, *The Leaderless Revolution* (London: Simon & Schuster, 2011), p. 103.

41. Ewen MacAskill, Ian Cobain, 'British forces' century of unbroken warfare set

to end with Afghanistan exit', *The Guardian*, 11 February 2014. See http://www. theguardian.com/uk-news/2014/feb/11/british-forces-century-warfare-end

42. Mike Davis, *Late Victorian Holocausts* (London: Verso, 2001), p. 7.

43. Mark Curtis, *Unpeople: Britain's Secret Human Rights Abuses* (London: Vintage, 2004), pp. 310–18.

44. William Blum, *Rogue State* (2000; revd edn, London: Zed Books, 2006); William Blum, *Killing Hope* (1995; revd edn, London: Zed Books, 2003).

45. There have since been a number of studies looking at the effects of Iraqi sanctions on mortality rates between 1991 and 2003. The results have varied widely. An often-cited figure, the result of the work of Columbia University's Richard Garfield, is 270,000 excess child deaths mostly as a result of sanctions between 1991 and 1998. (See: Richard Garfield, 'Morbidity and Mortality Among Iraqi Children from 1990 Through 1998', March 1999. See http://www.casi.org.uk/ info/garfield/dr-garfield.html). Continuing his research to include 1999 and 2000, he is reported to have arrived at the estimate of 350,000 excess child deaths. (See: Killing Sanctions in Iraq, *The Nation*, 21 January 2002. See http://www. thenation.com/article/killing-sanctions-iraq/). More recent research, however, suggests these figures may be too high and that they are based on inconsistent and unreliable data. (See: Working Group, 'The Impact of the Oil-For-Food Programme on the Iraqi People', Report of an Independent Working Group Established by the Independent Inquiry Committee, 2005. See www.iic-offp.org/ documents/Sept05/WG Impact.pdf.; Tim Dyson, 'New Evidence on Child Mortality in Iraq', *Economic and Political Weekly*, Vol. 44, No. 2, 10 January 2009, pp. 56–59.) All of that said, when evaluating the decision by the US and UK to keep the sanctions in place for twelve years, the morally relevant question is: what did the evidence suggest at the time these decisions were being taken? As we have seen, this is a much easier question to answer. It is clear that the deaths of hundreds of thousands of children under five, and many more above that age, were – for the US and UK – not reason enough to change policy.

46. John Mueller, Karl Mueller, 'Sanctions of Mass Destruction', *Foreign Affairs*, May/June 1999. See https://www.foreignaffairs.com/articles/iraq/1999-05-01/ sanctions-mass-destruction

47. 'US congressmen criticise Iraqi sanctions', BBC News, 17 February 2000. See http://news.bbc.co.uk/1/hi/world/middle_east/646783.stm.

48. The US and UK governments place the blame on Saddam Hussein. The people who helped to implement the programme see it differently. Starting in 1997, Denis Halliday coordinated the UN's Oil-for-Food programme. Thirteen

months into his role, after a distinguished thirty-four-year career with the UN, he resigned to protest the 'genocidal sanctions' being imposed on Iraq. His successor, Hans von Sponeck, ultimately resigned in protest too, as did head of the World Food Programme in Iraq, Jutta Burghardt. Halliday and Sponeck wrote an article in 2001 in which they argued: 'The death of some 5–6,000 children a month is mostly due to contaminated water, lack of medicines and malnutrition. The US and UK governments' delayed clearance of equipment and materials is responsible for this tragedy, not Baghdad.' (Hans von Sponeck, Denis Halliday, 'The Hostage Nation', *The Guardian*, 29 November 2001. See http://www.theguardian.com/world/2001/nov/29/iraq.comment.) This did not stop high-level denials from the establishment. In 2001, a British minister, Brian Wilson, maintained that 'there is no evidence that sanctions are hurting the Iraqi people' and Tony Blair had previously informed the House of Commons that 'we reject claims that the Iraqi people are suffering because of sanctions'. (Mark Curtis, *Web of Deceit: Britain's Real Role in the World*, [London: Vintage, 2003], p. 30.)

Carne Ross was a key member of the UK Foreign Office during the sanctions. His primary role for much of this period was to ensure that the sanctions agreed at the UN Security Council were implemented. 'Sanctions on Iraq had been imposed, I naively thought, because Iraq had not disarmed itself of its infamous "weapons of mass destruction" (WMD), in this case defined as nuclear, chemical and biological weapons, and ballistic missiles with a range of over 150 kilometres.' Yet when Ross asked one of his briefing officers whether, in fact, the UK really believed Iraq maintained significant stocks of WMD, he was shocked by the response: 'he looked a little sheepish. "Not really," he replied. How, then, do we justify sanctions, I asked, trying to contain my astonishment. He replied, on the basis that Iraq had failed to answer multiple questions about the destruction of its earlier stocks. In summary, sanctions were in place because Iraq had not correctly answered questions.' (Carne Ross, *The Leaderless Revolution: How Ordinary People will Take the Power and Change Politics in the 21st Century* [London: Simon and Schuster, 2011])

In an open letter to Tony Blair, Sponeck responded to Blair's account of the sanctions in his memoir, writing: 'Your officials must have told you that your policies translated into a meagre 51 US cents to finance a person's daily existence in Iraq. You acknowledge that 60 per cent of Iraqis were totally dependent on the goods that were allowed into their country under sanctions, but you make no reference in your book to how the UK and US governments blocked and delayed huge amounts of supplies that were needed for survival. In mid-2002, more than $5bn worth of supplies was blocked from entering the country. No other country on the Iraq sanctions committee of the UN Security Council supported you in this. The UN files are full of such evidence . . . You refuse to acknowledge that you and your policies had anything to do with this humanitarian crisis. You even argue that the death rate of children under five in Iraq, then among the highest in the world, was entirely due to the Iraqi government. I beg you to read Unicef's reports on this subject and what Carol Bellamy, Unicef's American executive director at the time, had to say to the Security Council. None of the UN officials involved in dealing with the crisis will subscribe to your view that Iraq "was free to buy as much food and medicines" as the government would allow. I wish that had been the case. During the Chilcot inquiry in July this year, a respected diplomat who represented the UK on the Security Council sanctions committee while I was in Baghdad observed: "UK officials and ministers were well aware of the negative effects of sanctions, but preferred to blame them on the Saddam regime's failure to implement the oil-for-food programme."' (Hans von Sponeck, 'After the journey – a UN man's open letter to Tony Blair', *New Statesman*, 23 September 2010. See http://www. newstatesman.com/middle-east/2010/09/iraq-humanitarian-sanctions)

49. Quoted in John Pilger, 'Squeezed to death', *The Guardian*, 4 March 2000. See http://www.theguardian.com/theguardian/2000/mar/04/weekend7.weekend9.

50. George F. Kennan, 'Policy Planning Study 23 (PPS/23)', *Foreign Relations of the United States (FRUS)*, 24 February 1948. The declassified document can be read in full. See https://en.wikisource.org/wiki/Memo_PPS23_by_George_Kennan

51. Mark Curtis, *Web of Deceit: Britain's Real Role in the World* (London: Vintage, 2003), p. 16.

52. Mark Curtis, *Web of Deceit*, p. 16.

53. Mark Curtis, *Web of Deceit*, p.16.

54. Mark Curtis, *Web of Deceit*, p.16.

55. 'Use It and Lose It: The Outsize Effect of U.S. Consumption on the Environment', *Scientific American*, 14 September 2012. See http://www.scientificamerican.com/article/american-consumption-habits/

56. Anna Fifield, 'Contractors reap $138bn from Iraq war', *Financial Times*, 18 March 2013. See http://www.ft.com/cms/s/0/7f435f04-8c05-11e2-b001-00144feabdc0.html

57. Anna Fifield, 'Contractors reap $138bn from Iraq war'.

58. Anna Fifield, 'Contractors reap $138bn from Iraq war'.

59. Tory Newmyer, 'The war on ISIS already has a winner: The defense industry',

Fortune, 13 September 2014. See http://fortune.com/2014/09/13/defense-industry-winner-against-isis/

60. Agence-Presse, 'Saudi Arabia Becomes World's Biggest Arms Importer', *The Guardian*, 9 March 2015. See http://www.theguardian.com/world/2015/mar/09/saudi-arabia-becomes-worlds-biggest-arms-importer

61. Jon Stone, 'British arms companies ramp up bomb sales to Saudi Arabia by 100 times despite air strikes on civilians', *The Independent*, 20 January 2016. See http://www.independent.co.uk/news/world/middle-east/british-arms-companies-cash-in-on-humanitarian-catastrophe-and-ramp-up-bomb-sales-to-saudi-arabia-by-a6822491.html

62. Jon Stone, 'British arms companies ramp up bomb sales to Saudi Arabia by 100 times despite air strikes on civilians'.

63. Matt Schivenza, 'Why the US is stuck with Saudi Arabia', *The Atlantic*, 24 January 2015. See http://www.theatlantic.com/international/archive/2015/01/why-the-us-is-stuck-with-saudi-arabia/384805/

64. Jonathan Aldred, *The Skeptical Economist* (Abingdon, Oxon: Earthscan, 2009), p. 148.

65. Jonathan Aldred, *The Skeptical Economist*, p. 145.

66. Raj Patel, *The Value of Nothing* (London: Portobello Books, 2009), p. 145.

67. Raj Patel, *The Value of Nothing*, p. 146.

68. 'David Livingstone Smith: Psychology of Violence,' *Forbes India*, 4 June 2010. See http://www.forbes.com/2010/06/15/forbes-india-david-livingstone-smith-psychology-of-violence-opinions-ideas-10-smith.html

69. David Hume, *A Treatise of Human Nature* (1738; London: Penguin, 1985), pp. 397–8.

70. 'Full Text: State of the Union Address', BBC News, 30 January 2002. See http://news.bbc.co.uk/1/hi/world/americas/1790537.stm

71. 'Bush Speech: Full Text', BBC News, 2 May 2003. See: http://news.bbc.co.uk/1/hi/world/americas/2994345.stm

72. Melanie Garunay, 'President Obama offers a statement on the attacks in Paris,' White House blog, 30 November 2015. See https://www.whitehouse.gov/blog/2015/11/13/watch-president-obamas-statement-attacks-paris

73. 'Chancellor George Osborne says UK has "got its mojo back" with air strikes', *Herald Scotland*, 8 December 2015. See http://www.heraldscotland.com/news/14129765.Osborne_UK_has_got_its_mojo_back_with_air_strikes/

74. Melanie Garunay, 'President Obama offers a statement on the attacks in Paris', White House blog, 30 November 2015. See https://www.whitehouse.gov/blog/2015/11/13/watch-president-obamas-statement-attacks-paris

75.   'Ex-US Intelligence Chief On Islamic State's Rise: "We Were Too Dumb"', Spiegel Online International, 29 November 2015. See http://www.spiegel.de/international/world/former-us-intelligence-chief-discusses-development-of-is-a-1065131.html

76.   'Iraq study estimates war-related deaths at 461,000', BBC News, October 2013. See http://www.bbc.co.uk/news/world-middle-east-24547256

77.   'Public continues to back U.S. drone attacks', Pew Research Center, 28 May 2015. See http://www.people-press.org/2015/05/28/public-continues-to-back-u-s-drone-attacks/

78.   Jana Kasperkevic, 'Poll: 30% of GOP voters support bombing Agrabah, the city from Aladdin', The Guardian, 18 December 2015. See http://www.theguardian.com/us-news/2015/dec/18/republican-voters-bomb-agrabah-disney-aladdin-donald-trump

79.   Mollie Reilly, 'Anti-Drone Activist Sentenced to 6 Months in Jail for Peaceful Protest', Huffington Post, 19 January 2016. See http://www.huffingtonpost.com/entry/mary-anne-grady-flores-drones_us_569e78a1e4b00f3e9863073d

80.   William Blum, Rogue State, p. 123.

81.   Johann Hari, 'Not his finest hour: the dark side of Winston Churchill', The Independent, 27 October 2010. See http://www.independent.co.uk/news/uk/politics/not-his-finest-hour-the-dark-side-of-winston-churchill-2118317.html

82.   Mihir Bose, 'Legacy of the Raj', New Statesman, 23 April 2009. See http://www.newstatesman.com/asia/2009/04/india-british-raj-pakistan

83.   Madhusree Mukerjee, Churchill's Secret War: The British Empire and the Ravaging of India During World War II (New York: Basic Books, 2010), p. 234.

84.   Peel Commission Report: Churchill Papers 2/317, quoted in Martin Gilbert, Churchill and the Jews (London: Simon and Shuster, 2007), p. 120.

85.   Chomsky's comments were made in an email exchange with Sam Harris which Harris subsequently published on his website. See http://www.samharris.org/blog/item/the-limits-of-discourse

86.   Owen Jones, Chavs: The Demonization of the Working Class (London: Verso, 2011), pp. 13–14.

87.   'Ending Newborn Deaths', Save the Children, 2014. See http://www.savethechildren.org/atf/cf/%7B9def2ebe-10ae-432c-9bd0-df91d2eba74a%7D/ENDING-NEWBORN-DEATHS_2014.PDF

88.   Sarah Boseley, 'UK child death rate among worst in Western Europe, say experts', The Guardian, 3 May 2014. See http://www.theguardian.com/society/2014/may/02/uk-child-death-rate-western-europe-health

89.   Tehila Kogut, Ilana Ritov, 'The "Identified Victim" Effect: An Identified Group,

or Just a Single Individual?', *Journal of Behavioral Decision Making*, Vol. 18, No. 3, July 2005, pp. 157–67.

90. Peter Singer, *Practical Ethics*, 2nd edn (Cambridge: Cambridge University Press, 1993), pp. 218–46, at p. 229.

91. Peter Singer, *Practical Ethics*, p. 230.

92. Peter Singer, *Practical Ethics*, p. 230.

93. Peter Singer, *Practical Ethics*, p. 232.

94. Lucy Ward, 'Poor give more generously than the rich', *The Guardian*, 21 December 2001. See http://www.theguardian.com/society/2001/dec/21/voluntarysector. fundraising

95. Ken Stern, 'Why the Rich Don't Give to Charity', *The Atlantic*, April 2013. See http://www.theatlantic.com/magazine/archive/2013/04/why-the-rich-dont-give/309254/

96. Ken Stern, 'Why the Rich Don't Give to Charity'.

97. Daisy Grewal, 'How Wealth Reduces Compassion', *Scientific American*, 10 April 2012. See http://www.scientificamerican.com/article/how-wealth-reduces-compassion/

98. Ian McEwan, 'Only love and then oblivion. Love was all they had to set against their murderers', *The Guardian*, 15 September 2001. See http://www.theguardian. com/world/2001/sep/15/september11.politicsphilosophyandsociety2

99. Adam Galinsky, Gordon Moskowitz, 'Perspective-taking: decreasing stereotype expression, stereotype accessibility, and in-group favoritism', *Journal of Personality and Social Psychology*, Vol. 78, No. 4, April, 2000, pp. 708–24.

100. Simon Baron-Cohen, *Zero Degrees of Empathy*, p. 105.

101. Daniel Voskoboynik, 'The Paris Agreement', *Medium*, 17 January 2016. See https://medium.com/@danielvoskoboy/the-paris-agreement-and-a-new-year-8671f7cdfce4#.x41kcv9g9

102. 'Jo Berry & Pat Magee (Northern Ireland)', The Forgiveness Project, 29 March 2010. See http://theforgivenessproject.com/stories/jo-berry-pat-magee-england/

103. 'Jo Berry & Pat Magee (Northern Ireland)', The Forgiveness Project.

104. Dr Patrick Magee, Building Bridges for Peace. See http://www.buildingbridg-esfor peace.org/about-building-bridges-for-peace/dr-patrick-magee/

105. Rebecca Solnit, *A Paradise Built in Hell* (London: Penguin Books, 2009), p. 2.

106. Rebecca Solnit, *A Paradise Built in Hell*, p. 2.

107. Rebecca Solnit, *A Paradise Built in Hell*, p. 105.

Index

Acknowledgements

I am grateful to a number of people who enabled me to immerse myself in the questions I find most interesting and provided valuable feedback, criticism and encouragement along the way. This book has been greatly improved by their help.

First of all, I want to thank my parents, my sister and her partner Kevin Hely, all of whom have been a constant source of support. My parents, Alex and Christina, read multiple drafts of the book, were always on hand to talk over my latest thoughts, and gave valuable feedback at every stage of the writing process. Perhaps most importantly, they taught me to question everyone and everything, including their own ideas, a lesson that has shaped my life ever since. My sister Francesca read a number of drafts and her instincts about what worked and what didn't were an invaluable guide that made all the difference at crucial points in the process. One of the freest people I know, she has been a constant source of inspiration and encouragement. Kevin did a thorough edit of the whole book over two drafts, pushing me to create a leaner, tighter text. His keen eye for detail is only matched by his work ethic and generosity.

Thanks also to Marienna Pope-Weidemann for her insightful notes and suggestions on the first eight chapters, and for many a stimulating conversation; to Daniel Voskoboynik for his feedback on Chapter 11 and some fact-checking on the early chapters; to Tatiana Garavito for her thoughts on Chapter 11; to Robin Hahnel for providing detailed feedback on several versions of Chapters 3 and 6, clarifying my understanding on a number of points; to Daniel O'Neill for his notes on Chapters 3 and 11; to Ha-Joon Chang for his comments on part of Chapter 3; and to Galen Strawson for reading an early draft of the first chapter and responding with encouragement.

Thanks to the late Alan Rickman, whose generous support made all the difference at the start of the Creating Freedom project; to Joshua van Praag, who brought his many talents to the project's first documentary, and to all those who kindly agreed to be interviewed along the way. In particular, Michael Albert, Noam Chomsky, Nick Davies, Daniel Dennett, Stuart Ewen, Bill Fletcher Jr., Amy Goodman, David Harvey, Chris Hedges, Janine Jackson, Helena Kennedy, Bill McKibben, George Monbiot, Helena Norberg-Hodge, Steven Pinker, Jeff Schmidt, Vandana Shiva, Kathleen Taylor, and the late Tony Benn and Howard Zinn.

Thanks to Nicoleta Carpineanu and Jonty Hurwitz, without whom the book might never have made it into print; to Jeannie Cohen for her early support; and to the whole Canongate team, especially Jamie Byng for having faith in the idea from the start, my editors Jenny Lord and Pantheon's Dan Frank for their patience and feedback, and my copy editor Jane Robertson.

I also want to acknowledge all the thinkers whose writings have inspired and challenged me over the years, many of whose names appear in these pages. Finally, I want to thank all those on the front lines of the fight to create freedom in the world. You are a constant source of hope and inspiration.